JOHN

America's Long Reckoning

BROWN

with Violence, Equality, & Change

STILL

R. Blakeslee Gilpin

LIVES!

THE UNIVERSITY OF NORTH CAROLINA PRESS   *Chapel Hill*

This book was published with the assistance of the Center for the Study of the American South of the University of North Carolina at Chapel Hill.

© 2011 The University of North Carolina Press

All rights reserved

Manufactured in the United States of America

Designed by Kimberly Bryant and set in Miller and DIN types by
Tseng Information Systems, Inc.

The paper in this book meets the guidelines for permanence and durability of the Committee on Production Guidelines for Book Longevity of the Council on Library Resources. The University of North Carolina Press has been a member of the Green Press Initiative since 2003.

Library of Congress Cataloging-in-Publication Data
Gilpin, R. Blakeslee.
John Brown still lives! : America's long reckoning with violence, equality, and change / R. Blakeslee Gilpin.
p. cm.
Includes bibliographical references and index.
ISBN 978-0-8078-3501-2 (cloth : alk. paper)
1. Brown, John, 1800–1859—Influence. 2. Brown, John, 1800–1859—In literature. 3. Harpers Ferry (W. Va.)—History—John Brown's Raid, 1859. 4. Abolitionists—United States—Biography. 5. Violence—Social aspects—United States—History. 6. Equality—United States—History. I. Title.
E451.G45 2011
973.7′114—dc22   2011008425

15 14 13 12 11   5 4 3 2 1

Chapter 7 has been reprinted in revised form from "The Fugitive Imagination: Robert Penn Warren's John Brown," in *Memory and Myth: The Civil War in Fiction and Film from "Uncle Tom's Cabin" to "Cold Mountain,"* edited by David B. Sachsman, S. Kittrell Rushing, and Roy Morris Jr. (West Lafayette, IN: Purdue University Press, 2007).

FOR ABBEY & PETER,

who would have been great friends

CONTENTS *Acknowledgments xi*

ILLUSTRATIONS

ACKNOWLEDGMENTS

In several years of chipping away at a legend, one incurs many debts, to places and institutions, but especially to people. I would not have pursued my PhD if it were not for the encouragement and enthusiasm of one of my undergraduate teachers at Yale, Eric Papenfuse. Eric now owns the Midtown Scholar Bookstore in Harrisburg, Pennsylvania, but he remains my model of teaching. His passion and expertise continue to inspire me.

Robert Johnston provided the foundation for my professional historical experience. His support, guidance, and candor about all aspects of academe have been a blessing. His friendship has meant the world to me since we first met—I think I looked all of fifteen years old. I hope we are sharing gossip, stories, and songs until we have nothing but gray hairs, but hopefully still have those!

John Merriman has been a friend since I took his lecture course as a sophomore in college. His maps tormented me during my oral exams, his work ethic has motivated me throughout graduate school, and his life convinces me that academics can live well.

I almost missed John Mack Faragher as an undergraduate but managed to slip in a readings course with him as I finished my master's thesis. His support for my project has stretched from Yale's Beinecke Library to the Huntington Library and back to the Howard Lamar Center for the Study of Frontiers and Borders. Johnny has been steadfast in his enthusiasm and faith in me, and I am delighted that my project has some piece of the West because of his influence.

Glenda Gilmore helped me get to England almost a decade ago, and when I was done she helped me return to New Haven. Despite having planted one foot so firmly in the antebellum world, Glenda has remained my ally, editor, and sounding board. She is dogged in making me a better thinker, writer, and teacher. This project would not be much without her blunt critiques and confidence in the ultimate outcome.

I met David W. Blight when he visited the American history reading group at Cambridge University. He had just accepted a job at Yale and was speaking about his brilliant book, *Race and Reunion*. I had never thought much about the Civil War, but his presentation thrilled me. I would not be working on John Brown if not for David's suggestion, during my first readings course, that someone ought to write a book about Brown's legacy. I took the bait. I have spent many mornings listening to David lecture; his ability to enchant and enthrall an audience of three hundred sleepy undergraduates is awesome. I feel lucky to have an adviser so keenly interested in my work and so willing to extend his support whenever I have needed it.

Many institutions supported my project, and Yale University is chief among them. At Yale, the Beinecke Library funded several chapters of research and writing, and the Howard Lamar Center for the Study of Frontiers and Borders sponsored a half year of extensive travel to Kansas, Tennessee, and beyond. I benefited greatly from my work as the Joan Nordell Fellow at the Houghton Library at Harvard and as a W. M. Keck Fellow at the Huntington Library in San Marino, California. Finally, my project really took shape with support from the Gilder Lehrman Institute of American History in New York. A yearlong fellowship from the Center for the Study of the American South at the University of North Carolina–Chapel Hill was an absolute godsend; to be among such a dynamic group of scholars at such an incredible university was an unparalleled opportunity for all manner of conversations, friendships, and mentors.

I am deeply grateful for the friendship of my fellow postdoc at UNC, Zoe Trodd. She is a first-rate scholar, and it was wonderful to be able to share time and ideas with her. Through Zoe, I am grateful for my relationship with the amazing John Stauffer, whose work first exposed me to Brown. John's insight, expertise, and enthusiasm have been essential to this project reaching its fullest potential.

As I prepared my manuscript, I was thrilled to get sage advice and boundless support from Harry Watson, Tim Marr, Fitz Brundage, and Joe Flora. Joyce Seltzer was also an enthusiastic source of calm counsel at various stages.

At the University of North Carolina Press, Kate Torrey and Chuck Grench were extremely patient at all stages of this process and offered much careful criticism and steady guidance. I am especially grateful to my two readers.

Bertram Wyatt-Brown has been particularly gracious with his encyclopedic knowledge, professional support, and enthusiasm. My project editor, Paula Wald, and copy editor, Alex Martin, were both a joy to work with, and their careful attention to this book has improved it immeasurably.

I am doubtful that I would have made it through the emotional roller-coaster that is graduate school without my friends and colleagues. I owe my orals success in French history to George Trumbull IV. I already miss the men's table—Gerry Cadava, Jake Lundberg, Bob Morrissey, and Sam Schaffer—who will have to settle for AHA and OAH meetings from now on.

Love to my second families: Dave and Ann Talbott, who saw me through long hair, meal money, Merlefests, and more—I love you guys; and the Martins, especially young Max, who will conquer the squash world—thanks for giving me an outlet to assist a young champion.

Thanks also to Anne Fadiman, whose enthusiasm, invitations, and friendship have simply made my life a brighter place; to Sam Chauncey, who has been generous with his wisdom since some squash bus trip a decade ago; to Amy Bloom, for all the many adventures since I cockily marched into your classroom; and to Patricio Zambrano-Barragán—helping each other keep on keeping on, brother, someday we'll get to Masa.

I probably wouldn't be in this business if not for my parents, who, beyond emotional and financial support, provided me with all the chalk dust. Critter and Alexa have remained a bit puzzled by my passion for so much school. My grandmother seems proud of all that I've done, though I think she'd like a visit to Florida most of all.

I keep George Musgrove in my heart every day, remembering his bemused looks over everything my enthusiasm generated.

Peter Fabrizio, the strange boy from Rome, New York, who so frightened me at nineteen, looms over everything I do. I miss him always and I hope I am making him proud.

Finally, it was ten years before we spoke, but I am more smitten every day. Smart as she is beautiful, tough as she is wise, my wife, Abbey, has made me a better person in every way. She has forced me to clarify this project when my rambling has not made sense to her. More than that, she often knows best what I hope to say. I am so grateful she found me and that we leaped and keep on leaping. I am forever in her debt for many reasons, not least for bringing Sal and Dolly into my heart. Never have I so eagerly anticipated todays and tomorrows. I cannot wait for the goats, the (small) dogs, and the bubs running around a bunch of acres somewhere.

John Brown Still Lives!

Nothing so charms the American people as personal bravery. . . . The trial for
life of one bold, and to some extent successful, man . . . would arouse more sympathy
throughout the nation than the accumulated wrongs and sufferings of more than
three million [slaves].
　　—John Brown, "Words of Advice"

Introduction

CAUSE AND CONSEQUENCE

John Brown in Nineteenth-Century America

John Brown believed that slavery would meet an end that matched its brutality. In 1859, his bold invasion of Harpers Ferry and polarizing trial by the
state of Virginia aroused the sympathy and anger that would spark the Civil
War. On the day of his execution, Brown seemed to predict the cause and
extent of that conflict. "I John Brown," he wrote, "am, now quite *certain* that
the crimes of this *guilty land* will never be purged away, but with Blood."[1]

Since December 2, 1859, all manner of writing, art, and memorial have
been employed to understand this man. While Brown's prophesizing underscores his keen understanding of antebellum tensions, the raid on Harpers
Ferry ignited a series of debates that have never stopped raging, prompted
an endless reckoning with the nature of this man's character, and provoked
swirling questions about the role and meaning of violence, equality, and
change. By tracing Brown's unique and nagging presence in the nation's
memory, this book illuminates the deep roots of America's continuing
struggles with these open questions.

In taking up arms to end slavery, Brown has forced generation after generation to clarify the morality and utility of violence. His progressive but
paternalistic relationships with black Americans mirror the troubling limits
of interracial efforts to redress the nation's mistakes.[2] Brown's martyrdom,
ultimately giving his life to liberate his enslaved brethren, admonishes us
to disentangle his web of interracial trailblazing, violent abolitionism, and
messianic paternalism to make sense of America's greatest trauma, slavery.

Biographers have tried to locate explanations to these knotty conundrums in the events of Brown's life, his psychological profile, and the cul-

tural currents of his time. In contrast, this book focuses on Brown's final decade and the 150 years since his death in order to reframe the debates over his meaning. When Brown was executed, Henry Wadsworth Longfellow wrote that "this will be a great day in our history, the date of a new revolution, quite as much needed as the old one. . . . [Brown's death] is sowing the wind to reap the whirlwind, which will soon come."[3] While the following chapters will familiarize readers with Brown's story, the multigenerational battle over his meaning reveals the true power and relevance of Brown's place in American memory. Exploring the whirlwinds Brown helped sow broadens our understanding of historical amnesia, systemic racism, and the indelible conservatism at the heart of America's understanding of its past, present, and future.

In 1882, Albion Tourgée, the Reconstruction-era judge and novelist, attempted to account for these contradictions and Brown's persistent presence. "Monster and Martyr," Tourgée called Brown in his novel *Hot Plowshares*, "Conspirator and Saint; Murderer and Liberator; Cause and Consequence! Alerting one-half of the land to emulate his example; stimulating the other to meet aggression; inciting both to shedding of blood!" Tourgée finished with a flourish, trying to situate Brown at the juncture of historical periods; "The climax of one age and the harbinger of another."[4]

Merging the contentious dialogues Tourgée so ably described with the endless repercussions that Longfellow predicted, this book explores the many symbolic John Browns and their significance to broader national debates. Incorporating art, literature, and history, the episodes in this book reveal how amnesia, hypocrisy, and conservatism still define America's perpetual negotiations with its founding principles. Facilitating these conversations, Brown continues to be used as a dynamic platform to debate America's evolving relationships with violence, equality, and change. Probing Brown's role as a conduit between these issues and the politics of the present highlights Americans' desire to maintain long-standing hierarchies of race, class, and gender. By following several generations' interpretations of Brown's symbolism, these chapters reveal the nation's difficulty in building a dynamic and nuanced relationship, in understanding and practice, with the American past.

Pithy assessments from Frederick Douglass, Abraham Lincoln, Malcolm X, and countless others testify to Brown's contentious timelessness, but the abolitionist's very ubiquity prompts the question of when and where we locate John Brown in American memory. Like any work of history, mine has involved subjective choices. Another scholar might dedicate a chapter to the ubiquitous Union marching song, "John Brown's Body," to a statue of Brown erected in Lake Placid, New York, or to any number of artists, writers, and historical moments. This book, however, examines the long history of John Brown in its most telling episodes, from Bleeding Kansas to the first efforts of the Progressive Era, from New Southern intellectual projects to the postracial art of the 1990s. The encounters I consider in these chapters are those when Brown served most intensely and provocatively as a symbolic foil to the legacies of the nation's founding principles. Brown's particular brand of heroic masculinity provided a platform for these conversations and helps explain how and why the writers, artists, and activists who sought to control Brown's story were bounded by his life and actions.[5]

For example, while W. E. B. Du Bois's deeply flawed 1909 biography of Brown sold miserably, I dedicate a chapter to circumstances surrounding the book's genesis and fate. Like each episode in this book, Du Bois's struggles with Brown sharpen our understanding of the swirl of events, personalities, and chance that occasioned the founding of the National Association for the Advancement of Colored People (NAACP). More important, this intersection offers a cogent and penetrating look at how memories of Brown helped and hindered early efforts to address the injustice and violence of American race relations in the early twentieth century.

The characters and events in this study span nearly two centuries, showing how Brown inspired his countrymen to search for answers to his perplexing existence beyond the confines of his life. Why have these conversations been mediated through him for so long? This book seeks answers by probing the meaning of slavery in dialogue with America's founding principles, slavery's violent destruction as it related to the nation's revolutionary origins, and the long-term effects of slavery's racial hierarchies on our national consciousness. Tracing these dialogues through Brown's aggressive interpretations and each subsequent recasting of Brown allows us to see the extent of slavery's disturbing hold on America's imagining of its past, the nation's understanding of its present problems, and the implications of both for the country's future.

In this study, those dialogues take root in John Brown's emergence as a public figure in the 1850s. While he became a national celebrity in October 1859, Brown was virtually unknown just ten years earlier. Making sense of that rise to fame (or infamy) is crucial to understanding Brown's importance to so many generations of Americans. The territorial contest in Kansas was the national event that transformed Brown and launched him as a public figure. After leading five brutal murders in Pottawatomie, Kansas, in 1856, the newly minted "Old Hero" gained fresh faith in his long-held dreams of fulfilling God's purpose, redeeming himself personally, and rescuing his wayward nation from its original sin. Having long discussed plans of invading the South to liberate slaves, Brown used his celebrity from Bleeding Kansas to realize some part of that vision. Even though Brown's detractors delighted in his failure at Harpers Ferry, the naysayers could not undo the propagandistic free-for-all that Brown's mission inspired. From the moment the old man and his ragtag interracial army were captured in Virginia on October 19, 1859, his words, significant and insignificant, achieved the status of antislavery gospel *and* proto-Confederate apocrypha.

On December 8, 1859, Jefferson Davis, then a Democratic U.S. senator from Mississippi, established the stakes of this endless tribunal. From the Senate floor, the future president of the Confederacy warned his countrymen of a vast Northern conspiracy. A cabal of abolitionists, politicians, and lunatics had fueled Brown's invasion of Harpers Ferry "with pike, with spear [and] rifles," Davis gravely described, to "take our niggers off." Admonishing his colleagues that "a thousand John Browns" were poised to follow, Davis maintained that "the only question for the South to decide" was how to combat these "traitor[s]."[6]

While most studies of Brown conclude with moments like Davis's speech or the opening of the Civil War, America's engagement with this character was only beginning in 1859. Indeed, the nation's long struggle with Brown did not cease with the shots at Fort Sumter, nor diminish with emancipation, nor fade with Robert E. Lee's surrender at Appomattox; Brown's actions echoed much further than anyone (even Brown himself) ever imagined.[7] Brown has continued to play a central role in conversations resonating since the antebellum years, thriving from Bleeding Kansas to Reconstruction, World War I to the New Deal, and the civil rights movement to the election of Barack Obama.

Explored through art, literature, and activism, the past 150 years reveal countless appropriations of Brown's life and mission.[8] Since John Brown unsheathed his broadsword in Kansas in 1856, he has forced his countrymen to reckon with violence in the name of freedom. Using Brown's beliefs, actions, and the rippling effects of both, generations of Americans have attempted to reconcile racial injustice with the founding principles of the nation. Accordingly, the abolitionist has provided a timeless platform to debate the place and process of change in American democracy. Throughout these conversations, Brown serves as a reminder of the irreconcilable fault lines in the nation's relationships with violence, equality, and change.

His willingness to die in a violent invasion to free his enslaved brethren made it impossible to separate change from violence, or violent change from equality. No other figure of such notoriety in American history so powerfully showcases the interconnectedness of these volatile subjects. Brown's principles and experiences convinced him that equality would only come with transformative change and that this change would be precipitated by righteous violence. It should be no surprise that attitudes toward the man have retained their potency since Brown's extreme actions unleashed a torrent of visual art, literature, and activism that continues to flow.

That torrent has carried Brown through many divergent and conflicting currents since 1859. He has been fashioned a cold-blooded killer of territorial Kansas, a redeeming hero of African Americans, a whipping boy for 1920s neo-Confederates, and a divinely inspired model of anti-abortion activists. Each of these incarnations of Brown draws on selective biography, partisan imagination, and grand historical framework. These representations, stretching from 1856 to 2010, help us to understand the meaning of this man's symbolic power to generations of Americans.

The very fluidity of Brown's symbolism has inspired each succeeding generation to tell his story; the man has been enticing biographers since his body was buried. James Redpath, one of Brown's Kansas compatriots, released his *Public Life of Captain John Brown* just weeks after the abolitionist's execution. In that book, Redpath labeled Brown a "saint" and "our bravest martyr," setting the worshipful tone that would dominate the next fifty years of biographies.[9] Among the dozens of books that followed, works by NAACP cofounders W. E. B. Du Bois and Oswald Garrison Villard in 1909 and 1910 did try to complicate Brown's story by presenting him respectively as a racial prophet and a moral example.[10] But by the 1920s Brown was being forced into a new pigeonhole, this time that of a madman.[11] Over the next century, debates about Brown were reduced to a one-dimensional contest of good versus evil and took on the rhythm of a ping-pong match. While the major works of the last decade have uncovered interesting material on Brown's life, recent biographies have fallen into many of the unfortunate patterns first established in 1860.[12] Despite an increase in factual detail, any survey of the extensive literature powerfully underscores the inherent limitations and diminishing returns of biography.

For a man like John Brown, whose life was a rather haphazard combination of the pedestrian and the exceptional, and whose actions and pronouncements are simultaneously incredible and contradictory, biography alone has proven an inadequate tool. Brown's story, which he described as a narrative "of follies and errors," hardly begins to explain his persistence as a symbol. While biographers have spent 150 years trying to parse which childhood trauma led to Brown's particular zeal, it is no longer fruitful to comb Brown's youth to label him a villain, madman, or transcendentalist.[13] In this book, I avoid purely biographical explanations in order to explore Brown's place in America's historical memory. By probing how Brown's meaning has shifted in his and others' hands, it is possible to understand the significance of our consuming interest in him. Brown has always served as a medium for America's endless debates on violence, equality, and change. From his self-creation in the battle over territorial Kansas to his emergence as a straw man of the New South; from a postbellum pacifist martyr to a hero of Harlem, Brown functions as a fluctuating emblem of evolving American attitudes. His unique place in our nation's memory facilitates this expansive look at such contentious topics.

This book utilizes Brown and his memory for the very essence of historical inquiry: the observance of change (or lack thereof) over time. The episodes herein force us to make sense of a multilayered past just as they reveal how historical actors did the same, even while they were making history themselves. By following each generation's exegesis of violence, equality, and change, all mediated through John Brown, it is possible to understand just how historical—rooted in the evidence and context of the past—a study of memory can be.[14] Through Brown and through other people's uses of him, we can better understand how interpretations of one man reflect on immutable truths about the American past, present, and future. Brown's trajectory as an emblem along the axes of violence, equality, and change reveals the nation's enduring struggle to fulfill the promise of its founding documents. While Brown helped various groups struggle against the status quo, the use and abuse of his symbolism demonstrate that resistance to substantive change has been built one generation at a time.[15] Our very understanding of the past provides the bricks and mortar for this ongoing construction.

As Brown evolved from abolitionist martyr to African American hero to neo-Confederate simulacrum and back again, his historical symbolism dramatically transcended the confines of his life and times. Tracking the changing shape of his meaning reveals the antislavery agitator being put to the service of many presents. Across these varied incidents and eras, the connecting thread is not just a man, but the many things he came to represent to a diverse assortment of Americans. In Brown, generations have found the perfect foil to debate the nation's evolving identity.

Brown quite consciously thought of himself as a symbol and recognized the potential power of his memory. As early as 1847, he fashioned himself as a vehicle for debate. His public emergence in Bleeding Kansas and Harpers Ferry coincided with his development of prescient self-consciousness. The first three chapters of this book follow that evolution, narrating Brown's emergence in the 1850s and exploring how he knowingly shaped the cultural symbol he left to American memory. Brown's final decade vividly demonstrates how he used long-standing national understandings of violence, equality, and change to achieve a specific sort of immortality. Chapter 4 surveys Brown's cultural ubiquity from 1859 to 1910, following the emergence of a vibrant African American relationship with Brown's memory, which corresponded and often conflicted with white memory, particularly the work of the transcendentalist chronicler and Brown confidant Franklin W. Sanborn. As the fight over the meaning of the Civil War began in earnest, it became increasingly important to white supporters to strip Brown of revolutionary violence, a shift that would exact devastating consequences. Chapter 5 locates Brown in the early twentieth century through two major biographers: Du Bois and Villard. Advanced in the midst of the NAACP's formation, their conflicting interpretations of Brown reveal an evolving paternalist narrative and underscore the limits of racial reform. Chapter 6 examines one of the best-selling poems of the twentieth century, Steven Vincent Benét's *John Brown's Body*. Prompted by continuing divides between North and South, Benét's work attempted to reunite the nation under a common banner, confronting Brown and the bloodshed of the Civil War by emphasizing America's destiny.

Following Brown south reveals a drastically different intellectual movement spearheaded by Robert Penn Warren and the Fugitive-Agrarians of the 1920s and 1930s. Examining Warren's first book, a biography of Brown, chapter 7 traces the efforts of these Southern intellectuals to refashion antebellum mythology for a new generation. Chapter 8 investigates the artistic explosion surrounding Brown in the 1930s through the murals of John Steuart Curry. While Curry's art drew on the vernacular of the progressive Left, his racial vision and historical narrative visually defined the anti-Brown school. Chapter 9 looks at Curry's contemporary, the Harlem painter Jacob Lawrence, through his twenty-two-painting historical series, *The Life of John Brown*. Lawrence's imagery and captions present Brown in a dynamic chronicle of interracial protest, biblical religion, and redemptive violence, questioning the nation's promise of liberty and equality. Finally, beginning with Orson Welles, the epilogue follows Brown's kaleidoscopic journey through another fifty years of American memory, landing in the bosom of the Black Panthers, the Weather Underground, and the pro-life movement before becoming a contradictory magnet in the so-called post-racial years. Through the writing of President Barack Obama and the work of the African American artist Kara Walker, the epilogue explores whether Brown has anything to offer twenty-first-century Americans. In clarifying the questions that Americans have long mediated through this man, Brown's symbolism highlights his utility as a powerful bridge between past and present as well as between black and white.

Each chapter traces the story of Brown's persistent presence in America's collective conversations and examines the role of memory in debates over the place of violence, equality, and change in pursuit of a more perfect union. These pages scrutinize Brown's various incarnations and highlight his importance to the nation's changing patterns of racial discrimination, cooperation, and construction. Approaching Brown through these different generations and contrasting settings reveals America's deep difficulties in coming to terms with its violent history, its checkered progress toward racial equality, and its resistance to substantive change. Brown's place in the nation's memory reveals Americans' eagerness to mediate these conversations through a historical personality (and our creations of him) rather than confront the frustrations, shame, and hope revealed by his memory.

A circumstance occurred that in the end made him a most determined abolitionist:
& led him to declare or swear: Eternal war with Slavery.
   —*John Brown to Henry L. Stearns, 1857*

1

SOME DEFINITE PLAN

The Early Life of John Brown

In the late 1850s, John Brown was often asked to recount the circumstances that led to his celebrity. No stranger to the grand narratives of the United States, Brown was particularly attracted to providential accounts of the American republic and the ways his life mimicked these themes. Accordingly, the abolitionist crafted autobiographical tales that fit his antislavery purpose, emphasizing his egalitarianism, tenacity, and constant service to God as the microcosm of his nation's narrative. Brown penned one such account for Henry Stearns, the twelve-year-old son of Boston factory owner (and abolitionist) George Stearns.[1] Brown wrote his anecdotal autobiography in the third person, providing young Henry with a primer in a patriotic and religious existence. Instructing the boy that his life should follow "some definite plan," Brown informed Stearns that he had been twelve years old when he watched a young black boy, dressed only in rags in the deepest of winter, beaten bloody with a shovel. The story was invented, but Brown was a man who relied on liberties, particularly when it fit his faith and his cause.[2]

Although Brown presented himself as destined from an early age for his raid on Harpers Ferry, his life was far more complicated, full of dead ends, disappointments, and defeats. Indeed, self-presentations aside, most of Brown's pronouncements, especially about his life's purpose and the fate of his nation, seemed to be realized only with his trip to the gallows and the events that followed his death. As a British newspaper editorial reminded readers in 1900, Brown's "last words prove that he foresaw, as plainly as man ever saw sunrise follow dawn, that blood, and blood alone, would loosen the shackles of the slave."[3] This self-awareness and prescience secured Brown some measure of lasting infamy. However, the meaning behind his proclamation that he wanted "to die at Harpers Ferry, for my death there will do more for my cause than anything I could do if I live" has never been adequately explained or analyzed.[4]

Brown's self-conscious marketing as a symbol of antislavery helps explain the lasting power of these statements. Prior to his formal agitations against slavery, Brown was a businessman sorting out his intertwining revolutionary, Calvinist, and capitalist influences. Until 1848, when Brown's final entrepreneurial venture, a wool concern, went bust, he was such a typical American he warranted no great notice at all. But for the man who would become "The Old Hero," anonymity was an ignominious circumstance. Brown's assertions about his genealogy spoke to his sense of historical entitlement. Although his claim to Mayflower ancestry was erroneous, his great-grandfather, Peter Brown, had served as a captain in the Revolutionary War. In the early years of the nineteenth century, being able to trace one's lineage to the founders of the Republic carried significant cultural capital, particularly to men like Brown.[5]

Brown was born on May 9, 1800, in a conventional New England farmhouse in the small town of Torrington, Connecticut. Brown's father, Owen, was a strict, religious man, whose Calvinism and patriotism formed the twin pillars of the household. Brown learned at the end of his father's lash about stealing and lying, quickly absorbing the idea that pain and doom awaited those who strayed from the righteous path. Beyond practical life lessons and careful study of the Bible, Owen Brown provided his son with a model of hard work, principled living, and engagement with the issues of the day.

Brown's early years were defined by hardships, including the death of his mother when he was eight years old. His father's remarriage and frequent relocation also steeled Brown for the unexpected. John was taken into his father's tannery business at the age of ten and developed an appreciation for hard work and fine animals. As an awkward teenager, Brown found meaning in Calvinism. Particularly devout members of Congregational and Presbyterian faiths, the Browns' Calvinism was a strident variation on the precariousness of one's status in the eyes of God.[6] This tension and uncertainty was grafted to a belief in salvation that meant life should be dedicated to atonement for one's inevitable sins and to fulfillment of one's spiritual mission. Brown embraced this faith passionately. The Bible provided confirmation of his intuitive beliefs on American slavery—particularly fueling a kinship with Hannibal—which seemed to justify vengeance against the perpetrators of so terrible an evil.

Starting at a young age, John Brown found several possible missions before settling on the broadsword and rifle in Kansas. When his family left Connecticut for a community of strict Calvinists in Ohio, Brown made two failed attempts at a professional religious education. Returning east to Moses Hallock's Plainfield, Massachusetts, school in 1816 and then to Morris Academy in Litchfield, Connecticut, Brown was thwarted by a combination of injury, poverty, and inadequacy. As a result of his failures, and within the Calvinist tradition in which he had been raised, Brown came to understand the Bible quite literally. Long before his involvement in radical abolitionism, Brown felt he had been called to help free America's slaves. While his course over the next forty years, through two wives and countless businesses, often seemed far removed from abolition, Brown was a casual believer in the cause from a young age.[7]

However, it was only after Brown was forced to join his father in Hudson, Ohio, in the 1820s and 1830s that he was exposed to the radical fringe of American antislavery thought. In this sense, Brown was less a lifelong soldier than someone in whom a seed had been planted. If in the 1850s Brown talked continually of his lifelong commitment to abolition, it is more accurate to say that Brown was, until the 1840s, a nonpracticing believer.[8] Like his father, Brown's life was consumed with providing for his family, teaching them religion and discipline, and searching out new financial opportunities.[9]

Although Brown had encountered William Lloyd Garrison's *Liberator*, the abolitionist newspaper started in 1831, Garrison's methods of agitation never spoke to Brown. It was not until the 1837 lynching of abolitionist printer Elijah Lovejoy that Brown publicly vowed to dedicate his life to overthrowing slavery.[10] Brown first heard about Lovejoy's death in church, listening to a Western Reserve professor ask his parishioners, "Are we free or are we slaves under Southern mob law?" Brown apparently felt called to respond and stood up at the back of the church. "Here, before God," Brown declared, "in the presence of these witnesses, from this time, I consecrate my life to the destruction of slavery!"[11]

Despite such passionate proclamations, in the early 1840s Brown was forced to focus his attention on financial security. Business, or the pursuit of business success, occupied Brown in the ensuing years, even as he spent his free time making grandiose plans to end American slavery. By the end of the decade, Brown had traveled across the Atlantic to make his fortune. Before the days of the striking white beard and the infamous adventures, Brown was merely an incompetent representative for the unfortunate American wool concern Perkins and Brown. Refusing what he considered insulting prices in the United States, Brown sailed to England. He tramped from London to Leeds and to the backwater markets of Wortley, Branley, and Bradford, attempting to unload two hundred thousand pounds of American wool. In the end, that wool was sold at a terrible loss. Brown wrote his son "in the midst of sickness and death," not sure if he would make it home.[12] If John Brown had succumbed to defeat and depression over the latest in his long series of catastrophic business failures, the course of American history might have turned out very differently. However, as was his nature, Brown escaped creditors and another round of bankruptcy, clawing his way into precarious poverty. Perhaps because of the dismal quality of his business interests, Brown's extracurricular passions began taking precedence over his business concerns. As he became one of the "misfit[s] of capitalism" that historian Scott Sandage chronicles in his book *Born Losers*, Brown made a concerted effort to transcend his circumstances by means other than money.[13]

In the middle of a lecture tour by Frederick Douglass in 1848, Brown contacted the famous former slave about "urgent business." Douglass dined with Brown and sat for an amateurish but enthusiastic presentation. Running his finger across a map of the Allegheny Mountains, Brown explained that God had made these features expressly for the purpose of slave liberation. Although Douglass was skeptical about Brown's plans, Brown's ideas about small bands of armed men raiding the South from strongholds in the mountains were certainly radical. Douglass's famous assessment in his newspaper *The North Star* anticipated the changes in Brown's temperament. Brown, "though a white gentleman," Douglass wrote, "is in sympathy, a black man, and as deeply interested in our cause, as though his own soul had been pierced with the iron of slavery."[14]

Brown had begun to understand himself in exactly these terms. Just as his financial situation bottomed out, Brown sat for two portraits by the African American photographer Augustus Washington. Washington was the son of a former Virginia slave, but he had grown up a free man in Trenton, New Jersey. Financing a Dartmouth degree through his portraits and the support of various abolitionists, Washington began mixing with like-minded New Englanders when he opened a studio in Hartford, Connecticut, in 1845. John Brown became one of his most famous clients.

Figure 1.1.
John Brown, quarter-
plate daguerreotype by
Augustus Washington,
1846–47. The Nelson-
Atkins Museum of Art,
Kansas City, Missouri;
Gift of the Hall Family
Foundation, 2008.6.4;
photograph by John
Lamberton.

In figure 1.1, Brown's arms are crossed forcefully.[15] While he appears confident and respectable in this portrait, his image was, quite literally, a pose.[16] Regardless of the intensity of his body language or expression, Brown's thoughts could not have been far from the bankruptcy courts he had been in and out of for the better part of the decade. While his imagination might have been running through revolutionary antislavery plans, Brown had to know the courts had not forgotten him. In this portrait, he plainly resists his creditors' labels for him: "failed surveyor, farmer, speculator, schoolteacher, tanner, and cattleman."[17] Accordingly, given Brown's capricious work history, it is no wonder that his true radicalization seemed to coincide with his most severe financial disappointments. As one business venture after another forced Brown deeper and deeper into debt, he became a more dedicated reader of abolitionist literature, a constant presence at antislavery meetings, and a vocal self-promoter.[18]

Washington's second portrait of Brown reflects this willed transformation; the abolitionist is no longer a determined capitalist but a revolution-

Figure 1.2.
John Brown, quarter-plate
daguerreotype by Augustus
Washington, 1847.
National Portrait Gallery,
Smithsonian Institution/
Art Resource, New York;
Purchased with major
acquisition funds and with
funds donated by Betty
Adler Schermer in honor
of her great grandfather,
August M. Bondi.

ary firebrand (figure 1.2). In this image, Brown clutches a flag in one hand and raises his other in a solemn oath. The portrait represents the kernel of Brown's eventual plans for the raid on Harpers Ferry. Brown's flag was his own creation—the standard of his "Subterranean Pass Way"—representing his militant alternative to the Underground Railroad. The flag's symbols illustrated the imagined raiding parties, based in the Alleghenies, that would attack plantations and protect fugitive slaves.[19] Brown was convinced the terrain was perfectly suited to hiding a roving insurrectionary force of armed slaves under his leadership. From the mountains, Brown would liberate one plantation after another, shuttling freed bondsmen north along the mountain range. Thus, Washington's image captured a John Brown that was to come, a true patriot who sought military liberation for those in bondage.[20]

Here was a latter-day American revolutionist, holding a homemade flag of freedom, pledging an oath to future sacrifice. But no matter how steely the glance or how determined Brown felt about his future abolitionist adventures, there were stark realities just outside the frame. Although only forty-seven at the time, Brown "looked sixty to credit reporters," according to Sandage. "Like many another misfit who pushed a doomed venture too far, he quit when he had no other choice."[21] When Brown, desperate and destitute, finally abandoned his financial scheming in 1848, he followed a path other misfits did not. He decided to *become* the man Augustus Washington had so strikingly photographed in the militant portrait. Turning to the wealthy philanthropist Gerrit Smith, Brown asked to become a resident patron to the free black community Smith was establishing on property he owned in upstate New York. Brown saw himself serving as a kind of father figure to the enterprising African Americans living in the densely wooded part of New York fifty miles west of Burlington, Vermont.

Brown's new mission drew him notice. In 1849, Richard Henry Dana, the midcentury novelist, became lost in the Adirondack Mountains with some associates. The men stumbled on a log house and Brown invited them inside. The men were immediately introduced to Mr. Jefferson and Mrs. Wait, a black couple. Brown introduced his black friends with egalitarian titles, and he and his guests were seated at the dining room table for dinner, where they ate with Jefferson and Wait as equals. Dana enthusiastically reported Brown's interracial trailblazing to friends across New England.[22]

The passage of the Fugitive Slave Act in 1850, mandating federal intervention in the return of runaway slaves, further cemented Brown's commitment to antislavery. In response to this legislation, Brown penned one of his most revealing documents, "Words of Advice to the United States League of Gileadites." Written as a series of suggestions to slaves, free blacks, and insurrectionists, Brown asked if his readers remembered "the names of Lovejoy and Torrey?"—the two martyred abolitionists of the 1830s and 1840s.[23] Brown even offered guidance for his own future efforts, steeling himself for imaginary missions; "*Stand by one another and your friends, while a drop of blood remains,*" Brown wrote in italics, "*and be hanged, if you must, but tell no tales out of school. Make no confession.*"[24]

Brown spent the next few years living in North Elba, New York, as a member of the fledgling black community of Timbucto, but he remained restless. Just as he had cast about for three decades to get rich, Brown spoke constantly about violent abolitionism but found few outlets for his passion.[25] Even the passage of the Kansas-Nebraska Act in 1854, which opened up the Kansas Territory to slavery by popular vote, did not immediately spur Brown to action. Sympathetic to his son John Brown Jr.'s Kansas emigration, Brown noted that he was "committed to operate in another part of the field," otherwise "I would be on my way this fall."[26] It was not until John Jr. wrote to him in March 1855 that opportunity seemed to cross with chance. "The interest of despotism has secured to its cause hundreds and thousands of the meanest and most desperate of men," John Jr. warned his father, "armed to the teeth with Revolvers, Bowie Knives, Rifles and Cannon." Using one of his father's favorite rhetorical flourishes, John Jr. explained the urgent need to "organize . . . in military companies." The younger Brown's proposal was very simple. "The remedy we propose," he told his father, "[is to] arm. . . . We see no other way." The Free Soil men were "thoroughly determined to fight" and were only lacking someone to "lead in the matter."[27] John Brown could not resist that call.[28]

It is better that ten guilty proslavery men should die, than that one
Free-State settler should be driven out.
  —*John Brown to Henry Townsley, 1856*

2

THE FINAL ARBITER

Bleeding Kansas and the Creation of the Old Hero

As John Brown made his way across Pennsylvania and Ohio in September 1855, he was a man still searching for his calling. Life in Timbucto had validated his beliefs in racial equality, but the experience had not offered much in the way of leadership. Brown had long maintained that liberty for all was impossible without intervention and benevolent guidance. "Forcible separation of the connection between master and slave," Brown argued, would be "necessary to fit the blacks for self-government." Brown told those willing to listen "that when the time came to fight against slavery" he would happily lead this forcible separation. Kansas provided more than a mere signal for that fight; the territorial conflict made Brown a new man.[1]

Less than two years later, Brown fled Kansas under threat of arrest. Suddenly infamous for his galvanizing role in what came to be known as Bleeding Kansas—the pressure-valve prelude to the Civil War—Brown provided an alternative to mainstream abolitionists in New England. He was a man of action, a man willing to fight for the principles of antislavery. The writer Ralph Waldo Emerson was one of many charmed when Brown came east to raise money and enlist support. Emerson wrote in his diary that Brown was "the rarest of heroes, a pure idealist, with no by-ends of his own." While Brown's 'by-ends' did include personally leading the new revolution, Emerson ignored such details to emphasize Brown's transformation in the Kansas territory. "He joins that perfect Puritan faith which brought his ancestor to Plymouth Rock," Emerson wrote, "with his grandfather's ardor in the Revolution. He believes in two articles—two instruments, shall I say—the Golden Rule and the Declaration of Independence; and he used this expression in conversation here concerning them: 'Better that a whole generation of men, women, and children should pass away by a violent death, than that one word of either should be violated in this country.'"[2] Emerson struck on the overriding question of Bleeding Kansas: How did John Brown, a man searching for meaning and purpose in 1855, become a revolutionary Puritan by 1856? John Brown used the territorial contest to redeem himself, to craft an image, and to harness the symbolism of a chaotic conflict just as he came to embody it. While the very real mayhem of Kansas's internecine civil war over slavery has complicated Brown's story, there is no doubt that his adventures in Kansas transformed him and changed the conflict as well.[3]

Brown's evolution into a symbol during Bleeding Kansas is central to understanding his changing shape in American memory.[4] Brown's embrace of violence in 1856 to further the cause of racial equality and his willingness to be the agent of that change must be understood in the context of the actual conflict in Kansas.[5] Indeed, Brown's actions, excusable and deplorable, only begin to make sense amid the increasingly haphazard violence of Bleeding Kansas, not solely at the vanguard of a sequentially coherent narrative.[6]

For Brown, and for countless others consumed by the political contests of the 1850s, the recently designated territory represented much more than a new home, it was a battleground for the most important issue of the day: slavery. Brown's son Jason was the first Brown to arrive in Kansas. Writing to the family in July 1855, Jason described the difficult journey to his new home in the crude hamlet of Osawatomie. Traveling through hostile proslavery territory powerfully confirmed to the Browns that slavery was truly "the sum of all villainies."[7] But despite the difficulties of emigration, which included the death of Jason's infant son, hardships were taken in stride. The territory had transcended the quotidian; Kansas was a bellwether for the growing sectionalism consuming North and South, a barometer of the health of the nation's founding documents, and the first violent test of America's imperfect union.

After the Kansas-Nebraska Act's deliberate retooling of the Missouri Compromise exploited Americans' eagerness for new land, economic opportunity, and a political proxy state, the nation's conflicts over slavery were translated into a territorial contest. Even the earliest settlers in the future state of Kansas became sophisticated interpreters and propagandists as they sought to influence the national slavery debate. Like his family members and the great majority of Kansan emigrants, Brown was drawn as much by economic opportunities as he was by grand political projects. For men like Brown, topically engaged and financially ambitious, the new territory promised economic opportunity as well as a religious and political battleground. That battleground soon housed as diverse a set of strivers as existed anywhere in the United States. There, "fire-eaters" (Southerners eager for secession and even war) lived alongside abolitionists trying to rid the nation of slavery, Unionists seeking to maintain the status quo, and countless others.[8] From the moment these clashing groups arrived, there was conflict. "Civil war exists in Kansas," one settler wrote, and it "will spread throughout the land.[9]

Throughout the next decade, the twin stars of opportunity and mission attracted Americans from every segment of the political and moral spectrum. This stew of personalities and attitudes escalated the slavery struggle in 1850s Kansas, lending uncertain momentum to a truly catastrophic national conflict. In his move to Kansas, Brown sought to improve his fortunes and accelerate this struggle. He arrived at the opportune moment. The Kansas Territory's electoral process had already gotten off to a disastrous start. On March 30, 1855, Missouri Senator David Atchison led several thousand armed and drunken citizens into Kansas to vote in the first territorial election. Free Soilers immediately denounced the election and refused to honor the results. "For freedom of speech [we] have imprisonment, for the sight of suffrage, dictation, and for giving liberty [to] the oppressed, Death," one settler described. "Is this America? The land of Freedom?"[10]

These outrages convinced John Brown to leave North Elba. News of similar violations of freedom and justice arrived nearly every day of Brown's trip west. Anticipating the new opportunities, Brown preserved his likeness in a daguerreotype en route to the territory (figure 2.1). This image, made by a portraitist in Ohio, shows the same clean-cut, formally dressed man from the first Augustus Washington daguerreotype.[11] Indeed, the image betrays no hint of the radical purpose of his journey, or of the revolutionary from the second Augustus Washington portrait.

On October 7, Brown arrived in Osawatomie, Kansas, hoping to firmly establish the territory as the model for a new era in American freedom. Brown was a fairly typical territorial emigrant, imagining himself as a shepherd in the Free State cause. His initial impressions of his new home were not favorable, however; the gusting winds and freezing temperatures of "Brownsville" (the family's name for its circle of "makeshift tents") were disconcerting. Brown was horrified to find his children and grandchildren in dismal health. Rather than inquire why the family's glowing reports of

Figure 2.1.
John Brown, photographic
print by Josiah J. Hawes, 1856.
The Boston Athenaeum.

a landscape unparalleled "in richness and in beauty" did not conform to what he saw, Brown got down to business.[12] Questioning his sons about the political situation, Brown asked about the neighbors and their sympathies. Brown had already given in to his impatience, his constant desire, in the words of his son Salmon, "to hurry up the fight."[13] Like most of the territory, the neighbors were a mixed bunch. "There are a few proslavery towns along the Mo. River and one or two on the Kansas," one of Brown's neighbors said, "hence the disturbances among them and the outrages so often reported."[14]

Despite the disagreeable factions, Osawatomie was relatively peaceful. Until the shooting of Charles Dow, a Free Soiler from Ohio, there was no open conflict. But when a land dispute near Lawrence, Kansas, became violent and a proslavery Virginian named Frank Coleman shot Dow, opportunity beckoned. The story had many Free Soilers up in arms; Coleman had been cutting timber on Dow's property until Dow protested and "received a charge of buck shot in his breast."[15]

It was a cold-blooded killing. When Lawrence's Free Soil citizens assembled in protest, the sheriff arrested one of them for disturbing the peace. Armed Free Soilers intercepted the sheriff and freed the protestor, but a group of "proslavers [followed] from all directions and demanded that he should be given up."[16] Federal troops arrived and a siege ensued. The call went out for men to defend Lawrence from an anticipated Missourian invasion.[17] Some proslavery men had threatened to destroy the Free State Hotel in Lawrence (a popular abolitionist meeting place) and throw the printing presses (where several Free State newspapers were printed) into the river. Understanding that "the people will never accept" these terms, even the elderly responded "like the old revolutionary" soldiers.[18] Invoking the legacy of the Revolutionary War was essential to Free Soilers' self-conception as the true inheritors of the principles of the founding generation.

John Brown joined Osawatomie's makeshift military company in that spirit, heading to Lawrence to do his part. Brown and his neighbors shared a belief that "the fall of Lawrence [would] open the flood gates for [proslavery supporters] to drench our land with the blood of peaceful settlers."[19] Imagining himself as the stopgap against such bloodletting, Brown saw Lawrence as the chance to realize the dream articulated in the Washington daguerreotype. By the time the company reached the town, Brown was thirsting for a real fight.[20] "Every man in the territory [is] compelled to take up arms and fight either on one side or the other," a *St. Louis Interpreter* article described, "war alone is the order of the day."[21]

The Osawatomie company found commotion in Lawrence: the streets thick with human and animal traffic, earthworks being dug, and every able man carrying a rifle.[22] Brown quickly discovered that despite the activity, a diplomatic solution had already been reached.[23] The "Wakarusa War" was over before Brown's arrival. He had come to Kansas to battle bands of evil Missourians bent on impinging Americans' God-given freedoms, but Kansas was turning out to be mostly hardship and talk. The general atmosphere was of "trickery . . . cowardice, folly and drunkenness," Brown said, even if the Free State forces were "well behaved, cool, determined men."[24] Brown noted that despite the lack of courageous leadership, Free Soilers all displayed "the high character of the Revolutionary fathers."[25] Brown's rhetoric testified to his awareness of the stakes of the territorial contest and its connection to the principles and methods of the American Revolution.

When the Osawatomie men returned to their homes, Brown and others noted the disturbing contrast between the idea of popular sovereignty and its actual execution. National politics loomed large through a frigid winter, and 1856 brought intense apprehension. Throughout January and February, the territory held a series of disputed elections, political contests where the slavery question would supposedly be determined. On January 15, Free Soil settlers held another election. Missourians were waiting and a gang of proslavery men seized a Free State settler in Lawrence named Reese Brown (no relation to John) and attacked him mercilessly with hatchets. His last words to his wife, "They murdered me like cowards," chilled Free Soilers.

Like Charles Dow before him, Reese Brown became a martyr for the Free State cause.[26]

The Free Soiler Charles Robinson won a three-to-one victory in the election, but President Franklin Pierce refused to honor the victory. Not long after, Missourians broke up further elections in Leavenworth. Wealthy Brown, Brown's daughter-in-law, wrote that voting Free Soilers were "attacked by about 30 Missourians and told to surrender." When their leader flew the white flag, "the wretches set upon him with knives, stones and hatchets and cut and mangled him in the most shocking manner, so that he died in a few hours."[27] Wealthy added matter-of-factly that "we expect to have war here in earnest in the Spring." Her husband, John Jr., put two notes in the margins for his sister in North Elba: "US troops disarm companies of 8 and 10 F.S. men and send companies of 50 Missourians and others from Slave States off *with* their *arms*" and "This is the protection we get from Pierce." Despite the imbalance, John Jr. had clearly been impressed by his father's dedication. "We expect to fight till the last," John Jr. explained. "I shall *not leave* Kansas till it is free or I fall on the field."[28]

The senior Brown would not let freedom be lost without a fight. When another call for help came from Lawrence on May 21, Brown convinced his son's Pottawatomie Rifle Company to begin the long march there. The men stopped at Prairie City when news arrived that Missourians had taken control of and then abandoned the Free State capital. Rumors swirled about greater catastrophes in the offing. In the short march, Brown had worked the Osawatomie men into a fervor, but no one could agree where to go. For a man outspokenly frustrated by abolitionists' reliance on words rather than action, Brown could not help his rage. The Wakarusa debacle sprung to mind, but so too did the unending stream of outrages, threats, and rumors that consumed life in the territory.[29] Brown shared his sons' belief that desperate proslavery men would give them no quarter, and so far no one seemed willing to fight back.

Thus, on the afternoon of May 23, Brown gathered the few men he thought worthy of what he labeled a "secret mission."[30] With eight of the Rifle Company with him, Brown set off for Pottawatomie Creek. His son Owen urged him to "commit no rash act," but the next night, Brown and his men posed as travelers and knocked on the door of James P. Doyle, a proslavery man from Tennessee.[31] The band took Doyle and his sons William, twenty-two years old, and Drury, twenty years old, as prisoners.

A dozen yards from the cabin, Brown gave the order. His men stabbed James Doyle and shot him multiple times; they split William and Drury's heads with broadswords. Brown told his men to leave the brothers in a ditch. The group proceeded to the home of another Tennessean, Allen Wilkinson, and cut his throat. Finally, the group arrived at the cabin of James Harris, in search of a notorious proslavery rabble-rouser named Henry Sherman. Finding only Sherman's brother William, Brown's troop split the man's skull in two places, put a hole in his chest, and left his hand dangling from his wrist.[32] No one in the company ever revealed definitively whose sword cut which man or which of the gang shot Doyle; but the entire group was present for each of the five murders.

One of Brown's Osawatomie neighbors, Bartow Darrach, deftly captured the aftermath of the massacre. "This settlement has been thrown into great commotion and placed in circumstances of great danger by the murder of 5 pro slavery men," Darrach wrote. Even though Brown's victims "had repeatedly threatened the lives and property of our free state men," Darrach said, "the murders [are] condemned as unjustifiable under any circumstances. I am sorry to say that the act was done by freestate men who heretofore have been highly respected."[33]

Darrach pointed out that these "freestate men" were close relatives of Brown's brother-in-law Samuel Adair.[34] Far from excusing the brutality of the massacre, Darrach noted that "the murderers," were "determined men and armed to the teeth."[35] On June 28, Owen Brown wrote the family in North Elba with his own account of the massacre. Owen described getting an "urgent call to arms . . . to defend the people of Lawrence," after which his father fled the area.[36]

The "murder of the 5 proslavery men had aroused the whole country," Jason Brown described in a letter, "and parties from Mo and about here were scouring about for the murderers." While Jason did not specifically name the culprits, he never denied his family's involvement and admitted that even when he and his brother were held captive by Federal troops, "we were kindly treated by the proslavery men." Of course, Jason continued, "there were a good many of the lower order about us . . . who were thirsting for our blood. I heard some of them say; 'If we could only get their Jesus (meaning John or Father), they could nail us all to a row of Posts and let us hang there till we would starve to death.'"[37]

Jason was anxious not for his safety but for "the worthless doughfaces of the North" to stop claiming, "'We have nothing to do with Slavery.'" He happily noted the departures of many proslavery settlers but cautioned that "murders and robbery are very frequent now. We are obliged to keep under arms night and day." The combat and fear were taking their toll.

We "would gladly go home," he wrote, "but feel safer here than on the *way* home." Finally, Jason repeated the flimsy rationale for his father's actions: "Some of the 5 Proslavery men who were killed had threatened the lives of Free State men near them, and also [threatened] to cut the throat of a young woman."[38] Despite the dubious veracity of these claims, there was no doubt that threats and killings had long been the lingua franca of territorial Kansas. Brown's brutal escapade on the Pottawatomie certainly raised the stakes, but it also seemed to give some form to the madness.

Territorial Kansas was already "a harrowing" environment, with night following "night of terror." But one Pottawatomie resident reported that after Brown's raid, Free Soilers and proslavery settlers alike lived in constant fear of "being mowed down in the darkness by an ambush[ing] foe."[39] Brown's murders convinced Free Soilers that their side could fight back. More important, Brown viscerally demonstrated to proslavery settlers and Missourians that Free Soilers would retaliate in kind. Of course, that demonstration alone did not create a stalemate; proslavery settlers responded to Brown's massacre by attacking the Free State capital of Lawrence, Kansas, leaving it barely recognizable. A proslavery posse torched the city, throwing the newspaper presses in the river.[40] The payback for Brown's viciousness on the Pottawatomie had begun.

Sitting in the ruins of Lawrence was a bearded Scotsman who would help Brown transcend Bleeding Kansas. James Redpath, the chief Kansas correspondent for Horace Greeley's *New York Tribune*, had witnessed the destruction of Lawrence firsthand.[41] Redpath had been perusing a newspaper, reading of Charles Sumner's brutal beating in the Senate chamber, when he heard the news that "five pro-slavery settlers had been murdered" in Pottawatomie by Free Soilers, "their bodies shockingly disfigured and mutilated." Through a shattered window, Redpath watched a "body of troops from Lecompton," all proslavery men, passing by, "destined for Osawatomie." As Redpath recalled, "not a moment was to be lost if John Brown . . . and his boys were to be warned of their coming and design." A longtime believer in the overlapping causes of journalism and activism, Redpath hired a horse and "started on the mission at once."[42]

Redpath was a precocious young man of twenty-two. Inspired by Frederick Law Olmsted's series of Southern dispatches for the *New York Times*, Redpath had traveled through the South in 1854 and 1855, interviewing whites and blacks, slaves and freedmen, in order to bring some detail to the "abstract evil" of slavery.[43] Although he had embarked on that journey a believer in gradualism or schemes to purchase freedom for slaves, in the midst of his reporting, Redpath wrote a friend that he was now a confirmed "fanatic" for violent abolition. As early as 1854, the journalist outlined radical invasion plans to end slavery in the *National Anti-slavery Standard* and *The Liberator*.[44] His move to Kansas, like that of so many, was motivated by both hope for professional success and belief in the territory's potential importance on the road to abolition.[45] Indeed, by 1856, Redpath happily supported violent uprising by and on behalf of slaves, welcoming "the approaching massacre" of "so desirable a revolution."[46]

Like Brown, Redpath recognized opportunity when it was in front of him. After riding out of Lawrence, Redpath was captured and released by Federal troops. He somehow managed to stumble upon John Brown's son Frederick on the Kansas prairie. After Redpath established his Free State credentials, Frederick showed the man to Brown's hidden camp, where the news of approaching hostile troops was greeted with nonchalance. John Brown was spoiling for a fight. Redpath recalled that the abolitionist's appearance was not particularly awe inspiring; Brown had "his shirt-sleeves rolled up" and was "poorly clad," with "his toes protrud[ing] from his boots."[47]

Having fulfilled his "altruistic" mission, Redpath inquired about the massacre. "Old Brown . . . respectfully but firmly forbade conversation on the Pottawatomie affair; and said that if I desired any information from the company . . . he, as their Captain, would answer for them whatever it was proper to communicate." Redpath was convinced by Brown's denial of any role in the killing. After a few hours in the camp, Redpath left with a single impression: "I had seen the predestined leader of the second and the holier American Revolution."[48]

Redpath did not make this pronouncement as a naive enthusiast in the antislavery cause. A well-read man of the world, Redpath had literary tastes that ran the gamut from Napoleonic histories to British economic analyses to obscure Eastern spiritual texts.[49] While his passions and ambition drove him to the extremes of reportage, Redpath was not the sort of man easily taken in by a gun-toting, Bible-quoting charlatan. Redpath saw something in Brown that harmonized with his own crusade for the abolition of slavery. "I am an Abolitionist," Redpath declared in the 1850s, "and something more. I am in favor, not only of abolishing the Curse, but of making reparation for the Crime. Not an Abolitionist only, but a Reparationist." Redpath earned a price on his head across many Southern states for his outspoken radicalism, a thousand-dollar bounty that filled him with pride.[50]

Redpath's involvement soon extended beyond observation. The young journalist became directly involved in many of Brown's adventures after Pottawatomie. The most notable came in June 1856, when one of Redpath's dispatches disclosing Brown's location was intercepted by the proslavery mercenary Captain Clay Pate. Pate led his makeshift militia to the town of Blackjack in hopes of capturing the leader of the Pottawatomie massacre.[51] Brown used his burgeoning legend to trick Pate, convincing him that his thirty men were surrounded. Redpath gloried in recounting Brown's heroic role in Pate's "unconditional surrender."[52]

Eastern audiences were eager for such news from Bleeding Kansas. Readers wanted dramatic events like those reported on June 6, 1856. In response to Brown's massacre, "about 80 mounted men from Westport and thereabouts made an invasion upon us," one local resident wrote to his family in Boston, "ransacking houses, breaking open trunks and stealing arms and money." The men searched for Brown, hoping to retaliate and intimidate. Brown's son Frederick was shot dead by proslavery men, but the elder Brown managed to evade capture. In the meantime, troops flooded Osawatomie. They knocked down houses, lit the town on fire, then "stole 12 of the best horses in the place."[53]

To be sure, with his five killings in May 1856, Brown dramatically altered the balance of power, mostly through the myths that grew up around the massacre. Jason Brown sent a letter to North Elba in August, explaining some but not all of what was happening in Pottawatomie. "I cannot write much for want of time and because of the continual trouble and excitement we are under here. I am trying to cut some hay," he wrote, "but am looking continually for it to be burned, and our cattle driven off." After a local militia attacked a group of proslavery Georgians and took "some good arms and provisions," Jason described the enormous symbolic power of John Brown's massacre. Every violent act directed at proslavery settlers and Missourians "was said to be done by Old Capt. John Brown's Co." Brown's name began to be invoked for every crime in the territory. Describing another skirmish, Jason noted that a group of settlers had "got word that Old Capt. Brown was coming with 200 Abolitionists to give them an *evening call on the next night*. They immediately rolled out and left."[54]

In this way the massacre transformed violence in the Kansas Territory, transforming Brown into a myth unto himself. Speaking to the fear rippling through proslavery Kansans, Jason wrote that "Old Capt. Brown can now be raised from every Prairie and thicket." Writing of the usefulness of such a symbolic threat, Jason indicated that all liberty-minded settlers would support Brown if they had suffered at the hands of their enemies. Until "free white State folks . . . had some horses taken by the Ruffians," they would not support John Brown's violence. "They will come out on the right side if their little town should get burnt," Jason wrote harshly. Alluding to the symbolic weight Brown now carried in the territory, Jason added that with one hundred men, "they would soon be called 1000 strong. . . . It is said in Mo that it will take 3 to 1 to take the Browns."[55]

Brown "was a tower of strength in time of need," one neighbor described, but more important, the abolitionist became "a veritable terror to the enemy."[56] After capturing another militia of Missourians, one of the captives made a single request: the prisoner wanted to see Brown with his own eyes. He was convinced there was no such man, only myth. "You wish to see me," Brown told the man. "Take a good look at me, and tell your friends, when you get back to Missouri, what sort of man I am. . . . We wish no harm to you or your companions. Stay at home, let us alone, and we shall be friends. I wish you well."[57]

But those prisoners did not stay home in peace. As one Osawatomie resident reported, not long after Brown had moved on, "the enemy plundered and burned our town, including both stores. . . . Many have lost every thing they had excepting the clothes they wore. . . . Our losses in killed is 5, wounded 3 and two or three are missing."[58] Perhaps fortunately for his neighbors, Brown continued his agitations elsewhere in Kansas, avoiding Federal troops and trigger-happy Missourians. When Brown did manage to capture proslavery prisoners, his lectures to them were impassioned. "You have been killing our men, terrorizing our women and children, and destroying our property—houses, crops, and animals," Brown told the men. "You stand here as criminals." After a dramatic pause, Brown continued. "You are fighting for slavery, you are fighting against liberty, which our Revolutionary fathers fought to establish in this Republic, where all men should be free and equal, with the inalienable rights of life, liberty and the pursuit of happiness. Therefore, you are traitors to liberty and to your country." After releasing the men, Brown simply instructed them to return "home and tell your neighbors and friends of your mistake." Then he took their guns.[59]

Brown's understanding of his symbolic importance was essential. His advocacy for the cause of liberty was accompanied by a strong sense of self-promotion. In this, Brown had allies. Since their first meeting, James Redpath promoted the abolitionist's exploits in the Eastern press. Redpath's field reporting was matched in spirit and kind by his colleague William Phillips at the *New York Tribune* and by Richard Hinton's Kansas dispatches for the *Boston Traveller*.[60] As a result, Brown's name circulated widely in New York, Boston, and beyond. When Brown fled arrest in Kansas during the winter of 1857 to raise money and support in New England, Redpath was already there soliciting donations. Redpath hyped Brown in the *New York Tribune*: "Old Brown of Osawatomie is in town. He is a hale and vigorous man of fifty-seven . . . with piercing dark blue-eyes, and face expressive of will."[61]

Since Brown had not and would never reveal his role in the Pottawatomie massacre, Redpath could not cite any concrete heroics on which to base the honorific "Old Brown of Osawatomie," but it was the first time the title had appeared in the Eastern press. Redpath, soon at Brown's specific urging, began to manipulate the old man's protomythic stature with an expert touch. Of course, the conceit was based on real exploits, even if neither Redpath nor Brown revealed the truth.

When Brown began barnstorming across New England in 1857, he shrewdly used his audience's ideas of the Kansas conflict to create an additional sense of danger and heroism. "I saw the ruins of many Free State men's houses . . . grain wasted and burning," Brown recounted; "saw the mangled and shockingly disfigured body of the murdered Hoyt, of Deerfield Mass. . . . I knew him well." Beyond his nods to politicized entertainment, peppering his accounts with asides that "it could not have cost the United States one dollar" to prevent the losses to life and property, Brown knew that the horror stories carried a voyeuristic thrill. In this vein, he developed a brilliant climax to his presentations. "I saw three mangled bodies of three young men," Brown would declare, "two of which were dead and had laid on the open ground for about eighteen hours for the flies to work at, the other living with twenty buckshot and bullet-holes in him. One of those two dead was my own son."[62]

In February 1857, Brown delivered a nearly identical speech to the Massachusetts Legislature. After detailing the huge financial losses his family had sustained, Brown described the everyday sights of murder and mayhem sure to horrify any upright New England man or woman. Brown told those assembled that he had "at his hotel, and would exhibit to the Committee[,] . . . the chains which one of his sons had worn" as he was taken to prison, an innocent man.[63]

Although Redpath had facilitated most of these meetings for Brown, relying on his previously cultivated "network of eastern supporters," aside from their meeting in May 1856, the two men had not spent substantial time together. Redpath was raising money for a new Free Soil newspaper, *The*

Doniphan Crusader of Freedom, which debuted in Doniphan, Kansas, on December 19, 1857.[64] While Redpath pursued this journalistic enterprise, he and fellow abolitionist reporter Richard Hinton often dined together. One evening in June 1858, John Brown, disguised with a long beard, interrupted their meal. Complaining that Free Soilers had "abandoned the rifle for the ballot box," Brown tried to recruit Redpath "to return East to help raise funds." Although Hinton already knew of Brown's plans to invade the South with an armed band, Redpath was delighted by Brown giving voice to fantasies so similar to his own. Redpath made a quick decision to help Brown raise money and support for the Southern invasion and slave insurrection.[65]

Wasting no time exploiting his contacts and Brown's symbolic power, Redpath began rewriting his personal narrative and Brown's as well. "You went to Kansas, when the troubles broke out there," Redpath wrote, addressing Brown, "not to 'settle' or 'speculate'—or from idle curiosity: but for one stern, solitary purpose—to have a shot at the South. So did I."[66]

One of Brown's Pottawatomie neighbors, Dr. W. Winkley, used a similar framework. "Brown was the cyclonic force, the lightning's flash in the darkness, that cleared and lighted the way for the men of that day."[67] Brown's partnership with Redpath distilled this imagery and commercialized the result. As the two men solicited money and support across New England, Brown's image was reproduced in prints, but especially *cartes-de-visite*.[68] The two frequently reproduced one image that became known as the Hudson daguerreotype (figure 2.2). This image shows the man that Brown and Redpath used to represent Bleeding Kansas and answer fears of the slave power conspiracy. Though apparently not deliberate, many contemporary reproductions of the original daguerreotype were overexposed, which tend to give an even greater impression of Brown's severity.[69] Beyond the weathered appearance and sunken features, Brown was putting forth a bolder image after his time in Kansas.[70] Following his infamous massacre in May 1856 and the subsequent armed skirmishes, Brown was a changed man, a take-no-nonsense fellow who had tangled with death. Indeed, Brown's disdain for the "milk and water" activism of William Lloyd Garrison is almost palpable in the intense gaze and defiantly crossed arms of the Hudson portrait.[71]

In tours of the Northeast, Brown's abundant opportunism and an overwhelming talent for manipulating his own symbolism allowed him to embody, in some grand sense, abolitionism. It was this legend, a legend Brown nurtured at every turn, that the Hudson daguerreotype captured. As a clear

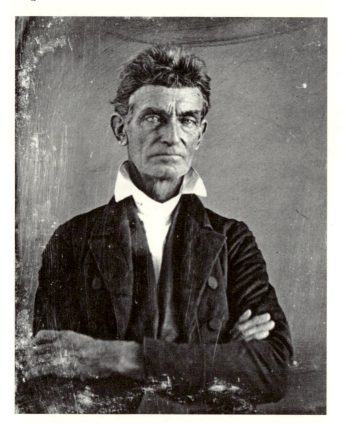

Figure 2.2.
John Brown in
Hudson, Ohio,
sixth-plate
daguerreotype,
1856. The Boston
Athenaeum.

threat to the slaveocracy, this imagery allowed Brown to solicit money and new opportunities to advance *his* cause of freedom. On these tours, Brown met with various luminaries and received the fawning attention of the region as he cultivated his plans for more dramatic projects. In parlors, churches, and lecture halls, "Osawatomie" Brown's exploits earned him enthusiastic audiences with Henry David Thoreau, Ralph Waldo Emerson, and dozens of other notable New England personalities.[72]

Less than two years after an almost-penniless Brown had moved to the Kansas prairies, he was filling seats and welcoming benefactors, rallying people to his mission and convincing them of his own heroism. The opportunities to use his symbolic presence were numerous with such impressionable audiences. After his meeting with Thoreau, Brown heard rumors that federal marshals from Kansas were going to arrest him. Taking refuge in the home of Judge Thomas Russell, Brown checked the windows dramatically, and told Mrs. Russell that he would die before he was arrested. He apologized gallantly, adding, "I should hate to spoil your carpet."[73]

With his friend Redpath's connections, Brown requested a personal audience with just one Bostonian: Charles Sumner. On May 21, 1856, Sumner had been beaten nearly to death on the Senate floor by South Carolina congressman Preston Brooks in response to Sumner's infamous 'Crime against Kansas' speech. Brown's request perfectly captured his savvy as a self-promoter. Sumner's beating was a perfect ex post facto justification for the Pottawatomie massacre on May 24: antislavery outrage answered by abolitionist justice.[74]

One evening, Redpath, Brown, and Sumner discussed the "assault of Brooks, under which Sumner then was suffering," but Brown focused the trio's attention. With Sumner "stretched in pain on the bed, Captain Brown suddenly asked if he had still the coat" he was wearing during the attack? "'Yes,' said Sumner, 'it is in that closet: [would] you like to see it?'" When Brown nodded, Sumner stood "slightly bent" and used the bed to guide himself across the room. "Brown, erect as a pillar," took the garment from the senator, "holding up the blood besmeared coat in his right hand and intently examining it." As Redpath recalled, Brown "said nothing . . . but I remember that his lips compressed and his eyes shone like polished steel."[75] As he thumbed the sleeves in silence, Brown's gaze invited conclusions about his next move.

We are abolitionists from the North, come to take and release your slaves; our organization is large and must succeed. I suffered much in Kansas, and expect to suffer here, in the cause of human freedom. Slaveholders I regard as robbers and murderers; and I have sworn to abolish slavery and liberate my fellow-men.
  —John Brown to the master of the Harpers Ferry Armory, October 16, 1859

3

NOT BURIED BUT PLANTED

Cultivating the Legend of John Brown

Although John Brown's invasion of Virginia generated much confusion, some grasped the man and his mission immediately. John Zittle, captain of one of the first military companies to arrive at Harpers Ferry, wrote that Brown's raid "was the signal gun of the great war."[1] Zittle, a native Virginian, was not the first, or the last, to assign such importance to the invasion. More than just a portent of America's Civil War, Harpers Ferry became the launching pad for Brown's immortality. Following Brown from Charles Sumner's cloakroom to a Charlestown scaffold highlights the abolitionist's path to martyrdom and the origins of his enigmatic place in American memory.

Brown's brief time as an abolitionist celebrity, the result of his adventures in Kansas, carried him to the small town of Harpers Ferry in 1859. In particular, Brown's tenacious desire to lead the revolution for black freedom convinced him that both God and the Founding Fathers authorized ever greater attacks on slavery. After Brown proved his revolutionary credentials in Kansas's territorial conflict, particularly after the brutal murders of the five proslavery settlers in Pottawatomie, he became known across the country. Brown did not merely rest on his Kansan laurels, he aggressively sought new ventures designed to threaten the institution of slavery. Brown stoked the flames of his burgeoning reputation, especially among African Americans, by returning to Kansas in 1858. Once there, he led a dramatic rescue of eleven slaves in Missouri, escorting them twenty-five hundred miles to Canada after "reparation" was "made for the wrongs that had been done."[2] Brown's friend Redpath wrote admiringly of the incident: "What [Brown] believed, he practiced." After asking the slaves "how much their services had been worth," the abolitionist "proceeded to take property to the amount thus due to the negroes," further infuriating their former masters.[3]

Brown himself wrote to the *New York Tribune* to celebrate his exploit. After explaining that his actions were partly in response to the senseless murder of "eleven quiet citizens" for the crime of "being Free-State men," Brown recalled a "negro man called Jim" coming to visit his cabin.[4] After Jim explained that his family was about to be sold, Brown "liberated" them, some nearby slaves, and other property.

"Now for a comparison," Brown wrote. "Eleven persons are forcibly restored to their natural and inalienable rights, with but one man killed, and all 'hell is stirred from beneath.' . . . Consider the two cases."[5] The incident, with Redpath running public relations, bolstered Brown's reputation even further. Black Americans began contacting Brown to express their appreciation and support. Here, for the first time, was a white abolitionist willing to take up arms for the cause. One admirer, James Newton Gloucester, a wealthy free black in Philadelphia, wrote to Brown to applaud his "very commendable measures to deliver the slave." Blacks, Gloucester warned, "suffer for the want of intelligence" and are "at sea without a commander or rudder."[6] Perhaps Brown was the man to give them that guidance.

In another letter, Gloucester edged toward Brown's extremism. Regardless of circumstances, Gloucester argued, no black Americans were truly free. "There is in truth no black man, north or south of Mason and Dixon line—a freeman whatever be his wealth, position or worth to the world." Thus, Gloucester wrote, we must "now use these means that God and nature have placed within our power . . . and join with you in holy energy and combat against the all damnable foe."[7] Gloucester's assessment captured Brown's peculiar magnetism. John Brown was "the man who most clearly saw the real crux of the conflict," W. E. B. Du Bois wrote of this period, "a man whose leadership lay not in his office, wealth or influence, but in the white flame of his utter devotion to an ideal."[8]

On Brown's tours of the Northeast, many noted the broad appeal of that devotion. In 1858, the eccentric writer A. Bronson Alcott attended a lecture by "the Captain" at the town hall in Concord, Massachusetts. "He spoke with a directness that so became him on the Kansas troubles," Alcott later recalled, "modestly alluding to the part he had taken in those encounters." The audience was impressed, as was Alcott, by Brown's "surpassing sense, courage, and religious earnestness. . . . He inspired a confidence in his integrity and good judgment. He seemed superior to any legal traditions. . . .

He did not conceal his hatred of Slavery, much less his readiness to strike a blow for freedom at the fitting moment. I thought him equal to any thing he should dare: the man to do the deed necessary to be done with the patriot's zeal, the martyr's temper and purpose." Alcott simply transcribed Brown's dramatic conclusion. "'What! Am I to wait for the Nation to do this righteous thing, for sluggish types and glib tongues to convert the country?' Brown asked his audience, 'No! I shall not wait for them; I must go and put myself, all I am, all Liberty is worth, into the Idea, body and soul, and take the consequences.'"[9]

Alcott's account revealed Brown's increasing radicalism and his eagerness to explain his plans. After he stated his destination as Virginia, Brown finally won his first black volunteer, a former slave named Richard Richardson.[10] In plainly detailing his plans, Brown relied on the advice of Frederick Douglass. Douglass, the former slave and prominent antislavery orator, frequently remarked that Brown "was the only man he had ever met who was without racism."[11] Brown stayed with Douglass at the latter's home in Rochester, New York, in January and February 1858. It was with Douglass that Brown drew up the first draft of the Provisional Constitution, the framework he intended to implement upon his invasion's success.[12] Douglass urged Brown to reconsider his plans, understanding slavery as Brown was unable to, but he could not help but be impressed and a little frightened by Brown's indifference toward the murder and mayhem of the imagined insurrection.[13]

By this point, Brown was convinced of his place in God's holy mission and equally confident that free and enslaved blacks would flock to his side. In the late winter of 1858, Brown had an encouraging meeting with a small group of blacks in Philadelphia, including Reverend Stephen Smith, Reverend Henry Highland Garnet, and William Still. These were the high points of black enthusiasm for Brown, but actual assistance was still remote. Garnet, who had urged outright slave rebellion as early as 1843, later claimed that he had specifically warned Brown that the timing was not right for the Harpers Ferry venture.[14]

Shrugging off these concerns, Brown traveled to Canada to recruit Harriet Tubman for his Virginia invasion. Tubman was enthusiastic and recalled Brown fondly in later years, but she made only vague commitments when Brown requested her help.[15] Writing to his son about the meeting, Brown revealed his eccentric egalitarian bent. Rather than just describe Tubman, Brown used the masculine pronoun to display just how heroic the slave liberator really was. "Tubman hooked on *his* whole team at once,"

Brown began. "He *Hariet* [*sic*] is the most of a *man* naturally; that *I ever* met with." Brown's experiences with Tubman earned him a nice reception in Chatham, Ontario, just east of Detroit. Some twenty blacks participated in a secret convention where Brown unveiled the draft of his Provisional Constitution. The crowd, largely drawn from the local community, filled Brown with confidence. The abolitionist believed that his warm reception was irrefutable proof of black interest in his plans and leadership. He was convinced such enthusiasm would translate into military recruits. "There is the most abundant material," he told John Brown Jr., "*& of the right quality*: in this quarter; beyond all doubt."[16]

In Chatham, Brown expounded on his study of Roman warfare, the Spanish revolt against the Romans, the rule of Schamyl (the Circassian chief), and Toussaint L'Ouverture's slave rebellion in Haiti. Brown positioned himself as the newest leader in this military and revolutionary lineage. The response to his ideas was spirited, and Brown cannot be blamed entirely for misreading that enthusiasm. For all his admirable foresight, Brown was a defiant, stubborn, and often enigmatic gentleman. His readiness to embrace violence made him especially susceptible to ambitious and violent rhetoric. The encouragement of Tubman and the Chatham convention convinced Brown of what he already believed: that an army would materialize when he needed it.[17]

Brown's Provisional Constitution was finalized at the convention and described the purpose of that imagined army: "Whereas slavery, throughout its entire existence in the United States, is none other than a most barbarous, unprovoked, and unjustifiable war of one portion of its citizens upon another portion, the only conditions of which are perpetual imprisonment and hopeless servitude or absolute extermination—in utter disregard and violation of those eternal and self-evident truths set forth in our Declaration of Independence." It was common in the 1850s, especially as the threat of secession increased, for both sides of the slavery debate to claim the mantle of the Declaration of Independence. "Therefore we," Brown wrote, "citizens of the United States, and the oppressed people who, by a recent decision of the Supreme Court, are declared to have no rights which the white man is bound to respect, establish for ourselves the following Provisional Constitution."[18]

For Brown, the Dred Scott decision of March 6, 1857, was the final straw. The case's impact spoke to the political stew in which Brown and his compatriots found themselves. The Provisional Constitution took the debates over these implications to particularly treasonous lengths. In addition to condemning slavery, the constitution authorized the confiscation of property, of "persons" as well as "money, plate, watches, or jewelry, captured by honorable warfare." The articles of Brown's constitution provided an extensive justification for the kind of armed raids that Brown had performed in Kansas and that he imagined continuing until slavery crumbled. Unlike a loosely organized Underground Railroad in the Alleghenies, Brown's Provisional Constitution had explicit goals. Seemingly aware of the document's dangerous implications, Brown's constitution claimed not to "in any way . . . encourage the overthrow of any State Government of the United States: and look to the dissolution of the Union." Instead, its purpose was "Amendment and Repeal" under the same flag "that our Fathers fought under in the Revolution."[19]

Brown saw himself as the vessel of the Revolution, the living defender of the Declaration of Independence. Accordingly, he believed that he would ultimately have to turn away recruits for his invasion. Surrounded by his raiders, numbering almost twenty, and the black community at Chatham, Brown believed that his charisma would carry the day. However, his faith that enslaved blacks would flock to his men when he attacked the South revealed a deep misunderstanding of the daily workings of Southern slavery.[20] Regardless, Brown soldiered on, convinced that vague commitments and faith would suffice.

In other quarters, his mission seemed to be gaining tremendous steam. When James Redpath published his collection of articles on his Southern travels, he dedicated the book to Brown. Indeed, *The Roving Editor*, first published in March 1859, sought out support for Brown's mission, however obliquely. "You, Old Hero!" Redpath declared in his dedication, "believe that the slave should be aided and urged to insurrection." Redpath even included new chapters outlining Brown's plans for "whites to foment a massive slave rebellion." Redpath summed up the meaning of the territorial conflict in similar terms: "Kansas was [the] Lexington" for the "Second American Revolution."[21]

By July 1859, that revolution seemed nearly hopeless. Brown's black support had not materialized, but his interracial liberation army, numbering only twenty men, moved ahead with its plans. The group moved into a farmhouse located just across the Potomac River from Harpers Ferry. Living under an alias, Isaac Smith, Brown used his rented farmhouse (part of Dr. Booth Kennedy's farm) as the center of operations. Here Brown and his men stockpiled weapons and strategized for the coming invasion. Even Brown's sixteen-year-old daughter played a part; she spent the summer as a lookout, responsible for sounding the alert if neighbors became curious. She dubbed her father's men the "Invisibles" because they lived completely out of sight for three months.

On a surreptitious mission just two months before the raid, Brown met Frederick Douglass at an abandoned stone quarry near Chambersburg, Pennsylvania. Douglass, in Chambersburg on a lecture tour, passionately warned Brown about the danger of his mission. Harpers Ferry was a "perfect steel-trap," Douglass told his friend; he and his men would "never get out alive."[22] "I wanted to get at John Brown before it was too late," Douglass recalled. "That is, I wished, if possible, to prevent him from going to Harper's Ferry. Some of us who knew of what he was about to do, not only felt sure that his attempt would fail, but we feared greatly that it would do serious harm to the whole anti-slavery movement."

Douglass noted that his lecture in Chambersburg "was a mere blind. If you had seen me the next morning, you would have seen me walking along the creek towards Kennedy's mill. . . . Not far from the town, an old man, whose slouched hat hung down over his face, was sitting on the bank of the creek, fishing. . . . That man was John Brown." As Douglass noted with regret, "I found that I could not budge him from going on with his plans. I was miserably troubled when I left him, and, as soon as possible I got away from that part of the country [and] it wasn't long after that that the terrible end came." Douglass did not mention that beyond ignoring his well-reasoned fears, Brown managed to convince Douglass's companion, Shields Green, to join his mission. Green simply turned to Douglass after hearing Brown make his case and said, "I b'leve I'll go wid de ole man."[23]

Men like Shields committed to Brown after only a few minutes and gave reassurance about the fate of the mission. If Virginia was anything like Kansas, Brown believed he and his men could survive on bluster, rumor, and the willingness to kill. Thus, as reconnaissance continued around the federal arsenal, their leader seemed eerily confident. On October 15, when Brown told the men at nightfall, "We will proceed to the Ferry," he led sixteen white and five black men to liberate slaves.[24]

The Reverend Vanderlip Leech, a revivalist Virginia preacher and witness to Brown's raid, recalled that the abolitionist "believed that if he could secure the arms and ammunition in" the armory, arsenal, and Hall's rifle works, he could "carry them into the [vastness] of the adjacent mountains, and then unfurl the flag of freedom for all slaves who would flock to his standard, the result would be a general uprising of the negro population throughout the border states." Even fifty years after the raid, Leech could not resist the obvious. "A more idiotic and senseless theory never entered an American mind," he described. "In the superlative degree it was unreasonable and ridiculous."[25]

At 8:00 P.M. on October 16, 1859, Brown left his son Owen to guard the farmhouse. He and his men—free blacks, runaway slaves, white soldiers of fortune, and others—crossed the Potomac River bridge at 10:00 P.M.[26] Contrary to later assessments of Brown's doomed plan, the early hours of the mission went well. Brown's men captured the railroad and armory watchmen without incident. The raiders cut telegraph wires and secured the arsenal and armory. Brown grew impatient for his army of bondsmen to arrive and he sent six men to alert local slaves that their liberator awaited them.[27] Whether these alerts ever reached their recipients is debated, but in the meantime Brown was forced to take prisoners. When Brown's men moved through the town, ladies "leaned out [windows] crying 'Murder.'" One of Brown's black compatriots yelled to "'take in your heads or I'll blow out your brains!' . . . leveling his gun at them as he spoke."[28] For the moment, Brown's men controlled the town.

Understanding the geography of Harpers Ferry underscores how precarious that grip was and the folly in Brown's choice of targets (figure 3.1). The town was a mere spit of land at the confluence of the Shenandoah and Potomac Rivers. Not only was the town at the bottom of this sloping peninsula, but the banks of the rivers rose in the characteristic hills of Virginia's countryside. Even if Brown could hold the town, he would still be trapped; the situation was a virtual turkey shoot. One could forgive antebellum Americans for speculating that only a fool or a madman would choose Harpers Ferry as a target.

After Brown's initial success, his luck changed rapidly. Around 1:00 A.M., Patrick Higgins, the night watchman for the Potomac River bridge, found his coworker missing (he was being held prisoner by Brown's men). After being shot at by Oliver Brown, Higgins tried to warn the incoming train from Wheeling, Virginia. Amid rifle fire and the chaos of the train's arrival, Brown's men shot the free black baggage handler Hayward Shepherd, the first fatality of Brown's mission. From there, things went from bad to worse. The same eastbound train was permitted to leave Harpers Ferry and continue its journey to Baltimore. As soon as the train left the town, news of an enormous "negro insurrection" traveled far and near.

John Brown thus accomplished one goal of his raid, to make headlines, but his army-in-waiting of local slaves failed to materialize. Contrary to

Figure 3.1. Harpers Ferry, Virginia, tinted lithograph by Augustus Weidenbach, ca. 1860–63. The New York Public Library/Art Resource, New York.

white Southern opinion, local blacks reacted ambivalently not out of loyalty to their masters but out of fear. Martha Tucker, a slave in Raleigh, North Carolina, at the time of Brown's raid, said her fellow bondsmen felt anything but loyalty. Focusing on the waves of fear that consumed slave owners, Tucker "spoke of the excitement" among her fellow slaves following "John Brown's raid." Describing Brown's being hung in effigy across North Carolina afterward, Tucker described the pleasure of seeing her master as he "brooded over the Brown uprising and feared that the slaves would be taken from him."[29]

Tucker's master had nothing to fear. By morning, church bells rang across Virginia, alerting local militias to the raid. "I was a lad of eighteen at the time," John Allstadt, a Harpers Ferry resident, noted. Held at gunpoint by Brown's raiders and informed that Brown had taken the armory and rifle works, Allstadt replied incredulously, "'That isn't much! . . . Only one watchman there!' . . . 'You shut your damned mouth or I'll blow your brains out!' [one of Brown's raiders told him] and ordered a negro to keep me quiet with a revolver at my breast."[30] Once "inside the Armory yard, there stood an old man 'This,' said [one of the raiders] by way of introduction, 'is John Brown.' 'Osawatomie Brown of Kansas,' added Brown." With Brown retaining his knack for self-promotion, even in the thick of combat, Allstadt watched the old man hand "pikes to our negroes, telling them to guard us carefully, to prevent our escape."[31]

Henry Clinton, a local slave, described his own restlessness and joy in hearing of the raid, just as he underscored its tragic consequences. Clinton noted that "the first time I ever struck a man I hit my master when he was beating my mother." This rage was channeled into hope when Brown hit Harpers Ferry. With some regret, Clinton recalled "holding a horse for my master to get on and go down to the Ferry to help kill John Brown if possible."[32]

The defenders of law who sought to capture and kill Brown arrived in hordes. "Received orders from the secretary of War in person," Robert E. Lee wrote, "to repair in evening train to Harper's Ferry. Reached Harper's Ferry at 11 P.M. . . . Posted marines in the United States Armory. Waited until daylight, as a number of citizens were held as hostages, whose lives were threatened."[33]

On the afternoon of October 17, two companies from Charlestown shot and killed Brown's man Dangerfield Newby, an ex-slave hoping to free his wife and children. Not long afterward, three more of Brown's men were killed at the rifle works. Just after dawn, Allstadt and other prisoners were taken into the armory watchhouse as the local militias arrived and began shooting. The first shootings there occurred when Brown tried to surrender, and Brown's son Watson and the raider Aaron Stevens were mortally wounded. "In the quiet of the night," Allstadt described, Brown's son Watson died. Watson "had begged again and again to be shot, in the agony of his wound, but his father had replied to him . . . 'If you must die, die like a man.' His father called to him, after a time. No answer. 'I guess he is dead,' said Brown."[34]

One of Brown's raiders shot the mayor of Harpers Ferry. In response, the townspeople shot the two remaining raiders-at-large, Willy Leeman and William Thompson. Brown was inside the engine house with his four remaining compatriots and their thirty captives. "Tuesday about sunrise," General Lee recounted, "with twelve marines, under Lieutenant Green, broke in the door of the engine-house, secured the insurgents, and relieved the prisoners unhurt. All the insurgents killed or mortally wounded, but four, John Brown, Stevens, Coppoc and Shields" (figure 3.2).[35] When the Marines finally entered the engine house, Allstadt maintained that it was "absolutely untrue that Brown had at any time proposed to put his prisoners to the fore in case of attack. Brown himself, at the moment of the break-

Figure 3.2. "The Harpers Ferry Insurrection—The U.S. Marines Storming the Engine House." From Frank Leslie's Illustrated Newspaper, *October 29, 1859. Library of Congress.*

ing of the door, was just back of the engine." Lee's second lieutenant, Israel Green, was the first to reach Brown. He slashed at the old man "with his [sheathed] sword, and the same sweeping stroke that cut Brown's head. . . . Brown fell as Green struck him and did not rise again."[36]

The events of October 1859 are notable above all for their folly and irony. The first man killed in Brown's dramatic war against slavery was a free black man. The raid bordered on the farcical considering Brown's inexplicable decisions. Fortunately for newspaper headlines, literary output, and many would argue, the nation, Brown survived the raid, escaping with a tolerable but dramatic bayonet wound in his side. Brown's trial for treason began immediately, a press event at the time without precedent or parallel.[37] Lawyers, reporters, well-wishers, lynch mobs; they all flocked to Harpers Ferry. Those who did not make the journey opined from afar.

White Southerners reacted fearfully.[38] "The panic among the women and children is . . . still most intense," one editorial complained. "People retire to their beds in doubt and uncertainty whether they will not be aroused before morning by the torch of the incendiary." Lashing out at Brown, the newspaper continued, "The truth is that all the blood of Kansas, all the blood of

Brown's victims, and at last, the blood of Brown himself, is in the skirts of the great Instigators," who, the paper explained, were the North and abolitionists.[39]

Those great instigators issued calls to liberate Brown from his prison cell. James Green, a former fugitive slave living in New York, urged one and all to purchase firearms and have them ready.[40] Despite the general atmosphere of betrayal and innuendo, the beleaguered Virginia governor, Henry A. Wise, conducted the trial with fairness and considerable equanimity. Brown, along with the other raiders captured in Harpers Ferry—Aaron Stevens, Shields Green, John Copeland, and Edwin Coppoc—were taken by train to Charlestown on October 18. A week later, Brown was in a courtroom shackled to Coppoc.

While Brown's invasion itself was an awful failure, his trial became the defining moment for his antislavery ambitions. A platoon of reporters took down Brown's every word. While his court-appointed and Northern-financed lawyers tried to argue that Brown was insane and his former compatriots circulated plots to break him out of his jail cell, the Old Hero began to truly embody an old hero.

Brown's capture prompted the widespread dissemination of two new images. In some sense, these contrasting portraits, one of the "mad" Brown, the other of the saintly hero, provided imagery to accompany the debates that began with Brown's capture and resonated long after his death. The portrait by John Whipple and J. W. Black was likely produced just after Brown returned from liberating slaves in Missouri in 1858 (figure 3.3). It was thought to be taken after Brown had a mild stroke, but it seems more likely that Brown merely had an itch or twitch during the portrait session. Regardless of the circumstances, Brown appears slightly deranged, and partisans would make hay with the image once Brown's sanity came under debate during his trial.

The image by J. B. Heywood is the John Brown that has been left to history (figure 3.4). The bearded patriarch became part of the timeless cultural imagery of the antebellum era. Reprinted widely in *cartes de visite*, frontispieces, and lithographs, this three-quarters portrait was the John Brown that materialized, seemingly out of nowhere, in a jail cell in Charlestown. Brought to prison the violent instigator of an invasion to destroy slavery, behind bars, Brown became a saint, a man of words and principle, not bayonets and violence.

Brown appeared courageous, well read, and calm, the very character from the Heywood portrait, as he faced certain execution. On October 31,

Figure 3.3.
John Brown in Boston, half-plate
daguerreotype by John A. Whipple
and J. W. Black, winter 1857–58.
The Boston Athenaeum.

after a trial of four days, Brown was found guilty of treason against Virginia as well as attempting to incite slave rebellion. Brown made a memorable speech at his sentencing on November 2, 1859. The Bible, Brown explained, taught him to "remember them that are in bonds, as bound with them." In this final address to the court, Brown explained that "I endeavored to act up to that instruction. . . . If it is deemed necessary that I should forfeit my life . . . and mingle my blood further with the blood of my children and with the blood of millions in this slave country whose rights are disregarded by wicked, cruel, and unjust enactments, — I submit; so let it be done!"[41]

Brown's codefendant, Edwin Coppoc, did not let down antislavery supporters, either. "The cause of everlasting truth and justice, will go on Conquering," Coppoc wrote, "to conquer, until our broad and beautiful land shall rest beneath the banner of freedom. I had hoped to see the dawn of that glorious day. I had hoped to live to see the principles of the Declarations of our Independence, fully realized. . . . But by the taking of my life, and the lives of My Comrades, Virginia is but hastening on that glorious day, when the Slave shall rejoice in his freedom. When he can say, *that I too am a man*, and am no more under the Yoke of oppression."[42]

With some foresight, or taking the recommendations of those most enraged by Brown's raid, Governor Wise would have required execution to

Figure 3.4.
John Brown, photographic
print by J. B. Heywood, 1859.
The Boston Athenaeum.

follow more swiftly. During the next month, the condemned abolitionist corresponded with hundreds of supporters and hosted visitors in his
Charlestown jail cell, achieving far more for the antislavery cause than the
raid had. "I do not feel conscious of guilt in taking up arms," he wrote one
supporter. "God will surely attend to his own cause in the best possible way
and time, and he will not forget the work of his own hands."[43] "Before I
began my work at Harpers Ferry," Brown recalled, "I felt assured that in the
worst event it would certainly pay. I often expressed that belief; and I can
see no possible cause to alter my mind."[44] Aside from reiterating his central
role in God's plans for slavery, Brown tried to sympathize with his griev-
ing family but could not help remarking to his wife that his mind was "very
tranquil, I may say joyous."[45]

Not only was Brown finally the object of the affection and attention he felt he had long deserved, but his role was thrust on him in clearer terms than even he had imagined. While James Redpath claimed that Brown "cared little for posthumous fame," Brown himself admitted to much more as the date of his execution drew near. "I cannot now better serve the cause I love so much than to die for it," he told a visiting pacifist Quaker woman.[46] When she told him that he would "be our martyr,"[47] the old man simply smiled.[48]

"I am quite cheerful . . . [at] the *near prospect* of the Gallows," Brown wrote to an admirer (figure 3.5). "Men cannot *imprison*, or *chain*; or *hang* the *soul*. I go joyfully in behalf of Millions that 'have no rights' that this 'great, & glorious'; 'this Christian Republic,' 'is bound to respect.'"[49] As the date neared, Brown's language became less ecstatic and more emphatic. Writing to his distraught wife and family, Brown's language was as sharp and declarative any of his statements. "Circumstances like my own . . . convince me beyond *all doubt* of our great need," Brown wrote, "of something more to rest our hopes on; than merely our own vague theories." He finished his letter in the third person; "John Brown writes to his children to abhor with *undiing hatred* [*sic*] . . . that 'sum of all vilanies [*sic*]' Slavery."[50] Brown's final note, written the morning of his execution, remains his most widely read and reproduced statement. "I John Brown," he wrote, "am, now quite *certain* that the crimes of this *guilty land* will never be purged away, but with Blood."[51]

One of the soldiers guarding the execution that day was a Maryland man named John Wilkes Booth.[52] At the time still an actor in his famous family troupe, Booth later claimed to have "aided in the capture and execution of John Brown." The young fire-eater had simply purchased a counterfeit uniform, however, in order to stand idly as Brown was hanged. Lincoln's future assassin was already a radical opponent of abolition, but spurred on by Brown's example, Booth claimed to be willing to take the law into his own hands. "I was proud of my little share in that transaction," Booth falsely recalled, "for I deemed it my duty, that I was helping our common country to perform an act of justice." Speaking to his own future, Booth reacted with disgust that "what was a crime in poor John Brown is now considered . . . the greatest and only virtue of the whole Republican party."[53] Booth concluded that "Abolitionists were the only traitors in the land."[54]

Among those gathered in Charlestown for Brown's execution were some of these traitors. Some impassioned abolitionists carried copies of a new

*Figure 3.5. "The Execution of John Brown," lithograph by
Robert P. Bennett, 1897. Library of Congress.*

poem by E. C. Stedman. "Scattered around" the streets of Charlestown,
Stedman's poem warned Governor Wise and the South about the consequences of taking revenge on Brown:

> And each drop from Old Brown's life veins, like the red gore of
> the dragon,
> May spring up a vengeful Fury, hissing through your slave-worn
> lands!

Figure 3.6. "John Brown Still Lives!," broadside, December 30, 1859. The Gilder Lehrman Collection, The Gilder Lehrman Institute of American History.

And Old Brown,
Osawatomie Brown,
May trouble you more than ever. When you've nailed his coffin
　down![55]

Stedman's poem, with its imagery of Brown rising again, was matched by one popular broadside. "John Brown Still Lives!" captured the meaning of Brown's hanging to sympathetic Americans (figure 3.6). The execution would not kill John Brown. Instead, his hanging unleashed the fury of Northern pens, a force far more effective than Brown's broadsword or the boxes of unused pikes. Soon Thoreau, Emerson, and others volleyed their barbs southward. "I meet John Brown at every turn," Thoreau declared. "He is more alive than ever he was. He has earned immortality."[56] The Northern eulogies and celebrations were everywhere. Of course, some celebrated Brown in more complex ways. The North's most famous abolitionist, William Lloyd Garrison, Brown's longtime bête noir, ridiculed the Old Hero for believing "in the method of Joshua rather than that of Jesus—in the sword of Gideon rather than the sword of the Spirit—in powder and ball rather than any moral instrumentalities."[57] Others, like the editor of the

Daily Cleveland Herald, condemned Brown's methods, but "while we say all this, it is a duty to defend Brown's fame and character." Even if his "head was wrong," the editorial continued, "while we see John Brown ascend the scaffold do not let us forget that his heart was in the right place."[58]

With every written word, Brown proved to be a more powerful means to argue and interpret the nation's relationship with violence, equality, and change. Because the Old Hero's life and symbolic death allowed proxy discussion and commentary on these vexing issues, there were not many who could resist. Violence, sectionalism, racism, and slavery were all fair game via the martyred Brown. The fiercely abolitionist *Oberlin (OH) Evangelist* wrote that "the Hero of Harper's Ferry, as we said some weeks since, has been a touchstone in the hands of Providence."[59] The Kansas newspaper *Freedom's Champion* waxed poetic about Brown. "Wounded, wracked with pain, almost dying . . . his courage is unshaken," the paper described, "correct and conscientious in all his dealing with his neighbors."[60] The *Cleveland Weekly Leader,* following Brown's lead of predicting the influence of his deeds, assessed the future. "The Martyr Brown has been 'permitted to die' for a cause," the paper intoned. "His death will illumine history, for all such records do. 'John Brown is dead, but his works do follow him.'"[61]

The *Ashtabula (OH) Sentinel* captured these thematic elements with particular passion. The newspaper argued that Brown had definitively demonstrated that "there can be no sense of social security in a system of slavery."[62] The Old Hero was "not buried but planted. He will spring up a hundred fold. I do not wonder at the solemn pomp of his death—they would have none but a Southern-made rope to hang him but that rope had two ends—one round the neck of a man, the other round the system."[63] Equally intriguing was the paper's mention of the town's Black String Organization, still in existence as late as 1908, which began "immediately after the attack on Harper's Ferry." Members took an oath "to defend with their property and their lives any refugee . . . in any way suspected of complicity in the John Brown conspiracy." As one member proudly noted, "all five of the survivors of the fight eventually came here for protection."[64]

White Southern opinion, of course, repudiated Brown's influence and symbolism with great fervor. Just like Northern celebrations of Brown, Southerners found in Brown the perfect means to address their rejection of racial equality, as well as abolitionist violence and social radicalism. As one ex-Confederate recalled, Brown's execution set Northern church bells tolling and "John Brown was mourned as a martyr on behalf of liberty and righteousness." Reverend J. H. McNeilly of Nashville wrote that Brown "was even compared with our Lord Jesus Christ, as a sufferer for humanity, while the Virginia authorities were held up to scorn and contempt as tyrants and murderers, like the Scribes and Pharisees who crucified the Savior of the world." McNeilly found it absurd that "New England—a section which had done more than any other to bring the negroes to America, and which had sold its own slaves to the South" would be responsible for this outpouring of "pious wrath . . . for a man whose past record was stained with brutal murders and assassinations."[65]

The Northern outcry over Brown's martyrdom helped prove to residents of the South that the Union was a dead letter. McNeilly explained that Southerners felt "that they could no longer remain in political association with a people who not only disregarded every right guaranteed to them by the common covenant of union, but who were ready to trample on the laws of our common humanity." Those traitors lived only according to "'a higher law' than the constitution—a higher law evolved out of the inner consciousness of New England, of which they were to be the sole judges, interpreters and executors." As a result, for Southerners like McNeilly, John Brown represented "the real sentiment and purpose of the dominant majority of the Northern people—the Republican party. . . . The only hope lay in a separation of the South from the Union."[66]

McNeilly was correct about Northern reactions to Brown's execution. December 2 became known as Martyr Day across many Northern cities, especially in black communities.[67] Brown was canonized by Reverend J. S. Martin at the Tremont Temple in Boston, where an interracial audience of more than four thousand gathered to pay tribute to the abolitionist on the day of his execution. Martin spoke eloquently to tremendous applause, particularly when he expressed his faith in "the success of the movement that [Brown] has inaugurated and of the final accomplishment of the great object of his soul." To explain his belief more literally, Martin invoked the hopes and dreams of slaves, adding prophetically that Brown would "slay more in his death than he ever slew in all his life."[68] As John Copeland, one of Brown's black soldiers, wrote from prison a week before his own execution, Harpers Ferry was merely "the prelude to [the] great event."[69]

In Detroit, "a densely crowded meeting of colored citizens" echoed Copeland, calling on the symbolism and passion that Brown had already inspired. At the Second Baptist Church, after religious songs and readings, the Reverend William Webb declared that Brown, "our much beloved and highly esteemed friend," had done more than just strike a blow against slavery. Brown "demonstrated to the world this sympathy and fidelity to the cause of the suffering slaves of this country, by bearding the hydra headed monster, Tyranny, in his den, and by his bold, effective, timely blow is now causing the South to tremble with a moral earthquake as he totally and freely delivered up his life to lay as a ransom for our enslaved race." "Solitary and alone," Webb told his congregation, "[Brown] has put a liberty ball in motion which shall continue to roll and gather strength until the last vestige of human slavery within this nation shall have been crushed beneath the ponderous weight."[70]

But where many preachers and pundits stopped, Webb turned the ideas of Brown's raid into a call for action: "The long lost rights and liberties of an oppressed people are only gained in proportion as they act in their own cause, therefore are we now loudly called upon to arouse to our own interest, and to concentrate our efforts in keeping the Old Brown liberty-ball in motion and thereby continue to kindle the fires of liberty upon the altar of every determined heart among men and continue to fan the same until the proper time, when a revolutionary blast from liberty's trump shall summon them simultaneously to unite for victorious and triumphant battle."[71] Webb's sermon was a call to arms, summoning those opposed to slavery to join Brown's revolution.

James Redpath, Brown's journalist friend, tried to match this passion with his prose. In many ways, Redpath obsessed over his old companion: publicizing Brown's name and cause along with his own. As soon as Brown was captured, Redpath began soliciting material for a biography at the suggestion of abolitionist publisher Eli Thayer. Redpath's solicitations were not without bias of course, for he rejected a genuine testimonial about Brown's direct involvement in the Pottawatomie massacre; such disturbing revelations would not sully Brown's first biography.

Redpath's *Public Life of Captain John Brown* began with three preeminent nineteenth-century personalities offering their thoughts. Ralph Waldo Emerson eulogized "the Saint . . . [who] will make the gallows glorious like the Cross." Henry David Thoreau declared that "no man in America has ever stood up so persistently for the dignity of human nature." Finally, Wendell Phillips argued that it was unimportant "whether the old man succeeded in a worldly sense or not [because] he stood a representative of law, of government, of right, of justice, of religion, and they were pirates that gathered about him, and sought to wreak vengeance by taking his life."[72]

In a short space, Redpath established a soaring tone for his biography. He presented Brown as an unparalleled Christ-like figure who exposed the hypocrisy and inhumanity of the South. Published just thirty days after

Brown's execution, *Public Life* was nothing if not polemical. Redpath's biography of Brown was the very first. Although the British De Witt Publishers rushed its *The Life, Trial and Execution of Captain John Brown* into print, this book was merely a hodgepodge of *Harper's* lithographs, court transcripts, and unacknowledged reprints of Redpath's *Tribune* columns.[73] In between efforts to assist surviving raiders, Redpath penned the first original biography of John Brown.[74] Both Redpath's *Public Life* and the DeWitt collection should be understood as forebears of the now ubiquitous accounts rushed to print following the latest hot scandal. Redpath did aspire to a greater social purpose, and his vision of Brown was disseminated more widely than any other. *Public Life* sold forty thousand copies in just five months. Before his publisher, Thayer and Eldridge, went bust, the biography had sold seventy-five thousand copies, which did not include three unauthorized British editions.[75]

Redpath was a promoter and publicist, and his work on Brown made him one of the earliest shapers of American celebrity culture.[76] While he skillfully combined activism, journalism, and salesmanship in his coverage of Brown in the 1850s, Redpath's biography demonstrated his shrewdest efforts at public relations. The biography made exclusive claims to Brown's name and story with a publisher's declaration that "a large percentage on each copy sold" would go to "the family of Captain John Brown." Thus, the publisher's note explained, "every purchaser thereby becomes a contributor . . . which appeals to all freemen with a force that is irresistible." This was no mere marketing ploy. Redpath raised substantial funds for Brown's family and the families of the other raiders. Brown's widow, Mary, received two thousand dollars by the end of 1860 alone, and Redpath eventually raised more than six thousand dollars for the other families.[77]

As if charity were not irresistible enough, Redpath offered more. Readers' desires for authentic accounts were substantiated by endorsements from Mary and Brown's son Salmon. Salmon declared that James Redpath was "THE MAN ABOVE ALL OTHERS to write the life of [his] beloved father." Mary indicated that Redpath, being "personally acquainted with [her husband] . . . will do him justice."[78] Mary's endorsement underscored the crucial distinction between Redpath's biography and all of those that have since followed; personal acquaintance. Not only did Redpath meet Brown, but he traveled and even fought with him during Brown's revolutionarily formative experience in Kansas.

Redpath dedicated the book, published just after Brown's execution, to the "Old Hero" himself. A simple dedication might be read benignly, but there was no mistaking the intent of Redpath's fifteen-paragraph epistle. "To you," Redpath wrote, "is due our homage for first showing how, and how alone, the gigantic crime of our age and nation can be effectually blotted out from our soil forever. You have proven that the slaver has a soul as cowardly as his own 'domestic institution.'" Redpath always combined praise with biblical imagery. "Rifle in hand," he continued, "you put the brave young men of Kansas to shame; truth in heart, you rendered insignificant the puerile programmes of anti-slavery politicians."[79]

In this incendiary spirit, Redpath laid down the first pages in the subsequent thousands that would be written to deride and praise John Brown. Redpath did more than explain Brown's experience at Harpers Ferry as "an eminent success"; he argued that Brown was taking his place "at the right hand of the Eternal. He had fought the good fight, and now wore the crown of victory." In characterizing Brown's fight as religiously righteous, Redpath offered a simple and chilling prophecy to the South. Eventually, Redpath, intoned, we will "see justice done" as Brown desired, "to clear God's earth of the Devil's lies, in the shortest time and at any cost."[80] It would be five years and at enormous cost, but at the very least the institution of slavery would be destroyed.

Redpath's biography justified that violent and deliberate sequence. From the first, Redpath showed no qualms about exposing his motives and biases (or what he considered a lack thereof). "When the news of the arrest of John Brown reached Boston," he recalled, "I could neither rest nor sleep; for I loved and reverenced the noble old man, and had perfect confidence in his plan of emancipation." Redpath's confidence demanded expression, for he "heard, on every side, people calling [Brown] a madman, and sneering at his 'crazy scheme.'" As Redpath reasoned, "now, or never, was the time to defend my friend, when no voice, however faint, was heard to praise him."[81]

Chronicling Brown's early years, Redpath gave a unique spin to Brown's failure to thrive in religious study. "God had higher work for this sedate, dignified young man. He was raising him up as a deliverer of captives and a teacher of righteousness to a nation; as the conserver of the light of true Christianity." Redpath, on the basis of his personal experience and his predictions about the future of American slavery, made Kansas the proving ground of Brown and his "heroic Christianity."[82]

But Redpath's greatest stroke in the retelling was what he withheld (or pretended to withhold) from his readers. The raid had failed and Brown was dead. After emphasizing the Kansas origins of Brown's invasion, Redpath chose to allude to grander schemes still afloat. He could divulge "at great length an admirably devised plan of an extended insurrection in the Southern States," he wrote, "but as its publication might prevent its successful execution," and Redpath was so sure of the plan's success, he deemed "it more prudent to suppress this portion."[83] Redpath was a shrewd man while Brown was living, but Brown's capture and execution transformed them both. When Brown was hung, Redpath and others harnessed the abolitionist's symbolic power, transforming him into a living myth.[84]

All the while, every politician, preacher, and pundit in the United States was compelled to contribute his or her opinion. Some, particularly those North of the Mason-Dixon line, echoed Thoreau, attempting to turn Brown into a Christ-figure for abolition. In Akron, Ohio, on the evening of Brown's execution, General L. V. Bierce celebrated Brown's words to Governor Wise, that "the people of the South had better prepare for a settlement of [the slavery] question." Bierce warned that the matter "must come up sooner than they are prepared for it, and the sooner they commence that preparation the better for them."[85] Even if "John Brown has this day perished on a scaffold," Bierce added, as "the first martyr in 'the irrepressible conflict' of Liberty with Slavery[,] his blood has sanctified the gallows."[86]

In Chicago Reverend W. W. Patton captured the national debate with similar flair: "A man who dies for the truth, who yields himself as a sacrifice for a righteous cause, is so far from perishing . . . that he actually multiplies his power a thousand fold. . . . No execution has ever excited so much interest in this country, or given rise to such conflicting opinions. There is no dispute as to what John Brown actually did; there is a wide difference of judgment as to the moral character of his conduct." Invoking a grand national narrative, Patton argued that Brown's "mind was just of the cast to imagine [ending slavery with his raid], direct descendant as he was of the Pilgrims, from the old May Flower stock, and kindred to the men who followed Cromwell, 'Trusting in God and keeping their powder dry.'"[87]

But in the competition for most gushing elegy that followed Brown's execution, none were more dramatic than those delivered in Concord, Massachusetts, by Henry David Thoreau and Ralph Waldo Emerson. Thoreau drew listeners and readers back to the past. "Some eighteen hundred years ago Christ was crucified," Thoreau echoed; "this morning, perchance, Captain Brown was hung. These are two ends of a chain which is not without its links. He is not Old Brown any longer; he is an angel of light."[88] Emerson spoke to Brown's future. "Of all the men who were said to be my contemporaries," Emerson told his biographer Franklin Sanborn, "it seemed to me that John Brown was the only one who had not died. I meet him at every turn. He is more alive than ever he was. He is no longer working in secret; he works in public, and in the clearest light that shines on this land."[89]

Granting Brown sainthood would have enormous consequences as the abolitionist became a living part of American memory. Indeed, the contours of his afterlife would be as hotly contested as any debate in the history of the United States.

*[John Brown] was a mild and humble Christian ... a practical disciple
of Jefferson ... a pioneer and hero of emancipation.*
    —*Franklin Sanborn, 1909*

4

A SAINT IN SUSPENSE

Competing Visions of John Brown

On December 3, 1860, a riot broke out at Boston's Tremont Temple. *Harper's Weekly* provided a vivid illustration of the incident, revealing the tensions consuming the nation on the eve of the Civil War (figure 4.1). The event was meant to be a peaceful celebration for the abolitionist martyr John Brown. However, when free blacks began entering the hall, a group of white Bostonians, outraged that the country was on the brink of war, began attacking them. Over chants of "Put the niggers out!," Frederick Douglass (shown in a rather poor likeness) shouted the kind of radical Brown-inspired rhetoric that was polarizing the nation and had spurred the mob. Slaveholders must feel the threat of "death all around" them, Douglass declared. "All methods" of antislavery agitation were fair game, even "war."[1] But as his fellow blacks were beaten and arrested, Douglass gave up the stage. Testifying to the perverse race relations of 1860s America, the chaos erupted in Boston, the very heart of abolitionist activity, at a memorial for a white man who had given his life to destroy slavery.

One of the white audience members at the Tremont Temple celebration, Franklin Sanborn, former ringleader of Brown's "Secret Six," believed his old friend must be honored properly or he would be forgotten. Over the next five decades, Sanborn became the loudest voice in the ongoing debate over Brown's memory. Although he would never dream of actually shouting down Frederick Douglass, Sanborn's feelings about Brown and racial reform defined a certain paternalistic memory that would echo for many years. Beneath the veneer of honoring the antislavery martyr, men like Sanborn decided that stripping Brown of his violence and radicalism was the

*Figure 4.1. "Expulsion of Negroes and Abolitionists from Tremont Temple, Boston."
From* Harper's Weekly, *December 15, 1860. The Boston Athenaeum.*

only way for the abolitionist to join the pantheon of American heroes. Emphasizing Brown's ideals over his methods soon gained cultural currency, helping establish the paternalistic racial reform that would exact great costs into the twentieth century.

The Tremont Temple riot exemplified these costs and underscored just how seriously African Americans' ideas about Brown differed from white conceptions of the abolitionist. From 1859 to 1920, whites and blacks used Brown to focus the same struggles for social justice and racial equality, but they took different lessons from his radical project of freedom. For many black Americans, Brown could be a violent *and* heroic liberator, but for whites, he soon became a man of ideals alone. Beyond revealing the growing chasm between African American and white opinions of this polarizing character, the period's brilliant array of prose, imagery, and memorial exposed the difficulty of interracial partnership in pursuit of Brown's mission.

In 1861, the sole surviving black raider from Harpers Ferry, Osborne Anderson, tried to put forward a positive, forward-looking remembrance of those means and ends. Although Anderson called his memoir a "plain, unadorned, truthful story," he dramatically hinted at greater, violent plans for the destruction of slavery; schemes beyond Brown's that had yet to be consummated. At the outset of the contest over Brown's memory, Anderson described an "unbroken chain of sentiment and purpose from Moses of the Jews to John Brown of America." Grouping Brown with the slave rebels Gabriel Prosser and Nat Turner, Anderson identified Brown as the leader of the final American slave rebellion.[2] "John Brown did not only capture and hold Harper's Ferry for twenty hours, but he held the whole South," Anderson declared, "he captured President Buchanan and his Cabinet, convulsed the whole country, killed Governor Wise, and dug the mine and laid the train which will eventually dissolve the union between Freedom and Slavery." Brown's actions in Virginia revealed "the truth," Anderson concluded. "So let it be!"[3] Anderson's *Voice from Harper's Ferry* was more than a first-person account of the raid; it was a radical call to arms inside a prediction and a plea. With this volatile mix of recollection and elegy, Anderson used his own memories of Brown to mediate a broader memory. In so doing, Anderson captured the defiant and unique relationship that black Americans would enjoy with John Brown. Despite the passion and dedication that characterized black memories of Brown, the relationship was a precarious one, always threatened by mainstream opinions of Brown.

The opening shots at Fort Sumter began this contest in earnest. One month later, "The John Brown Song," most often referred to as "John Brown's Body," was first played at a flag-raising ceremony at Fort Warren, near Boston, on Sunday, May 12, 1861 (figure 4.2).[4] Although the tune originated in religious music from early nineteenth-century camp meetings, secession motivated many Northerners (dozens took credit) to put new words and meaning to the song.[5] Union troops were first reported singing "John Brown's body lies a mouldering in the grave" while marching through Boston on July 18, 1861.[6] With the song's adoption as the Union standard, Brown reached his first real milestone of immortality, even if the lyrics bounded him in rather dull martyrdom.

The popularity of "John Brown's Body" helped spread awareness of Brown's name if not the specifics of his final decade. Although his radical violence and racial egalitarianism occasionally seemed distant from the meaning of the Civil War as it was waged, he was constantly being invoked through this song. Northerners and Southerners, free and enslaved, all heard "John Brown's Body" as the war consumed the nation. Despite its smoothing-out of Brown's revolutionary violence and racial radicalism,

the song itself did provide opportunities to contest Brown's memory. On Union-occupied St. Helena's Island in Beaufort, South Carolina, the African American writer and teacher Charlotte Forten taught her black schoolchildren the song, which she tellingly described in a diary entry simply as "John Brown." As she wrote, "I felt to the full the significance of that song being sung here in SC by little negro children, by those whom he—the glorious old man—died to save."[7] Black regiments, like the one pictured in a *Harper's Weekly* illustration from 1865, took up this notion of "John Brown's Body" and defiantly sang the anthem while liberating Charleston (figure 4.3). The *Harper's* image clarifies Brown's importance as a cultural symbol,

Figure 4.3. "Colored Regiment Singing 'John Brown's Body' in Charleston."
From Harper's Weekly, *March 18, 1865. The Boston Athenaeum.*

particularly for African Americans; the recently freed slaves and spectators appear to be singing and celebrating the most boisterously, signaling their embrace of actual freedom and, on some level, John Brown.

Nonetheless, the song, with its explicit Unionism, was most popularly understood and embraced without any endorsement of revolutionary violence in the service of freedom. In fact, the most provocative verse merely called for hanging Confederate president "Jeff Davis to a tree," a message far more Unionist than revolutionary. Apart from the idea that Brown's soul was marching on, the song, especially after its transformation into the "Battle Hymn of the Republic," helped transform Brown from a radical racial revolutionary into an idealized (and eventually absentee) martyr in the Unionist cause.[8]

Black Americans had long articulated their own John Brown. For twenty years, the Shiloh Presbyterian Church in New York City held annual celebrations on the anniversary of his execution.[9] In 1879, the church was elaborately decorated for the twentieth memorial, with an American flag over the reading desk, a portrait of Lincoln on one wall, "surrounded by fern leaves and flowers," and a portrait of John Brown on the other, "encircled by a wreath of laurel and bay."[10]

Reverend Henry Highland Garnet, a famous pastor and abolitionist orator, conducted the memorial service that day. Born into slavery, Garnet befriended Brown in the 1850s, when they bonded over the notion that violence might be useful and even necessary for black liberation. After singing "John Brown's Body," Garnet meditated on the chorus, clarifying its different messages that "John Brown's spirit is marching on." Garnet argued that for the blacks gathered in the church that day, Brown's spirit "still has sympathy and intelligence."[11] Brown's lasting and living memory was evident to the parishioners. "For twenty years," Garnet told the congregation, "it has been the custom of the friends in this city of the cause in which John Brown laid down his life to meet and commemorate this day. . . . It was a great work that [Brown] did, for it was he who moved the South to rebellion, and rebellion led to the destruction of slavery. Without him there would have been no civil war, and without civil war there would have been no emancipation."[12]

Garnet identified the crux of the matter — emancipation — the fundamental goal and unfinished business of Brown's life. Garnet spoke to his nation's continuing struggles with this question because the unrealized promises that were supposed to accompany emancipation continued to elude black Americans. With his closing remarks, Garnet revealed the purpose of the day's celebration. "Slavery still abounds to a fearful extent on Southern soil. . . . The work is not yet all done." For Garnet and those gathered in celebration, Brown was more than a memory; he was an active reminder and motivator.[13] "If old John Brown could address us here to-night," Garnet concluded, "he would say: 'Spare your eulogies and inquire into present needs and present duties.'"[14]

The sharp dilemma posed by "present needs and present duties" and by their seeming call for Brown's violence and radicalism underscores the differences between black and white memories of the abolitionist. As a result, those memories would forever be doomed to echo one another but only rarely to harmonize. Just as in Brown's life, these disconnects were not due to any lack of opportunity. By this time, however, as Reconstruction was fully eclipsed, the sadness of that reality became more widely understood.

Brown's friend Frederick Douglass understood the bitterness of the war's aftermath more personally than most. In the 1860s, Douglass connected with fellow Brown associate James Redpath and was represented by his speaking bureau. Settling into the role of an elder abolitionist spokesman,

Douglass lectured regularly to audiences about Brown, emancipation, and the sad unfolding of Reconstruction. Douglass's evangelizing was more than just a sinecure for a former slave; he consistently tried to inform his audiences of what still hung in the balance.

The Civil War and Reconstruction had not fulfilled the promises of America's founding documents; instead, the years following them saw a consistent retreat into white supremacy and the beginning of the dark night of Jim Crow. Expressing his frustrations about the limited subject matter his audiences were interested in, Douglass remarked to his agent that "Fredk. Douglass the self educated fugitive slave" was palatable, but no one wanted to hear about John Brown the radical hero or the frustrating heartbreaks of Reconstruction.[15] At the fourteenth anniversary of Storer College in Harpers Ferry, Douglass finally found a willing audience. He used the opportunity to passionately memorialize John Brown and survey the sad remains of Reconstruction.

Self-deprecating as always, Douglass declared that Brown's "zeal in the cause of my race was far greater than mine. . . . I could live for the slave, but he could die for him."[16] Douglass ended his speech with a brilliant rhetorical device. He repeated the question "Did John Brown fail?" again and again, answering each time with a different Confederate personality who underscored Brown's triumph. Pointing out how much the United States had progressed from 1850 until the end of the war, Douglass asked his audience about Henry A. Wise. It was in Wise's own house, Douglass reminded his audience, less than two years after the Civil War, that "a school for the emancipated slaves" was started. Did John Brown fail? "Ask James M. Mason, the author of the inhuman fugitive slave bill," who was jailed as a traitor, "less than two years from the time that he stood over the prostrate body of John Brown." The list went on until Douglass thundered, "If John Brown did not end the war that ended slavery, he did at least begin the war that ended slavery. . . . Until this blow was struck, the prospect for freedom was dim, shadowy and uncertain. . . . When John Brown stretched his arm forth the sky was cleared . . . and the clash of arms was at hand."[17]

But the John Brown who struck blows and cleared the sky with clash of arms was not the character settling into a benign afterlife in popular American memory. The search for a benevolent and peaceful martyr had begun in earnest even before Brown's execution. One particular myth captures this process and underscores the conflicts facing any racially revolutionary depiction of Brown. The passionately abolitionist *New York Tribune* had assigned a special correspondent, Edward H. House, to cover Brown's trial. On December 5, 1859, an article appeared in the newspaper with House's byline, describing Brown's path to the gallows.

"As he stepped out of the door a black woman, with her little child in arms, stood near his way," the writer recounted. "His thoughts at the moment none can know except as his acts interpret them. He stopped for a moment in his course, stooped over, and with the tenderness of one whose love is as broad as the brotherhood of man, kissed it affectionately."

The scene was dramatic, but it never took place; House was not even in Charlestown for Brown's execution. He had fled to Baltimore after earlier dispatches prompted death threats. Henry S. Olcott, the *Tribune*'s Southern agricultural correspondent, concocted the scene, and the story instantly grew wings.[18] Not three weeks later, the abolitionist poet John Greenleaf Whittier immortalized the apocryphal scene in verse. Whittier's *Brown of Osawatomie* described the martyr on the way to his execution, when "a poor slave-mother with her little child" approached. Shirking off "the jeering ranks" Brown "kissed the negro's child!" and in his "Christian's sacrifice" Brown achieved his "generous purpose unstained with human blood!"[19] Whittier's florid poetry was not especially notable in the din of Northern eulogies, but he gave the spurious kissing tale a staying power that Emerson, Thoreau, and Melville never matched with their metaphorical flights. Whittier's poem, distributed widely across the Northeast, provided the seed from which white devotees' hagiography would flower.

In late 1859 or early 1860, the *Tribune* scene was transformed again, this time into a painting by the artist Louis Liscolm Ransom.[20] Ransom's *John Brown on His Way to Execution* was inspired by the artist's "profound admiration," even "veneration for old John Brown."[21] Ransom kept his studio in New York City, and the canvas enjoyed some renown there, even during the Civil War. When P. T. Barnum showed Ransom's painting at his museum in Manhattan in May 1863, the *Harper's* columnist George William Curtis wrote favorably of its exhibition. "It is one of the incidents that history will always fondly record and art delineate," Curtis wrote, noting that "the fierce and bitter judgment of the moment upon the old man is already tempered. Despised and forsaken in his own day, the heart of another generation may treat him as he treated the little outcast child."[22]

The story of that fictional child was illuminated by Ransom's canvas. When the artist donated his painting to Oberlin College in 1886, a broadside thought to be written by Ransom himself explained the imagery. Aside from Brown, the painting showed seven other figures. Two were representatives of "the slave power." "Strongly marked by passion and a domineering Spirit," according to the pamphlet's description, one figure is shown in Virginia military uniform, "which happens to be that worn by the minions of European despotism, and whose gorgeous trappings fitly symbolize the 'pride which cometh before destruction.'" The other soldier wears "in the service of oppression the uniform of the old 'Continentals.'" The jailor and a friend, "in civilian's clothes" appear beside Brown in the doorway. In the lower left-hand corner, "among neglected rubbish," rests "a mutilated and discarded statue of Justice."[23]

"Seated on the stone balustrade is the slave-mother and her child, already immortalized in the verse of Whittier," the pamphlet described. "The artist does not spare slavery here." Behind them is "a contemptible little 'overseer' or hired slave-driver, parading in militia uniform, who forgets his assumed soldierly bearing, and reverts to his true character, in his unseemly rush to push the 'nigger woman' out of the way." The soldier's movement loosens his "yellow silk ensign . . . to swell out so that the sunlight falling upon a portion of it forms a background and a halo for the head of John Brown." Ransom made his protagonist even more beatific by framing him inside that halo. The pamphlet explained the symbolic resonance. "Above his head, upon the silken banner, are the arms of Virginia, a conqueror trampling upon his prostrate foe, and the motto 'Sic Semper Tyrannis.' The terrible irony of that motto, on that occasion, drives home to every beholder the question, 'Who is the tyrant, who the conqueror?'"[24]

For the central figure of the painting, Ransom relied heavily on Heywood's 1859 print of Brown (see figure 3.4). Because the artist essentially reproduced Heywood's portrait, Brown appears rather aloof and distant from the rest of the scene. His body and gaze barely acknowledge the slave woman and her child; there is no real gesture to a kiss in the painting. Brown is, the pamphlet noted, "of course, the central figure. Standing on the upper Step he overtops all others, calm and dignified, with the bearing of one altogether assured of the final triumph of his cause. His eyes are upon the little child."[25]

Those eyes were enough. The image was lithographed and widely circulated by the printmakers Nathaniel Currier and James Merritt Ives, going through several variations on Ransom's original painting. The differences between these efforts underscore Brown's volatility as postbellum symbol. In Ransom's painting, the abolitionist appeared under a halo and the slave child had noticeably lighter skin than its mother.[26] Ransom explained that by representing slave mother as "half white," and her child as even "lighter

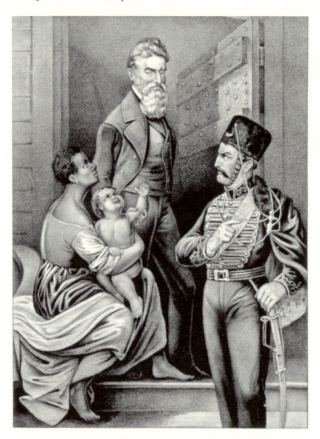

Figure 4.4.
After Louis Ransom,
John Brown—The
Martyr, *lithograph*
by Currier and Ives,
1870. Library of
Congress.

than herself," he sought to combat "the oft repeated sneer at abolitionists, 'Would you wish your daughter to marry a nigger?'" This symbolism was lost by 1870, when Currier and Ives's lithographs reached their third iteration (figure 4.4). By then, the printmakers had stripped Ransom's painting to its bare essentials, preserving only the relevant elements for heroic simplicity. Gone were the halo, the racially mixed figures, and most of the scene to boot. All that remained were Brown, slave mother, child, and jailer.[27]

The popularity of Ransom's image inspired others to paint the scene, but it was not until 1883 that the Irish immigrant and painter Thomas Hovenden created the defining work of this apocryphal kiss.[28] With his imposing canvas, *The Last Moments of John Brown,* Hovenden articulated a heroic and peaceful John Brown for the ages.

Classically trained in France, Hovenden arrived in America during the last gasps of Reconstruction and married into a family of passionate Pennsylvania abolitionists. His painting studio was known locally as "Antislavery or Abolition Hall" for the meetings held there since before the Civil War; both William Lloyd Garrison and Lucretia Mott had spoken there. Hovenden painted several African American genre works and other historical paintings before he received his defining commission. The New York industrialist and Mayflower descendant Robin Battell encountered Hovenden's paintings of incidents from America's past and immediately commissioned "a historical picture of the last moments of John Brown." Although Hovenden was sympathetic to Battell's subject of choice, the particular scene struck him as apocryphal. Battell sent the artist the spurious *Tribune* piece from 1859 as proof and told Hovenden that "the incident of the kissing of the child must have occurred as stated and published at the time." "You are familiar I suppose with Whittier's beautiful allusion to it written a few weeks afterward," Battell continued. "It has probably occurred to you that you might represent the child in its mother's arms, extending one or both of its little hands toward the man, with a wistful look which he pleasantly recognizes, and is about to kiss it."[29]

Ignoring these entreaties, Hovenden made an initial painting of the scene of Brown's capture.[30] Eventually, the artist conceded to his benefactor's requests and embarked on extensive research to accurately document Brown's final moments, visiting Harpers Ferry and Charlestown and even interviewing the martyr's aged jailer. Hovenden studied all the available visual sources for his reinterpretation of the fictional incident.[31] The resulting product was an enormous canvas, almost seven feet tall and five feet wide, that clearly shows its debts to Ransom but surpasses all previous interpretations of the kiss (figure 4.5).[32]

Hovenden's protagonist is dramatically more Christ-like then his predecessors. Brown is shown in full grandfatherly beard wearing bedroom slippers as he peacefully descends the steps to be transported to the gallows and his awaiting martyrdom. A noose already around his neck, Brown is the center of a scene drawn with religious reverence and significance. As the art historian Gwendolyn DuBois Shaw observes, Hovenden's drew on "a larger discourse" that sought to sanitize and enshrine Brown as an "Old Testament patriarch." But with its peaceful Christian hero, Hovenden's Brown better represented a New Testament Christ of love, tolerance, and compassion.[33] The slave mother offers Brown her child for his blessing, and Brown tilts his neck to receive the child. The offering and kiss pacify Brown's radical violence and put Brown in an exalted position in relation to his black counterparts.[34] Complicit with Brown's own efforts from his Charlestown cell, the heroic aura of the work helped transform this racial revolutionary

Figure 4.5. Thomas Hovenden, The Last Moments of John Brown,
etching, 1885. Library of Congress.

from a gun-toting murderer into a peaceful martyr. By creating an acceptable Christian symbol for white audiences, Hovenden and other artists used
Brown as a righteous symbol of national atonement for the collective sin of
slavery and the bloodletting of the Civil War.

While Hovenden researched and painted this powerful interpretation of
Brown, the artist's brothers-in-arms polished the written briefs for the old
hero's martyrdom. In particular, there was one man, Brown's compatriot

Figure 4.6.
Franklin Benjamin Sanborn.
From Harper's New Monthly Magazine,
June 1875. Library of Congress.

Franklin Sanborn (figure 4.6), who created a virtual encyclopedia of the martyr's Christian grace and courage. Between 1870 and 1916, Sanborn penned more than seventy-five articles and published four major books on Brown.[35] Sanborn's message strengthened the themes of Hovenden's painting. Brown was "a simple, brave, heroic person incapable of anything selfish or base," Sanborn wrote in 1883. Brown "has become, to the world in general, one of the immortal champions of liberty—historical or mythical."[36] Sanborn's heroic accounts of the abolitionist show the overlapping purposes of the popular Brown imagery and written accounts. Probing Sanborn's self-appointed role as Brown's defender highlights the powerful differences between the saintly Brown and African American visions of a violent radical.

Franklin Sanborn was the quintessential blue-blooded New Englander. Born in 1831 in Hampton Falls, New Hampshire, on the same farm his family had owned since the seventeenth century, Sanborn was raised in the farmhouse his grandfather, who fought in the American Revolution, built in 1743. The farm was a near-perfect microcosm of democracy, Sanborn would argue, exactly as the Founding Fathers had intended.[37] After graduating from Phillips Exeter Academy, Sanborn went to Harvard in the fall of 1852. An eager if presumptuous student, Sanborn attended Theodore Parker's lectures in lieu of chapel services, cultivated local authors like Harriet Beecher

Stowe, and constantly wrote poetry and book reviews.[38] The young man took it upon himself to visit Ralph Waldo Emerson as a sophomore (walking from Cambridge to Concord in the spring of 1853) and was welcomed into his home, where Emerson encouraged him to stoke Harvard students' interest in transcendentalism.[39] When Henry David Thoreau's *Walden* was published, Sanborn's enthusiastic review of the book in the *Harvard Magazine* prompted a visit from Thoreau to Sanborn's dorm room. These encounters, which first struck Sanborn's lifelong balance between luck and pluck, began his lasting and intimate associations with Concord's most famous sons.

Just as formatively, a month before his senior year, Sanborn's childhood sweetheart became gravely ill, and the two were married a week before she died. Sanborn remembered the marriage as an important gesture of youthful idealism.[40] His bold act, against the rules of Harvard and propriety, revealed Sanborn as a young man dedicated to principles, damn the costs. Sanborn's budding friendship with Emerson was built on this very foundation. The two men shared a belief in the importance of idealism and activism. It was not long before Emerson asked the young Sanborn if he would start a primary school in Concord.

For the next eight years, Sanborn ran this school, teaching not only Emerson's sons but two of John Brown's daughters, Henry James's older brothers, and the children of numerous local notables.[41] Sanborn quickly became a man-about-town, for as he wrote, "Emerson's introduction passed current everywhere in Concord."[42] Sanborn was absorbed into the regular meetings of Bronson Alcott (father of Louisa May), poet William Channing, Thoreau, Emerson, and others. As one Brown biographer described, Sanborn "attached himself to the town's celebrated intellectual community" as "a sort of . . . apprentice," "making up in enthusiasm for what he lacked in experience."[43] Indeed, Sanborn seemed to be everywhere at once, and in the midst of the Concord salon and his teaching responsibilities, he also became deeply involved in the Kansas territorial conflict, raising money and awareness to ensure that Kansas entered the Union as a free state. Traveling to Iowa and Nebraska, and skirting Kansas in the summer of 1856, Sanborn became positively enthralled with the fight against slavery. Only months later, an important visitor arrived at his office in Concord.

It was January 1857 when John Brown knocked on Sanborn's door, carrying a letter of introduction from a Sanborn relative in Illinois. As Sanborn looked at the old man before him, he recognized the gravity of the moment in the grand scheme of his life, or so he later recalled: "The greatness of

Brown's nature and mission . . . [was] not seen by all, but there is a divining quality in youth and in genius which lets them behold [things others
cannot]." To Sanborn, Emerson, and Thoreau (whom Sanborn soon introduced to Brown), "it was clear . . . that [Brown] was no common man." These
early meetings convinced the Concord glitterati that Brown "had a purpose"
much greater than milk-and-water abolition, and, more important, he had
the will to achieve that purpose. Sanborn, a "romantic idealist . . . [and] impressionable" youth, was immediately "swept off his feet" by Brown's rugged
worldliness and fierce dedication.[44]

Notwithstanding Sanborn's long friendships with Thoreau, Emerson and
others, and despite eventually becoming Concord's James Boswell to these
men (of whom Sanborn would go on to write "a procession of worshipful
biographies"), Sanborn seemed to consider Brown his true Samuel Johnson.[45] As Sanborn told it, speaking both to his approach to history and to
life, sometimes what was needed most was "a *man*—the man of the moment, the man of destiny."[46]

Soon after their first meeting, Sanborn corralled Brown into the Massachusetts state legislature and numerous other venues as *that* man. Sanborn
passed the hat while Brown displayed his wounds, the chains that held his
son Frederick, or the captured bowie knife of Captain Clay Pate.[47] Going
from town to town, Sanborn and Brown asked New Englanders to contribute money and arms to causes disclosed and undisclosed. As Brown's
plots moved more decisively into secret planning for an invasion of the
South, Sanborn became increasingly enchanted. Sanborn later claimed,
however, seemingly with some hindsight, that the fundraising was fraught
with doubt. Moreover, he maintained that when Brown fully revealed the
Harpers Ferry plan at Gerrit Smith's estate near Syracuse, New York, reactions were tinged with fatalism rather than faith.

Sanborn took a long walk with Smith to discuss Brown's proposal, and
the two men agreed that they could not "give [Brown] up to die alone; [they]
must support him."[48] Nonetheless, Sanborn recalled in his memoir that "it
was done far more from our regard for the man than from hopes of immediate success."[49] In fact, according to Sanborn, both men were fairly convinced that Brown's plan would fail. But, having tried "proposing objections and raising difficulties," to which Brown responded with scripture, the
two men accepted his prediction that God would ensure the gambit "would
pay."[50]

Sanborn spent the next year playing cloak and dagger with Brown, writing anonymous or encoded letters and generally spearheading the group of

men that came to be known as the "Secret Six."[51] Writing about this group of conspirators, Sanborn always referred to himself in the third person, and his tone was steadfastly impersonal. He employed the same approach for Harpers Ferry, which in Sanborn's analysis was made dramatic not by the raid itself but by what it meant to Brown's martyrdom. In Sanborn's memoirs, the historic raid, from Brown's arrival at Harpers Ferry to his trial and execution, occupies less than a page.[52]

Sanborn was at great personal risk following Brown's capture. His compatriots in the Secret Six reacted in varying states of alarm, belying the detached and even tone of Sanborn's later writing. Gerrit Smith checked himself into the insane asylum in Utica, New York, to avoid arrest; Frederick Douglass (not a member of the Secret Six but a longtime supporter of Brown) fled to England. Sanborn wrote his mother on the eve of Brown's execution, supposedly to calm her but exhibiting more bluster than concern. "In the first place," he wrote, "there is no evidence against me [that anyone could bring] in any fair court." No one "will even attempt to arrest me," he assured her, so "feel no fear of it." Sanborn's justifications in this letter offered the clearest glimpse into his mindset during Brown's trial. "What I have really done to aid Brown is nothing more than all men ought to do," he wrote self-righteously. "I am sorry to give my friends and you so much anxiety, but . . . if my name is remembered at all, it will be in an honorable way—the fruits of Brown's acts are to be a great good, I have no doubt."[53]

While his calm statements were a fine front, Sanborn's brashness was tinged with panic. Sanborn pestered Thoreau not to speak in public about Brown, for fear that any Concordian agitation would be traced to him.[54] In Sanborn's memoirs, he presented these October days as ones of courage, when he broke the law to destroy letters that might incriminate his compatriots and hid evidence from the "hands of the slaveholding authorities."[55] In fact, within days of Brown's capture, Sanborn fled to Canada (and ended up doing so more than once) in fear of being arrested. Sheepishly returning when friends informed him there was no immediate legal threat, he remained ready to bolt at the slightest provocation.

Despite his fears, Sanborn was unprepared when the moment finally arrived. Although he later looked back on the incident as his proudest and most defiant, it really was his worst nightmare come true. Like many abolitionists, Sanborn was a thinker, writer, and talker; this was partly why Brown intrigued him so.[56] He was not very interested in being on the front lines of the battle; he wanted to remain behind the scenes. But on April 3, 1860, after 9:00 P.M., a stranger appeared in Sanborn's doorway and handcuffed him. Three men emerged from the shadows and attempted to force Sanborn into a waiting carriage, bound for Boston, and eventually to Washington, where Sanborn would be made to testify in front of the Senate about his role in planning Harpers Ferry. Sanborn's sister roused the neighbors, who surrounded the carriage until Sanborn's attorney arrived with a writ of habeas corpus. This shady legal maneuver sufficed for fiercely antislavery Concord, and Sanborn was shuttled to a secret hiding place.

After this harrowing incident, scenes of which were colorfully reported in Massachusetts newspapers, Sanborn all but disappeared from the limelight. The episode effectively removed him from antislavery agitation for more than a decade. At first, with Sanborn's absence, it seemed possible that Brown's memory might thrive in a dynamic, radical, and interracial afterlife. Sanborn's Concord neighbor Bronson Alcott made overtures to this vision when he invoked Brown in 1864, calling him "the martyr of the age, for he risked his life for a race not his own, and struck the first stroke of a Revolution that is freeing us all."[57] But the radical and revolutionary overtones of Brown's mission remained in a tense dynamic with his potential martyrdom. That martyrdom took on fewer forms after Fort Sumter, First Manassas, and the battles and developments of the nation's deadliest war.

That war transformed Brown. It was so bloody and so long that it dampened Americans' appetite for regional tensions and for Brown's revolutionary violence. The war also drove Sanborn away. Whereas some abolitionists had joined the Union Army to fight the good fight, Sanborn's involvement in abolition politics continued to wane. In fact, he spent most of the 1860s directing public charities, avoiding Brown, Thoreau, and Emerson for his own work. But just as Sanborn became independent of the great men of his past, he sensed that attitudes toward Brown, along with a national understanding that the South's defense of slavery was the root cause of the Civil War, were being forgotten or even intentionally obscured. Sanborn reemerged as an abolitionist when he began publishing a series of John Brown memoirs in the *Atlantic Monthly*. Throughout the 1870s, the *Atlantic* published dozens of chapters of Sanborn's Brown history, including an incredible seventy pages on what he dubbed "The Virginia Campaign of John Brown," a campaign, we should remember, that lasted just over one day.

Sanborn's *Atlantic* articles represented a distinct shift. No longer was Brown a principled and visionary revolutionary. By 1871, for Sanborn and others weary of bloodshed, Brown simply became a principled and peaceful visionary. Sanborn's portrait defined late nineteenth-century white attitudes toward Brown, aggressively minimizing the man's morally questionable acts. Brown did not kill anyone in Kansas himself, Sanborn often explicitly argued; the Old Man only hoped to free slaves. By stripping Brown of his violence, Sanborn concealed Brown's most potent attribute, the radicalism of that force and its meaning. Sanborn removed the taint of Brown's revolutionary stance in order to focus attention on the man's ideals.

To do so, Sanborn stretched his interpretations when this was required. Brown's Provisional Constitution was designed to govern the territory he conquered but also to establish himself as a sort of president of an inter-racial utopia. Using that document, Sanborn marveled at Brown's patriotic fervor. "Brown's devotion to the flag and principles of the [American] revolution" was the same "as it had been in the hearts of his two grandfathers who fought under Washington."[58] Sanborn's argument required *only* the preamble of Brown's document, which spoke of "barbarous" slavery as an "unjustifiable war" of whites against blacks, "in utter disregard and violation of . . . our Declaration of Independence."[59] But the subsequent forty-eight articles of Brown's document mimicked the U.S. Constitution and outlined an alternative government following the forceful takeover of the Southern states. Even cursory attention to Brown's plainly treasonous Constitution underscores that the document was *one* man's interpretation of what American liberty should be.[60]

Sanborn's enthusiasm for Brown grew out of a shared faith in his own interpretations of American liberty's ideal shape. In an extended biography, Sanborn began by erroneously connecting Brown to a Mayflower passenger named Peter Brown, in a trademark gambit to illustrate that the martyr of Harpers Ferry had roots in the very origins of the United States. In Sanborn's hands, Brown, the leader of the Pottawatomie massacre, veteran of Bleeding Kansas, mastermind of the murderous raid on Harpers Ferry, somehow became "a puritan soldier" whose "heart was averse to bloodshed." Sometimes Sanborn's linguistic flourishes and solemn passion bordered on the ridiculous, as when he wrote that Brown had "the keen senses of an Indian warrior," which allowed him to "perceive the frying of donuts at a distance of five miles." But in moments of greatest gravity, Sanborn applied a hyperbolic touch in order to will his vision of Brown into popular consciousness. Not only had Brown single-handedly "secured the harvest of freedom in Kansas," but according to Sanborn, he also "led the way to" Lincoln's freeing of the slaves, just as Brown, not Lincoln, had won over the "great heart of the people" to that cause. Furthermore, Sanborn told readers, "history now agrees that Brown was a hero."[61]

But in the muddled aftermath of Reconstruction, writers focused on new heroes with fewer ties to painful episodes in the American past. Brown was a relic that roiled up all sorts of difficult associations and unfinished business. Despite these complexities, Sanborn continued to believe that Brown could be a guiding moral light for the nation. As passionate as he was, Sanborn saw that the tides of historical judgment could be fickle and contrarian, that they might turn against his friend John Brown at any moment. Sanborn's mission was simple. Get rid of Brown's radicalism and ignore his violence in order to hold him up as a Christian hero for posterity. Sanborn was not alone in this effort. At the unveiling of a John Brown monument in Kansas, the former governor (and later Brown critic) Charles Robinson spoke: "The soul of John Brown was the inspiration of the armies of the Union in the war. It is and will be the inspiration of all men in all struggles against tyranny." Brown had become "a traitor to the government that he might be loyal to freedom," Robinson reasoned. "John Brown was deemed a traitor by men of his generation, and so was Jesus Christ. The one died to save a world from sin, the other died the saviour of [a] race from bondage."[62]

But even with men like Robinson unveiling monuments and preaching the gospel, Sanborn did not rest easy. A vivid and definitive account of Brown's life was needed to bolster men like Robinson. Published in 1885, the book largely reprinted Sanborn's previous writings in slightly reworked form.[63] *The Life and Letters of John Brown* was as much a document collection as a biography, but for some twenty-five years after its publication, it was the most thorough and coherent account of Brown's life. Passages abound in the book capturing Sanborn's evangelical fervor for Brown and his ability to make the Old Hero a nearly nonviolent martyr, but certain moments capture his particular grandiosity. "History seeks in vain for parallels to [Brown's] achievement," Sanborn wrote about Brown in prison. "A defeated, dying old man, who had been prying and fighting, pleading and toiling, for years, to persuade a great people that their national life was all wrong, suddenly converting millions to his cause by the silent magnanimity or the spoken wisdom of his last days."

At a Brown birthday centennial celebration in Boston in May 1900, Sanborn refined this appeal for the abolitionist's permanence. "No man of our century has done more," Sanborn wrote, "by his career and its result, to vindicate the ways of God to man." "Service and Sacrifice give Brown's biography in two words." Sanborn described the honor he felt at having known Brown, then lit into his favorite quasi-poetics. Recalling a snowy walk they had taken together, Sanborn described the abolitionist "gazing thoughtfully forward upon the untrodden expanse—and then silently and thoughtfully backward" on the footprints in the snow. "'I like to see my tracks behind me,'" Brown told Sanborn. "Already the aged hero at my side left his unmistakable tracks in Kansas, which have never melted with her snows, and never will, and which her true sons will always 'like to see,' to guard with reverence and honor, and in spirit to follow."[64] "Brown's memory only grows clearer and brighter with lapse of time."[65]

Sanborn's praise was far from the last word on Brown. On the heels of a cursory dismissal by Lincoln's biographers John Nicolay and John Hay, Brown's place in the American imagination seemed headed for a brief and derisive footnote.[66] Part of the problem was the very hero worship that Sanborn and his compatriots so passionately practiced. Writing for *Harper's Monthly* in 1894, William Dean Howells, an aspiring young Brown biographer, described a meeting with Thoreau that revealed these clashing agendas. Thoreau's Brown was a different man than Howells imagined, "a sort of John Brown type, a John Brown ideal, a John Brown principle, which we were somehow (with long pauses between the vague, orphic phrases) to cherish, and to nourish ourselves upon." Howells wanted a concrete vision, or as he described it, "the warm, palpable, loving, fearful old man of my conception." But Thoreau gave him a "type," where Brown's "principle alone existed."[67]

Howells's dissatisfaction with Brown as a disembodied principle spoke to the failures of Sanborn's impassioned hagiography. "Sanborn I have little respect for," wrote the editor of the *Harvard Alumni Magazine*, William Roscoe Thayer. "He has successfully exploited for fifty years his very secondary associations with celebrities. Like Little Lacky Honey, when he pulls out a plum, he says 'What a great boy am *I*?' . . . What a perfect specimen of Puritan hickory John Brown was!"[68]

Sanborn did habitually parade these associations, and did so again when he revised his *Life and Letters* for a new and expanded printing. The publication prompted another round of Sanborn's championing Brown the humble Christian martyr as well as himself. When a harsh review appeared in *The Nation* and the *New York Evening Post*, Sanborn wrote a vituperative letter to the editor (and fellow Brown biographer) Oswald Garrison Villard.[69] Sanborn had been unfairly criticized, even insulted. "I began to write the remarkable story of John Brown in 1871," Sanborn recalled, "knowing that I had the material." Since then, Sanborn had published "more than 1000 closely printed pages." It would be impossible to "find any essential change in my manner during this whole period." Furthermore, Sanborn explained impatiently to Villard, no one could best his unique perspective or his expertise.[70] Sanborn alone could explain Brown, the Concordian always maintained, because he knew him.

With the publication of Sanborn's two-volume autobiography in 1909, there was another opportunity for reflection. Sanborn's account sped across the personal events of his own life, his first love and marriage, for instance, and revolved around three characters: Ralph Waldo Emerson, Henry David Thoreau, and John Brown. While Sanborn considered Thoreau and Emerson his college education, John Brown occupied the roles of father figure and spiritual leader. Drawn to Brown's masculine heroism, Sanborn (like Redpath before him) saw something in the abolitionist that seemed intriguingly beyond his own limits. Thoreau shared this fascination. According to the scholar Bruce Ronda, Thoreau put Brown forward as a "heroic American male" at "the center of northern, reformist culture rather than out on its lawless margins."[71] Brown's actions obviously put him outside the norm, but so did his beliefs. For these reasons, Sanborn felt that Brown should play the role of moral guide and figurehead to the nation. "John Brown fastened the gaze of the whole world upon his acts and his fate," Sanborn wrote, and "each succeeding generation" had proven "the interest of mankind in his life and death."[72]

As Sanborn entered his final decade, in the midst of yet another of these succeeding generations, he continued to stoke enthusiasm for John Brown. Surprisingly, Sanborn's later work occasionally flirted with a more complicated idol. Brown's faith in destiny, Sanborn revealed, led him into "dark heroic ways." But "that descendent of Mayflower Pilgrims," Sanborn explained, returning to the heroic narrative, was led by his fidelity to both "the forcible destruction of slavery, and his own immortality of fame." So while Sanborn had known many men of genius, "Brown stands by himself—an occasion for dispute and blame as well as praise and song."[73]

Until his death in 1917, however, Sanborn reacted viciously to anyone who tried to explore the dark side of Brown's heroism or offer anything less than praise and song. Sanborn kept up this fight for as long as he could. At the age of eighty-five, he traveled to Lake Placid, New York, to speak at a John Brown memorial and monument dedication.[74] But by that time, the elusive Brown had already gotten away from Sanborn. In fact, Villard's 1910 biography, with its exhaustive research, trumped Sanborn with more accurately reproduced documents, not to mention greater nuance and depth.

Until the end, Sanborn did his damnedest to keep some grip on the popular representations of his fellows, putting forth his very particular "great man" school of history and biography. As Sanborn wrote in 1910, "A Boston reviewer announced the other day that he was going to indicate 'John Brown's place in history.' Such authors have yet to learn that original characters fix their own place in history; it is for the rest of us to find it out, not by argument, but by appreciation."[75] Positively appreciating Brown was Sanborn's central task for the final forty-five years of his life because he wanted Americans to accept a very specific myth. This John Brown was a "mild and humble Christian," Sanborn wrote, a "practical disciple of Jefferson . . . [and] a pioneer and hero of emancipation."[76]

A very different John Brown was thriving in black communities, spurring black civic organizations and inspiring memorials and celebrations. Making Brown a Jeffersonian, a peaceful (not Old Testament) Christian, showed Sanborn picking and choosing parts of Brown to fashion a myth.

In 1903, an Augusta, Maine, newspaper told the story of the pioneering California entrepreneur and activist Mary E. Pleasant, a black woman who supplied Brown with money for the raid at Harpers Ferry.[77] When Brown was captured, he carried a letter which read that "the axe is laid at the foot of the tree and as soon as the first blow is struck, there will be plenty more money coming." On her deathbed, no longer fearful of repercussions, Pleasant revealed her secret—she had made a small fortune in California and had traveled east in 1858 "to help John Brown." Although "it seemed at first like a failure," Pleasant told the *Augusta Comfort*, "time proved that the money was well spent. It paved the way for the war and the war freed the slaves. I always felt that John Brown started the Civil War. . . . It was the greatest pleasure of my life to give [him] money. When I die, all I want on my tombstone is: 'She was a friend of John Brown.'"[78]

Anniversary celebrations of Brown highlighted a similar depth of black identification with the abolitionist.[79] Newspapers in Springfield, Massachusetts, wrote of the memorial celebrations of 1907, where addresses were delivered "by former slaves."[80] The *Weekly Republican* called it "a voluntary recognition by the colored people of a place and generation far removed from the scene and time of his sacrifice on their behalf."[81] Events like the one in Springfield underscore the racially divided memories of Brown and the reason they grew so contentious. Later that year, the Brown biographers Thomas Featherstonhaugh and Oswald Garrison Villard complained that "the darkies have not as yet done one thing for the memory of John Brown and it is high time they were stirring."[82] For white aficionados, until blacks built concrete memorials to Brown, their meetings, speeches, and events were meaningless.

Unlike the racially homogenous effort of former Confederates that so deftly managed Civil War memory in the South, memorializing Brown was fraught with difficulties.[83] Discussing the plight of Brown family members in a later letter, Featherstonhaugh wrote that it was "to the everlasting disgrace of the negroes that any member of his family is allowed to suffer. I got a bunch of darkies together on [December 2, 1907] The 48th anniversary of John Brown's execution, and gave them a good raking over."[84] Clearly, these patriarchal attitudes shifted at the slightest whim, but only rarely did they take African American attitudes and efforts seriously.

In contrast, Featherstonhaugh and his fellow enthusiasts rejoiced at the efforts of their white counterparts. There was cause for celebration when groups like the Woman's Relief Corps of Kansas preserved the "Battle Field of Osawatomie." The corps wanted to honor "that masterful spirit, that forceful man, John Brown" because "he was not as other men are. . . . He saw eternal truth with undazzled vision." In the battle over Brown's memory, white memorials, writings, and art made the abolitionist "our herald," who "grasped the thousand spears of prejudice to his heart . . . and cried with the same uplifting fervor, 'Make way for Liberty.'"[85]

For these supporters, Brown had to be cleansed of revolutionary violence to be revered. If America was to remember the man, his example had to be moral, not practical. Of course, for blacks, a different vision of Brown had thrived. Brown became a conduit to a different set of ideals, beliefs, and practices. Black imaginings of Brown as an inspiration, literally and figuratively, for the battles of their own lives allowed the martyr of Harpers Ferry to live on in a different way. More important, invoking Brown's name and deeds contained the possibility that his mission might one day be fulfilled.

The Niagara Movement, a group of black reformers and one of the direct antecedents of the NAACP, took up that mission. In the movement's short life, its members contributed much commentary on John Brown. Eager to make a new mark on American racial reform, fifty-nine black men met at Niagara Falls on July 10, 1905, and brainstormed radical alternatives to racial reform. The name of their organization captured the spirit they hoped to follow. The founders had been barred from hotels on the American side, and the men hoped their radicalism would be part of a "mighty current" of racial reform. In this first meeting, they argued that "agitation [was] the way to liberty," encouraging real protest in response to every racial injustice.[86] Imagining themselves in competition with the model offered by Booker T. Washington, the youthful upstarts of the Niagara Movement wanted blacks not merely to aspire, but to demand.

At the group's second meeting, in Harpers Ferry in 1906, the sixty men and women came as true believers, expressing their faith in a new movement. On the ground where John Brown had made a similarly heartfelt and embryonic stab for black freedom, the Niagara conventioneers spoke at length about the Civil War, the failures of Reconstruction, and the overriding need to fight for equality and justice.

Reverend Reverdy Ransom, pastor of the Charles Street African Methodist Episcopal Church in Boston, was given the central speaking role at the event. In observance of "John Brown Day," which the Niagara conventioneers celebrated on August 17, 1906, Ransom gave an oration he called "The Spirit of John Brown." The Brown he described was not Franklin Sanborn's. This was not the John Brown of moral light and peace. Brown was important, Ransom told his audience, because of "his attempt to organize and arm the slaves to arise and strike for their freedom." Brown's goal was not simply to "break their chains, in order [that they could] flee . . . but to forcibly assert and maintain their freedom."

Ransom's speech clarified Brown's radical meaning to African Americans. Brown became a lasting symbol not merely because he contributed to breaking the chains of slavery but because these efforts were defined as the forcible assertion *and* maintenance of that freedom. As unpalatable as this violent and radical John Brown might be, until white America could come to terms with him and the black Americans who embraced him, conversations about violence, equality, and change would continue to be fractured and divisive.

The Negro American faces his destiny and doggedly strives to realize it.
—W. E. B. Du Bois, 1909

5

DISCRIMINATION AND DESTINY

John Brown and the NAACP

The keynote speaker at the Harpers Ferry Niagara convention in August 1906 was Reverend Reverdy Ransom, but his volatile cofounder of the Niagara Movement, W. E. B. Du Bois, delivered the weekend's closing speech (figure 5.1). The convention was "in significance if not in numbers one of the greatest meetings that American Negroes ever held," Du Bois wrote in his *Autobiography*. Congregating at the scene "of John Brown's raid" was essential, not least for the barefooted "pilgrimage at dawn . . . to the scene of Brown's martyrdom." There, Du Bois wrote, "we talked some of the plainest English that had been given voice by black men in America."[1]

Du Bois's remarks in August 1906 articulated the goals of his fledgling organization and its intense connections to John Brown. We "believe in John Brown," Du Bois told the Niagara attendees, "in that incarnate spirit of justice, that hatred of a lie, that willingness to sacrifice money, reputation, and life itself on the altar of right. And here on the scene of John Brown's martyrdom, we reconsecrate ourselves, our honor, our property to the final emancipation of the race which John Brown died to make free."[2] As he would do on numerous occasions, Du Bois used John Brown to engage the past as a means to make sense of the present and put forth plans for the future.[3]

During the next three years, Du Bois made dramatic efforts to combine these strategies, publishing what he considered his finest work, a short biography of John Brown, in the fall of 1909. However, Du Bois's plans for the book's role in the final emancipation were short-lived; as soon as *John Brown* appeared in print, it received crushing reviews in *The Nation* and the

Figure 5.1. Niagara Movement delegates, Harpers Ferry, August 17, 1906.
Special Collections and University Archives, University of Massachusetts at Amherst.

New York Evening Post. Oswald Garrison Villard, Du Bois's eventual NAACP
colleague and fellow Brown biographer, wrote these hatchet jobs anonymously. But long before the two men began their respective Brown projects,
Du Bois and Villard were far from friends. Their tumultuous relationship
and competing portraits of Brown took shape while they helped found the
most important black organization in American history, the National Association for the Advancement of Colored People.

These dovetailing narratives underscore the importance of controlling
Brown's memory, an increasingly volatile commodity, particularly as activists began to articulate the needs, desires, and demands of black Americans.[4] Throughout the early decades of the twentieth century, outwardly
progressive philanthropists like Villard frustrated and were frustrated by
the opinions and personalities of outspoken blacks like Du Bois. Observed
through the prism of John Brown, their story reveals the strategies and
conflicts involved in the greater project for racial equality, the longest and
most significant struggle in American history. As part of that centuries-long
process, the stories of Du Bois and Villard reveal the limits of interracial
partnership and understanding, limitations Brown exposed with particular

Figure 5.2.
W. E. B. Du Bois, 1907. Special
Collections and University
Archives, University of
Massachusetts at Amherst.

clarity because he forced these men to mesh their reforming impulses with his methods and beliefs. Exploring Du Bois, Villard, and the formational moment of the NAACP also reveals the degree to which each man identified with Brown and appropriated his memory in the service of broad social reform and individual ego.

Du Bois's approach to Brown does much to explain his past, his fiery endorsements of violent change, and many of his struggles in the first half of the twentieth century. William Edward Burghardt Du Bois, was born in Great Barrington, Massachusetts, in 1868, seemingly far removed from the world that Brown sought so desperately to change (figure 5.2). Boasting distinguished backgrounds on both sides of his family, Du Bois could trace ancestors back to both Revolutionary War soldiers and the French aristocracy in Haiti. Unlike the majority of his black countrymen, Du Bois enjoyed the advantages of this lineage and a relatively accepting environment. An exceptionally gifted student, Du Bois attended Fisk University in Nashville, Tennessee. Summer teaching in rural Tennessee exposed the young Yankee to the ugly realities of race in America. In the midst of the intense poverty and exploitation, Du Bois saw that slavery was still quite powerfully casting its shadow over the United States.[5]

After continuing graduate studies begun at Harvard in Germany, Du Bois returned to America intent on making a difference with his scholarship. When he was asked to contribute a biography to the popular American Crisis series in 1904, Du Bois chose as his subject Frederick Douglass.[6] Being contracted to write the biography for the series (other installments included bestselling volumes on Stonewall Jackson and Robert E. Lee) was largely the result of Du Bois's status as the most prominent black leader in America after Booker T. Washington.[7] When Washington was informed of Du Bois's Douglass biography, the elder reformer seized the opportunity to frustrate his young rival; Washington convinced the American Crisis series editor to let *him* write Douglass's life. Bitter but determined, Du Bois suggested Nat Turner as a possible replacement before his editor suggested that a biography of John Brown would be a more salable subject.[8]

Du Bois spent the next five years researching John Brown, a period that overlapped with many of the most dramatic developments in his long life, stretching from his experiences during the Atlanta Race Riot of 1906 to his role in the formation of the NAACP in 1909 and his editorship of *The Crisis* beginning in 1910. My "career as a scientist," Du Bois wrote of the period, "was to be swallowed up in my role as a master of propaganda."[9] *John Brown* captured Du Bois in the midst of that transformation just as it punctuated the struggles that swung him into full-scale activism. Throughout, Du Bois worked sporadically on his 220-page volume, which reflected little original research and relied heavily on other works. Still, *John Brown*, published in 1909, was a unique distillation of Du Bois's ideas and dreams for black Americans. Despite his efforts, but partly because of the book's radical interpretation, the biography was a commercial failure that sold only 660 copies in the seven years following publication.[10] Directly testifying to that dim commercial fate, Du Bois wrote that the gun-wielding martyr of Harpers Ferry was "the man who of all Americans has perhaps come nearest to touching the real souls of black folk."[11]

"John Brown worked not simply for Black Men," Du Bois told readers more eager for reunion than division, Brown "worked with them." Du Bois's Brown was blacks' "companion [in] daily life, knew their faults and virtues, and felt, as few white Americans have felt, the bitter tragedy of their lot."[12] Quite obviously, Du Bois's conclusions were not meant to coddle readers; *John Brown* explored a radical and violent vision of the abolitionist that

stirred little enthusiasm in the America of the 1910s. While Du Bois's abstract and optimistic endorsement of violence would soon be repudiated by
the American and black experience in World War I (a war that largely validated Villard's outspoken pacifism), this largely abandoned biography highlights Brown's problematic and nagging presence.

Du Bois inscribed the martyr inside a broader exploration of black
American history, a framework systematically marginalized by historians
since Du Bois first told his story in print.[13] To understand Du Bois's Brown
is to trace black perceptions of the antislavery crusader's involvement in
Bleeding Kansas, his friendships with blacks dating to the 1840s, his catastrophic invasion of the South, his execution, and, finally, the many facets
of his martyrdom.

Du Bois imagined a Brown in stark contrast to prevailing historical interpretations. He launched a preemptive strike on the emerging Revisionist
school and its arguments that the Civil War was unnecessary by focusing
his biography of Brown on the horrors of slavery and the absolute necessity and urgency of its demise. Du Bois confronted Lost Cause arguments,
which glorified the purpose and people of the Old South, by developing a
vibrant counternarrative of the nature of antebellum slavery. In these ways,
Du Bois offered a forceful alternative interpretation of America's continuing struggle with race, radicalism, and the legacy of slavery. Keenly aware
of this tangled web, Du Bois placed John Brown as the symbolic confluence
of centuries of African American subjugation and resistance.[14] What better
symbol of the ironies, heartbreaks, and hypocrisies of America's claims to
liberty and freedom than a descendant of a Revolutionary War captain sac-
rificing his life to end slavery?

Du Bois saw the power of black connections with Brown and radical
violence because he had lived through many of the contradictions, duali-
ties, and frustrations of being black in America. These struggles were put
in great relief through the memory of John Brown, especially as Du Bois
attended celebrations for Brown at North Elba, made his own pilgrimage
to Harpers Ferry in 1906, and became embroiled with paternalistic white
counterparts over Brown's true meaning to American history. It remains
a source of scholarly derision that Du Bois admired his own biography of
Brown as much as he did. However, Du Bois's interest in the work exposes
the central issues of his activism, that mixture of brilliance, principle, and
stubborn egotism that drove him.[15] Du Bois was ever the obstinate icono-
clast, and his opinion of the biography grew in direct proportion to how obscure it became.[16]

His uncompromising attitude notwithstanding, there were specific reasons why Du Bois's take on Brown was so unpopular. The biography is terribly flawed and was almost immediately supplanted by better-researched volumes (most notably Villard's). Nonetheless, *John Brown*'s unique strengths and glaring weaknesses clarify the unique questions (about violence, interracial cooperation, and radicalism) Brown posed to civil rights leadership at this crucial time.

After Du Bois agitated for fifty years to have the book reprinted, International Publishers agreed to reissue the biography on the centenary, not of Brown's death, but of the Emancipation Proclamation. In this and so many other ways, Du Bois wanted to dramatically resituate Brown inside an African American timeline.[17] As Du Bois wrote in his second autobiography, "one of my jobs was to disinter [blacks'] unknown past, and help make certain a splendid future."[18] Du Bois told readers, most unprepared to even glance in his direction, that they had all gotten the story wrong. He referred to more than Brown's life; the grand narrative of the United States of America, that Whiggish story of freedom, prosperity, and destiny, needed to be reimagined.[19]

Accordingly, Du Bois did not make Brown a facsimile of the hero of abolitionist legend, that martyr Sanborn and Hovenden helped enshrine. Instead, Du Bois's arguments spoke to a half century of black relationships with Brown and Du Bois's belief that the abolitionist should play a central role in movements for human equality. Accordingly, *John Brown* grafts the extralegal crusades of Kansas and Harpers Ferry onto the central narrative of America's ongoing national struggle for freedom. That story, Du Bois argued through Brown, should stretch from the slave ships to the Revolution, from Jefferson to emancipation, from Reconstruction to the present day. The guiding light in that story, Du Bois made clear, was unfulfilled promise. The biography's significance is simple: Du Bois explicitly connected the martyred abolitionist to a devastating critique of the American past, present, and future.

Du Bois's biography is fascinating and frustrating in equal measure.[20] For all of the book's adventurous presentism, it is plagued by factual errors and a lack of serious research. Curiously, Du Bois was aware of these critiques even before he wrote the biography. As Du Bois admitted in the opening pages, he used "little new material." Indeed, his "only excuse for another life of John Brown [was the] opportunity to lay new emphasis . . . and to treat [the] facts from a different point of view."[21] While the book suffers from these shortcomings, Du Bois's ability to raise Brown as a vehicle of

racial radicalism and revolutionary violence should reorient criticisms of
the book.

Du Bois titled the biography's opening chapter "Africa and America," discussing slavery rather than John Brown's birth, the raid on Harpers Ferry,
or the 1859 hanging. Du Bois invoked "the mystic spell of Africa," a spell that
"is and ever was over all America."[22] There is no question about where Du
Bois stood on the ultimate meaning of Brown's life as well the abolitionist's
significance to the overall narrative of the United States. For Du Bois, these
stories were only meaningful if Brown's example illuminated the horrors of
slavery and emphasized violent solutions to that violent system. While the
source material was derivative, the interpretation was radical to the core.[23]
For this purpose, Du Bois demonstrated a keen eye for the telling detail. Describing Brown's appearance in bankruptcy court in June 1854, which other
historians used to illustrate Brown's profligacy, incompetence, or worse, Du
Bois focused on the news of fugitive slave Anthony Burns's arrest in Boston. Brown informed his weary lawyer he was "going to Boston. . . . Anthony
Burns must be released or I will die in the attempt."[24] This was not Sanborn's Brown or the horse thief who would be pilloried by historians for the
next fifty years; Du Bois's Brown was a new creation.

At every turn, Du Bois invoked the horrors of slavery but also, and
most important, the unfinished national business still at hand in 1909. Du
Bois's straightforward narrative strategies have often been ignored, but
they served to establish Brown's context. For instance, his only mention of
Brown's birth invoked Toussaint L'Ouverture: "John Brown was born just
as the shudder of Haiti was running through all the Americas, and from his
earliest boyhood he saw and felt the price of repression—the fearful cost
that the western world was paying for slavery."[25] Du Bois had Brown inherit
that shudder and feel the spirit of L'Ouverture at birth. These connections
were the basis of Du Bois's central argument: America past, present, and
future needed Brown because he was very nearly an idiot savant of abolitionism, a white man uniquely and profoundly aware of the brutality in his
midst.[26]

Du Bois was well aware of the high stakes of this history. "Men and
women of the South, and honest ones, too, have striven feverishly to paint
Negro slavery in bright alluring colors, Du Bois wrote, "They have told of
childlike devotion, faithful service and light-hearted irresponsibility, in the
fine old aristocracy of the plantation." To this sunny picture, Du Bois contrasted the realities of chattel slavery. "As a school of brutality and human
suffering, of female prostitution and male debauchery; as a mockery of mar-

riage and defilement of family life; as a darkening of reason, and spiritual death, it had no parallel in its day." Sure, Du Bois conceded, slavery "was not all as dark as it might have been. Human life, thank God, is never as bad as it may be, but it is too often desperately bad."[27]

Like slavery, Du Bois emphasized, Brown was integral to the path of American history. Du Bois began his narrative with the first African slaves in Virginia looking prophetically westward to Kansas. The Midwestern territory "was big with the tragic fate" of American blacks, Du Bois wrote, because "the center of the slavery battle had swung westward."[28] Brown and his family, of course, were to be intimately involved in that battle. Du Bois anticipated future scholarship in describing Bleeding Kansas, often cast as an intermittent skirmish, as a "war" where even the smallest daily dispute quickly turned "to force and blood."[29] Brown's role in Kansas was "to strike the blow for freedom," Du Bois wrote, because he "saw the real crux of the conflict, most definitely knew his own convictions and was readiest at the crisis for decisive action[,] . . . a man whose leadership lay not in his office, wealth or influence, but in the white flame of his utter devotion to an ideal."[30]

Unlike many of the abolitionist's hagiographers, Du Bois readily admitted the facts: Brown played the central role in the Pottawatomie massacre. But Du Bois went a step further. Bloodshed and murder, he wrote, "such were the cost of freedom."[31] "When a prophet like John Brown appears," he asked readers, "how must we the world receive him?"[32] The question was a demanding one. Du Bois, like Brown, thought noble aims justified questionable means. Any methods available to Brown were appropriate "to confront and overcome traditional, often white supremacist versions of American history."[33] Within this mission, Du Bois's Brown took on different meanings, perhaps less historically factual, but crucial for the challenges ahead. Brown's soul was a light for the nation, shining as brightly in 1865 as it did in 1909, revealing that "slavery is wrong. . . . Kill it." Du Bois asked readers if Brown was wrong to take such an extreme position, then answered for them. "To-day at last we know. John Brown was right."[34]

Beyond his explicit endorsement of Brown's means and ends, Du Bois contrasted the abolitionist with white America. "To most Americans the inner striving of the Negro was a veiled and unknown tale," but "John Brown sought to know individuals among them intimately and personally. . . . He talked to them, and listened to the history of their trials, advised them, and took advice from them. His dream was to enlist the boldest and most daring spirits among them in his great plan."[35]

Brown's plan was surely bold, but its greatness could just as surely be called into question. Du Bois hoped to release Brown from the confines of his life and its mistakes. "Was John Brown simply an episode," he asked, "or was he an eternal truth? If a truth, how speaks that truth to-day?" Brown's legacy "to the twentieth century" was that "the cost of liberty is greater than the price of repression." In other words, blood can and sometimes must be shed to achieve liberty.[36] Here was the fault line of Du Bois's *John Brown*. Within this divisive argument was the root of the regrettable conflict between Du Bois and Oswald Garrison Villard.

Villard's story clarifies the extent of this division, showing how Du Bois's conceptions of means and ends made their cooperation nearly impossible. Villard, the grandson of John Brown's bête noir, William Lloyd Garrison, was the son of the German-born industrialist Henry Villard. Henry began as a Civil War reporter but after the Panic of 1873 parlayed this experience into great fortune, becoming a railroad agent for holders of Western railroad securities. As the Pacific Northwest burst with economic opportunity, Henry was able to obtain a controlling interest in the Northern Pacific, and became president of that railroad in 1881. His fortune meant more than creature comforts or a cosmopolitan childhood for young Oswald; Henry was an empire builder. Owning a railroad did not say enough about a man, so, in an effort to crown his ascendancy, and perhaps to stay connected to his journalistic past, Henry purchased the *New York Evening Post* and *The Nation* on July 1, 1881. At the time of his purchase, the Villard family's personal fortune was valued at over $1 billion in today's currency.

The family built houses in Manhattan and Dobbs Ferry, designed by the legendary architects and designers Louis Comfort Tiffany and Charles McKim, where the Villards enjoyed every luxury; they even boasted ownership of the first elevator in New York City.[37] The sociocultural mindset this wealth fostered was essential to Villard's philanthropic and journalistic projects. The private railroad cars, the "magnificent country house," the awesome extent of "the family fortunes," were the fabric of daily life for Oswald Villard throughout his life.[38]

Beyond every material advantage, Villard also had the privilege of important associates. His father was a lifelong friend and one of the first supporters of Thomas Edison, who was frequently at the Villard homes showing off his latest inventions. On visits to Germany, the family spent time in the company of Otto von Bismarck and other European notables. In short, growing up a Villard meant an endless sequence of exceptional places and people. Just after Villard had completed his undergraduate studies at Harvard in 1893, his family began a long vacation in Europe and North Africa. Greece, Constantinople, Vienna, Lake Geneva, Italy; young Oswald had seen much of the world before he ever held a job.

Regarding John Brown (and Du Bois), Villard's father passed on two crucial beliefs to his son, one concerned the Civil War, the other, the best method of reform in America. When the Civil War began, Henry was a field correspondent for Horace Greeley's *New York Tribune*.[39] In addition to meeting and writing about many of the great military leaders of the war, Henry personally covered almost every major battle—Bull Run, Shiloh, Perryville, Fredericksburg, the Wilderness campaign—only missing Appomattox because of his father's poor health. Henry's war experiences were profoundly affecting, and he spoke of the battles often. At Shiloh, viewing the thousands of blue and gray clad corpses, he was repelled by the horror, sadness, and "bloody evidence in every direction."[40]

Haunted by the war's brutalities, Henry Villard was equally inspired by the heroism and mistreatment he saw traveling with various black troops. After scoring a huge scoop onboard the ironclad *New Ironsides* during the naval assault of Fort Sumter on April 7, 1863, Henry was feted by the *New York Tribune* and received a one-hundred-dollar bonus. On his editor's suggestion, Henry took his riches to Boston, where he met with William Lloyd Garrison, and his life took a dramatic turn.

Visiting the famous editor, Henry met Garrison's daughter Fanny and fell deeply in love. So in addition to his critiques of the means the United States had utilized to preserve the Union and emancipate the slaves, Henry soon began incorporating Garrison's pacifist mantle. Oswald Garrison Villard celebrated his grandfather in his memoir, writing that no one felt the lashes and "brandings upon their own limbs" quite so much as Garrison. Quoting John Jay Chapman's 1913 hagiography, Villard agreed that neither "Cromwell [n]or Milton could have rivaled Garrison" in speechmaking or writing, for the Liberator possessed "as dreadful a weapon as any which the human intellect can forge."[41] Villard felt that force from an early age; his "earliest memories" were the family's frequent visits to Grandpapa Garrison's home in Brookline, Massachusetts. When Garrison turned seventy-four, his daughter finally convinced him to move in with her family in New York. For one month at the impressionable age of seven, young Oswald tended to his grandfather along with his siblings, parents, and uncles, witnessing firsthand the great outpouring of grief when Garrison died on May 23, 1879.

Oswald Villard's father also provided a powerful example. While "Mr. Garrison had staked his life for many years on liberty for the Negro slaves," Villard maintained that Henry had "risked his existence . . . for the same cause." Villard's opinion was somewhat grandiose given his father's strictly journalistic duties, but the connection between his forebears transcended these specifics. "Mr. Garrison died under my father's roof," Villard continued, "in complete sympathy and deep affection, for both sought to serve their generation and their time with all the means at their command." Serving *his* generation convinced Oswald Villard to adopt the intellectual and moral mantle of his grandfather.[42] As Garrison's own son Francis wrote, Villard was the "natural successor to the custodianship" of what Villard described as "dear Grandpapa's principles."[43]

Villard saw himself as the rightful heir to his family's tradition of service and was bolstered by his father's overwhelming emphasis on a particular set of life choices (figure 5.3). Money was not something worth pursuing, "it was something to be used, pragmatically and conscientiously, to reach a higher goal."[44] Villard was inspired by his father's "ideals and his character" and wrote that he was eternally grateful "for an idealistic father who held his wealth to be merely a trusteeship."[45] This high-mindedness, which was tempered by a potent cocktail of principle and realism, deeply influenced Villard's opinion of both John Brown and W. E. B. Du Bois.

Villard once wrote that his father's spirit had come to rest in his own "soul." In particular, he felt that his father's "integrity and his ideals" survived in him. Henry never discriminated against any "man for his color," and "four years of battle and of carnage had made of him an uncompromising foe of war." Villard absorbed his father's pacifism, gleaned from his war reporting, and blended it with his grandfather's pacifism. In particular, Villard took inspiration from family principles of a worthwhile life; the Garrisons and Villards shared an abhorrence for "those who seek by metes and bounds to stake out for their selfish selves a part of the world to have it all their own." For Villard, Du Bois personified this quality. Moreover, Villard judged both Brown and Du Bois by their inability to practice his father's greatest skill and his own greatest inheritance, besides the vast fortune and publishing empire: selfless ambition. Above all else, the Villards valued the ability to "foresee consequences where others were conscious only of the deeds of the moment, the circumstances of the hour, caring not at all how these might mold the future."[46]

Of course, Villard's story—his own set of personal achievements—was rather less distinguished than that of his father or grandfather. Villard had a

Figure 5.3.
Oswald Garrison Villard,
1910. Special Collections and
University Archives, University
of Massachusetts at Amherst.

thoroughly mediocre collegiate career, mainly cultivating even greater elit-
ism at Harvard. Even as Villard critiqued his alma matter for being so "entirely satisfied with itself," he admitted the school's reputation was well deserved because students and faculty represented "the flowering of an age."
Not one to wear "rosy spectacles," Villard maintained that "Harvard especially typified" the best that the nation had to offer.[47] It was at Harvard
that Villard first imagined a career in writing, and he toyed with a book on
John Brown as early as the mid-1890s. He began his journalistic career as
a sophomore, becoming the college's official correspondent for his family's
New York Evening Post.[48] It was *The Nation* (then a weekly supplement),
however, that Villard would eventually wield as a club to beat enemies into
submission, express his views, and spread his influence.[49]

   The Nation became more than Villard's mouthpiece, the magazine highlighted its owner's domineering self-righteousness and high-principled
moralizing. Villard was upfront about his allegiances and beliefs, which
were deeply rooted in his family history. Theorizing that greater wealth
might have corrupted the Villards, Oswald wrote that their comparatively
limited riches meant his "socially minded parents, with their compelling

sense of community obligation and public spirit" were never "hostile to progress."[50]

Villard's own take on the obligations of wealth was a curious combination of real selflessness—giving time, money, and resources toward projects for those in need—and principled snobbery—lashing out at those who for whatever reason did not meet his exacting standards. The most important outlet for his charity and judgment arrived in 1909, when Villard was asked by three activists to clarify their mission statement for a new African American reform movement. Despite his numerous philanthropic projects, and his responsibilities to *The Nation* and the *New York Evening Post*, the looming spirit of grandfather Garrison made it impossible to refuse an early role in what would become the NAACP. Garrison was omnipresent in Villard's many statements and recollections but also in the very character of his involvement in the NAACP.[51]

The organization had its roots in many places, but the final spark was provided by the August 14, 1908, riot that erupted in Springfield, Illinois. In a single day, three blacks were lynched and thousands fled the city. William Walling, a socialist journalist and Southerner, responded to the Springfield massacre with an article titled "Race War in the North."[52] Walling called on one of Du Bois's few white confidants, Mary White Ovington, and the Jewish philanthropist Henry Moskowitz, for a meeting of sympathetic friends.[53]

At that meeting, the "three progenitors" decided that their best hope was to ally themselves with someone of power, financial means, and influence. They contacted Villard to help "issue a call for a larger meeting."[54] What came to be known as *The Call* was published in Villard's *Evening Post* on February 12, 1909, the hundredth anniversary of Abraham Lincoln's birth. *The Call* declared that "if Mr. Lincoln could visit this country he would be disheartened by the nation's failure." Not only was there widespread "disfranchising [of] the negro" but the Supreme Court had abandoned civil rights; the legal framework of education, miscegenation, and taxation had all turned against blacks.[55] The document was a call to action. "Silence under these conditions means tacit approval," *The Call* explained, announcing "a national conference for the discussion of present evils, the voicing of protests, and the renewal of the struggle for civil and political liberty."[56]

The Call was signed by sixty supporters and "Prof. W. E. B. Du Bois, Atlanta," was at the top of the right-hand column.[57] At the unnamed organization's first meeting on May 25, 1910, Du Bois was named director of publicity and research and Villard was made treasurer and member of the board. Villard's recollection of the meeting captured the paternalistic tone that characterized his involvement. "We have raised up leaders of their people," Villard recalled, "and we have given older leaders the opportunity to stand forth, as when we aided Dr. W. E. B. Du Bois to found *The Crisis*."[58] In his retelling, Villard made no mention of the many reform organizations that had preceded the NAACP. Instead, Villard made the NAACP the logical culmination of his family history and personal story. His John Brown project was soon shoehorned into the same narrative arc: descendant of Garrison makes good. Villard did boast a proud heritage, but it was his financial means and publishing opportunities that were truly impressive.

Villard's upbringing and education had instilled in him a powerful belief in noblesse oblige. Villard believed that members of the privileged classes had a responsibility to uplift those beneath them.[59] Beyond his own feelings of obligation, Villard was guided in his involvement with the NAACP by feelings of responsibility to his long-deceased grandfather and father.[60] Villard was continuously astonished to see so little of this spirit in his Harvard classmates and still less among his peers in the elegant parlors of New York's elite. Villard's outrage over the apparent lack of social responsibility spurred his desire to lead, not just contribute to, philanthropic efforts.[61]

The NAACP, of course, had deep roots in black reform groups of the previous decades. Du Bois's Niagara Movement was a specific model, especially for Ovington, who Du Bois had befriended and invited to the Harpers Ferry convention. In her autobiography, Ovington cited Du Bois's Niagara resolution as an inspiration for all three instigators of *The Call*. Du Bois's demand for "every right that belongs to a free-born American—political, civil, and social" and his promise to "never cease to protest and assail the ears of America with the story of its shameful deeds towards us," Ovington recalled, were the cornerstones of the new organization's vision. Du Bois's statement and William Walling's 1908 warning that "either the spirit of Lincoln and Lovejoy must be revived and we must come to treat the Negro on a plane of absolute political and social equality or [we] will soon have transferred race war to the North" were foundational.[62] "Out of these two statements," Ovington explained, "the militant National Association for the Advancement of Colored People was born."[63] For this reason, Ovington was especially intent that Du Bois be given a prominent role in the new organization, and despite earlier disagreements with Du Bois over Booker T. Washington, Villard was made amenable to the idea.[64] It was an auspicious beginning; in addition to the initial donation of "room-rent in the *Evening Post* building," Ovington recalled that Villard "won friends for us, and gave us much publicity in his paper."[65] This generosity came with a price; Villard strongly pushed his own agenda for the organization, particularly trying to explicitly link the movement to a new era of Garrisonian agitation.[66]

The debate over the exact caste of the organization found Villard deeply wary of one self-styled descendant of John Brown, the relentlessly combative Du Bois. Du Bois, for his part, was cautiously optimistic about Villard, observing that the initial conferences for the NAACP gave him confidence in Villard's leadership. However, the two men soon found themselves at loggerheads.[67] Only nine months after Villard's *Call* was released, the philanthropist attacked Du Bois's Brown biography in his publications.[68] At work on his own biography since 1903, Villard contributed a scathing and unsigned indictment of Du Bois's *John Brown* to the literature section of *The Nation*.[69]

Villard conceded that Du Bois was a "gifted" author, but he said Du Bois had made a "most regrettable" mistake in choosing Brown's story. Considering the book's flaws, Villard argued, it was easy to understand Du Bois's impulse to "write a new life of John Brown from the point of view of the negro." Villard's paternalism came through as he lamented how little "negroes [had] done to honor the memory of John Brown." Although Du Bois offered a "readable" restitution, Villard challenged the quality of the tribute. *John Brown* was not "impartial" and trafficked recklessly "in inaccuracies."[70]

Du Bois's book, Villard maintained, was filled with unsupportable theories, which, to make things worse, rested "upon untrustworthy staves." The review provided a litany of the biography's inaccuracies, facts Villard had paid a researcher to uncover. While the criticisms of Du Bois were well deserved, Villard made no attempt to confront the volume's overarching questions about violence, equality, and change. Instead, Villard concluded anonymously, "a page of *The Nation* would not suffice to record the other slips which make it impossible to accept this volume."[71]

Du Bois was outraged and demanded the reviewer's name as well as the chance to respond in *The Nation*.[72] In his first letter to editor Paul Elmer More, Du Bois thanked the magazine for pointing out some regrettable inaccuracies, but Du Bois took pains to call attention to several misrepresentations of his work.[73] None of his concerns were printed in *The Nation*.[74] While the magazine might "at least have the courtesy to allow me a word in self defense," Du Bois wrote again to More, "I receive a letter little short of insulting." Indicating that he knew full well the man responsible for the review and its toxicity, Du Bois added that he hoped "that both you and

Mr. Villard will on second thought have the grace to grant me this slight reparation after your peculiarly wanton assault."[75]

As Du Bois added in another angry letter to *The Nation*, he would "not think of seating myself at the feet of Mr. Villard for instruction either in History or English."[76] Unfortunately, Du Bois could not have known that kowtowing was a requirement with Villard, especially when it came to African Americans. To make matters worse, Villard saw in Du Bois's reaction a volatile and angry man, exactly the type of reformer who might compromise the goals of the fledgling NAACP.[77]

Villard's private correspondence at the time captures the disturbing condescension and subtle racism of Villard's noblesse oblige philanthropy. Du Bois's careless biography and his anger at Villard's hatchet job in *The Nation* simply revealed "the super-sensitiveness of one whose color constantly subjects him to insult and contempt."[78] Du Bois was not to blame, Villard admitted; his race made it impossible for him to act otherwise. Ill will began to calcify, and when the two men met at the second annual NAACP conference in May 1910, they "shook hands across" what was now quite definitively a "chasm."[79]

That chasm did not prevent the five individuals from incorporating the NAACP: Du Bois, Villard, Ovington, Walters Sachs (one of the founding partners of the investment firm Goldman Sachs), and John Hayne Holmes, a prominent social reformer. Notwithstanding the organization's mission and its unparalleled success, Du Bois remained the only black member of its executive board until 1917. While the racial makeup was tacitly ignored at first, when the issue was simply getting the NAACP off of the ground, the absence of black executives became highly contentious after the initial months.

In the fall of 1910, Du Bois launched *The Crisis*, the NAACP's monthly journal, which within a year had a circulation of twelve thousand. In its inaugural issue, Du Bois enumerated the goals of the organization, strongly echoing his statements about John Brown. The NAACP was designed "to fight the wrong of race prejudice." In the interest of "meeting the forces of evil," he added, his compatriots would "fight the wrong with every weapon in every civilized way."[80] In response, the black-run *Washington (DC) Bee* ran a highly critical series of articles about *The Crisis*, focusing particularly on the degree to which Du Bois and the magazine were beholden to white benefactors.[81] Given such critiques, the NAACP made it a priority to retain Du Bois's participation.

But moving together as an organization *and* keeping Du Bois happy often proved difficult. Throughout, Villard was both instigator and obstacle. In 1910, the philanthropist claimed that Du Bois was obstructing "his" project, also known as the NAACP.[82] Villard's sense of ownership had long been a source of strife, but in this crucial period, when the organization was especially vulnerable to attacks, Villard's possessiveness posed a real threat. True to his self-proclaimed crusading roots, however, Villard stuck almost blindly to his principles, following his self-righteous and sanctimonious agenda.[83]

Unfortunately, Villard and Du Bois felt similarly about their penchant for and responsibility to truth-telling. These shared qualities largely ruled out diplomacy, professional courtesy, and any doubts over the wisdom of their judgment.[84] Both Du Bois and Villard were crippled by ego, but Villard was additionally restrained by the tradition of high principle he inherited and felt bound by. Villard identified with Brown because of their dedication to lofty principles. Villard found it nearly impossible to imagine that this connection might blind him to the majority of Brown's actions and beliefs. But the publishing scion often revealed rather limited self-awareness. In one of the most unintentionally ironic passages in his autobiography, following some self-congratulation about his role in founding the NAACP, Villard recalled the organization's origins. Beyond editing and releasing *The Call*, Villard's most important contribution was naming the organization, which was initially dubbed the National Negro Committee.[85] But Villard, like any man of leisure, had many things on his plate. "My work for the colored people was by no means my only professional activity," Villard wrote. "On January 1, 1907, there appeared the first issue of *Yachting*, a creation of mine."[86] It did not strike Villard as odd to publish a magazine intended only for yacht-owning Americans on the eve of the formation of an organization dedicated to racial justice and equality.

Villard's most consuming hobby was his biography of John Brown. Conceived from the start as a project deeply rooted in his family history, Villard's book on Brown allowed him to celebrate the influence of his grandfather, his father, and his beloved mother. Villard was very close to the former Fanny Garrison, and his two biographers maintain that the bond was the most significant in Villard's life. Therefore, tales of the meeting between seventeen-year-old Fanny Garrison and John Brown "under her father's roof" were crucial. Fanny had told her son of the encounter, in which Brown ridiculed Garrison's "milk and water" abolitionism. Villard's mother acknowledged that Brown might have been the "curtain raiser" to the Civil War, but she condemned the man and his methods.[87]

Villard's actual training for the writing of the biography is harder to

quantify. After wandering across the better parts of Europe for a year following his graduation, Villard became a graduate student and part-time
instructor for the eminent Harvard historian Albert Bushnell Hart. Hart's
interest in Villard had nothing to do with his intellect. "Professor Hart con-
fided to me," Villard recalled, "that he had selected me because of my social
standing, the fact that I wore nice clothes, and was a member of a couple
of good clubs." Such experiences reinforced Villard's belief that only men
of "leisure and of good manners" could produce scholarship untainted by
propaganda. The Boston Brahmin class had generated a "notable scholastic
senate" which, Villard lamented, "cannot be replaced today."[88] Villard's inherited fortune and distinguished background fit that mold quite nicely.

Hart's guidance was the seed for Villard's Brown biography. Villard's first
lecture for his advisor was about Brown, a task he performed so miserably
that the audience reacted with "shuffling of feet, uncalled for applause, and
laughter at nothing." Villard recalled his "desperation," but that single difficult morning "led in time to my biography . . . the only first-class job I have
ever done." Villard rightly called the biography a "first class job," but also
called it *his*. In the midst of his NAACP leadership, his many businesses, and
his editorial responsibilities at the *New York Evening Post* and *The Nation*,
Villard claimed to have written the book "on Wednesday afternoons, Satur-
days, Sundays, holidays, and occasional evenings."[89]

In his autobiography, however, Villard revealed that the Brown project
depended largely on the work of his assistant Katherine Mayo. Mayo was
already a world traveler and accomplished journalist when Villard recruited
her for the biography; she would go on to write several books, including a
definitive account of India's struggle for independence.[90] Villard recalled
that he was deeply in debt for "her enthusiasm in collating the material
and rare skill in interviewing the survivors of the John Brown period all
over the United States."[91] Villard's papers show the true extent of Mayo's
contributions. Applauding one of Mayo's dozens of interviews, her analysis
convinced Villard "once more," he wrote, "that you ought to write the book
and not I."[92] Villard, who received daily infusions of Brown material from
Mayo, was quickly overwhelmed by the volume and quality of his assistant's
contributions. Even today, Mayo's interviews are startling, not merely for
their breadth and insight into the last living witnesses and descendants of
Brown, but also for her intrepid and exhaustive work in tracking them to
every corner of the nation.[93]

"I certainly need your aid," Villard wrote Mayo in 1908. "There is lots of
work to be done here and I can find only odd moments myself. I am quite

in despair about my own share of the work."[94] In the biography itself, Villard only admitted a "lasting indebtedness to Miss Katherine Mayo, whose journeys in search of material for his use have covered a period of more than two years and many thousands of miles. But for her judgment, her tact and skill, and her enthusiasm for the work, it could hardly have approached its present comprehensiveness."[95] Villard seeming generosity only told part of the story. "How well it was," Villard revealed privately to Mayo, "that we wrote J. B. when we did."[96]

The biography began with a quotation from Charles Eliot, Villard's favorite Harvard president, which appeared in the *Atlantic Monthly* of March 1860. "There never was more need," Eliot wrote, "for a good life of any man than there was for one of John Brown." Villard then quoted an 1886 *Atlantic* article lamenting that while "so grand a subject cannot fail to inspire a writer. . . . the ill-starred 'martyr' suffers a prolongation of martyrdom . . . riddled with the odious arrows of fulsome panegyrists."[97] Villard agreed. His preface pilloried the five major biographies since 1886, among them those by Sanborn and Du Bois, as one-dimensional briefs "for Brown and his men."[98] In contrast, "fifty years after the Harper's Ferry tragedy," Villard maintained, "the time is ripe for a study of John Brown, free from bias, from the errors in taste and fact of the mere panegyrist." Not only would he avoid all of these pitfalls, Villard declared, he would "make accurate the smallest detail; the original documents, contemporary letters and living witnesses have been examined in every quarter of the United States."[99]

Villard captured the volatile contest between fact and interpretation that plagues every student of Brown. Apologizing for his extensive quotations, Villard explained "that already a hundred myths have attached themselves to John Brown's name. . . . Over some of them have raged long and bitter controversies which give little evidence to the softening effects of time." Acting as mediator, "the historian's task is made heavier since nearly all characterizations of the man have been at one extreme or another." Finally, Villard revealed that for his biographical purposes, he would use "accepted ethical standards . . . to pass a deliberate and accurate historical judgment, to bestow praise and blame without favor or sectional partisanship."[100]

In that tumultuous historiography of a hundred myths, Villard managed to carve out an impressively measured and thoughtful biography. Even as Villard debunked Brown's Mayflower roots or affirmed Owen Brown's Underground Railroad credentials, he also showed a deep understanding of and sympathy for Brown's role in abolition, the Civil War, and emancipation. It was his pleasure, Villard wrote, to write the life of a man "who for a brief day challenged the attention of a great nation, compelled it to heart searchings most beneficent in their results, and through his death of apparent ignominy achieved not only an historical immortality, but a far-reaching victory over forces of evil against which he had dared and lost his life."[101]

Still, as the grandson of the Liberator, Villard drew on some grandiloquent conceptions of abolitionism and pacifism. In *John Brown*, Villard's overriding question was "From what midnight star did [Brown] draw his inspiration to go forth and kill?" Villard was dogged about pinning down the exact date of Brown's "conversion" to antislavery, an obsession designed to find a parallel to Garrison's well-known epiphany at the age of twenty-five.[102] Despite these personal agendas, Villard showed a unique talent in highlighting the contradictions between Brown's business failures and his antislavery beliefs. Though not the first to explore Brown's financial mishaps, Villard elided hackneyed labels by making Brown both a product of his time *and* a figure who transcended that time.[103] Mayo's interviews illuminated these exact themes. "It is a Brown trait to be migratory," Brown's son Jason explained to Mayo, "sanguine about what they think they can do, to speculate, to go into debt, and to make a good many failures."[104]

Villard used such insights to show Brown's attraction to a new kind of speculation: territorial Kansas. Kansas gave "Brown the opportunity to test himself as a guerrilla-leader. . . . For no other purpose did he proceed to the Territory." Once in Kansas, Brown found an outlet for his instinct for leadership. To his "intense nature" was added "the driving force of a mighty and unselfish purpose." Villard's refrain for the violent closing chapters was his argument that "however one may dislike the methods adopted . . . [this was] the explanation of the forging of this rough, natural leader of men.[105]

While Villard isolated Brown from the historical chaos of territorial Kansas, his explanations of Brown's behavior remain insightful. Brown "came to Kansas bringing arms and ammunition," Villard wrote, "convinced that force alone would save Kansas, to shed blood to defend the voters." But after the skirmish known as the Wakarusa War, Brown came to believe, in Villard's opinion, that "a collision was inevitable."[106] Remarkable given his distaste for violence, Villard grasped the psychology and motivation of his subject better than most.

"Fired with indignation at the wrongs he witnessed on every hand," Villard wrote, "impelled by the Covenanter's spirit that made him so strange a figure in the nineteenth century, and believing that there should be an eye for an eye and a tooth for a tooth, he killed his men in the conscientious belief that he was a faithful servant of Kansas and of the Lord." But even when Villard seemed to justify the Pottawatomie massacre, he reminded his readers that the murder of the proslavery men on May 24, 1856, by Brown and his posse "must ever remain a complete indictment of his judgment and wisdom; a dark blot upon his memory; a proof that, however self-controlled, he had neither true respect for the laws nor for human life, nor a knowledge that two wrongs never make a right." In his final judgment Villard argued that if Brown "deserves to live in history, it is not because of his cruel, gruesome, reprehensible acts on the Pottawatomie, but despite them."[107] While Villard was cautious about awarding Brown real heroism, he seamlessly wove Brown's beliefs into a broader discussion of his mental health, the morass of an endless succession of historians. Anyone "who sacrifices business prospects, a quiet ordinary life, his family's happiness, and the lives of himself and his children, in a crusade which the world has since declared to have been righteous . . . cannot . . . be adjudged a maniac."[108]

For a Garrisonian descendant and pacifist like Villard, Brown's physical attacks on slavery were less important than his writing and symbolism. "For all his years of dreaming that he might become another [Toussaint L'Ouverture]" Villard admitted, it took a "humble pen to bring him glory." In this sense, Brown's violence simply ended up showing him the wisdom of Garrison's methods for his last month on earth. "Stripped of his liberty," Villard wrote, "the great power of the spirit within was revealed . . . to the hearts of all who sympathized with him, and of many who abhorred his methods." Brown's timelessness was due to "the innate nobility of the man," Villard argued, "his essential unselfishness and his readiness for the supreme sacrifice." So "misguided as he was, here was another martyr whose blood was to be the seed."[109]

Villard's solution did not strike the same balance he had achieved in the rest of the volume. "In Virginia," he argued, "John Brown atoned for Pottawatomie by the nobility of his philosophy and his sublime devotion to principle, even to the gallows."[110] By setting Brown's "nobility" in opposition to his violence, Villard echoed the conflicts over Brown that created the peaceful patriarch of Franklin Sanborn and Thomas Hovenden. Admitting that Brown was "and must remain a great and lasting figure in American history," the author maintained the Old Hero was wrong to imagine he could "undo one wrong by committing another." Here, Villard's Garrisonian judgment was brought to bear. Maintaining that Brown's actions were pure folly, Villard argued that it was only "by words . . . that he stirred his Northern countrymen."[111]

For Villard, Brown made amends for his sins by writing letters and stirring his fellow Americans. But the biographer wanted to have things both ways, particularly when it came to Brown's seemingly sanctifying the blood-letting of the next five years. Downplaying Brown's influence, Villard maintained that "the south was on the brink of a volcano the day before the blow at Harper's Ferry, as it was the day after." But "because slavery was intolerable morally and economically, it was bound to be overthrown because, in the long run, truth and righteousness prevail."[112]

Through Brown, Villard furthered a murky argument about historical causality and contingency. Was there a destiny for the nation—a fate for black Americans—that was simply inevitable because "in the long run, truth and righteousness prevail"? Or would that destiny have to be struggled for, sometimes by laying down life? Brown clearly believed the latter. But in Villard's answers to these questions, we understand his stance about violence, equality, and change; we see to the heart of his conflicts with Du Bois.

The biography quickly became a bestseller and reviewers celebrated Villard's work. The *Emporia (KS) Gazette* offered typical praise: "No life of John Brown, of the old days, has told the whole truth. This book should be read by every citizen who would understand the forces that led to the American Civil War; for everything is set down here. . . . Here is a hero . . . painted 'warts and all'—but still a hero who did his day's work in the world, gave himself freely for an ideal in the sublime faith that some way in the scheme of things the sacrifice would count in the balance for good."[113]

Perhaps the most interesting review, given Du Bois's drubbing by *The Nation*, was the review that appeared in Villard's publications. Focusing largely on the historical conundrum that Brown posed, William Mac-Donald pointed out that in contrast to Du Bois, Villard kept to the most "salient point for the historian and the moralist": "slavery was doomed before Brown began his attack upon it." Just as Villard had done in his conclusions, his mouthpiece publication underscored that Brown's principles, not his methods, were noble.[114]

"The success [*sic*] d'estime of that book," Villard wrote about the reception of his biography, "filled me with an amazement that has never passed."[115] The book's success even seemed to provide temporary salve for Villard and Du Bois's relationship. Indeed, in the heady atmosphere of his glowing reviews, Villard temporarily showed enough grace to support the debut of Du Bois's *The Crisis*. However, each passing day sparked new conflicts between the two men.[116] In particular, Du Bois's persistent antagonizing of his colleagues within the NAACP caused Villard to complain about Du Bois's "almost racial" disposition for controversy.[117] Villard's efforts on behalf of black Americans notwithstanding, since his initial involvement with reform movements he expressed alarm at how "colored people fight among themselves."[118]

Before too long, that alarm focused entirely on Du Bois. When Villard learned that his rival was at work on a new book, effectively splitting his time between *The Crisis* and personal projects, Villard went on a crusade. The two sparred over the issue, but Du Bois had worked a provision for independent projects into his first contract with the NAACP. While this infuriated Villard, he became even angrier when Du Bois refused to comply with his "suggestion" for a crime column in *The Crisis*. Entirely keeping with his curious racial attitudes, Villard wanted Du Bois's column, which documented crimes committed against blacks, to include crimes being committed *by* blacks as well.[119] In what became a standard routine, the board sided with Du Bois, even though it pointed out that he was antagonizing Villard.

By 1913, the situation had reached a breaking point. Villard, as chairman of the board, thought he should exercise total authority over all NAACP employees, including Du Bois. When that demand was refused, Villard insisted his name be taken off the masthead of *The Crisis*.[120] After Villard resigned as the chairman of the board, Du Bois reached out to him personally. "I am told that since the passage of words between us in the board meeting you do not think further co-operation between us in the work of the association is possible," Du Bois wrote. "It does not seem to me that this conclusion is at all necessary. So far as I am concerned the incident will make no difference in my continued endeavor to give my best service to a great cause and to act harmoniously with all my fellow workers." These inaccurate platitudes aside, Du Bois clarified his grievance and the fundamental issue. "I count myself not as your subordinate but as a fellow officer," he wrote. "Any suggestions made to me by you will always receive careful attention, but I decline to receive orders from anyone but the board."[121]

Du Bois's statements only further antagonized Villard, who doubled his efforts to oust Du Bois. Arguing that "the removal of Dr. Du Bois as editor" was a necessary step forward, Villard offered himself as a replacement.[122] It was an audacious attempt at a coup, particularly because Du Bois had made *The Crisis* an unfettered success and was still the only black member of the board.[123] But as the battle over their Brown biographies revealed, these men could barely see past their personal differences, much less their ideological ones. Villard's correspondence with Mary Ovington reveals the extent of his troubling approach. When Ovington asked Villard to reconsider one of his many resignations, she explained that his actions were "a confession to the world that we cannot work with colored people unless they are our subordinates. And everyone who believes in segregation will become a little more firmly convinced that he is right."[124] While Ovington admitted her own favorable feelings toward Du Bois, she asked Villard to appreciate the bigger picture: "When we demand that some colored man be put in office and given a place in which he will be the equal of a white man, we shall be told, 'You can't give a nigger a big job. Haven't you found it out yourselves.' It puts us back five years."[125]

But Villard's pattern of threats continued in spite of this symbolism. Ovington wrote Villard again in 1915, trying to reason with him. Her letter perfectly captured the tragic dimension of these power struggles. "I do admire [Du Bois's] genius and his business ability . . . and it doubtless prejudices me in his favor," Ovington admitted, "but if I disliked him I think I should want him on *The Crisis* just the same." Admitting that Du Bois had his obstinate side, Ovington wrote that she agreed "with his ideals for the Negro and with his methods of work. He does do dangerous things. He strikes at people with a harshness and directness that appalls me, but the blow is often deserved and it is never below the belt."[126]

Ovington's letter did nothing to change Villard's mind. In fact, he privately marveled at how many blacks hated Du Bois.[127] "I have felt for some time past that [the NAACP] must get on without him or without me," Villard maintained. "It would not hurt my feelings at all if the decision should be that Dr. Du Bois should remain [but] it has certainly gotten to a pass where I cannot have any further personal relations with him."[128] When asked to write a review of Du Bois's book *Darkwater* in 1920, Villard explained his intense dislike: "I think I pity Dr. Du Bois almost more than any man in America, but I do not want to work with him; nor do I believe in his editing of *The Crisis*."[129] Villard's "pity" is perplexing but understandable given his background. Du Bois, in his embrace of propagandistic history for racial progress, violated noblesse oblige and upended the pacifist abolitionist spirit of honorable and paternalistic reform. Villard could not help but feel sorry for someone so caught in the undertow of his skin color.

Circumstances would continue to throw Du Bois and Villard into contact with one another for another twenty years. Perhaps the defining moment in that conflict occurred on May 21, 1932. On a pleasant spring day, five busloads of NAACP delegates, including Villard and Du Bois, traveled from their national convention in Washington, DC, to Harpers Ferry. Du Bois carried a single piece of cargo: a veiled stone tablet. The delegates were welcomed by Henry T. McDonald, the white president of the black Baptist Storer College, founded in 1867 in the river-bound village.[130] McDonald showed the visitors to the "John Brown Fort," the engine house where Brown was finally captured.[131] Storer's trustees had purchased the landmark from an amusement park owner, moved it to their campus, and solicited the NAACP for an appropriate commemorative plaque, one they hoped would simply read "John Brown—His Soul Goes Marching On."[132] The NAACP had informed McDonald that W. E. B. Du Bois had written a more detailed inscription which read: "Here John Brown Aimed at Human Slavery A Blow That woke a guilty nation. With him fought Seven slaves and sons of slaves. Over his crucified corpse Marched 200,000 black soldiers And 4,000,000 freedmen Singing, 'John Brown's body lies a-mouldering in the grave But his Soul goes marching on.'"[133]

The NAACP brought Du Bois's tablet, but McDonald informed some members that he would not accept it because it would "perpetuate racial hostilities."[134] The day thus proved to be much more than a simple dedication. Instead, the event became another moment fraught with the difficulties of interracial cooperation and the pitfalls of divining an appropriate John Brown. At Storer College in 1932, in the shadow of Brown's infamous raid, these divisions were powerfully reinscribed.[135]

Given the racial politics surrounding the event, McDonald had asked Villard to give remarks following his own.[136] Villard toed his usual line: Brown was a crusading inspiration whose example was not to be taken literally.[137] "More than ever today," Villard told the audience, "it is necessary to discriminate between John Brown the man and the methods that that man chose to do his will." Along with mild declarations about Brown being "a tremendously potent figure throughout the North," Villard cautioned his audience that to embrace Brown's doctrine would "do violence to the best lessons of [his] life." Villard maintained that "the nobility, the majesty, the calmness and the fearlessness of [John Brown] . . . made it possible for his country to acknowledge the divine that was in him, while admitting his mistakes of judgment and policy and morals." Villard reminded the racially mixed audience of his central interpretation and belief: "force gets one nowhere" because "bloodshed never advances this unhappy sphere."[138]

Villard argued that Brown stood for "absolute equality, for the abolition of all special privilege, against all discriminations of race and color, for the original American doctrine . . . that all men are free and equal." These remarks captured the curious mixture of activism and restraint as well as sympathy and paternalism that defined Villard's involvement in the NAACP.

"What we would not give today for a John Brown to strike a Vulcan-like blow," Villard fantasized. "Not that I would for a moment in the remotest degree suggest approval of John Brown's methods."[139]

Dr. Jesse Max Barber, the black Philadelphian and president of the John Brown Memorial Association, was scheduled to follow Villard with a celebratory speech titled "Freedom's Rosary." Newspaper reports captured the tension of the event, explaining that McDonald and Villard had both "characterized the use of force by the martyr as a wrong way of obtaining reforms." In response, Barber threw out his prepared remarks. "I am not particular about how John Brown struck his blow at slavery," he told the audience, as Storer trustees and other whites stood up to leave. "When John Brown appeared at Harpers Ferry more than 3,000,000 Negroes were literally chained to the dung heaps of civilization," Barber continued. "Our women were forced to become the cloaks for the lechery of diseased white men in order that white womanhood might be protected." Barber explained that "it was in this abattoir of sin, into this lair of the damned that John Brown burst like an avenging knight of God. He came with a sword in his hand and prayer on his lips. He came prepared to help God strangle slavery." The contrasts between white and black conceptions of John Brown were never more obvious. In these competing visions of John Brown was the contentious fight to define appropriate means for racial equality.[140]

Du Bois's remarks brought that contentiousness to a fever pitch. Titled "The Use of Force in Reform," Du Bois's speech rejected Villard's premise and the politics of their hosts point by point. Highlighting the absurdity of McDonald's stance on Brown's violence, Du Bois angrily declared that these hypocrites would only accept "a colorless inscription" that would not offend "the sensibilities of the Daughters of the Confederacy." Du Bois, as he had done so many times in the previous thirty years, trumpeted Brown's intentions. Brown "took human lives," Du Bois admitted. "He took them in Kansas and he took them here. He meant to take them. He meant to use force to wipe out an evil he could no longer endure." Questioning the depth of McDonald's commitment to the cause of black equality, Du Bois sarcastically quipped that he "did not think there remained anyone who still defended slavery and the Lost Cause."[141]

Du Bois finished his speech by continually slamming the Storer administration. Over John Brown's "crucified corpse marched 200,000 black soldiers," Du Bois declared, but "Black soldiers of the Civil War no longer march in our text books. I doubt whether they march in the text books of Storer College." Working his deeply divided audience up even further, Du

Bois expressed his regret that "the president and trustees of Storer College did not have the courage to have the tablet left here."[142]

When Du Bois finished, the NAACP delegates angrily boarded their buses, tablet in tow, and headed back to New York City.[143] The tablet sat in a closet until sometime in the 1950s, when it disappeared. Du Bois's personal connection to Harpers Ferry and John Brown underscored the disappointment and irony of the tablet's ignominious end. For Du Bois, the event symbolized the frustrations of a lifetime of racial agitation and propagandizing.

As the buses motored away from Storer College in 1932, no one was overly surprised by the day's events. Du Bois never could have settled for an inscription that would satisfy white *and* black visitors, Northerners *and* Southerners. Du Bois's commitment to Brown's mission was cast in much more personal terms. While Villard shared many of the same hopes, his beliefs stood in the way of a truly cooperative path to achieving them. Unlike Villard, who dreamed of racial reform without "John Brown's methods," Du Bois found it impossible to separate the mission for racial equality from whatever could be done to realize that goal. "Thus to-day," Du Bois wrote at the conclusion of his Brown biography, "the Negro American faces his destiny and doggedly strives to realize it."[144] The project of striving for this destiny remained unfinished; and the conflicts over violence, equality, and change continued to churn.

John Brown's body lies a-mouldering in the grave
Spread over it is the bloodstained flag of his song,
For the sun to bleach, the wind and the birds to tear.
   —*Stephen Vincent Benét, 1928*

6

THE SOUL RESTS

Stephen Vincent Benét and the Silencing of John Brown's Body

Stephen Vincent Benét's epic poem, *John Brown's Body*, arrived in book-stores in 1928. In its structure, content, and message, the poem mediated long-standing divisions, not just those that had raged between W. E. B. Du Bois and Oswald Garrison Villard, but even the conflict that had consumed the Union and the Confederacy some seventy years before. While Benét's choice of protagonist might indicate another hagiography, *John Brown's Body* situated the infamous abolitionist in a broader narrative of reunion and patriotic destiny. So just as Du Bois and Villard urged readers of *The Crisis* to wrestle with John Brown's meaning, Benét snatched Brown from their hands and gave him a symbolic role in a triumphal story of American progress.

In a manner almost inconceivable to modern readers and likely impos-sible in the modern literary world, Benét's poem swallowed the marketplace whole in a matter of weeks.[1] In addition to being selected by the Book-of-the-Month Club and eventually winning the Pulitzer Prize, *John Brown's Body* became Alfred A. Knopf's bestselling book for over a decade, going through dozens of editions in its first few years in print. Benét wrapped the story of John Brown in a celebratory Civil War drama and sold an incredible 130,000 copies in 1928 and 1929 alone. Benét's poem offered an amalgam of Brown's life and the great themes of nineteenth-century America. The story and structure of *John Brown's Body* powerfully reveal Benét's vision of the grand historical narrative of the United States. The poem's reception exposed America's desire to justify the brutal sacrifices of the Civil War. By celebrating the rationales and heroism of both Union and Confederacy,

John Brown's Body argued that Brown was merely a cog in America's traumatic but triumphal adolescence. Benét's upbringing helps clarify how *John Brown's Body* satisfied the poet's desire to thematically unite the country's disparate regions. More troubling, the reception of his poem underscores the nation's deep need for a narrative that minimized its compromised relationships with violence, equality, and change.

Stephen Vincent Benét was born in Pennsylvania in 1898 to Colonel James Walker Benét, an Army ordnance officer, and his wife, Frances. The colonel's post required great mobility, and the Benét family was forced to move across the country many times. Stephen spent most of his childhood in Pennsylvania, New York, and California and his teenage years in Georgia. As Benét later recalled, growing up in such disparate parts of the country gave him a unique set of attitudes, tethered to no specific region or geographic prejudice. "I was a Northern boy in a Southern town, and then a Southern boy in a Northern town," Benét maintained; "that taught me a great deal."[2]

Both of Benét's grandfathers had fought in the Civil War, but on opposing sides. Despite the divide in Benét's Civil War heritage, his father "talked endlessly" of the skirmishes, personalities, and principles from that not-so-distant conflict. The family's time in Pennsylvania fueled Benét's engagement with the war through visits to the battlefields and monuments that dotted the Northern edge of Civil War country. By the time the Benéts moved to Augusta, Georgia, in 1911, young Stephen could feed his interests in the cradle of the former Confederacy. The picturesque plantations and local history inspired Benét, and he pursued his talent for writing largely through his passion for the Civil War. Being surrounded by the persistent contradictions of life in the South was as exhilarating as it was disorienting. For a fiercely patriotic American proud of the legacy of Union, Benét felt strange celebrating the birthday of Jefferson Davis, former president of the Confederacy. Indeed, these years in Georgia illuminated the living side of a conflict that had existed for Benét mostly in quaint memorials and greened-over battlefields.[3] In that sense, Augusta planted seeds of tension, loss, and regeneration that would gestate in Benét for some time to come.

For nearly a decade the young poet put that colorful past behind him. When Benét followed his older brother to Yale University in the fall of 1915, he moved on to new and different subject matter. Benét's first book of poetry, *Five Men and Pompey*, a collection of monologues by classical Roman figures, was published before his freshman year. *Five Men* showcased

Benét's most important influence, the epic poetry of the ancient Romans and Greeks. This ambitious effort revealed Benét's early hopes for his writing, and the young man quickly became a pillar of the university's elite literary society, the Elizabethan Club. Benét also found himself at the center of a dynamic set of intellectuals, including William DeVane, Thornton Wilder, and Henry Luce, all of whom would go on to play major roles in American letters. Midway through his college career, Benét had surpassed even his outstanding friends, publishing two more books of poetry. Benét had been stunned by the lyrical flights and stunning performances of the Midwestern poet Vachel Lindsay, whom Benét met twice in New Haven.[4] Benét's *Young Adventure* (1918) and *Heavens and Earth* (1920) revealed Lindsay's influence as well as Benét's fondness for the Victorian Renaissance man William Morris.[5] Benét's command of these disparate styles and his prodigious publications earned him legendary status among Ivy League literati. In the *Harvard Advocate*, the writer and editor Malcolm Cowley called Benét "the bright star not only of Yale but of all the Eastern colleges," and in *This Side of Paradise*, F. Scott Fitzgerald called attention to his generation's ubiquitous discussions of the "young poet, Stephen Vincent Benét."[6]

Unfortunately for Benét, following a postgraduate year at Yale, his many successes receded rather quickly into the past. After becoming a freelance writer in 1920, he had no luck finding a publisher for his first novel. Struggling financially, he managed to sell the book as a serial to *Harper's Bazaar* and began to write commercial fiction for *Redbook*, *Cosmopolitan*, and other magazines. Even though the work was steady, the burdens—generating page after page of mediocre and formulaic prose—soon became tiresome. While Benét periodically indulged his historical interests, winning *The Nation*'s poetry prize in 1922 for a poem on King David, he was tethered to the steady income of his hack writing. Even with the work, within five years, his family responsibilities and high standard of living made it nearly impossible to break even. Given his output since finishing college—three novels, six volumes of poetry, and over thirty short stories published—his financial straits were hard to believe. But when Benét put his wife and children on a train to Chicago for the holidays in 1925, the poet had five dollars to his name.[7]

Benét realized that if he did not change his circumstances, he would be doomed to the emotional and financial vicissitudes of magazine writing for the remainder of his career. As his friend and Yale classmate Douglas Moore recalled, Benét "had reached a point of exhaustion [with] short story writing," which he considered a glorified "form of drudgery."[8] In his application to the Guggenheim Foundation in 1925, Benét explained that he hoped, more than anything, "to do a long poem on some American subject."[9] As he later recalled, Benét had told the committee he was simply "sick of writing short-stories and . . . had several ideas—including the Civil War one—but couldn't say which one I'd take—and that seemed all right with them."[10]

After being awarded the first Guggenheim ever for poetry, Benét gathered his family and left for Paris in the fall of 1926. The city of light might seem a strange locale for writing an epic American poem, but, as Benét argued a bit humorously, not only was Paris cheaper, but living there "intensified my Americanism."[11] Still, mere patriotism would not suffice to carry the Civil War poem he had settled on. Easily the biggest undertaking of his professional life, Benét's new poem required new skills, and he was frequently humbled by the difficulties. His brother, William Rose Benét, a writer and editor in New York, periodically reassured Stephen that "ups and downs" were to be expected and that he would eventually write himself "out of the woods."[12]

Of course, the work was not all trial and tribulation; Benét did most of his research inside the extravagant American Library in Paris, a former palace on the rue de l'Elysée with an extensive collection. Not content to rely on his general knowledge of the period, Benét was inspired by Villard's biography of Brown and by Villard's professed desire for objective neutrality. In this spirit, Benét endeavored to learn more about the personalities and events of the Civil War. He used Nicolay and Hay's exhaustive *Abraham Lincoln* (1887) and extracted battlefield descriptions from Robert Goldthwaite's *Four Brothers in Blue*, the first-person account of the Army of the Potomac. Being judicious, Benét also studied Southerners' memoirs and intimate accounts like John B. Jones's *A Rebel War Clerk's Diary* so that he might understand the conflict equally from both sides.[13]

As Benét wrote in 1928, "It is worthy to assemble facts, to put truth in the face of legend, to investigate impartially [and] to throw new light on an old problem."[14] This desire for impartiality was the hallmark of Benét's approach. The John Brown sections of the poem provided its narrative engine, but the Civil War was a more difficult beast to tame. As Benét wrote to his brother, "Sometimes I think it is good and sometimes wonder who will read it but the typesetters—but I shall finish it or explode in loud fragments of *Battles and Leaders of the Civil War* all over my quaint little room."[15] Even with the occasional frustrations, writing *John Brown's Body* was the only period during Benét's career when he was able to write without worrying about money or the demands of popular magazines.[16]

At times, however, Benét keenly missed the ready formulas of commercial fiction. "My poem is staggering toward the end of its fourth part," he wrote to his brother in 1927. In the times when his progress slowed, Benét simply hoped he would "be able to finish the damn thing sooner or later." The process required "about a million books on the Civil War that aren't in the American Library," Benét complained, "but then I am having trouble enough with the ones I can use—people lie so, especially when they write their reminiscences."[17] Just a few weeks later, Benét had decided that despite the poem's focus on the Civil War writ large, John Brown was the symbol that provided the framework for the epic. "I think now I'll call my thing *John Brown's Body* definitely," he wrote confidently, a decision that helped reveal the "way ahead to the finish."[18] But Benét's confidence was often short-lived, and his occasional bouts with writer's block filled him with dismay. "I am at present extinguished under the tall foolscap of this long poem," he wrote to his friend, the poet and novelist Robert Nathan. "Nobody will read it, nobody will buy it, and the linotypers will just shrdlu [*sic*] all over it."[19]

Fortunately, Benét overcame his doubts and finished the manuscript in late 1927. After publishing the poem's invocation in his brother's *Saturday Review of Literature* in June, Benét's final months revising *John Brown's Body* partially convinced him of the poem's value. The responses to the excerpt were overwhelmingly positive, and his publisher and editor spoke grandly about the book's prospects. "I have just run through *John Brown's Body*," Benét's brother wrote in November. "I am amazed and exultant. There is no doubt in my own mind but that you have done a magnificent thing. . . . Such enormous vitality in it, such intensity, such beauty and wisdom in abundance that the thing is going to stand. . . . You have achieved something. . . . It is an event in American letters."[20]

By the summer of 1928, William Benét's bold declarations were proven out. In a few short months, the book sold fifty-two thousand copies, and as Benét wrote to his wife, "The press has really been remarkable—space everywhere and some of the praise so overdone it makes me feel ashamed."[21] *John Brown's Body*, without exaggeration, made Benét the preeminent poet in the country.[22] When the Book-of-the-Month-Club selected *John Brown's Body*'s just weeks later, the poem's prodigious sales and continued financial success seemed unshakable. In May 1929, Benét was informed that his poem had won "the prize of one thousand dollars established by the Will of the late Joseph Pulitzer for the best volume of American verse."[23] With the

Pulitzer and royalties flowing steadily, Benét's gambit with *John Brown's Body* had clearly paid off.

The poem itself is quite an unusual piece of literature.[24] Following the lead of the exultant Northerners and outraged Southerners of John Brown's own generation, Benét chose to connect the martyr of Harpers Ferry quite explicitly to the events of the Civil War. Just titling the epic poem after the infamous song and its namesake gave credence to Herman Melville's claim that Brown was "the meteor of the war."[25] As the introduction to the 1941 edition put it, Benét chose "for his theme the effect of four years of civil strife, and for his symbol, John Brown, the fierce, liberty-loving abolitionist with the Old Testament eyes." Benét's own introduction further elucidated the ideas he hoped to explore. "*John Brown's Body*," Benét wrote, "is a long poem dealing with some of the things that happened in our Civil War and how they affected various kinds of Americans." He concluded, in his even-handed way, that more important than assigning blame, the war produced "on both sides, men and deeds of the heroic kind."[26]

Benét attempted to distinguish himself from his contemporaries by declaring the Civil War a positive and necessary experience for the nation, even if the poem itself often contradicted that argument. The Civil War, Benét argued, "decided how we were going to live as a nation—whether we were going to live as two nations or as one—and all the America we know today is built upon that decision."[27] In this conception, the Civil War was not incidental but crucial for the ultimate growth of the United States. But Benét's desire to give evenhanded treatment required some incredible interpretive contortions. The poet completely ignored the systemic violence and moral contradictions of Southern slavery just as he valorized the Confederacy's willingness to defend the system under arms. Benét was forced to celebrate the North's willingness to brutally preserve the Union just as he downplayed the contradictions so crucial to that mission. By presenting the conflict as a necessity in America's maturation as a nation, *John Brown's Body* glossed over the devastating effects the war would have on racial equality, the relationship between regions, and the national consciousness.

Benét's focus on extracting the truth about the war and its protagonists "from the legend" also presented difficulties.[28] Just as the poet decried the unfortunate myths about the war, he muted the force of these statements by focusing on the "look of mountains and the flow of rivers" and the natural synchronicity of the grand partnership of Americans. Rather than dwell on seventy years of misinterpretation and legend, Benét valorized the "millions upon millions of ordinary men and women who lived through war and peace, strove, struggled, succeeded, failed, built something together."[29] As a result, *John Brown's Body* validated the experience of both North and South by historicizing the war's terrible violence, ignoring the war's immediate and long-standing effects on black Americans, and trivializing the nation's compact with difficult change. In this sense, Benét reinforced the dominant legend of the war by emphasizing America's historical destiny over these complicating factors.

Contrary to this interpretive quagmire, Benét began his epic poem in a captivating way, one that seemed to belie the underlying message of a universally principled and heroic Civil War. Rather than encountering the poem's namesake at Harpers Ferry or in the battles of Bleeding Kansas, Benét followed the lead of W. E. B. Du Bois's *John Brown* and located the origins of his American epic on a slave ship bearing its human cargo to New England's shores. In this choice, Benét emphasized the contradiction that Brown obsessed over and that the Civil War would clumsily provide a piecemeal resolution of: American slavery. Inscribing the war and Brown's life in a story of America's compromising embrace of slavery was an admirable gambit. Benét hoped to show that both North and South had dirtied their hands with slavery, making both sides equally responsible for the war.

Accordingly, the poem's cast of characters included the most important stock figure of slavery apologia: the conflicted slave master. In this case, the role is played by the captain of the slave ship; "a strange mixture of ruthlessness and Puritan religion," that is, a character used to cast doubts on the brutality and totality of slavery through his own doubts in the system, doubts that Benét depicted as representative. Benét's choice universalized the guilt and conflict over slavery to America as a whole. The antagonist of the poem's opening section is the delicately named "Tarbarrel," the biggest and blackest slave shackled in the hold, who, Benét sarcastically noted, "claimed he was once a king." The other black characters in Benét's American epic include another caricature, "Fat Aunt Bess," whom the poet described as the "devoted slave," and finally, the equally delicate "Spade," the runaway slave.[30] Without belaboring the point, these characters do not represent the countless three-dimensional black men and women that populate the American past. Benét showed that when seeking to validate the mutual guilt and glory of the Civil War, black Americans could not share the historical stage without complicating the distorted picture of past, present, and future.

Structurally, Benét's poem recalls the work of Homer and Virgil, but in its language and organization, *John Brown's Body* drew equally on Benét's college hero Vachel Lindsay; Benét's nineteenth-century historical model, William Morris; as well as a distinctly American vernacular. The poem is organized into ten sections: an invocation, a prelude, and eight books. Two fictional characters, a Northerner, Jack Ellyat, and a Southerner, Clay Wingate, guide the reader through daily life in the Union and the Confederacy, alongside real historical personalities like Abraham Lincoln, Ulysses S. Grant, Robert E. Lee, and Stonewall Jackson.

Benét's introductory sections for each book of verse are particularly important for understanding the purpose of *John Brown's Body*. In the first of these sections, Benét located his readers in October 1859 with his representative Yankee, the fictional Jack Ellyat, a farmer who, above all, is "glad to be Connecticut-born." At work in his fields, Ellyat's "mind shivers with the wind of premonition [as] he finds himself thinking of the rumors he hears of dissension on the slavery question between the North and the South; of catch-word phrases; of conventional pictures of the South in the books he has read; of remarks made by bitter abolitionists in Massachusetts." Benét immediately shifts the reader's attention to Clay Wingate of Georgia, a descendant of Stuart kings, and owner of "one of the great plantations of the South." On the "same autumn day" Wingate was "riding home after a day's hunting [and] feels the chill wind of premonition."[31] After introducing these fictional characters, proxies of the sentiments and foibles of North and South, Benét deftly shifted the narrative.

"Meanwhile at Harper's Ferry," Benét intoned ominously, "John Brown, the famous abolitionist of Kansas, with twenty-two followers, takes possession of the Maryland bridge. Colonel Robert E. Lee and Lieut. J. E. B. Stuart, later General Stuart, one of the most dashing figures of the Civil War, are ordered to join the marines and surround the arsenal held by Brown and his followers." In just two sentences, Benét tied two of the key personalities of the Civil War to John Brown. Moreover, with the arrival of Lee and Stuart, Brown's fate, and that of the nation, already hung in the balance. "John Brown is vanquished," Benét wrote, "he is brought to trial; sentenced to be hanged; is hanged. And with that hanging is kindled a great conflagration between the North and the South." But Benét did more than simply highlight Brown's causal role in that "great conflagration." Invoking the memory of Brown, Benét wrote that the martyred abolitionist's "body cannot rest. His story renews the old legend of the bones of one who, feeling himself unjustly killed, tells the tale until he is avenged. John Brown's body may be moldering in the grave, but the cause of freedom for which he sacrificed his life becomes a common cause."[32]

Benét described Brown's cause as freedom, rather than the elimination of slavery. This framework was both a narrative strategy and an interpretation. While the poem's message generally obscures Brown's self-professed purpose in life, the liberation of black Americans, Benét paid close attention to Brown's psyche. The verse includes many wonderful descriptions of the infamous martyr. "For fifty-nine unsparing years," Benét wrote of Brown's prayers to God, "Thy Grace hath worked apart / To mould a man of iron tears / With a bullet for a heart." Benét's verse has a declarative strength that biographers, memorialists, and even painters had trouble matching.

Brown's religiosity and his time in Kansas, for instance, were especially well-served by Benét's method. "I heard Thee when Thou bade me spurn / Destruction from my hand," Benét wrote of Brown's thoughts in May 1856. "And, though all Kansas bleed and burn / It was at thy command." For many of Brown's admirers and detractors, the abolitionist's religious justifications were the most difficult to comprehend, but Benét captured Brown as a devout believer. Benét's delicately crafted verse revealed Brown's inability to forget the meaning of Bleeding Kansas. "All night long," Benét described Brown's thoughts, "I staunch a wound that ever bleeds afresh." It is a superlative description of the martyr's mindset during his final decade.

To his credit, the poet also documented the darker side of Brown's life, and his verse illuminated the abolitionist's troubling extremism. "If we live, we free the slave," Benét wrote in Brown's voice. "And if we die, we die."[33] Benét beautifully distilled the plaguing questions of Brown's meaning when he wrote, "You can weigh John Brown's body well enough / But how and in what balance weigh John Brown?" Unlike Du Bois, Sanborn, and countless others, Benét self-consciously resisted choosing a side with Brown. But of course, in his objective abstaining, the poet passed a series of judgments about Brown's continued relevance as a racial and violent revolutionary, the meaning of the Civil War, and the trajectory of the history of the United States. Benét muted Brown by reducing him to the stray spark of an inevitable explosion. "He had the shepherd's gift, but that was all," Benét argued. "He had no other single gift for life." For those who felt distaste for the violence of Brown's pursuit of liberty, Benét lamented, "Slaves will be slaves next year, in spite of the bones / Nothing is changed, John Brown, nothing is changed."[34]

After exploring the war through a combination of exploits by his fictional characters and the high political machinations of Lincoln and Davis, Benét returned to Brown, as he would throughout the poem. Betraying a slight bias toward the Union, Benét wrote that on the eve of war, "The great stone gate of the Union crumbles and totters / The cotton blossoms are pushing the blocks apart."[35] Here, the threat that secession posed to the project of the American republic was very real and potentially devastating. In this formulation, Benét fashioned Brown less as a provocateur or meteor and more as a symptom of a sickness that both North and South had contracted. Accordingly, the Civil War was a traumatic remedy, but a remedy nonetheless.

As Benét described finishing the manuscript, the balance between the North and the South was necessary for the poem to surpass mere polemic. Both the Union and the Confederacy "must be in the poem," Benét wrote. "Of course the lost cause is always the romantic one, and I suppose something of that gets into the verse." However, when Benét invoked the language of 1860, he declared himself "a Union man or a Lincoln man." It was the poet's admiration for Lincoln that led to his distaste for "Phillips and Greeley and the rest of the rather loud-mouthed people who did their best to hinder him whenever they got a chance—oh, all with the finest and purest motives, but with so little sense or vision!"[36]

This transparent anti-abolitionism fed into Benét's overarching interpretation. Benét's private correspondence showed the poet's true feelings about the sectional conflict, which clearly colored the content and themes of *John Brown's Body*. In the poem's final pages, Benét interspersed meditations on Brown with italicized lyrics from the famous Union marching song. Invoking black spirituals, Benét wrote dramatically, "Go down, John Brown, and set that people free!" But he pointed out the futility of Brown's raid on Harpers Ferry when he said that "the fight will be over, the slaves will be slaves forever." Even more significant was Benét's cutting critique of the Northern conception of slavery embodied by Brown. "You fought for a people you did not comprehend / For a symbol chained by a symbol in your own mind."[37] In this case, by emphasizing the ignorance, error, and mistakes made by the North in the antebellum years, Benét celebrated the crucial purpose of coming together as a nation.

The poem's final stanzas forcefully make this case by rendering Brown nearly inanimate. Brown "was a stone / this man who lies so still / A stone flung from a sling against a wall / A sacrificial instrument of kill." Benét made the abolitionist necessary for American adulthood, but not heroic in the least. Instead, the poem ends in a strange swirl of imagery designed to show the dangers of the nation's contested history. To move on, to make the country "whole again," each American must keep "your distance and your soul from" those worshiping or despairing over the past.[38]

While these closing verses were somewhat contradictory, millions of Americans were captivated by the poem's overall message of reunion. Readers made sense of these seeming contradictions, particularly parsing culpability for the Civil War, by imagining a shared sense of sin and a united future. As David Blight has persuasively argued, by 1920, national memories of the Civil War had coalesced "in a core master narrative that led inexorably to reunion of the sections," a process that excused both sides from guilt or responsibility.[39] In this sense, it is possible to see just how intensely Benét tapped into the national consciousness with *John Brown's Body*, particularly with his efforts to validate and valorize both sides of the Civil War.

In the scheme of the poem, slavery was a problem that belonged as much to the North as to the South, and John Brown was both a product and a symbol of that problem. Jack Ellyat and Clay Wingate must be taken as equals to understand America's national story. The implications of this reunion were significant. Bringing partisans on both sides of the conflict together to honor the heroism and bravery of the men as well as the ideals of the Union and the Confederacy; this was reunion. Benét's message generated enormous sympathy across the geographic and political spectrum, perfectly capturing the pervading spirit of Civil War memory that dominated the interwar period. The process that lay beneath these sentiments, the reunion and reconciliation of the valorous North and the equally heroic South, dramatically divided white and black Americans.[40] The very act of enshrining North and South marginalized the role of black Americans and trivialized the nature and impact of American slavery.

The ingenious structure of *John Brown's Body* gracefully developed this troubling interpretation. Benét's epic is not overwhelmed by Brown because it appears to hold no brief for North or South. Instead, Benét managed to embed his reunionist message in a story of heroism and freedom that valorized the nation. Not surprisingly, this vibrant patriotism proved incredibly popular. The poem sold millions of copies and Benét received thousands of fan letters for *John Brown's Body*. Two letters in particular, one from a Northerner and the other from a Southerner, wonderfully capture the poem's persuasive and comprehensive message of reunion.

William Minor Lile, the dean of the University of Virginia Law School, wrote Benét in 1929, declaring his Southern bona fides up front. He had grown up on "a cotton plantation in Alabama[,] . . . six years old at the end of the Civil War[,] . . . in close association with my father's slaves and former slaves and their descendants."[41] Beyond thinking of Yankees as "blue devils," Lile assured Benét that he was passionately "loyal to my birth and breeding." Even Benét's title had stirred up "the childish prejudices of sixty years before, though I had thought these as dead as the carcass of Brown himself." But Benét's poem won over even this staunch Southerner. "You have handled the delicate situation between the Northern and Southern viewpoint with remarkable balance, and skill," Lile wrote, "and have accomplished what I had thought impossible. You have produced an epic of the Civil War which should appeal to the Northern worshippers of Brown and Sherman (with his practically unopposed march to the sea, burning the homes of the helpless as he marched) as well as to Southerners, with General Lee, their Sir Galahad, whom they have enshrined forever in their memories."[42]

A letter from Meredith Nicholson of Indiana just a week earlier had struck a similar chord, albeit from the opposite sectional persuasion. Nicholson's father had fought for the Union forces, and she wrote to Benét thanking him "for the pleasure and deep satisfaction I have found in *John Brown's Body*." Nicholson told Benét of her intense connection to the war; in addition to counting her "father's sword . . . among my playthings; I have read well nigh everything written about that conflict. . . . Your characterizations of the leaders are splendid—of Lee particularly penetrating. I wept over it." Ms. Nicholson explained why her emotional reaction to Lee was so astonishing: "My father was with Sherman on the March to the Sea!"[43]

Clearly, Benét had produced a narrative of John Brown and the Civil War that pleased a broad spectrum of readers. Lile's letter underscored the most troubling aspect of Benét's poem and its captivating hold on American readers: "No sensible Southerner could wish a more faithful chronicler of Lee and Jackson and their heroic followers. . . . You have portrayed the faithful negro slaves, as I knew them—with here and there the faithless one . . . their loyalty and childlike devotion to the white women and children, left defenseless on the great plantations by the absence of their natural defenders."[44]

John Brown's Body's subtle narrative broadcast these messages to millions of readers. Because Benét worked so diligently to balance North and South in his poem, because his imagery was so compelling, but mostly because his reunionist and patriotic messages allowed readers to feel that no one was to blame for America's national trauma, the poem catapulted Benét to the forefront of American letters.

Like his college admirer F. Scott Fitzgerald, Benét's success led to Hollywood, where Benét became involved with the first great filmmaker of the twentieth century, D. W. Griffith. A decade earlier, *The Birth of a Nation*, Griffith's adaptation of Thomas Dixon's brief for the Ku Klux Klan, *The Clansman*, had embedded a white supremacist vision of the past, present, and future in America's consciousness.[45] "Ku Klux Fever" gripped the South, where the film was treated as a "sacred epic," but the rest of the United States also showed "overwhelming enthusiasm" for Griffith's film. Leaving a screening, one New Englander remarked that the film made him "want to go out and kill the first Negro I see."[46] The power of Griffith's art form demanded writers who knew how to control the loose ends of a historical narrative. Griffith recognized in Benét a man who never let the contradictions of history overwhelm a satisfying message.

Benét's screenplay for Griffith's decidedly neo-Confederate *Abraham Lincoln* (1930) depicted Lincoln as a hard-liner whose decisions seem nearly preordained throughout the film. Benét chose dramatic narrative over historical verity, but one historically probable incident is particularly revealing. Benét's script juxtaposes an apocryphal scene of Lincoln being offered the Republican nomination (an offer made in the film because of Lincoln's opposition to secession) with an imagined scene of Virginians reacting to news of Brown's raid. In the latter, a group of well-to-do whites, including John Wilkes Booth, surround a slave, played by a white actor in blackface, whom we learn Brown attempted to recruit.

From a wide shot of the crowd, a voice declares: "They started it—this is gonna mean war." As the camera cuts to a tighter view, a distinguished looking man explains.

"This darky saw it himself. John Brown and a gang of abolitionists have captured the armory at Harpers Ferry, arming the slaves to rise up and murder us all."

"Yup, they gived us all rifles," the slave explains.

"And what'd you do with yours?"

"What'd I do? I throwed it down and I said feet, you run."

With that, Benét had given new emphasis and meaning to the loyal slaves, not just of his epic poem, but also of Griffith's *Birth of a Nation*. The distinguished looking gentleman further clarifies the historical import of the scene. "Boys, go home and get your guns," he tells the crowd, "or we'll be murdered in our beds by our own slaves." In Benét's script, both Brown and Lincoln are merely tools in the same narrative: America's traumatic but necessary Civil War for genuine unification.[47]

Perhaps unsurprisingly given these boilerplate scenes, Benét also crossed paths with the other great cinematic source for America's popular imagining of the South, Margaret Mitchell. As she toiled on *Gone With the Wind* in the late 1920s, a friend brought her Benét's newly published *John Brown's Body*. When Mitchell read Benét's treatment of Clay Wingate and her native Georgia, her shaky self-confidence was nearly shattered. Refusing to read any more but unable not to, Mitchell later told Benét that he "had caught so clearly, so vividly and so simply everything in the world that I was sweating to catch, done it in a way I could never hope to do it and with a heartbreaking beauty. . . . Just listening to it made me realize my own inadequacies so much that I knew if I heard more I wouldn't be able to write." As she explained, Benét had struck a delicate balance; "It's hard to make people understand that North Georgia wasn't all white columns and singing darkies and magnolias."[48]

Mitchell took another eight years to publish her novel, that tableau of an antebellum Georgia of white columns, singing darkies, and magnolias. She wrote Benét after the book's publication to inform him that *John Brown's Body* "is my favorite poem, my favorite book. I know more of it by heart than I do any other poetry. It means more to me, is realer than anything I've ever read by any poet, bar none, and I've read an awful lot of poetry."[49] Benét's influence on Mitchell's work was significant and their mutual enthusiasm spoke to their dovetailing purposes. Of course, like Benét, Mitchell could not have known that her vision of the antebellum and Reconstruction South would shape a century of romanticized narratives centered on gorgeous plantations and charming slaves. While Benét's story was a subtler, national one, his fondness for a past in service of the present opened the door for Mitchell and other writers, artists, and historians who followed.

The closing stanzas of *John Brown's Body* speak to these troubling fruits. The poet wonders if it is useful to "Bury the South together with this man / Bury the bygone South," along with "The sick magnolias of the false romance / And all the chivalry that went to seed." Benét reveals that it is not necessary to bury the South or forget John Brown's murderous justice, because the future of a united nation beckons. Out of this trauma inevitably comes triumph; "Out of John Brown's strong sinews the tall skyscrapers grow," Benét declared, "Out of his heart the chanting buildings rise."[50] The epic poet of America declared his country one. With Brown dead, the North and South could finally become the United States. In that transition from adolescence to adulthood, Benét's poem makes the present and the future unanswerable for the tragedies of the past.

Bayonets and bullets and God's will . . . with a "little touch of insanity." . . . Captain Brown was a "higher law man." He was "superior to any legal tradition"—just as most of these people felt themselves to be—and if he claimed to have a divine commission, they could understand what he meant, for they too were privy to God.

—*Robert Penn Warren, 1929*

7

THE FUGITIVE IMAGINATION

A John Brown for the Old South

In July 1925, Tennessee was thrust into national headlines. John Scopes, a Rhea County biology teacher, was charged with illegally explaining evolution in his high school science class. A bonanza for journalists, the trial exposed America's sectional fault lines and reinforced long-standing national stereotypes of the South. H. L. Mencken, a writer for the *Baltimore Sun* and the country's best-known columnist, aggressively chronicled what he considered the perfect encapsulation of an American backwater. Mencken's columns on the trial were filled with references to the "yokels," "primates," "morons," "half-wits," and "hillbillies" who populated the South.[1]

In the hands of writers like Mencken, the trial crystallized the national perception of the South as intellectually, religiously, and culturally backward.[2] For Southerners, the trial became, in the words of Fred Hobson, "a prototypic event, the single event that . . . brought to the surface all of the forces and tensions that had characterized the post-war South, the event that most forcefully dramatized the struggle between southern provincialism and the modern, secular world."[3]

In nearby Nashville, an influential group of writers and intellectuals at Vanderbilt University were radicalized by that prototypic event. In no uncertain terms, the Scopes trial galvanized a new Southern intellectual movement and revealed the battlefield where the cultural honor of this maligned region could be reclaimed. Beyond making "Southern intellectual" an oxymoron, the Scopes trial showed that this battle would be fought not with bayonets but with words. The dynamic group of poets, writers, and academics who answered that call to arms included Robert Penn Warren,

Allen Tate, Donald Davidson, John Crowe Ransom, and Andrew Lytle—a collective known in the 1920s as the Fugitives. In their post-Scopes fervor, these men pursued a broad range of intellectual, cultural, and social projects to contrast the halcyon days of the antebellum years with the encroaching problems of the industrial North. Spearheaded by some of the leading writers of the period, the Fugitives revived the personalities and conflicts of the antebellum and Civil War eras in fiction, poetry, and biography. Often using the conflict-ridden language of the Civil War itself, the Fugitives set out to rewrite the past to create the future. The Scopes trial demonstrated to them the urgency of seizing the memory and future of the South, since failure to do so would be tantamount to conceding another defeat.

The most intriguing response to the Scopes debacle came from a young Kentuckian named Robert Penn Warren. The only writer to win Pulitzer Prizes in both fiction and poetry, Warren began his career with a biography straight from the belly of the Fugitive beast: *John Brown: The Making of a Martyr*. Warren's study embodied the collective Fugitive campaign, a movement that culminated with the controversial volume of essays *I'll Take My Stand*. While the Fugitives are mostly remembered for the literary impact of their individual members, this generation of Southern intellectuals and their propagandistic biographies, utopian schemes, and agrarian manifestoes successfully shifted national understandings of the New South as well as the Old. The insinuatory impact of their advocacy reveals the deep roots of America's fractured national identity and the national traumas that continue to haunt us.

In an unpublished essay from 1963, Warren wrote that although he had lived all over the world, "I have always felt myself identified with [the South]." He described his intense relationship with the region: "By blood, education, and formative experience, I was Southern. My two Grandfathers were at Shiloh, for what I consider good and sufficient reason, and I am proud of the fact. All the books I have written are about the South, for life there engaged my imagination more deeply than any other topic."[4] Warren's conjured South, revealed through his publications and private correspondence, allows us to trace the Fugitives' manipulation of John Brown and the imagined past they sought to revive. Using the authority of history, the group's collective projects rehabilitated national opinion of not just a region but its past and future.

In his essay on the South's place in his imagination, Warren wrote that Nashville was "the city I know—or knew—best in the world, the city which more than any other, with all the thinning of old ties and the work of time, was still 'home.'"[5] Nashville was also the place that launched the Fugitives into intellectual combat. As the twentieth century began Nashville was a city of aspirations. The self-pronounced "Athens of the South" had constructed a replica of the Parthenon in its main public park alongside the Kentucky cabin that Jefferson Davis grew up in. It remains a vivid illustration of the South's living conflict between its Confederate past and its hopes for a cultured future. But aside from a collection of emerging universities, Nashville had very little to distinguish itself from other Southern cities.[6] In fact, many of Nashville's educational institutions, Vanderbilt chief among them, were having trouble shedding intellectually crippling religious influences. Indeed, it was not until 1914 that the "progress"-minded chancellor of Vanderbilt, James Kirkland, finally managed to wrest control from the school's board of Methodist Episcopal bishops. John Crowe Ransom, a Vanderbilt-trained Tennessean and the recipient of one of the first Rhodes scholarships, returned to Nashville to help bolster his alma matter's changing reputation. On joining Vanderbilt's English department, Ransom's first Shakespeare seminar included a student named Donald Davidson, whom Ransom helped shape into the rabble-rouser of the Fugitive-Agrarian movement.

Davidson, a fellow Tennessean, was raised among Confederate veterans who traded horrific stories of the Northern occupation during the war, tales full of boilerplate fare depicting marauding Yankee troops shooting loved ones "in cold blood on the main street[s]" of every hometown in the South.[7] Davidson's grandmother grew up next door to Nathan Bedford Forrest, founder of the Ku Klux Klan, and spun heroic tales starring him.[8] The Rebel spirit ran strong in Davidson. Ransom and his pupil became fast friends and started regular discussions about literature and the South. In 1916, these conversations took on a new form. Ransom was walking with Davidson in a quiet corner of the Vanderbilt campus when he pulled out a sheet of paper. He told Davidson he had written a poem. In that moment, the Fugitives were born.

By the end of World War I, Davidson and Ransom were both teaching at Vanderbilt, writing poetry, and cultivating a group of dedicated writers. This group, introduced formally to the world in 1921 through their poetry magazine, *The Fugitive*, held biweekly meetings to discuss literature, philosophy, and their poetry. At these early Fugitive meetings, conversation often drifted to the dismal state of Southern letters. With Southern roots in common and a desire to foster Southern writing, these complaints led directly to *The Fugitive*. As part of that same mission, Davidson soon recruited a precocious Vanderbilt undergraduate named Allen Tate into the group.

Tate was born in Kentucky, raised on spurious stories of his Virginia roots as a descendent of Southern aristocracy. Ransom, the informal leader of the group, recognized Tate's prodigious talent from the start, seeing his youth and mysterious Southern background as the key strengths of his writerly temperament. In the spring of 1923, Tate was typing a poem for the group when a gangly and awkward boy approached him from behind, asking quietly if he might like to trade poems. A friendship was immediately struck and Robert Penn Warren, a sixteen-year-old from Guthrie, Kentucky, who called himself "Red," moved in with Tate just a week later.

Tate nurtured Warren's writing and boosted the nervous freshman's confidence in his work. After arriving home one evening to see that Warren had illustrated the walls of their room with scenes from T. S. Eliot's "The Wasteland," Tate observed that Warren "was perhaps the most gifted and . . . fiercely dedicated writer" he knew.[9] Tate had a ready ally in Donald Davidson, who had Warren in his freshman English class. Davidson, who admitted to being slightly intimidated by Warren's precociousness, described him as "a freckled, angular, gawky boy, yet a prodigy whom at birth the Muse had apparently vested with complete literary equipment."[10] For Davidson, Warren was "the brightest student they had ever seen around here."[11]

The addition of Warren certainly bolstered the Fugitives writerly talent, but the Scopes trial strengthened their bond and ultimately gave shape to the projects they would collectively pursue. Ransom and Davidson were particularly inflamed by the trial. The two men hoped to transform Vanderbilt into a "veritable citadel" of Southern values, a stronghold "in defense of their sectional heritage."[12] When the group's members began to conceive of themselves as defending the intellectual life, memory, and future of the South, they began referring to each other as "the brethren."[13] The group's bonding in the crucible of the Scopes trial helped them develop an almost spiritual belief in their imagined antebellum South.[14]

In 1927, Tate wrote his fellow Fugitives with plans for a Southern symposium to confront the issues raised by the trial and the infuriating Northern press treatment.[15] Davidson responded by relating his transformative visit to a Confederate graveyard. Here was the Fugitives' initial imagining of the world they sought to rescue. Walking through the gravestones, David-son was convinced that the Old South would rise again. The inscriptions of "bold, generous and free" soldiers, "firm in conviction of the right, ready at their country's call, [and] steadfast in their duty" spoke to the values that could revive the South.[16] As Davidson proudly wrote to his fellow Fugitives, "the principles for which they fought can never die."[17]

Tate took these principles to the next level, giving the romanticized Con-federacy the authority of history. Planning a biography of Virginia war hero Stonewall Jackson, Tate wrote to Davidson that the Fugitives' shared "doc-trine" was the backbone of the study.[18] The South "should now be a separate nation," Tate maintained.[19] "I'm doing a stirring partizan [*sic*] account," he wrote. "The stars and bars forever!"[20] "I don't want it to be obvious," Tate revealed, but the book will enshrine "the bright hopes of the Confederacy."[21] In the place of slavery, Tate would celebrate a set of imagined Confederate values, using historical narrative to sell this vision of the South to readers.

Tate's invocation of "the bright hopes of the Confederacy" reveals the Fugitives' deep engagement with the mythology of the Lost Cause. The popularity of these beliefs had facilitated Southern groups' effective orga-nization after the Civil War. Confederate veterans and the United Daugh-ters of the Confederacy drew on the mysticism of the Lost Cause to present the Southern soldier as the eternally valiant defender, depicting the Con-federacy as a steady alternative to undesirable societal changes, from the troubling industrial transformations wrought by the North to the pervasive racial problems created by emancipation. Through civic committees and monument construction, Southern groups managed to assume control of the meaning of the war. As the historian David Blight explains, "A nostal-gic Lost Cause reinvigorated white supremacy, [with] arguments [that] re-inforced Southern pride, nationalized the Lost Cause, and racialized Civil War memory for the postwar generations."[22]

The most ingenious aspect of the Lost Cause was not organizational; rather, through the siege mentality it encouraged, this ideology convinced Southerners that they were constantly under some form of attack from the North. Clearly for the Fugitives, the Scopes trial functioned in exactly this way. Tate, Ransom, Davidson, and Warren identified the Lost Cause with terrorist organizations like the Klan, hereditary organizations like the United Daughters of the Confederacy, or veterans groups like the United Confederate Veterans.[23] The Fugitives saw themselves at the vanguard of something new, progressive, and different.[24] Ironically, the group drew its approach most directly from the same set of beliefs as the Lost Cause. But, instead of building monuments and terrorizing blacks, the Fugitives saw literature and history, particularly the nexus of these two disciplines, as the key to creating a New South.

Again adopting Lost Cause arguments, the Fugitives tried to shift blame northward for the unnecessary war. Slavery was gradually going to end itself, the group maintained; there was no reason for the North's cavalier intervention.[25] The 1928 publication of Tate's *Stonewall Jackson* brought these arguments into print. Using a Confederate war hero as his historical agent, Tate made Unionists the true traitors, hell-bent on destroying the Constitution.[26] In this framework, Jackson's life became an allegory for the tragic decline of the region. Tate's message was clear; people must revive the Old South "if only through memory."[27] Tate fully grasped the contemporary implications of this argument; depicting Jackson and the Confederacy as heroic victims should ignite a national reappraisal of the true moral and cultural heart of America.

Of course, in pursuit of that agenda, Tate had to paint the rosy pictures of the antebellum South that the Fugitives had decried in the Lost Cause. In particular, it was left to Tate to figure out how to rationalize slavery. In service of the broader Southern mythology, Tate explained that enslaving blacks was truly a "positive good" because "it had become a necessary element in a stable society."[28] Slavery was merely "benevolent protection: the elite man was in every sense responsible for the Black," Tate wrote. "The Black man, 'free,' would have been exploited."[29]

Tate's biography created the pattern that Warren and the other Fugitives would follow. *Stonewall Jackson* articulated the Fugitive belief that the Old South was the archetypal America, or at the very least, the model for the South's future. By shaping that world into their utopia, the Fugitives could properly critique the North as an industrial region bereft of morality, principles, and soul.[30]

To embody this critique of Northern reprobation, Tate used John Brown, an antihero Warren would soon perfect in his biography. Tate erroneously described Brown in Kansas splitting the skulls of slave owners and cutting "off [their] fingers," scenes he would pepper with the quotable Brown canon, as if to prove deed by word. Brown's argument that "without the shedding of blood, there is no remission of sins" delighted Tate. All "men in New England," Tate argued, shared Brown's belief in the treasonous rationale of higher law. This belief, that an understanding of God's law trumped the laws of man, had led William Lloyd Garrison to decry the Constitution as a pact with the devil and eventually sent Brown under arms into Virginia. Tate mockingly inquired how "an illiterate fanatic like John Brown was as privy to God as the Reverend Lyman Beecher."[31] Tate finished his tirade against the actually quite literate abolitionist with a flourish characteristic of the Fugitive mindset. "In New England," he wrote, "educated and ignorant alike believed in the same things . . . [and] saw nothing irregular in the antics of a homicidal maniac."[32]

Tate's biography got mixed reviews, but the book sold extremely well. Earle Balch, Tate's publisher, solicited another biography. The Fugitives' collective project reached a new stage with Tate's biography and the promise of others to come. Articulating the Fugitives' shared sentiments did not simply revalorize the Old South, these biographies brought the group's forceful advocacy into the public sphere. Tate wrote a friend that the Jackson biography proved that the Old South could "be made into a convenient symbol of the good life for everybody."[33] Fashioning the South into that symbol could not happen without concrete efforts by all the brethren. Tennessean Andrew Lytle, a late recruit to the Fugitives, was a dedicated comrade and wanted to be involved. Along with Tate, Lytle imagined this written work as part of their new "society, something like the *Action Francaise* group," with "a whole religious, philosophical, literary and social program."[34] Warren went him one better when he wrote to Tate that "the Nashville brothers are on fire with crusading zeal and the determination to lynch carpet baggers."[35] That zeal led Tate to his unused notes from *Stonewall Jackson*. He decided to add another salvo to the Fugitives' written arsenal with a biography of Confederate president Jefferson Davis. *Jefferson Davis: His Rise and Fall*, published in 1929, underscored what Tate hoped was a "greater Southern movement" that would be carried "to the most extreme ends."[36]

Having enjoyed commercial success with *Stonewall Jackson*, Tate convinced his publishers to give Andrew Lytle a contract for a biography of Nathan Bedford Forrest. Tate then introduced Mavis MacIntosh, a literary agent in New York, to Warren. MacIntosh quickly secured Warren a contract with Payson and Clarke for a study of John Brown.[37] Warren's choice might seem striking given his friends' projects, but the intense collaboration among these men insured that Tate, Lytle, and Warren were on parallel tracks with their biographies. In other words, the subjects of these studies already had a fixed meaning; the writing was primarily a matter of shoehorning characters and evidence into the Fugitives' predetermined interpretive framework.

In addition to celebrating the antebellum South at all costs, slavery had to be rationalized, even celebrated, and the North must be blamed for the Civil War, that pointless bloodbath begun by fanatics. While some critics have dismissed these biographies as "exercise[s], done to earn bread and to shock the Brahmins[,] . . . game[s] played for the fun of it," this light-hearted attitude ignores the wellspring of belief that created the works as well as the Fugitives' polemical vision of past and present.[38] By making these biographies out to be incidental exercises, many have failed to grasp the implications of the very real propagandistic program behind them. The program was a dangerous one, particularly for the Jim Crow South, because the Fugitives were attempting to bring back a lost world of their imagining. By rendering slavery benign and the antebellum South a model for the future, these writers sought to obliterate the piecemeal progress that had been made toward racial equality, economic advancement, and regional integration.

As Tate wrote in 1927, "interesting things are . . . at last stirring in the South, and in that part of the South which we cannot help taking about with us forever, wherever we may go."[39] Tate recognized the progress the Fugitives had already made and keenly invoked the imagined space they had created together. Tate's biographies were the first published counterattacks to perpetual Northern invasions; a call to arms for his fellow Southerners to craft similar tales. In February 1928, Warren learned that he had won a Rhodes scholarship and signed his *John Brown* contract. It was time for the Kentuckian to do his part.

That spring, Tate and Lytle, researching their biographies, embarked on a thirty-five-hundred mile tour of Civil War battlefields.[40] Tate labeled the group, which included his wife and daughter, a Southern "battalion." Lytle wrote that they were on a "quest for our common historic past."[41] By their own account, their visit to Antietam, better known to them as the Battle of Sharpsburg, revealed the root of their identities as Southerners. Standing where the Union army made its famous and tragic charge, Tate whispered reverently to Lytle that the "enemy" had died there by the thousands. Genuinely moved by this connection to the heroic Southern past, and a glimpse of Northern vulnerability, Tate and Lytle were deliriously happy for the rest of the day.[42]

The battalion moved on to Harpers Ferry, where Warren was soaking up John Brown tales. In that river-bound village so heavy with symbolism, the men discussed their common pursuit of Southern history.[43] Tate triumphantly declared, "Here we are all working on the same idea."[44] Tate had his Confederate warriors, Lytle, Nathan Bedford Forrest, and Warren, an abolitionist straw man.[45] As the group traveled and camped together for the next few weeks, the journey took on greater spiritual meaning for all three men. As Tate recalled, "I feel like the Confederate States—still alive but not the man I was."[46]

For Warren, the infamous abolitionist represented an irresistible and insidious juxtaposition of man and myth. Warren would forever be captivated by these conundrums, but he had long identified Brown's most disturbing aftereffect as the Civil War itself.[47] "The Civil War," Warren wrote in 1961, "draws us as an oracle, darkly unriddled and portentous, of personal, as well as national fate."[48] Warren saw an opportunity with Brown to confront the false riddles and terrible fate of his region. For the young author, Brown symbolized the most delusional and destructive American myth, just as he personified the North's Pyrrhic victory in the Civil War. Warren believed that the Civil War and its memory had been tragically usurped, manipulated into a series of self-serving legends that not only compromised truthful understanding but marginalized the intellectual and cultural supremacy of the South. From the moment Warren began listening to stories about Shiloh at his grandfathers' knees, he became determined to challenge these falsehoods.

In the biography, Warren made Brown the idol of these Northern myths. Through the abolitionist, Warren sought to dislodge national narratives that had corrupted accounts of the path to war. Beyond his belief that Brown was nothing more than a common criminal, Warren long professed to abhor manhandling the past for a cause.[49] Brown symbolized his region's willingness to follow its beliefs to unknown ends, regardless of the consequences. Practically speaking, Brown and the North were responsible for a horrific and unnecessary war. Warren was disgusted and fascinated by the hubris of this Northern mindset.

Andrew Lytle articulated this Fugitive sentiment in a letter to Tate, in which he decried the North's "short-sighted greed" in the "murder of the South." Lytle expressed his horror that "we've had to submit to our enemies in the presentation of our case to the world." Much more was at stake than an interpretation. Their analysis of the war's causes, Lytle made clear, would show the South's refusal to submit any longer to the indignities of these pervasive Northern myths.[50]

While the battlefield tour brought thematic and spiritual coherence to Warren's work, his encounter with Tate and Lytle did not help with the most serious task of the Brown biography: the historical research. Warren tried to put a positive spin on his progress in a letter to his publisher in September 1928: "In Harpers Ferry I had a long talk with Mr. Boerly, the last living witness of the raid."[51] But beyond the trip to Harpers Ferry and that single interview, Warren conducted most of his research in the pages of the best-known biographies of Brown, bringing a rather arbitrary lens to the task. Although Warren summarily dismissed James Redpath's biography along with Oswald Garrison Villard's for their "abolitionist bias," he extracted whole documents from Franklin Sanborn's hagiographic *The Life and Letters of John Brown.*[52]

Warren relied most heavily on two notoriously partisan biographies: Richard Hinton's specious *John Brown and His Men* and Hill Peebles Wilson's vituperative *John Brown, Soldier of Fortune: A Critique.*[53] Wilson's interpretation, especially his portrait of Brown as an amoral opportunist, had a profound influence on Warren's understanding of Brown and his era. But even with these aids, Warren noted in a letter that he could not find evidence to support his belief in Brown's "sundry swindling operations."[54] Selected precisely *because* Warren wanted to show that like all Northerners, Brown was a foe of order, tradition, and, most important, thoughtful change, the Fugitives' perfect straw man was difficult to pin down.

Recounting the trials of research, Warren recalled finding "nothing but snags for quite a time, but now the business has been running smoothly and I am considerably more optimistic. . . . I learned finally that I was not writing an epic."[55] In the fall of 1928, Warren left for Oxford University. He soon set to work finishing the biography, now overdue. Updating his friends on his progress, Warren described the project as explicitly connected to the war, writing that with his new bride "and the Civil War, I have had two very agreeable occupations for the past two months."[56] For a book that never explores the Civil War explicitly, a biography of a man who died in 1859, Warren's conception of the book's purpose is fascinating.

In fact, by articulating his concern for the Civil War, not Brown, Warren exposed just how pervasive the Fugitive program for these biographies truly was. With Allen Tate in Paris on a Guggenheim fellowship, the two corresponded frequently, and Tate visited Warren several times in England, reading drafts of the Brown biography and giving his friend ideas for improving various aspects of the book.[57] Tate previewed the book for Lytle in 1929, writing that he was "all applause. [*John Brown* is] a great piece of work— very deceptive at first glance . . . but very soon you are amazed at the subtlety of the presentation—at the way small facts connect with other small facts further on, and at the quiet, dawning case that is being built up against the pseudomartyr. It's going to be a great book."[58]

Warren began *John Brown: The Making of a Martyr* with a caustic device. He told the story of the execution, in 1511, of a man in Kent, England, named John Brown who held so tightly to his vision of God that he was put to death. In addition to establishing the biting tone that characterizes the biography, Warren used the Kent story as a narrative hook and a thematic trope. Pointing out that the John Brown of Harpers Ferry erroneously claimed to descend from a Mayflower passenger named Peter Brown, Warren suggested that it would be equally ridiculous, but perhaps more consistent with Brown's "higher law" proclamations, if he claimed to descend from this executed Kent namesake.

Warren opened Brown's personal story by casting doubt on the family's involvement in the Revolutionary War. Warren used this device throughout the biography, in this case to underscore the incongruities between Brown's connections with the founding conflict of the nation and Brown's pursuit of "liberty" in Kansas and Harpers Ferry. Even in the opening pages, Warren loudly complained about the veracity of the sources utilized in heroic accounts of Brown's life. The young author showed particular delight in pointing out absurdities in the man's legend, and Brown's relentless and factually flexible self-promotion provided countless opportunities. The abolitionist's hagiographic tales of his own life included an entry from his time in Ohio, when a runaway slave appeared at his family's door and young Brown took the man in, hiding him in the underbrush. Brown recalled later of "hearing his heart beating before I reached him." Skewering Brown's claims at superhuman hearing, Warren was especially pleased to parody Brown's being afforded yet another "opportunity to again swear eternal enmity against slavery."[59] The biographer seriously questioned Brown's heartfelt belief in abolition; his "eternal enmity against slavery" seemed to Warren merely a cover for the pursuit of personal fame and fortune. Warren made plain that he considered tales like these to be the inventions of a deluded and misguided zealot.

However, Warren did not simply refute any of these anecdotes because he had not done research to disprove them. Instead, he used language to great dramatic effect, dressing these passages with enough sarcasm to render Brown's story ridiculous. Throughout the biography, Warren alluded to Brown's supposed hypocrisy on slavery, arguing that Brown adopted a changing opinion to fit any given situation. Warren employed an 1834 letter from Brown to serve this end. As Brown wrote, "I have been trying to devise some means whereby I might do something in a practical way for my poor fellowmen who are in bondage." Warren juxtaposed Brown's noble proclamation with the fact that "the state of John Brown's birth" had just passed a law enforcing segregation in schools.[60] By implication, Warren asked his readers why Northerners like Brown were so concerned with the South when they had plenty of racial bugaboos in their own region. These forceful insertions of doubt, together with Warren's focus on contradictory but irrelevant information, synthesized a narrative that made Brown seem shifty and hypocritical.

Warren used Northern racism to accentuate this hypocrisy. Describing Brown's time in Ohio, Warren highlighted the restrictive black laws of the 1830s, passed because "free negroes were generally unpopular in Ohio." Of course, Warren asserted, "black laws or no black laws, Ohio was a better home to them than the jungle." Thus, not only were Warren's Yankees hypocritical opponents of slavery for enacting racist laws, but blacks in *John Brown* were hardly human: unwitting participants in a drama they could not comprehend. Throughout the biography, Warren's treatment of blacks underscores the unacknowledged Fugitive dream of resurrecting the rigid racial hierarchy dismantled during the Civil War. Describing the mixed feelings of Brown's interracial raiders, Warren explained that the "negroes, knowing nothing of Harpers Ferry, naturally held no opinions."[61]

The mental capacity of black Americans was a crucial component of Warren's arguments about the hypocrisy of the Northern mindset. Warren blithely depicted the slave as a happy and contented creature never bothering "his kinky head about the moral issue" of bondage. Instead, those concerns were the exclusive provenance of meddling Yankees. Slavery, the object of Brown's rage, should be considered "in the more human terms of its practical workings," Warren argued, and not in an abolitionist's conception of its "abstract morality." Southern slavery, Warren continued, had none of "the horrors of West Indian slavery," because "immediate contact existed between master and slave," encouraging "an exercise of obligation [that] reached downward as well as upward." In Warren's view, basic economics insured there was no serious mistreatment because "the slave was valuable property and it was only natural that the master would take care to . . . not jeopardize its value." While Warren admitted "the system was subject to grave abuse," he argued that "the negro's condition was tolerable enough." Being enslaved was merely a matter "of convenience" to Southern bonds-men.[62]

Taking much of this defense of slavery from Lost Cause boilerplate, Warren argued that in contrast, liberty had only brought "inconvenience" to Southern slaves. Warren explained that because blacks had become so "accustomed to explicit directions" under slavery, they were mentally un-prepared for freedom. "Negroes," Warren explained, "as the experience of emancipation was to show, could not work for themselves."[63] This assertion, of course, was not a historical one but an argument loaded with contemporary implications.[64]

These contemporary concerns ran throughout Warren's study. Within what is supposed to be a biography of John Brown was an extensive polemic on the history of American slavery and the meaning of the Civil War to the South and its consequences for black Americans. Because slavery was such a benevolent system of mutual kindness, Warren wrote, "there was, by consequence, no great reservoir of hate and rancor which . . . would convert every slave into a [Union] soldier." In fact, the author maintained, abolitionists were so misled that when the slave owners marched off to war, they left "their families and estates in the care of those same negroes for whose liberty, presumably, the North was fighting."[65]

Warren's sheer ignorance, willful or not, of the physical and psychological horrors of slavery is notable, but he further minimized the system's brutalities by focusing on the North's celebration of Brown's martyrdom. Warren's title spoke to his interest in this Northern mythmaking, but the author was particularly interested in the period from Brown's execution until the shots were fired on Fort Sumter. Describing his disdain for James Redpath's celebratory biography, Warren wrote that "the Civil War, which confounded so many problems and clarified so few, followed close on the heels of Redpath's book to supplement the confusion which [Brown] had already contributed."[66] Warren developed the argument in Tate's biographies that Northern actions violated the democratic principles of the nation.[67] Brown personified higher-law thinking and the danger of unconstitutional activism, but his execution and Northern martyrdom showed the North controlling the Civil War narrative before the war even began. Warren used Brown to expose a North hell-bent on destroying an evil so theoretical it lacked even a basic historical, moral, or human context. In Warren's biography, Brown was a self-conscious exploiter of an abstract moral cause that helped him justify his actions, profit from his misdeeds, and carry the North into an unconstitutional war.[68]

While the main agenda of the biography was blaming the North for the Civil War and excusing the South for slavery, Brown the scoundrel provided the narrative means toward these larger ends. Indeed, the abolitionist's "dishonest" business practices were Warren's favorite trope in the biography. As Warren wrote, "only once in these confused years of business did John Brown see, as many more honest men have seen, the very unattractive inside of a jail."[69] Warren's picture of Brown's financial dealings was far from "confused" and can better be described as intentionally pathological. For Warren, Brown's business practices, in which he saw dishonesty and deception where others observed mere incompetence, held the key to John Brown's entire life.[70] After describing Brown's bloody killings at Pottawatomie Creek in May 1856, Warren highlighted only one fact: Brown stole his victims' horses and traded them on the profitable black market of territorial Kansas.

The exploitation of this trope was one of Warren's shrewdest thematic strategies. What better way to vilify Brown than to make him not just spiritually misled but also a common criminal? Warren's biography shows an almost obsessive attention to the debated incidents in Brown's life, specifically the continual lies about his presence at the Pottawatomie massacre: "The truth was out at last, and the world had prepared a motive—a motive which would fit the martyr. . . . The world had justified the murderer. . . . It is a little more difficult to justify a horse thief." Warren was most incensed that Brown's defenders justified his actions while stolen property was on its "way north to be sold."[71] Here Warren was able to condemn Brown, his mythmakers, and the North all in one stroke.

Warren's critique of Villard's exhaustive 1910 biography highlighted his obsession with Brown's thievery. "Mr. Villard has a great deal to say about the murders [at Pottawatomie], which, of course, he does not attempt to justify, but he has very little to say about the theft of murdered men's horses, which, one feels sure he would not attempt to justify."[72] Warren was unwilling to admit how widespread the theft of horses, property, and money actually was during the Kansas conflict. In fact, he went so far as to suggest that "lone Missourians did not penetrate into Free State Kansas and appropriate anything."[73] A cursory glance at contemporary accounts of Bleeding Kansas quickly reveals how rampant thievery was on both sides of the conflict.[74] Warren did no such research for *John Brown*. Instead, he relied exclusively on his highly selective reading of Villard's biography and on the interpretive slant of the anti-Brown school. This focus on trivialities was intentional. While readers were distracted by Brown's pettiness, Warren advanced the Fugitives' overarching case for the Old South.

In truth, Brown was a charismatic and intriguing fellow, particularly after his symbolic military triumphs in the Bleeding Kansas struggle. But describing the choice of Brown's raiders to join his invasion of the South, Warren could not bring himself to give the Northern martyr any compelling qualities. As a result, Warren argued, people were taken in by Brown because "their ignorance, their recklessness" and "their ambition" made them susceptible to any charlatan. Furthermore, Warren depicted the twenty-one men of the Harpers Ferry raid as weakly principled opportunists. "They didn't like slavery," he revealed, "but they were ready to capitalize [on] the process and profit from the wreckage."[75]

Most important, Warren connected the Harpers Ferry raid to Bleeding Kansas as if one was the inevitable result of the other. As he wrote, Bleeding Kansas and the raid on Harpers Ferry became "one big *coup* which would obscure [Brown's] shabby past." To reinforce this idea, Warren even invoked historical inevitability, writing that Brown "marched down the road to Harpers Ferry because he could not do otherwise." Warren's real argument was that Brown's actions were the unavoidable outcome of the New England mindset; the logical, if slightly extreme, products of the region's vices. In one pivotal description, Warren deftly combined these various threads: "The stooped but rigid old man with his neat rural dress, his talk about bayonets and bullets and God's will, his immense awkward dignity, immense egotism, his white beard and hard grey-blue eyes which glittered, as one host put it, with a 'little touch of insanity,' moved impressively about the albums and pleasant china of those New England parlors."[76]

Having impugned the abolitionist's mental health and his principles, Warren then set on the misled souls who supported Brown's crusade: "Most of the people who sat about him in those parlors, and gave their earnest attention to his words, found something peculiarly congenial to their own prejudices and beliefs. Captain Brown was a 'higher law man.' He was 'superior to any legal tradition'—just as most of these people felt themselves to be—and if he claimed to have a divine commission, they could understand what he meant, for they too were privy to God." With Brown and his compatriots condemned for their false religiosity, Warren leaped on the North writ large, blaming the entire Civil War on the Yankees.[77]

"The Southerner pointed to the Constitution and said: 'There is the law and the bargain; keep them and give us justice,'" Warren wrote, but

"Garrison burned the Constitution as a 'covenant with Hell'; and many other countrymen of his, if they were not ready to do this, could still call on conscience and the higher law." Higher law was enough to cause the war, but Warren wanted a culprit for Reconstruction and the trials of the New South. "Unhappily, the corollary of this divine revelation was to make the South pay, and pay again," he wrote. "The disagreement might conceivably have been settled under terms of law, but when it was transposed into terms of theology there was no hope of settlement. There is only one way to conclude a theological argument: bayonets and bullets."[78]

With the North condemned, and the war accounted for, Warren painted Brown in even starker terms. "As the years passed," Warren wrote, Brown "had tried many ways to get to the head of the heap and had failed and failed again, but with each failure the desire had become more insatiable, more absolute." And with these failures, Warren earnestly believed, Brown, like his fellow abolitionists, fell victim "to meanness, to chicanery, to bitter, querulous intolerance, to dishonesty, to vindictive and ruthless brutality."[79] This was the John Brown that Robert Penn Warren left to the ages.

Published in the fall of 1929, Warren's biography arrived in an extremely unwelcoming marketplace. Stephen Vincent Benét's epic poem, *John Brown's Body*, was generating unprecedented sales, and Warren's book went to the printers just three weeks before Black Tuesday. Like many publishers at the time, Warren's publishing house, Payson and Clark, was bankrupted by the stock market crash.[80] Not surprisingly, the firm's fiduciary troubles had a debilitating effect on the prospects of the biography. After the crash, the company was in a state of serious disarray, and book distribution was plagued with difficulties. Still, perhaps because of Brown's new visibility (thanks to Benét), *John Brown: The Making of a Martyr* was reviewed by hundreds of publications.[81] In fact, the sheer extent of critical response to the biography revealed how resonant the Fugitives' ideas were with a wide swath of Americans.

One of the most intriguing reviews was penned by a young professor of history at the University of Chicago named Avery Craven.[82] Craven, who became one of the key figures in the group known as the Revisionist historians, eventually echoed many Fugitive arguments. The Revisionists, who ranged from blatant neo-Confederates to subtle iconoclasts, helped shift national understandings of the meaning and causes of the Civil War. Much like the Fugitives, the Revisionists tried to prove that Northern impatience, not slavery, was to blame for the war. To Craven, Warren's biography was portentous because its analytical framework was nearly identical to the Revisionists' burgeoning project. Warren's explicitly pro-Southern program, however, threatened to delegitimize what Craven considered to be the Revisionists' transparently objective interpretations. Given these overlapping concerns, Craven jumped at the chance to review Warren's biography for the *New York Herald Tribune*. Under the headline, "The John Brown the South Saw," Craven took on the air of professional superiority toward a popular historian, writing that "Mr. Warren, with pen a trifle caustic," had written the biography for "the South . . . in days of old." Reflecting his fear that the Fugitives' over-the-top neo-Confederacy would undercut the seriousness of his own interpretation, Craven argued that Warren was transparently courting "the Southern group who still get a bit excited at the mention of the name of 'Old John Brown.'"[83] Craven did not want stars-and-bars dilettantes rendering the Revisionist doctrine stillborn.[84]

Craven's review struck at the heart of Donald Davidson's fears, using the specter of Southern provincialism to dismiss the Fugitives' new project. For Davidson, this was proof positive that the Lost Cause siege mentality was more than justified. Reacting to another Northern assault, a *New York Times* review Davidson called "an abomination," the elder Fugitive wrote to Warren offering to review *John Brown* himself. Davidson would "waive [his] lack of qualification" in order to celebrate Warren's "study of that consummate old scoundrel." Personally, Davidson offered his congratulations to Warren for the "very substantial, well-balanced, and intelligent biography—I am full of admiration,—the book is a remarkable performance all the way through, and it means, among other things, that you are able to do practically anything you wish in a literary way." Reminding Warren of the feelings of "all of your old Fugitive comrades," Davidson added that *John Brown* proved "the world is your apple, Red."[85]

Davidson's laudatory review appeared in dozens of papers across Tennessee, rallying support for Warren's book under a pro-Southern banner. Rather than respond to Craven or other negative reviewers, Davidson laid out the Fugitives' historical arguments in the combative vernacular of the Lost Cause. Warren, Davidson argued, clarified the "profound difference in historical point of view between the North and South." Fortunately, that difference would no longer "lead, as it once did, to a tragic effusion of blood; but it is still much more than a cold academic matter. It relates to differences of temper, social tradition, economics, geography, and much more." These differences were at the crux of the Fugitives' project.[86] It was not enough to change the nation's understanding of Southern history; the Fugitives hoped, through Warren's biography and reviews like these, to create a model for the future.

Davidson's review was really a manifesto for the superiority of Southern values, which he clarified with flair. "The North holds for abstraction," Davidson wrote, "the South for concreteness." "In the long struggle between North and South," he continued, "the North fought for abstractions: freedom of the slaves (in whom the North had no material interest), preservation of the Union; and the South for concrete things; family, home, property, an established and pragmatic social order." Davidson maintained that Warren's book had objectively explored those differences. *John Brown* was "a cool, thoroughly documented study, covering every detail of Brown's career." The book was being called biased, Davidson elaborated, simply because Warren did not make "excuses for John Brown's villainies." But that accurate approach did not make the biography "a wrathy, fire-eating book."[87]

Davidson's review contained the clearest statement of the Fugitives' mission that had ever appeared in print. Speaking to the national usurpation of their past and present, that process that had marginalized the South and blamed the region's institutions for the country's greatest national trauma, Davidson explained the importance of forcefully rejecting such interpretations of the causes, course, and aftermath of the Civil War. Plumbing the soulful Southern values that he and his friends sought to exploit, Davidson recalled "a mountain saying . . . 'A lie can run around the world while the truth is gittin' on his clothes.' . . . After three-quarters of a century surely the truth can 'get on its clothes' and make a favorable public appearance." Warren's "excellent book will disturb and dislocate the legend," Davidson wrote. "If anything will lay John Brown's ghost, this book will."[88]

Davidson was delighted that these propagandistic goals were so effective in Warren's hands. Texas newspapers sprang to Warren's support, applauding the accuracy of his portrait of Brown as "an embezzler, a horse thief, a murderer, and an egotist. Probably he was all these and more besides."[89] Another Texas columnist argued that Warren "shows pretty conclusively that . . . Brown's performance at Harper's Ferry seems to have been conceived not so much to free the slaves as to start a rebellion which would create a new government, presumably with him at its head. . . . He was probably less guilty, broadly speaking, than some of those who fed his mind on silly stories about the slaves."[90] In addition to accepting Warren's portrait of Brown as truth, this column shows the success of the Fugitive project. In attributing the Civil War to what this reviewer called "silly stories about the slaves," Warren had spread a new interpretation of the war's cause throughout the nation.

Illustrating the shrewdness and talent of the Fugitive writers, H. L. Mencken, general of the 1925 invasion of Tennessee, ringleader of the mocking treatment of the South during the Scopes trial, also applauded Warren's efforts. Warren's biography, Mencken wrote, was "the first attempt to tell the story of Old Osawatomie objectively, with no bias either for or against him." Offered despite Warren's neo-Confederate polemic, Mencken's celebratory words speak to the powerful cloak that history offered to the Fugitives' ideas. "It is a capital piece of work, careful, thorough and judicious," Mencken continued. "Its merits are not diminished by the somewhat surprising fact that the author is but twenty-five years old."[91] Even if it had taken five years, Mencken implicitly acknowledged the fruits of his insulting journalism. Warren's biography signified the success of those Mencken had lured into combat.

Not all Northerners were convinced by the Fugitives' historical maneuvers. *John Brown* "is as much argument as biography," was the summary in the most important black newspaper in New York City, the *New York Amsterdam News*.[92] "After a few pages the reader knows that it was written by a Southerner, and as it goes on the Southern bias comes out bitterly," the review explained. "The author never has a good word for any of the enemies of slavery [and no bad words for their] friends."[93] These biases were evident to other reviewers as well, even if most of them resided north of the Mason-Dixon line. "Warren's narrative method," wrote one Pennsylvania reviewer, "gives that final rakish twist to the material that identifies it as primarily the work of a Southerner on a ramp, and only secondarily that of a simple minded biographer with his fingers uncrossed."[94]

These judgments bolstered the Fugitives' siege mentality, convincing the group that their legitimate views would never receive fair treatment by the Yankee press. The fate of Warren's debunking of the North's false martyr revealed to the Fugitives that their fears were totally legitimate. When a single negative review appeared after ten positive notices, the group was outraged. William MacDonald, writing in *The Nation*, embodied that Yankee conspiracy just as he recognized the Fugitives' fears. Pointing out Warren's "failure to add much of importance to what was already known of Brown's career," MacDonald argued that Warren's biography was "deeply tinged with his bias and sneering hostility toward Brown and his supporters." The review was relentless on this point. "To topple an idol from its pedestal was not enough," he wrote. "The idol must be hacked to pieces and the pieces trampled in the mud of innuendo and scorn." MacDonald attacked the very foundation of the Fugitive project, writing that "the heart of John Brown and his antislavery supporters is a subject about which Mr. Warren's prejudices hardly entitle him to speak." Finally, acknowledging the inherent power of a sparkling new biography, regardless of its merits, MacDonald lamented that "here or there some unreconstructed Southerner, ignorant of what has been written hitherto, may rejoice that the horrid truth about John Brown has at last been told."[95] MacDonald spoke not only to the Fugitives' fears of Northern condescension but also to the deep cultural, intellectual, and historical chasms between North and South. It was these divides that the Fugitives would confront in their crowning work.

MacDonald's review, among others, proved to these men that they could not afford to rest. As proud as Davidson, Ransom, Tate, Warren, and Lytle were of the four biographies the group had produced, there were already new plans afoot. With some new recruits the Fugitives embarked on the project that would earn the group a new label and instant notoriety. Just a few months after Warren's *John Brown* was released, Harper and Brothers would publish a book by "Twelve Southerners," *I'll Take My Stand: The South and the Agrarian Tradition.* The title was borrowed from a stanza of "Dixie," Daniel Emmett's seminal song of the Confederacy:

> Then I wish I was in Dixie, Hooray! Hooray!
> In Dixie Land, I'll take my stand, to live and die in Dixie.
> Away! Away! Away! Down South in Dixie.
> Away! Away! Away! Down South in Dixie.[96]

With the book's publication, the Fugitives became known as the Agrarians. Plans for expanding the Fugitive project had been circulating among Tate, Warren, Davidson, and Ransom since the late 1920s. Tate had floated the idea of founding a Southern literary community as early as 1929.[97] Inviting Warren and Lytle, Tate imagined the men and their families would raise animals, get into "the chicken business," and everyone would work "as neighbors."[98] In fact, Tate's vision extended well beyond a Confederate biography or two, he dreamed of writing an entire "history of the South."[99]

When Ransom wrote Warren in early 1930 to congratulate him on the Brown biography—"a beautiful piece of work"—Ransom added that "as to the sentimental background, you know that I shared that from the start." Ransom described his idea to purchase a country newspaper "say at Franklin, Tennessee," where "one or more of us could make a living." The point here was to "provide our group with a press, with which we could issue pamphlets and particularly a periodical, for circulation Southern and country-wide. We need to write furiously, and we will have the stuff to write." The plans, though remarkably close to fruition, never materialized. Ransom, still hopeful, assured Warren that "we are getting an option on one or more Tennessee papers. I think we will put this thing over."[100]

But Ransom also had a specific request; "What is immediately on my mind is to say: Now is the time for all good men to come to the aid of the party." Ransom continued that, "Don, Andrew Lytle, Tate, and I have got things cooked up to the point where they can't be stopped. I refer to the Old South movement, about which we had a few flying words last summer. Our project is immediate to this extent: —We must at once get out that symposium of essays on the South old and new, and aim for early fall publication."[101] Ransom appealed to Warren as a Southerner: "We have been counting on you as one of the faithful. I don't mean to mortgage your career, but only for the time being to get your article and your signature. Haven't you a burning message on the subject of ruralism as the salvation of the negro?"[102]

Donald Davidson wrote to Warren the very same day, recruiting him for the "book on The South." "We now have our ideas fairly well defined," he told Warren, "and are making enlistments for the cause." Davidson ended his letter urging Warren to respond to his "eager and excited conspirators back home."[103] Writing again in March 1930, Davidson told Warren that "Tate has just come in from New York, and day after tomorrow we are holding a Council of the Confederates (Ransom, Tate, Owsley, Lanier, Wade, Lytle, and I) to discuss final plans for the book."[104] In a postcard from 1931, Davidson's enthusiasm spoke to the group's momentum. "The Rebels gathered in full force," he wrote. "Tate, Ransom, Lytle, Lanier, all led their troops into action."[105]

Warren was an integral part of this world of "Confederates" and "conspirators" in the late 1920s and early 1930s. As Tate's biographer, Thomas Underwood, has explained, Warren and his friends had all "undergone Southern conversions" that bolstered their belief in the redemptive force of the antebellum South. Moreover, Tate, Lytle, and Warren "had written biographies that radicalized them."[106] Keeping their Southern conversions in mind, Warren's essay for *I'll Take My Stand*, "The Briar Patch," clearly and explicitly amplified the exact themes developed in *John Brown* and the Fugitive program.

Davidson wrote Warren on March 17, 1930, trying to clarify the shape of Warren's contribution. In the letter, Davidson told Warren that "we have held our big pow-wow, have talked things out, and are ready to march on the enemy. . . . It's up to you, Red, to prove that negroes are country folks [the word 'animals' is crossed out]—'bawn and bred in a briar-patch.' Go to it."[107]

I'll Take My Stand was published in 1930, with Warren's essay taking its title from Davidson's letter.[108] While their private correspondence was rife with references to the battle of this new Confederacy, the Fugitives were keenly aware of the need to properly disguise some of these ideas. Arguments over the book's title exposed these concerns. Warren wrote to Tate that the title was "the god damnedest thing" he'd ever heard.[109] Tate and Warren feared that the title was "likely to rouse antagonistic prejudices" in equal proportion "to the sympathetic ones latent in the Southern reader."[110] The two were convinced that anti-Southern sentiment in the media would manifest itself in low sales and the contentious title would only encourage the Yankees to dismiss the book. Conflict over the title eventually led Ransom and Davidson to question Warren's dedication to the cause.[111] When it came to this small cadre of fierce pro-Southerners, Tate wrote that "we all watch one another like Mexican revolutionists."[112]

Indeed, tempers were running high because the group felt Warren's essay, "The Briar Patch," raised unnecessary questions about Southern race relations. Davidson reacted to Warren's essay in a letter to Tate, writing that it "hardly seems worthy of Red." Davidson initially wanted to reject the essay, furious about the way Warren chose to "discuss the negro problem."[113] Davidson had hoped Warren would make a forceful case for the return to the rigid racial hierarchies of the antebellum years, but Davidson believed that the essay had failed. The dispute over whether Warren had held the party line revealed the group's increasing radicalism.

A mere eighteen pages, "The Briar Patch" opened with the historical image of the first American slaves arriving at Jamestown. "When the bluecoats and bayonets disappeared," Warren maintained, "when certain gentlemen packed their carpet-bags and silently departed, and when scalawags settled down to enjoy their profits or sought them elsewhere, the year of jubilo drew to a close and the negro found himself in a jungle as puzzling and mysterious, and as little answering his desires, as the forgotten jungles of Africa."[114] Davidson's disappointment with Warren's depiction of slavery is difficult to understand.

The "practical workings" of the "humane" system of Southern slavery, Warren had informed readers in *John Brown*, insured utter loyalty, with "house-negroes" more inclined to side with their benevolent white masters than the emancipating forces of Brown, Lincoln, or anyone else.[115] It followed naturally that after the Civil War, as Warren wrote in "Briar Patch," "the negro was as little equipped to establish himself as he would have been to live again, with spear and breech-cloth, in the Sudan or Bantu country."[116]

Warren's professed goal with the essay was to chart that dilemma; it was "[an] attempt to find . . . the story of the negro since 1865." A defense of rural Southern labor in its social and racial dimensions, Warren's essay stressed the transparency of the idyllic world that was that imagined antebellum South. Poor whites, Warren claimed, were "just as much the victim of the slave system as the negro." Again ignoring slavery's brutalities, Warren argued that Southern whites suffered from the lack of an open labor market. Once slavery was gone, it was clear that "if a negro mason lays a brick as well as a white mason and asks less pay for the job or is content with longer hours, the negro mason in the end will get the job and keep it." These were false assertions that ignored the actual mechanics of contemporary racism. Citing Booker T. Washington (another terrible gesture in Davidson's opinion), Warren called for some variety of benevolent segregation: provide education for blacks as long as they maintain their place in the system. "The Southern negro has always been a creature of the small town and farm," he wrote. "That is where he still chiefly belongs, by temperament and capacity."[117]

I'll Take My Stand, and Warren's essay particularly, patently ignored the actual racial realities of the interwar South. Warren's ideological gymnastics perfected the polemic he had been crafting with his fellow Fugitive-Agrarians throughout the previous decade. With the same historical background, arguments, and deftly crafted prose he had used in *John Brown*, "The Briar Patch" represented an attempt to convince and mobilize. Both book and essay sought believers in the ways of the Old South, particularly those sympathetic to the cultural values, social system, and racial hierarchies of this imagined world.

The Fugitive-Agrarian publications reveal the successful appropriation of history in the campaign to wrest control of the South's present and the future. Warren's *John Brown* and his contribution to *I'll Take My Stand* were part of an organized effort to convince the nation that their imagined South (past and present) was real. This impressive intellectual uprising effectively created a history of the Old South that could be used as a model for the New South. In the hands of these talented men, historical writing gave legitimacy to what otherwise would have been dismissed as the rantings of hillbillies straight out of Mencken's Scopes columns. Instead, Warren and his compatriots transformed the South, an amalgamation of historical reality, imagined past, and hopes for the future, into the torchbearer of the American republic.

While this uniquely Southern project would continue to reverberate through literature, art, and history for much of the twentieth century, its roots were in an impassioned plea for regional redemption. The Fugitive-Agrarian project was designed to transform the present and direct the future. But the "Dixie" invoked in these texts, that land of happy, kinky-headed slaves, beholden to kindly, benevolent masters, had never existed. The antebellum South, in reality, *depended* on subjecting blacks to all manner of degradation: of body, of mind, and of spirit. When we understand these interdependent arguments, the Fugitive-Agrarian invocation of Daniel Emmett's "Dixie" is particularly disturbing. "In Dixie Land, I'll take my stand, to live and die in Dixie. / . . . O, I wish I was in the land of cotton. / Old times there are not forgotten. / . . . I wish I was in Dixie."

Within a decade, the Fugitives' arguments had found overwhelming national sympathy. The group's romanticization of an imagined "land of cotton" was not just eerily effective, it spoke to the long shadows that the Civil War continued to cast over American culture and society. That great national trauma allowed this intellectual tradition not just to embed itself powerfully in a regional culture and identity but to reforge the zeitgeist of our national past. The American impulse to imagine Southern plantations at the far end of a tree-shaded drive rather than at the slave quarters speaks to this understanding. Our insistence that the Civil War was a valorous tragedy without blame owes much to Warren and his compatriots. This is the legacy of the Fugitive imagination.

8

REVISING KANSAS

John Steuart Curry and the Fanaticism of John Brown

John Brown had long inspired artists, but his memory produced an explosion of art in the 1930s unequaled since the 1860s.[1] Just as Revisionist historians converged on an interpretation of Brown that mirrored Robert Penn Warren's, artists began giving visual expression to similar ideas. Painters, playwrights, and writers were galvanized by Stephen Vincent Benét's popular poem, but the radical politics of the New Deal and the daunting specter of World War II also generated new interest in Brown. Inevitably, these intertwining political, social, and historical currents made for intriguing new imaginings of the abolitionist.

Just before his death in March 1943, Benét began an illustrated edition of *John Brown's Body*, still dominating Knopf's bestseller list. Benét commissioned artwork for the book from a native Kansan named John Steuart Curry, noted for his enormous mural of John Brown that covered a wall in the Topeka, Kansas, statehouse. While Benét's death prevented completion of this edition of the poem, Curry's work harmonized with *John Brown's Body* and spoke to shared concerns over Brown's extremism and his role in America's grand narrative.

Curry was one of several major artists attracted to Brown during the 1930s. During a decade when public art became a popular and exciting frontier, Curry's mural showed the abolitionist's importance to a new generation's negotiations with the past. In his work, Curry made Brown a fanatic extremist who began the nation's terrible fratricidal war in Kansas in 1856. Curry's vision of Brown, the visual companion to Warren's higher-law martyr, underscores America's continued reckoning with the utility of violence, the promise of racial equality, and the possibility of substantive change. Painting Brown as a figure of religious violence with the blood of the Civil War literally on his hands, Curry rejected Brown as a racial progressive in order to condemn the mindset that led to war.

Along with Thomas Hart Benton and Grant Wood, John Steuart Curry was part of a triumvirate of artists in the 1930s who, because of their attraction to the people, places, and themes of Middle America, came to be called the American Regionalists. Curry's designation as a Regionalist, however, has obscured rather than clarified the importance of his work, particularly the enormous John Brown mural he completed for the Kansas state capitol in 1942. Curry's artistic interests ranged far beyond the rigid and somewhat arbitrary boundaries of strictly Midwestern art. At the height of his powers, Curry painted political art with sharp social messages, and his John Brown mural remains the most compelling example of these efforts.[2] While his political goals stretched the parochial associations of the Regionalist label, Curry also tailored his social commentary to reinterpret the American past, present, and future.[3]

Born to Dunavant, Kansas, farmers in November 1897, Curry left home at nineteen, determined to make his fortune as a painter. After saving money working on a Missouri Pacific section gang, he moved to Chicago to attend the city's famed Art Institute. A few years later, he was living in an artists' community in Westport, Connecticut, but his skills had not yet caught up with his ambition. Curry spent most of the 1920s as a magazine illustrator, but the community in Westport saw enough promise in him that its members collected money so he could study art in Paris.

When Curry returned to the United States, he painted a water-tank baptism set in his native Kansas. With the canvas, Curry stumbled on the magic formula. *Baptism in Kansas* "was painted in August, 1928," the artist told *Life Magazine* in 1942. "I was in a state of desperation trying to get along at illustration, or anything I could do. I took a month off and painted this picture. It was painted without notes or sketches from memory of a baptism that took place in 1915."[4] The canvas changed Curry's life, establishing him as a financially successful and critically celebrated painter. As Edward Jewell, the art critic for the *New York Times*, described, "Kansas has found her Homer."[5] The praise was welcome, but, more important, *Baptism* secured the patronage of Gertrude Vanderbilt, who not only purchased the painting but sponsored Curry for the next two years at fifty dollars per week, a tidy sum in the middle of the Depression.

With free license to paint as he pleased, Curry did not content himself with quaint images of folks from the plains. He consistently pushed the limits of his subject matter, spending a year with the Ringling Brothers Circus and doing hundreds of sketches, studies, and paintings of life with the performers. Above all, the circus work showed Curry striving; trying to bring more meaningful content and themes to his art. Throughout his career, Curry sought dramatic subject matter that he believed was historically important.[6]

Unfortunately, the public showed greater interest in Curry as a Regionalist. Thomas Hart Benton spoke to the difficulties of this label. "We came in the popular mind to represent a homegrown, grass-roots artistry which damned 'furrin' influence," Benton explained, and "cared nothing for the traditions of art [according to] cultivated city snobs. . . . A play was written and a stage erected for us. Grant Wood became the typical Iowa small towner, John Curry the typical Kansas farmer, and I just an Ozark hill billy. We accepted our roles."[7]

Of course, it was somewhat absurd that Curry had been "discovered" as a Regionalist representing the Kansan farmer after his training in Paris and longtime residence in Westport, Connecticut, but Curry seized the opportunity nonetheless. After being invited to Grant Wood's Stone City art colony in Iowa in 1933, Curry put on overalls and the men rolled up their shirtsleeves for publicity shots, looking to the world like Midwestern farmers. Despite Curry's distaste for the Regionalist label, these moments helped establish him as a potential savior of genuine American art.

Like many of the left-leaning artists of the period, Curry was increasingly drawn to social causes for his art. The murder of department store scion Brooke Hart in San Francisco and the lynching of his murderers inspired Curry to approach mob justice in a painting. The Hart lynching came in the midst of a series of legal fiascoes like the Scottsboro case in Alabama and increasingly brazen lynchings across the South.[8] Because Hart was a white victim, the outcry over uncontrollable mob action provided the NAACP with a pretext to reinvigorate the campaign for federal antilynching legislation.[9] This public momentum inspired an accompanying art show, and Curry was asked by the NAACP to contribute to the exhibition.[10]

Curry's contribution, *The Fugitive*, showed a black man hiding from a lynch mob in a tree, arms spread as in a crucifixion. The image graced the

Figure 8.1. John Steuart Curry, The Freeing of the Slaves, *1942. University of Wisconsin–Madison; © Board of Regents for the University of Wisconsin System; photograph by Greg Anderson.*

cover of the exhibition catalog.[11] This painting channeled Curry's passions and spurred his desire for social agitation. On the heels of the experience, Curry declared his most earnest hope to the *New York Herald Tribune* in 1935: "I would like nothing better than to be given a free hand to paint the Kansas scene on the walls of some state institution."[12]

Curry's desire came at an opportune moment: Franklin Roosevelt had authorized a new division of the federal government with the specific mission of decorating public buildings.[13] Because of his increasing celebrity, Curry was appointed in late 1934 to produce a mural for the Department of Justice Building in Washington, DC. Inspired by the Mexican muralist José Clemente Orozco, Curry was thrilled about the possibilities of a public mural with social content.[14] As the mural took shape, Curry began to clarify his own ideas about public art, which he wanted to be recognizable in shape, form, and associations to anyone who saw it.[15] Curry was not alone in his beliefs; these years saw the emergence of murals as a popular forum for social critique.[16] Curry's mission for the Justice Building spoke to the importance of social themes for paintings in the 1930s and the value of choosing subject matter with an important "political, social, and even moral background."[17]

In Curry's sketches for the Justice Building mural, a freed black slave stands above fallen Union and Confederate soldiers (figure 8.1).[18] The central figure is flanked on the left by a mule-drawn wagon with two passengers, and an old man prays behind a woman in the characteristic dress of a plantation cook. Behind them, a storm head veined with lightning looms. On the right, three black figures, identifiable as slaves, raise their hands in religious ecstasy. This trio was liberated in the wake of marching Union troops and welcomes the crystal-clear skies of post-1865 America.[19] Curry's ideas for the Justice Building reflected more than a stereotype of black Americans' religious exaltation and the simple rewards of the postbellum United States. In the midst of terribly real discrimination throughout the United States, Curry's choice of imagery spoke to the past, to the moment of emancipation, but not to the racial troubles of the present or to solutions for the future.[20] In the short term, the sketches' historicity was immaterial. Informed that his chosen theme "might stir up racial controversy," Curry had to abandon the mural, titled *The Freeing of the Slaves*, for the time being.[21]

Curry was deeply disappointed with the mural's rejection, but he circled back to a generic tableau about lynching. With its air of racial injustice, Curry hoped to give the project a racial dimension until he was again urged to make the mural more generically about mob violence. When Curry finished *Justice Defeating Mob Violence*, the mural bore virtually no resemblance to his original submission.

While many have emphasized Curry's smooth career path until his frustrations in Topeka, the Justice Building commission familiarized the artist with controversy. Curry's quashed submissions taught him that public and socially minded art must tread a fine line to succeed but not offend.[22] Curry continued to revisit Kansas for subject matter, keeping alive his desire to meld his interest in his home state with his overarching artistic goals. At the same time, Curry was increasingly linked with more self-conscious Regionalism through Benton in Missouri and Wood in Iowa. Wood, who wore the Regionalist label with pride, encouraged Curry to come to the Midwest to become a resident Regionalist as Benton had done in Missouri. After a few heavily publicized visits, Curry moved to Madison, Wisconsin, in 1936, becoming the first artist-in-residence at the state's college of agriculture.

The Justice Department commission did not sour Curry on mural painting and public art. The combination of grand federal projects and socially relevant subject matter took on greater importance for him as public murals began to be produced with greater frequency. In a speech to the Madison Art Association in January 1937, Curry announced his profound optimism for the future of his country, American art, and their intersecting paths. "The ushering in of the Roosevelt Administration and the New Deal," Curry argued, "emphatically ushered in a new deal in American painting . . . [and their initiatives are] of tremendous importance to the American art of the present and of the future." Meanwhile, Curry blasted away at the triumphal civic art of the past. For Curry, "flowing robes" and "the noble youth posed in a noble attitude doing nothing" were no longer needed. "Now," Curry proudly declared, the "luscious arm" will hold "a business-like broom." Rather than the derivative grandiosity of classical art, artistic projects of the New Deal should immortalize the everyday experiences of everyday people. "My sole interest and conception of subject matter deals with American life," Curry added, "its spirit and its actualities."[23]

Throughout the 1930s, Curry and his agent tried to convince Kansans to appreciate the artist's paintings, hoping to use such interest to generate a commission for a public art project. But Curry's work, particularly the rural baptisms, country preachers, and tornadoes, had not gone over well with Kansans. The people of the state reacted very negatively to a local exhibition of Curry's work in 1931 and largely ignored the positive press the artist received during the early 1930s. It was not until 1935 that Curry sold his first painting in Kansas. The news was so surprising that the New York newspapers and the Associated Press covered the sale. The Justice mural also helped improve Curry's dismal reception in Kansas. The artist's move to Wisconsin was seen by his handful of Kansas supporters as another dangerous affront. Moreover, by the mid-1930s, Curry's achievements had been validated by the national press; he, Thomas Hart Benton, and Grant Wood had made the cover of *Time* in December 1934, and the premier issue of Henry Luce's new *Life Magazine* in 1936 had a four-page spread on "Curry of Kansas."[24]

The *Life* article intensified Kansans' worries that they might have neglected their best hope for a cultural representative of national importance. At the center of these fears was a growing realization that Wisconsin had stolen "Curry from his native state, which had . . . failed to buy his pictures."[25] This idea gained further traction with the growing reputation of Curry's friend Benton, who unveiled his signature work, *Social History of Missouri*, in the Jefferson City statehouse in 1935. While Benton's mural was controversial in its depiction of slavery and outlaw figures like Jesse James, the artist cemented his status as a Missourian with the work. In addition to immersing himself in state history for his mural research, Benton took a teaching position and permanent residence in Kansas City. These elements brought matters to a head for his friend Curry, and agitation increased in Kansas for the state to be painted under official auspices.

Henry J. Allen, editor of the *Topeka State Journal* and owner of a house designed by Frank Lloyd Wright, wrote to Curry asking him to produce some civic art for Kansas. "While we haven't any Jesse James to work on as Benton had in Missouri," Allen wrote, alluding to the controversial Benton murals, "you could think up some mighty good substitutes in the person of John Brown and Jim Lane."[26] The timing was perfect for Allen's efforts. Prompted largely by the success, albeit controversial, of Benton's murals in neighboring Missouri, the press surrounding Curry and his compatriots forced Kansans' hand in hiring him or forcing the artist to choose another state as his muse.

Focusing on the Kansas statehouse in Topeka, Curry's enthusiasts realized that Kansans would not support a government-funded project, so the money would need to be raised from other sources. Even this process was plagued by debate over potential subject matter and concerns about the artist. Henry Allen's own wife accurately captured the opinion of most Kansans toward the native son's work: "Cyclones, gospel trains, the medicine man, the man hunt are certainly to be found in Kansas but why must Mr. Curry paint these freakish subjects?"[27]

As I have noted, even though Benton's artwork was ultimately accepted and celebrated, the Missouri mural's initial reception was rather rocky. As one article explained, "Mr. Benton painted murals with a slashing and perhaps bitter satire, using the caricature technique and emphasizing the ungainly peculiarities of Missouri hill-billies . . . [and other] unorthodox characters." The analogies were obvious to concerned Kansans: "Curry's work has been of somewhat similar flavor. He has emphasized Kansas tornadoes, baptisms in watering troughs, hogs killing snakes, and other subjects which do not have any particular connection with the significant achievements of the state. Those who are not now enthusiastic about his technique fear that he will emphasize the ugly and repulsive features of Kansas history."[28]

Despite the concerns, the *Topeka State Journal* reported that Curry's art was being considered for the statehouse. The artist did not hide his hopes for the assignment. "I would be tremendously happy," Curry told reporters. "I have my own ideas about telling the story of the pioneers coming into Kansas. I want to paint this war with nature and I want to paint the things I feel as a native Kansan." Nonetheless, Curry cautioned that the murals "must not be dead paintings" but "something that will live . . . the true story of Kansas and her struggle through adversity."[29]

In his detailed proposals and accompanying sketches, Curry described the murals. On either side of the corridor doors on the main floor of the capitol were "Coronado and Padre Padilla, the Franciscan missionary, look[ing] out across the Kingdom of Quivira, above which float the omnipresent buzzards." On the facing wall, Curry would paint "the figure of the plainsman and buffalo hunter, behind him the slain buffalo, and behind them the thundering herds of buffalo pursued by Indians—and behind all, a lurid sun which lights the scenes of both walls." Finally, in the center of the north wall, the most important panel in the rotunda, was "the gigantic figure of John Brown. In his outstretched left hand the word of God and in the right a 'Beecher's Bible.' Beside him facing each other are the contending free soil and pro-slavery forces. At their feet, two figures symbolic of the million and a half dead of the North and South." As Curry explained, the centerpiece of the mural "expressed the fratricidal fury that first flamed on the plains of Kansas, the tragic prelude to the last bloody feud of the English-speaking people. Back of this group are the pioneers and their wagons on the endless trek to the West, and back of all, the tornado and the raging prairie fire, fitting symbols of the destruction of the coming Civil War."[30]

There was conflict from the very first. *Art Digest* reported in August 1937 that Kansas's "native son, has been invited . . . to depict Kansas history on the walls of the state capitol in a 'sane sensible manner.'"[31] Members of the Kansas commission, the article read, "were emphatic in asserting there would be no 'outlandish characterizations' of historical Kansas figures such as John Brown and Carry A. Nation, no controversial paintings such as those of Thomas H. Benton, which aroused a furor at the Missouri Capitol. Also there must not be 'too much modernism.'"[32] It was a long list of demands that Curry immediately challenged; he was not willing to paint "a soft, soppy presentation," he told the commission.[33] "I don't see how I can leave out John Brown or Carry Nation," he argued. "They were expressions of militant Free Soil and a militant prohibition sentiment."[34] What Curry did not mention was that, being fond of drink, he never intended to portray the temperance advocate Carry Nation, whose personality and beliefs he found absurd. John Brown was another matter altogether.[35]

In the end, the commission needed Curry more than he needed it; he was given free rein with the murals. The artist was ecstatic as he began his formal sketches. "It is up to me!" he told one reporter excitedly. "There are no restrictions! I can paint the things I love! I want these murals to be my best work, a monument to my State that will stand for a long time!"[36] Studying the statehouse interiors and completing the preliminary work for the murals, Curry assured Kansans that there would "be no bent towards sensationalism in his murals," but he would not "sidestep unpleasant incidents in" the state's history. "I'm excited about the Kansas project," Curry added. "I think I can do things for the architecture of this building."

Bolstered by his belief that he would not "be censored by the committee," Curry became bolder in predicting Brown's role in the mural.[37] "Kansas was the starting place for the war between the North and South," he explained. "You can't paint Kansas history without painting that. And you can't paint that without including John Brown."[38] Even though Curry sometimes showed a deaf ear to Kansans' likes or dislikes, he realized the advantages of shifting attention to the other panels of the mural. "I have been accused of seeing only the dark and seamy side of my native state," he wrote in his proposal. "In these panels I shall show the beauty of real things under the hand of beneficent Nature . . . so that we as farmers, patrons, and artists can shout happily together, 'Ad Astra Per Aspera.'"[39] Curry's invocation of Kansas's state motto ("To the Stars through Difficulties") helped smooth over growing objections. Although the John Brown centerpiece, titled *The Tragic Prelude*, was the largest panel of the mural, Curry's public statements focused on the naturalistic panels and the large canvases of Coronado and Kansas farm scenes.

Curry's clever management of his patrons created a brief window of support for his mural. The commission agreed to Curry's design, in particular to Curry's specification of "John Brown in the center of a struggle between pro and anti-slavery forces [which] shows the Osawatomie crusader towering above a struggling crowd."[40] As the artist's wife recalled of the Topeka mural and especially of the centrality of Brown, Curry "thought [Brown] was what represented Kansas."[41]

However, Curry's knowledge of the abolitionist was rather meager, consisting mainly of vague schoolboy memories. Moreover, the only written work the artist consulted was a single pamphlet by Alfred A. Santway, "an aged negro," the work's frontispiece described, "who had remembered [Brown] from boyhood and whose family had been liberated through the [abolitionist's] efforts." Regardless of the dubious accuracy of this claim, Santway's 1934 reminiscence laid out the heroic vision of Brown that detractors had decried since 1859. Recalling Albion Tourgée, Santway described "John Brown, The Traitor, John Brown, The Fanatic, John Brown, The Martyr. . . . Thus has this man, one of the most dramatic characters of all times, been denounced and acclaimed."[42] Curry ignored that history of acclaim and focused almost exclusively on Brown as a traitor and fanatic. Curry's canvas shows this very man: fire in his eyes, Bible and rifle in hand, amid a sea of destruction.

The main question for Curry was how to translate these ideas into a more interactive form of art. For the first time, instead of painting and transfer-

Figure 8.2. John Steuart Curry at work on The Tragic Prelude, *1940.*
Kansas State Historical Society.

ring sections of the mural, Curry used lantern slides as he painted, allowing for more sudden changes influenced by both the subject matter and
the actual surroundings (figure 8.2).[43] Early reports of his work gave Curry
great confidence. "The Curry murals are everything Kansas has a right to
expect," a local newspaper hopefully reported in November 1937. "They are
conceived in a spirit of dignity and respect to the traditions of the state, and
other generations seeing them will understand the story of Kansas from the
days of Coronado to today."[44]

The centerpiece of the Topeka mural owed much to Curry's rejected
sketches for the Justice Building. When he designed *Tragic Prelude* (figure
8.3), Curry reshuffled elements from the sketches for *The Freeing of the
Slaves*, painted in 1943 for the University of Wisconsin Law Library. Most
notably, the central foreground figure of the freed slave is replaced in the
Kansas mural by a Moses-like John Brown. Unlike the rejoicing black slave
of the Justice sketch, John Brown, rifle in one bloody hand and New Testament in the other, does not praise God for freedom, he demands it. Both
figures stand over the bodies of Union and Confederate soldiers, but in the
background of *The Tragic Prelude*, Curry depicts representatives of both
sides of the territorial conflict as well as the prairie fires and tornadoes

Figure 8.3. John Steuart Curry, The Tragic Prelude, *1937–42.*
Kansas State Historical Society.

that Kansans had dealt with since long before Brown's time. In the context of Brown, the weather is as foreboding as the dead bodies Brown towers above, speaking to the biblical plagues and catastrophes the abolitionist predicted if America did not end slavery.

Who was the John Brown that Curry presented? As he described it, "I portray John Brown as a bloodthirsty, god-fearing maniac." Throughout American history, Curry argued, men "like [Brown]" had "brought on" wars. Curry was an isolationist and saw his nation on the "eve of conflict," a second world war in Europe. When decisions were made by "pious cranks" like John Brown, only bloodshed, death, and destruction would ensue.[45]

Because of the scope of the mural, Brown as an isolationist icon was the least of Curry's problems. Soon after Curry enjoyed a moment of acceptance, his overall plans for the Topeka mural were tabled. In proposals submitted to the Topeka commission, Curry sketched rotunda panels depicting the homesteaders and barbed wire that changed the state's landscape. He showed scenes documenting the plagues of drought, grasshoppers, and soil erosion the people faced. Finally, Curry intended to paint the fruitful harvest of corn, wheat, and oil fields. To install these panels, slabs of Italian marble in the rotunda were slated for removal. By 1939, however, midway through Curry's painting of the mural, it became clear that no marble would be displaced.

When Kansas voters and politicians encountered Curry's unfinished mural, particularly the enraged Brown, forces began aligning to prevent the artist from finishing the project. When newspapers reported that marble would be removed, people searched for and discovered flaws, real and imagined, in Curry's half-finished artwork. The pigs' tails curled the wrong way, the tornado resembled an elephant's trunk; the list of objections was virtually endless.[46] Curry, hoping to stave off disaster, rescued his sketches before objections could be raised to work not even yet begun.[47] Finally, the *Kansas City Times* reported that "the marble wainscoting will not be removed from the walls of the Kansas statehouse corridors and John Curry will have to make his murals fit the space on the walls."[48] As far as the artist was concerned the critiques were the last straw; he privately resigned himself to finishing the existing panels, but the process was heartbreaking.

The marble was really beside the point, the slabs of rock were simply a cloak for Kansans' worries about Curry's chosen subject matter.[49] The most aggressive denouncers were a collection of civic organizations, the Kansas Council of Women, the American War Mothers, and the Topeka Women's Club, all of whom protested the mural. The groups claimed that the artist's murals, "while true in a sense, do not portray the true Kansas."[50] In highlighting Brown, Kansans were outraged that, as they had feared, the artist had "emphasized the freaks in history."[51]

By 1941, Kansas politicians had swung completely behind their incensed citizens. "John Brown's murals may rank tops with the art experts," the *Topeka State Journal* snidely noted, "but the legislature is thumbs down on them. For the second time during the session the Curry paintings were denounced from the floor." Several state representatives let reporters know just how much they disliked the mural. "I don't know how the rest of you feel about John Brown," Representative Van De Mark explained, "but I think he was [an] erratic, crazy old coot and a murderer."

Van De Mark's comments are jarring. Curry's John Brown was exactly the character the representative described: an erratic, crazy old coot and a murderer. Furthermore, Curry hoped to alert the nation to the danger of such men. If anything, Curry had honored Kansas by showing how Brown had used the territory as a platform to launch an extremist campaign against slavery. However, because these conversations were being mediated through Brown, Curry's painting was totally misunderstood by people outspokenly sympathetic to his interpretation.

Perhaps Kansans just did not want Brown as the centerpiece of their statehouse? Other legislators called Curry's murals "modernistic and cheap." In this sense, Curry had erred just by including Brown. Kansas was not ready for the kind of public art being promoted by the Works Progress Administration and the Federal Art Project. Kansans wanted the flowing robes and noble youths that Curry derided in the 1930s. Kansas Representative Towers-Wyandotte simply wanted the murals erased from the statehouse walls. Dejected and disappointed, Curry finally left Topeka on March 24, 1942. His final parting shot to the newspapers was that "the value per square foot of his paintings is probably considerably more than the value per similar unit of the marble."[52]

In the end, Curry could only refuse to sign his murals. "The work in the east and west wings stands as disjointed and un-united fragments," the artist explained from Wisconsin, where he was painting *The Freeing of the Slaves* for Madison's Law Library. "Because this project is uncompleted and does not represent my true idea," Curry reasoned, "I am not signing these works."[53] The artist also issued a direct rebuke to his critics. "I sincerely believe that in the fragments, particularly the panel of John Brown, I have accomplished the greatest paintings I have yet done," he told the *Topeka Capital.* The murals, Curry believed, "will stand as historical monuments. To the Mural Commission and to the children who donated their pennies, as well as to all others who have believed in me, I wish to express my appreciation and to assure you that I have done the best I could with the space at my command."[54] The Kansas state legislature answered with a bill appropriating $1.15 "from the state sewage disposal fund to complete the murals" and place them "in all Statehouse rest rooms [because] there was no place else suitable for such art."[55]

The mural controversy, which quickly devolved into outright mockery, destroyed Curry's confidence. As his wife recalled, the experience was "shattering, absolutely shattering. I think it really contributed toward his death. . . . I think John felt that this was his great mural . . . this was his home, and he wanted to do the very finest for his state."[56] Instead, Curry left the experience utterly dejected. As his daughter added, more than anything else the mural ordeal was "a humiliation . . . because he looked on Kansas sort of the way you look on motherhood and the flag and so forth. You know, it was home."[57]

Of course, the man at the center of the hoopla had long been a source of division and rage. But beyond refusing to ignore this polemical figure, Curry had, despite the paucity of his research, articulated swelling popular understandings of the man. Mirroring the works of Stephen Vincent Benét, Robert Penn Warren, and the Revisionist historical movement, Curry gave American public art the widely accepted vision of the abolitionist: the wild-eyed and dangerous John Brown whose extremism led to war. Unfortunately, Curry's venue happened to strangely twist the kaleidoscopic controversies of Brown's place in American memory. While Kansans were understandably upset about the seeming celebration of a violent fanatic on their statehouse walls, Curry's mural was also an unwelcome reminder of the state's role in the racial and social upheavals of the nineteenth century.

Curry hoped to provoke Kansans with his murals, but his Brown was designed for a more conservative purpose. Curry painted Brown to highlight the costs of moral righteousness and violent radicalism; the artist had decided to mediate his isolationism and pacifism toward war in Europe though the abolitionist. Kansans' rejection of Curry's work reveals both the underlying fears of righteous violence, racial equality, and societal change as well as the awkward bluntness of using Brown as a political tool.

Curry paid dearly for these murals and his selection of Brown. "I'd have done better to stay on the farm," Curry said just before his death. "No one seems interested in my pictures. Nobody thinks I can paint. If I am any good, I lived at the wrong time."[58] Curry's experiences with the Topeka statehouse mural prove that no matter what the timing, Brown's memory still could have dangerous and unpredictable consequences.

The inspiration to paint [John Brown] was motivated by historical events
as told to us by the adults of our community . . . the black community.
—Jacob Lawrence, 1978

9

TOGETHER UNDER ARMS

Jacob Lawrence Paints Black History

Whereas John Steuart Curry suffered because of John Brown's contentious legacy, another painter thrived. At the very same moment Curry worked in the Kansas statehouse, Jacob Lawrence, a young black painter from Harlem, finished a series of paintings called *The Life of John Brown*. These twenty-two captioned images were the culmination of more than 170 scenes of African American history Lawrence painted from 1937 to 1941.[1] After series based on Toussaint L'Ouverture, Frederick Douglass, Harriet Tubman, and black migration in the United States, Lawrence selected Brown for his final historical cycle. The painter was drawn to black history to provoke discussion about America's present and future.[2] The alternate narrative of America's past that Lawrence created in these paintings cultivated pride in black historical struggles and was designed to inspire the ongoing pursuit of freedom, justice, and equality.[3]

Celebrated as one of the great American painters before he was twenty-five, Lawrence was an artist whose subject matter, method, and background all contributed to his enormous success. The art world delighted in his achievements partly because it finally claimed a black American painter. However, Lawrence's John Brown series, first exhibited in 1945 then restored and screen-printed in 1977, radically reinterpreted white artistic and historical traditions.[4] By exploring the genesis of Lawrence's Brown imagery and his broader narrative of black struggle, it is possible to situate the painter's vision in a rich tradition of both white and African American celebration and memorialization. While Lawrence presented his protagonist as a radical interracial leader, he did not make the abolitionist an uncomplicated hero. Instead, *The Life of John Brown* presented a tormented soul and interrogated his martyrdom. For Lawrence, that assignation still depended on the realization of black equality. Through his quirky choice of historical moments, challenging imagery, and plainspoken captions, the painter engaged his audience with open questions about Brown and the country's history. These methods helped Lawrence interrogate the potential use of religion, violence, and interracial partnership in the struggle for freedom and change.

Born in Atlantic City, New Jersey, on September 7, 1917, Lawrence came of age during the Great Depression. After his father, a Pullman cook, disappeared, Lawrence and his mother moved to Harlem. As an early teen, Lawrence frequented the progressive Utopia Children's House, a community center that served hot lunches and provided after-school activities. The center was Lawrence's first exposure to paint—the dramatically colored gouaches that became his hallmark.[5] It was also at Utopia that Lawrence began learning about African American history; he later recalled learning about Toussaint L'Ouverture at the age of fifteen.[6]

In response to his new home and new tools, Lawrence built intricately detailed dioramas of Harlem street scenes. The young artist was "keenly aware of the special character of the sights and sounds of" Harlem.[7] As his early paintings reveal, Harlem's environment influenced him profoundly. "My motivation and my desire to be an artist," Lawrence explained, was "the black community."[8] From the people and the streets of Harlem, Lawrence became a visual storyteller.[9]

Equally crucial was "the black experience," the artist recalled, "which is our heritage—an experience that gives inspiration, motivation, and stimulation." Central to his success, Lawrence always argued, was the "encouragement which came from the black community," as important to his subject matter as the aesthetic "beauty and poignancy of our environment."[10] Lawrence's earliest paintings powerfully showed how Harlem pervaded his outlook.[11] It was the community, the painter maintained, that nurtured him until he could support himself. "I had acceptance at a very early age from the community, and that does a lot," he recalled. "The people . . . didn't necessarily know about art, but they encouraged me."[12]

Harlem in the 1930s was an exciting place for a teenager of Lawrence's talents; the community helped him bask in the afterglow of the Harlem Renaissance, learning from its heartiest practitioners as the next generation took the helm.[13] Cultural figures like W. E. B. Du Bois, James Weldon John-son, Alain Locke, and writers like Langston Hughes, Zora Neale Hurston, and Richard Wright encouraged blacks to look to the past for inspiration. The Harlem literati believed that honoring black contributions to Ameri-can history would provide the foundation for a social, political, and cultural identity.[14] In this sense, Du Bois's plea in 1920 to "let us train ourselves to see beauty in black" spoke to more than just self-esteem; it also revealed a burgeoning pursuit of black art and black history.[15] Lawrence heard these messages on the street, in church, and even at home and began looking past the strictly experiential to illustrate black history.

As Lawrence came of age, there was tremendous ferment around the cul-tivation and expression of that history; Harlem was literally bursting with speeches, pamphlets, and sermons drawing Lawrence to the past.[16] One afternoon in the mid-1930s, the painter was shooting pool at the YMCA and heard someone on the street declare that "black people were never going to get anywhere until they knew their own history and took pride in it."[17] The speaker was known honorifically as Professor Seifert, and, as Lawrence recalled, Seifert "believed that through their pictures [artists] could show black people their history and inspire them."[18] At the time, the young art-ist only partly grasped how essential this message would be to his career. Seifert personified Harlem's historical passion, and Lawrence responded enthusiastically to his message "to select as our content black history." In addition to being "a most inspiring and exciting man," Lawrence recalled, Seifert "helped to give us something that we needed at the time."[19]

The artistic establishment in Harlem also fed the young painter's inter-ests. Successful artists and writers mingled with the younger generation at the Harlem Artists Guild, the Harlem Arts Center, the Schomburg Library, and especially at 306 West 141st Street, which became known simply as "306." A studio workshop run by the artist Charles Alston and the sculptor Henry W. Bannarn, 306 was "the main center in Harlem for creative black people."[20] Lawrence rented a small studio at 306 and enjoyed teenage en-counters with people like "Katherine Dunham, Aaron Douglas, Leigh Whip-per, Countee Cullen, Richard Wright, Ralph Ellison, Alain Locke, William Attaway, [and] O. Richard Reid." A shy young man, Lawrence mainly lis-tened carefully to these artists "discuss the topics of the day—as well as phi-losophy and creative processes pertaining to their own fields." These con-versations often circled back to what Lawrence recalled as the dominant collective "interest in Black history and the social and political issues of the day."[21]

Charles Alston was a driving force in these preoccupations. At 306, Alston was at work on a pair of historical murals for the Harlem hospital and directed much of the mural activities of the Works Progress Administration (WPA) from his studios. Across Harlem, New York City, and other parts of the country, the WPA was funding and encouraging the production of murals, many done in narrative sequence.[22] This work, telling stories through large-format paintings or series of panels, spoke to Lawrence's desire to paint more extensive and complex narratives.[23]

When Lawrence was asked to attend WPA art classes at 306, Alston's partner Henry Bannarn exerted a significant influence on the young painter's evolution. Commissioned by Howard University for a bust of Frederick Douglass, the sculptor lamented the history that young blacks were taught in school. "They know about George Washington . . . and not about Crispus Attucks—about Admiral Peary and not Matt Henson," Bannarn told the *New York Amsterdam News*. "This is not as it should be. I want to be a means of them knowing the Attuckses, the Hensons, the Pushkins and the Douglasses. I will not rest until they do. . . . I want to contribute in the field of art to the culture of the Negro in the same manner that the subjects I portray have contributed to Negro culture and the general culture of America."[24]

Within the year, Lawrence took up Bannarn's cause as his own. When the classes at 306 ended, a scholarship to the American Artists School materialized, and art became Lawrence's permanent focus. The YMCA's Negro History Club bolstered Lawrence's burgeoning interest. "The stories of Frederick Douglass, Harriet Tubman, Toussaint L'Ouverture, Nat Turner, Denmark Vesey, and John Brown," Lawrence recalled, "were told in a very dramatic way."[25] The painter was reassured in his historical choices by the William Du Bois play *Haiti* at the Lafayette Theater, which told the story of the Haitian revolution.[26] Lawrence had already installed himself in Harlem's Schomburg Library, studying L'Ouverture and the history of the Republic of Haiti.

The Schomburg, part of the 135th Street branch of the New York Public Library, was a vital resource as Lawrence searched for source material for his art. Started by Arturo Alfonso Schomburg, a black Puerto Rican historian and bibliophile, the library housed an unparalleled collection of literature about and by blacks. "I remember Mr. Schomburg well," Lawrence told one interviewer. "I was too young to know him as a personal friend, but I recall seeing him and speaking with him there at the library. What an atmosphere he created in that special room of the library during the thirties—

what with African sculpture and other items of our ancient and contemporary culture!"[27]

For Lawrence's interest in storytelling and black history, the Schomburg was the only destination. "I was doing research at the time," he wrote, "both emotional and intellectual."[28] For Lawrence and many others, the Schomburg was, in the words of art historian Leslie King-Hammond, "a natural haven in their quest to reclaim their historical legacy."[29] The library was crucial in promoting what one librarian described as "negro genius."[30] It was through lectures, research, and the atmosphere of the Library, 306, and the YMCA that Lawrence learned about the myriad accomplishments of black historical figures.

This research fed Lawrence's first series of paintings on black history, *The Life of Toussaint L'Ouverture*, a forty-one-painting cycle that Lawrence began in 1937 and completed in early 1938.[31] Although Lawrence claimed practical reasons for narrating L'Ouverture's story in multiple paintings—"I couldn't get it all in one picture, so I made it into a series"—the influence of 306 was plain.[32] In the L'Ouverture cycle, Lawrence was visibly figuring out how to use history and make narrative art. The series is the painter's most simplistic in its didactic presentation of a black hero, an unfortunate circumstance considering the complexity and brutality of the Haitian Revolution.[33] Nevertheless, the L'Ouverture series was a radical departure for an American artist. Lawrence showed a revolution, with provocative imagery of armed blacks taking their freedom and future into their own hands.[34] Although the series included moments of proslavery boilerplate (L'Ouverture's sheltering of his master and mistress in panel 13), Lawrence managed to forcefully illustrate the fears of black rebellion that haunted the antebellum Southern psyche. Using violent tableaus, quiet scenes of L'Ouverture, and historical incidents, the young painter celebrated the heroism, nobility, and humanity of the Haitian leader. Above all, Lawrence wanted the paintings to show that even struggles as great as the one against slavery were winnable.[35]

The Life of Toussaint L'Ouverture established Lawrence's visual style, as well as an emerging process for his historical paintings. Eventually celebrated for being both primitive and modernist, Lawrence's images were simple and bold. Throughout his work, the painter utilized strong lines, vivid geometric shapes, and extensive symbolism. Lawrence's series paintings consist of gessoed panels painted with a limited palette of powdered tempera. Lawrence worked on an entire series at once by lining the panels up and painting the dark colors on each panel, then painting the light colors. As the art historian Patricia Hills discovered in personal interviews with Lawrence, this procedure "ensured that hues would have the same values and intensities throughout . . . the parts were integral to the whole structure."[36]

Lawrence's other innovation was to caption each painting in plain and instructive prose, captions meant to describe, inform, or challenge the visual content.[37] In the tenth panel of the Toussaint series, for example, a white slave owner (with gold cross prominently around his neck) savagely beats a bound man in front of a half-dozen chained slaves. "The cruelty of the planters towards the slaves drove the slaves to revolt, 1776," the caption reads. "Those revolts, which kept cropping up from time to time, finally came to a head in the rebellion." While the planters' cruelty is vividly depicted, the caption also narrated a series of offstage responses to this abuse. Lawrence hoped viewers would imagine (and visualize) the narrative taking place between and outside the captions and paintings. This bold step gave interpretative power to the series by situating the panels and captions within African American oral traditions.[38]

The response to Lawrence's Toussaint series was immediate. Prominent Harlem cultural figures were captivated by the paintings. "What impresses me about Lawrence is his ability to combine social interest and interpretation . . . with a straight art approach," Alain Locke wrote. "There is little or no hint of social propaganda in his pictures, and no slighting of the artistic problems involved, such as one finds in many of the contemporary painters of social themes. Yet his work has a stirring social and racial appeal."[39] The L'Ouverture paintings were the first to be shown by an African American artist in a major museum, and Lawrence was featured in New York's preeminent black newspaper under the heading: "An Artist of Merit: Pictorial History of Haiti Set on Canvas."[40]

Encouraged by this success, Lawrence painted 130 more scenes over the next three years. In these paintings, Lawrence depicted nearly two hundred years of black history, visual biographies of Frederick Douglass, Harriet Tubman, black migration, and finally, John Brown. While the paintings occasionally drew on legend and myth, Lawrence's historical series are more than heroic and one-dimensional highlight reels of black history. Drawn to heroic figures willing to sacrifice for a greater cause, Lawrence hoped his art would force viewers to take positions on the ambiguities, open questions, and narrative gaps in the lives of these characters and their involvement in ongoing struggles.[41] Lawrence explicitly hoped that his art would provoke action and reform; each of his historical series used epic narratives to con-

Figure 9.1. Jacob Lawrence, The Life of Frederick Douglass, No. 23, 1939: *"It was in 1847 at Springfield, Massachusetts, that Frederick Douglass first met Captain John Brown, one of the strongest fighters for the abolishment of slavery. Here, John Brown talked with Douglass about his plan to fight slavery. He had long been looking for a man such as Douglass, as an admirer and champion of Negro rights—he had found the man." Collection of Hampton University Museum; © 2010 The Jacob and Gwendolyn Lawrence Foundation, Seattle/ Artists Rights Society (ARS), New York.*

front far-reaching and troubling questions about race, violence, and radicalism.

Lawrence's treatment of race changed markedly across his various series. In the L'Ouverture and Douglass series, whites almost exclusively appear "as agents of violent oppression or exploitation."[42] John Brown was an exception. Before he chose Brown for a series of paintings, Lawrence used the abolitionist in his narratives of Douglass and Tubman. For *The Life of Frederick Douglass*, which Lawrence painted in 1938 and 1939, Lawrence chose the ex-slave's first meeting with Brown for panel 23 (figure 9.1).[43] The previous twenty-two images depicted Douglass's life from afar; there was a certain narrative distance even when Lawrence painted Douglass in his home editing *The North Star*. In contrast, the artist showed Brown and Douglass in extreme close-up, confronting viewers with this radical white man.

Lawrence's caption calls Brown by the honorific "Captain John Brown,"

Figure 9.2. Jacob Lawrence, The Life of Frederick Douglass, No. 24, *1939:*
"John Brown discussed with Frederick Douglass his plan to attack Harper's Ferry,
an arsenal of the United States Government. Brown's idea was to attack the arsenal
and seize the guns. Douglass argued against this plan, his reason being that the
abolishment of slavery should not occur through revolution." Collection of Hampton
University Museum; © 2010 The Jacob and Gwendolyn Lawrence Foundation,
Seattle/Artists Rights Society (ARS), New York.

a title he would not earn for another nine years. Describing the abolitionist
as "one of the strongest fighters for the abolishment of slavery," the caption
does not mention Brown's total lack of abolitionist experience during their
1847 meeting. In the scene, Brown and Douglass are, according to Lawrence, discussing Brown's "plan to fight slavery." Lawrence drew on American artistic tradition by painting Brown with flowing white hair and a dramatic beard. In truth, Brown was brown-haired and beardless until the late
1850s; he first met Douglass just after Augustus Washington made his second daguerreotype. With this allegorical Brown, Lawrence asked viewers to
consider white and black efforts for "Negro rights" and whether cooperation
was possible or beneficial.

The following painting in the cycle shows Brown and Douglass at a table
with an ominously curling black document—Lawrence's representation of
Brown's plans to invade Virginia (figure 9.2). Brown is trying to convince a

reluctant Douglass to assist in the raid at Harpers Ferry. Brown straddles a high red chair dramatically, with Douglass across the table in a smaller yellow one. A cross hangs directly above Brown's plans, potentially blessing the sanctity of revolutionary violence. Through his imagery and contentious caption, Lawrence asked viewers what role religion had played in struggles for equality and what that role might be in the future.

Lawrence expressed these ideas even more powerfully in *The Life of Harriet Tubman*, painted in 1939 and 1940. In panel 25, Brown sits at the head of a round table, with Tubman on his right and Douglass on his left (figure 9.3). A large cross covers the floor opposite Brown and a large black Bible rests on the table. All three figures have their faces covered by hands locked in prayer. "Harriet Tubman was one of John Brown's friends," the caption reads. "Douglass had arranged for a meeting with 'Moses,' . . . the woman John Brown came to for help. . . . 'I will help,' she said." Lawrence's emphasis on interracial cooperation was meant to be suggestive to those working for racial justice in the 1930s. It was not enough to pray and agitate separately, racial reform required unity.

Lawrence placed John Brown at the center of these black heroes. In many ways, the image is a dialogue of methods. In Douglass, there is the orator and writer; in Tubman, the peaceful antislavery guerrilla; and in Brown, the violent fanatic. The painting's cross and bluish rug point emphatically to Brown, since his method represented the next stage in this long struggle. Again, Lawrence asked challenging questions. Was Brown the result of prayers? Was he the culmination of the antislavery agitation of leaders like Tubman and Douglass? The doorway at the top of the scene is especially provocative in this regard. It soon led both Brown and Lawrence to Harpers Ferry. As the artist finished the Tubman series, he was increasingly aware of the intertwining purposes of these historical figures, and the powerful lessons black history could offer contemporary America. With his

(opposite) *Figure 9.3. Jacob Lawrence,* The Life of Harriet Tubman, *No. 25, 1940: "Harriet Tubman was one of John Brown's friends. John Brown and Frederick Douglass crossed into Canada and arrived at the town of St. Catherines, a settlement of fugitive slaves, former 'freight' of the Underground Railroad. Here, Douglass had arranged for a meeting with 'Moses.' She was Harriet Tubman: huge, deepest ebony, muscled as a giant, with a small close-curled head and anguished eyes—this was the woman John Brown came to for help. 'I will help,' she said." Collection of Hampton University Museum;* © 2010 *The Jacob and Gwendolyn Lawrence Foundation, Seattle/Artists Rights Society (ARS), New York.*

Brown series, the artist became especially explicit about his desire to use the dramatic narratives of Douglass, Tubman, and Brown to assess present circumstances and probe future actions.[44]

In 1939, Lawrence joined the Federal Art Project (FAP), which, in addition to being a life preserver for many artists during the 1930s, was the perfect incubator for Lawrence's talents and his thinking about radical racial reform. "It was my education," he said later, "an exciting, fermenting period. The concept of social content in art . . . had become the overriding conviction."[45] This period was absolutely essential to the painter's evolution. Government support of the arts through the FAP helped sustain many novice artists, allowing them to paint full time and receive recognition for their work.[46] The FAP also exposed Lawrence to an interracial group of like-minded painters, sculptors, and writers just as he was honing his artistic skills and discovering his historical interests.[47] Equally crucial was the untaxed $23.86 he received every week with the requirement to keep busy; two paintings needed to be finished every six weeks.

In 1941, Lawrence began painting the story of John Brown. As he wrote proposals to fund the paintings, Lawrence reaffirmed the purpose of his historical work. "I've always been interested in history," he wrote, "but they never taught Negro history in the public schools." Lawrence imagined the Brown series, with its white protagonist, as a crucial piece of his project. Simply situating Brown in this history was a radical proposition. "Having no Negro history makes the Negro people feel inferior to the rest of the world," Lawrence explained. "I don't see how a history of the United States can be written honestly without including the Negro."[48] With Brown, the painter sought to show blacks and whites the interracial partnership and radical change that was fought for in their not-so-distant past.

Lawrence believed that lack of historical knowledge and the legacies of slavery "tie up the Negro today."[49] "We don't have a physical slavery, but an economic slavery," he wrote in 1940. "If these people, who were so much worse off than the people today, could conquer their slavery, we certainly can do the same thing." Lawrence believed that interacting with the stories of L'Ouverture, Douglass, Tubman, and Brown could help end black subjugation. Lawrence asked, "How will it come about?" and answered, "I don't know, I'm not a politician. . . . I'm an artist, just trying to do my part to bring this thing about. . . . It's the same thing Douglass meant when he said, 'Judge me not by the heights to which I have risen but by the depths from which I have come.'"[50] Here was Lawrence's rationale for exploring black history; he hoped to show the hardships endured during America's traumatic history to inspire the continuing struggle for true equality.

Lawrence's research quickly underscored Brown's polarizing trajectory through American history. The painter relied heavily on Franklin Sanborn's *The Life and Letters of John Brown*, with its heroic white savior rescuing a downtrodden people from the depths of slavery. As we saw in chapter 4, Sanborn personified a wider movement in art and literature to canonize Brown as a peaceful martyr. Sanborn's typical depiction of Brown was "the simple, brave, heroic" man who "set in motion" an "avalanche" known as the Civil War.[51] Sanborn made Brown the true father of emancipation, and his book celebrated Emerson's famous statement that Brown was the "new saint . . . none purer or more brave was ever led by love of men into conflict and death,—the new saint awaiting his martyrdom, and who, if he shall suffer, will make the gallows glorious like the cross."[52]

While Sanborn's text was Lawrence's "principal source in writing the captions for each image," the captions and imagery were ultimately his own. Although he borrowed from the artistic tradition of portraying Brown as a saintly hero, Lawrence channeled his visual and written research in new ways. The Brown cycle begins and ends with crucifixion scenes. The first panel addresses analogies between Brown and Christ, while the final image raises the question of his martyrdom. The accompanying captions utilize the language of Sanborn's biblically inflected hagiography and reinforce the religious themes of Lawrence's paintings. The series' historical interpretation is a hybrid of disparate sources, evoking both the violent crusader of African American tradition and the peaceful martyr of nineteenth-century white America. The resulting protagonist is equally derived from the passion for black history in 1930s Harlem and the artist's mixed feelings about the role of violence in bringing change.[53]

Lawrence's palette helped sharpen these interpretative challenges; he used color to reinforce his thematic choices. In contrast to the earlier series, *The Life of John Brown* paintings are bleak.[54] Lawrence depended on blacks, grays, and browns to bring gravity to Brown's story. These colors put Lawrence's sparing use of blood red, bright yellow, and rich blues into even greater relief.

The first panel of the series shows a crucified figure nailed to a bodeful black cross (figure 9.4). His hair hangs in jagged streaks, obscuring his face. Lawrence used this same technique to paint Brown throughout the series, making the Christ figure's identity ambiguous. Another man stands in the

shadow of the cross, alluding to the biblical figure John the Apostle, who alone stayed by Jesus during his crucifixion. The shared name suggests an association with Brown, who fashioned himself a latter-day apostle.[55]

Against a backdrop of black and deep blue storm clouds, red blood spills into the soil, portending the events of Virginia in 1859. Yellow nails hammered into the crucified body become weaponry in the hands of Brown and his men in later panels. Both in theme and color, Lawrence's first painting echoes Brown's final statement that the sin of slavery would "never be purged away but with blood." The imagery presents Brown as both Christ and disciple, but the painting's caption calls the abolitionist's religiosity into question. "John Brown," it identifies him, "a man who had a fanatical belief he was chosen by God to overthrow black slavery in America." Lawrence invoked the abolitionist's martyrdom by visually comparing him to Christ, but the caption questions Brown's extremism and Christ's own fanaticism. Thus, in addition to raising broader questions about violence, belief, and change, Lawrence complicated Brown's mythic stature from the very beginning of the series.

In the second panel, Lawrence began to narrate Brown's personal religiosity, his willingness to use violence, and his anguished need to find a solution to the evil of slavery (figure 9.5). Brown leads a prayer, flanked by obedient family members, weaponry, and a large Bible reminiscent of the Tubman painting. Out an open doorway stands a foreboding and leafless tree. Lawrence used the tree throughout the series to herald Brown's hanging, but he also included trees extensively in the Douglass and Tubman series.[56] In these earlier works, the tree represents the twisted and morally barren system of slavery, and Lawrence certainly cultivated the same associations in the Brown series. The rifles and broadswords evoke the abolitionist's eventual solution to his nation's original sin. The blood-red Bible pages summon Brown's particularly Old Testament–styled solution to slavery, highlighting Christ's blood as a cleansing agent. The bright yellow nails from the first panel now hold up Brown's rifles. In the abolitionist's first appearance, he is no hero, but he is certainly a patriarch.

Lawrence used these opening panels to establish Brown's bleak past.

(OPPOSITE) *Figure 9.4. Jacob Lawrence,* The Legend of John Brown, No. 1, *1977: "John Brown, a man who had a fanatical belief that he was chosen by God to overthrow black slavery in America." Ackland Art Museum, University of North Carolina at Chapel Hill; Ackland Fund;* © *2010 The Jacob and Gwendolyn Lawrence Foundation, Seattle/Artists Rights Society (ARS), New York.*

Lawrence hoped to paint more than Brown's antislavery triumphs. In panel 3, Brown surveys land. The caption describes his many business ventures and his hope that they would finance "his greater work[,] which was the abolishment of slavery." In the following panel, the result of these ventures has Brown praying desperately in a sparsely decorated room. The text explains that "his adventures failing him, he accepted poverty." The next painting shows Brown in the center of a huddled mass of people. The caption describes the abolitionist enlisting others for an attack on "slavery by force." Again, the result is far from heroic. Lawrence illustrated Brown's fanaticism, his dedication to abolition over the demands of his family and well-being. These scenes underscore the Brown family's haphazard existence before Kansas and Harpers Ferry and show a man struggling to figure out the relationship between his faith, his beliefs, and the circumstances of his life.

Lawrence also hoped to rekindle interest in Brown's kinship with black Americans. In panel 6, Brown offers weapons to three "colored people of the Adirondack woods." In panel 7, he reaches out in friendship to two blacks at his table. The caption informs viewers that these men were "worthy of his trust," so they could hear "his plans." In the Douglass series, Brown's invasion plans are painted as an ominous black document. Lawrence gave them clearer form in the Brown series's panel 8. Visually sparse, the painting shows the craggy Allegheny Mountains, the natural shelter for Brown's Underground Railroad of armed stations. In his provocative melding of past, present, and future, Lawrence colored the mountains in the Garveyite colors of African liberation.

Panels 9 through 12 bring viewers into the hagiographers' morass: Bleeding Kansas. Lawrence labeled the territory "the skirmish ground of the Civil War." The ninth painting firmly locates the Civil War's origins in the Kansas territorial battle; the ground runs red with blood and a burned-out cabin sits beneath the crooked tree of slavery, from which a body hangs. Unlike Brown's hagiographers, Lawrence did not avoid the violence and ambiguities of the Kansas conflict.

Panel 10's violent imagery belies the passive tone of the caption: "Those

(OPPOSITE) *Figure 9.5.* Jacob Lawrence, The Legend of John Brown, No. 2, *1977: "For 40 years, John Brown reflected on the hopeless and miserable condition of the slaves." Ackland Art Museum, University of North Carolina at Chapel Hill; Ackland Fund; © 2010 The Jacob and Gwendolyn Lawrence Foundation, Seattle/Artists Rights Society (ARS), New York.*

Figure 9.6. Jacob Lawrence, The Legend of John Brown, No. 10, *1977:*
"Those pro-slavery were murdered by those anti-slavery." Ackland Art Museum,
University of North Carolina at Chapel Hill; Ackland Fund; © *2010 The Jacob and*
Gwendolyn Lawrence Foundations, Seattle/Artists Rights Society (ARS), New York.

pro-slavery were murdered by those anti-slavery" (figure 9.6). The absence
of murderers from the image recalls Brown's vagueness about the Pottawatomie massacre, while the text treats this territorial violence as somewhat inevitable. The painting shows five murdered men: Brown's five Pottawatomie victims. A yellow spike juts out of the back of the central figure as
blood spills from the wound. A green and black snake slithers across the
foreground. The artist had used snakes before; in the fifth image of the Tubman cycle, Lawrence painted a black snake with forked tongue reaching out
toward an inert Tubman; "she first felt the sting of slavery when as a young
girl she was struck on the head with an iron bar by an enraged overseer."

In the tenth panel of *The Life of Harriet Tubman*, that same reptile
chases the slave liberator during her own escape from bondage. In that
series, black snakes are a clear metaphor for slavery. The green and black
snake, however, invokes an image well known to antebellum America, particularly to men like John Brown who claimed kinship with the Revolutionary generation and believed their actions were justified by this tradition.

Benjamin Franklin's snake woodcut of 1854, with the slogan "Join, or Die," introduced serpentine imagery into the American visual lexicon. Franklin's disjointed snake was meant to drive home the message that American liberty depended on the colonies' unity of purpose. That image was modified for Paul Revere's newspaper in the mid-1770s before being coiled and emblazoned on the first flag of the American Revolution (the Gadsden Flag) with the motto, "Don't Tread on Me." This same coiled snake appeared on the 1775 flag of the Culpeper, Virginia, Minutemen (with the accompanying motto "Liberty or Death") as well as the seal from a 1778 Georgia twenty-dollar bill (on which the Latin motto read, "Nemo me impune lacesset [No one will provoke me with impunity]"). Finally, an elongated yellow snake with red markings appeared on early flags of the United States Navy with the motto "Don't Tread on Me." In each of its applications, this snake was meant to represent the choice between liberty and death.

When Lawrence applied the reptile to territorial Kansas, particularly to the victims of Brown's Pottawatomie massacre, the message was twofold. Of course, these men were slavery supporters; they rejected liberty and must suffer the consequences. But the painter also drew on Franklin's snake. In an abolitionist context, "Join, or Die" meant that unity on the slavery question was a prerequisite for the United States to atone for its original sin. Brown could not profit from his role in the blood atonement because the painting vividly shows his rotting victims, one of whom has been stabbed in the back. Lawrence's snake situates both Bleeding Kansas and the Civil War in a timeline marked by the painful past and the ultimate destiny of the republic.[57]

Meditating over destiny drew Lawrence to characters poring over maps and plans.[58] Brown first appears in such a scenario in the Douglass series with his ominous black document. In panel 11 of *The Life of John Brown*, the abolitionist stoops over a map of the United States, now blood red. Over Harpers Ferry are railroad tracks, Brown's imagined armed pathway out of the South. An oil lamp illuminates the cross on the wall but leaves the abolitionist, his Bible, and three sidearms in relative darkness.[59] The painting is Lawrence's bluntest challenge to Brown as a legend; the use of light and color condemns using the abolitionist's religion as justification for his violence.[60]

While Brown presented himself to New England as a battle-hardened hero, Lawrence painted him in panel 14 as a humble beggar, dwarfed by looming images of Christ and the Virgin Mary. In this image, Christ's face is clearly visible, and Lawrence painted Brown to look very similar. Midway

Figure 9.7. Jacob Lawrence, The Legend of John Brown, No. 17, 1977: *"John Brown remained a full winter in Canada, drilling Negroes for his coming raid on Harpers Ferry." Ackland Art Museum, University of North Carolina at Chapel Hill; Ackland Fund;* © *2010 The Jacob and Gwendolyn Lawrence Foundation, Seattle/Artists Rights Society (ARS), New York.*

through the series, the painter sought again to interrogate this man's faith and his status as a Christian martyr. A few coins litter the tiny table that the abolitionist cowers behind. This is not the hero Sanborn and others marketed so aggressively. Lawrence avoided showing the abolitionist charming Thoreau, Emerson, or Charles Sumner. Instead, Brown is alone, with color and scale making him nearly pitiable.

Lawrence further reduced Brown's stature in panel 15. Brown appears tiny as he looks up for approval from his eight black recruits. The artist used panel 16 to showcase Brown's rescue of eleven (Lawrence mistakenly said twelve) enslaved blacks in Missouri. For one of Brown's most self-consciously heroic moments, Lawrence painted only half of his skulking figure. The image consists of footprints in the snow, blood shed in liberation, and the crooked tree of slavery.

Lawrence used more explicit juxtaposition for panel 17, which shows Brown "drilling Negroes for his coming raid on Harpers Ferry" (figure 9.7).

Much like the Missouri image, Brown appears stooped over, diminutive in contrast to the looming black soldiers. The abolitionist martyr is anonymous, faceless, and smaller than every one of his men. This painting is Lawrence's most explicit illustration of Brown's violent solution to slavery. Moreover, these are black revolutionaries and renegades taking the racial struggle into their own hands under arms. This was a radical message in 1941.

Panel 18 interrogates this racial revolution even more provocatively.[61] The painting shows a room overflowing with rifles, bullets, and revolvers. A ladder, mimicking the railroad tracks on the Alleghenies in Brown's map, leads to the open window of freedom. The weapons come together to form abstract illustrations of Brown's armed encampments in the mountains—that pathway to freedom he hoped to establish after the raid on Harpers Ferry. "John Brown stocked an old barn with guns and ammunition," Lawrence wrote. "He was ready to strike his first blow at slavery." The painter again asked his audience to consider if this historical violence was acceptable and whether it could be useful in the present and future. The caption made clear that Brown's invasion of Harpers Ferry was just the first blow in that long struggle for black freedom.

Two themes resonate throughout the final panels of the series: Brown's personal sacrifice to end slavery and the interracial partnership involved in the broader struggle for equality. Only the yellow pikes of the twenty-two raiders are visible in panel 19; it is tellingly impossible to determine which weapons are held by black raiders and which by white ones.[62] The caption explains that on "Sunday, October 16, 1859, John Brown with a company of 21 men, white and black, marched on Harpers Ferry." The bright yellow pikes, painted with Christ, in Kansas, and finally in slave country, underscore the artist's questions about the sordid legacy of slavery, violence, and the long struggle for racial justice. In the artist's hands, the pikes become symbols of the righteous and the damned.

Lawrence's final panels question the future shape of that continuing struggle. Panel 20 shows Brown and his men in the heat of battle. The caption explains that despite the golden pikes thrust overhead and Brown's golden cross broadsword, "defeat was a few hours off." In contrast to this commotion, Brown is slumped at the center of the penultimate panel, grasping a blood red cross, his face covered with the same jagged hair of the crucified figure from panel 1. Lawrence wanted viewers to contemplate Brown's martyrdom when his legacy was far from assured. In the image's almost despairing tone, Lawrence sought to remind his audience of Brown's (and America's) unfinished business.

Figure 9.8. Jacob Lawrence, The Legend of John Brown, No. 22, 1977:
*"John Brown was found 'Guilty of treason and murder in the 1st degree' and was
hanged in Charles Town, Virginia on December 2, 1859." Ackland Art Museum,
University of North Carolina at Chapel Hill; Ackland Fund; © 2010 The Jacob and
Gwendolyn Lawrence Foundation, Seattle/Artists Rights Society (ARS), New York.*

Understanding Brown's story and dramatizing past struggles for freedom could change the present and future.[63] Nowhere is that message plainer than in the final panel. In the first painting in the series, storm clouds form in the background of the crucifixion and blood takes root in the land. Lawrence used a very different crucifixion for the final panel.

Lawrence's conclusion does not enshrine Brown (figure 9.8). The abolitionist's body, stiff and angular, appears to float, not soar. Unlike Curry's Brown, who consumes the Kansas statehouse rotunda, Lawrence's Brown remains confined in a spacious canvas, suspended by the hangman's rope. The inclusion of that rope shows that Brown was still connected to the earth, not released to his heavenly afterlife. In this sense, he was hanged but also still hung; the jury was deadlocked as to his memory and meaning. These judgments rested in the outcome of the struggle he so doggedly pursued.[64]

Lawrence hoped Brown's story would raise questions, ones rooted in a communal experience and a desire to continue fighting for freedom and equality. "The inspiration to paint the Frederick Douglass, Harriet Tubman and John Brown series was motivated by historical events as told to us by the adults of our community . . . the black community," he recalled. "The relating of those events, for many of us, was not only very informative but also most exciting. To us, the men and women of these stories were strong, daring and heroic; therefore we could and did relate to these heroes by means of poetry, song and paint."[65]

The Life of John Brown was Lawrence's final historical series based on a single figure. Each series was designed to inspire viewers with the nation's history. The artist's vision of Brown narrated a black history that thrived in dialogue with the history of all America.[66] To be sure, the artist repeated elements of the black counternarrative of Brown that made the abolitionist a unique white man who could be trusted and even revered. From Frederick Douglass, who deftly navigated the hazards of that hagiography, to W. E. B. Du Bois, who embraced it sometimes at the expense of logic, Brown exposed frayed nerves at the racial divide. Lawrence drew on these understandings by situating Brown in a more complex narrative. Brown upended the notion that blacks and whites in the United States had separate fates just as he challenged the limits of interracial partnership with his example. He also inadvertently reenshrined foundational racial hierarchies as a white man worthy of worship. Lawrence tweaked this formula by plainly depicting Brown's violence, religion, and desire to personally fulfill Jefferson's infamous line, that the "tree of liberty must be refreshed from time to time with the blood of patriots & tyrants."[67]

Lawrence's eagerness to reconnect Brown to the glories of African American history certainly slanted the series' content. Viewed in concert with his other historical series, however, Brown was Lawrence's most sophisticated interrogation of the past, present, and future of America's racial struggle. The painter's approach to Brown as an artistic symbol and open question demanded answers about his nation's unfulfilled promises, particularly regarding the role of violence in precipitating the full measure of justice and equality.

John Brown is a symbol; a symbol of tragic futility, of unleashed human
emotion, of misguided fervor. But [he] is also a living part of the folklore
of the American people.

—Bert Loewenberg, 1941

Epilogue

CLIMAX AND HARBINGER

A Life as a Common Cause

The stage directions of Orson Welles's 1932 play *The Marching Song* described "a great unearthly light fall[ing] full upon" the "transfigured" protagonist. The play investigates one man's life through conflicting recollections to explore how myth can permanently obscure the truth. While Welles used an almost identical method in *Citizen Kane*, his 1941 cinematic masterpiece, the script explains that the unearthly light falls not on Charles Foster Kane but on "THE SWORD OF THE LORD AND OF GIDEON!": the abolitionist John Brown.[1]

While the enigmatic Kane will forever be his greatest creation, Welles first explored the creation of conflicting and contradictory myths through Brown. As many film historians and biographers have noted, *The Marching Song* articulated one of Welles's "lifelong obsessions," the distortion of memory and myth.[2] He observed many of these qualities in Brown, "an enigmatic public [figure] who is not really a three-dimensional personality, but a mask, a name, a voice, a cobweb of legends."[3] Exploring Brown through conflicting sounds and images, *The Marching Song* utilized contrasting screen projections of newspaper headlines from both sides of the Mason-Dixon line, offstage singing of "John Brown's Body," and other media underscoring the mystery of a man's life and its meaning.[4]

For Welles, Brown captured a series of irresolvable myths. In this vein, the abolitionist has stubbornly remained in the nation's consciousness into the new millennium. We continue to discuss Brown because of the intertwining fates of righteous violence, racial equality, and societal change. In Brown, Americans have long located a fractured reflection of our very

understanding of our past: its glorious moments of transformation, its horrific betrayals of principle, and the lessons it holds for our own lives. Since
his time in Kansas, Brown has powerfully inspired this ongoing argument.
Considering these qualities, the use of Brown's memory will likely never be
exhausted; his body will continue a-mouldering, and the abolitionist will
continue to be manipulated and misused.

By following Brown's more recent manifestations, particularly through
two wildly different icons of contemporary black America, the artist Kara
Walker and President Barack Obama, it is possible to underscore the difficulty of laying Brown to rest. In their art and writing, Walker and Obama
underscore Brown's living relevance and his potent symbolism. The abolitionist continues to allow Americans to wrestle with the meaning of the
past, the state of the present, and the shape of the county's future.

Following Brown from the 1950s to 2010, we are reminded of how furiously this figure resists the divisions that are typically applied to American
history. He is not bound by the antebellum era where he lived and died or
by the Civil War in which his name became the marching cry of the Union
army. Throughout Reconstruction, the Progressive Era, the New Deal, and
beyond, Brown resists periodization; any end date obscures his place in
American memory. With a rifle and a fervent belief in American freedom,
Brown transformed himself into a symbol on the Kansas prairies and became a martyr of interracial radicalism in Virginia in 1859. Embracing the
principles and means of his Revolutionary War forebears, Brown tried to
force Americans to honor the commitments of the nation's founding documents.

He failed in that mission. Although many have argued that the civil war
that quickly followed his execution was his legacy, from the moment of
his death, Brown became the property of Americans of all faiths, colors,
and political leanings. As Stephen Vincent Benét observed, with Brown
"moldering in the grave," his life became "a common cause."[5] While a dizzy-
ing range of Americans have found in Brown the symbol of their own cause,
at no time has the man been able to unite his countrymen. Each generation
has reinterpreted Brown according to the divisive politics of its time.

That volatile persistence has created anything but consensus. By the
1950s, there was as little accord as ever about the man and his deeds.
Whereas the first fifty years of his memory were dominated by hagiogra-
phies of Brown as an idealized (and often peaceful) martyr of freedom,
Brown's place in the popular imagination suffered after World War I. De-

spite the efforts of some on the left, a collection of artists, writers, and historians succeeded in transforming Brown into a criminal and a madman.

In the midst of the civil rights movement, the legendary Southern historian C. Vann Woodward synthesized these visions of Brown. Woodward contributed his essay "John Brown's Private War" to the collection *America in Crisis: Fourteen Crucial Episodes in American History*.[6] The essay was later featured in Woodward's *The Burden of Southern History* (1960), published just after the hundredth anniversary of Brown's execution. Woodward's essay summarized the meaning of this martyr for a new generation of students, academics, and laypeople.[7]

Decrying the efforts of the fourteen biographers that had preceded Robert Penn Warren, Woodward dismissed these "legend makers" and the man they had enshrined. Among his other critiques of Brown, Woodward derided the abolitionist for dragging his family "along in want and at times in something approaching destitution."[8] Accepting the precarious conclusions of Kansas historian James Malin, Woodward labeled Brown a petty criminal, arguing that the Pottawatomie massacre "would seem to have put [Brown] forever beyond the pale of association with intelligent opponents of slavery."[9] Woodward explained that Brown had not led the murders for the cause of abolition, but in order to steal horses. Underpinning this baseless assertion, Woodward argued that "intelligent" opponents of slavery could not and should not accept violence as a means to end slavery, a position that conveniently ignored the brutality and violence of American slavery and the system's role in Brown's personal evolution.

Attacking Brown's supporters for their higher-law hypocrisy, Woodward ridiculed the cultural and moral aristocracy of the antebellum North. These misguided men, Thoreau, Emerson, and dozens of others, formed a "cult dedicated" to "idealizing [John Brown] as a symbol of the moral order and social purpose of the Northern cause."[10] Woodward quoted Warren's 1929 potshot that Brown "should not have deceived a child, but [he] deceived a generation."[11] Like John Steuart Curry, Woodward saw Brown's violence as inexcusable, not just for the part that bloodshed played in the sectional collapse, but for its place in America's present and future.

More insidiously, Woodward echoed the Revisionist historians in decrying Brown for unnecessarily arousing antagonism between North and South.[12] Woodward argued that the Civil War was caused not by slavery or Southern extremism but by the swirling of depersonalized and blameless forces. "Paranoia continued to induce counterparanoia, each antagonist infecting the other reciprocally, until the vicious spiral ended in war."[13] Brown began that vicious spiral, Woodward reasoned; the war could have been avoided if this violent criminal had not indulged the misguided North.

Woodward condemned Brown's violence and ridiculed his beliefs. Brown's false righteousness prompted his invasion of Virginia, which in turn, created the atmosphere of extremism and mistrust that boiled over into the Civil War. With busloads of Northerners about to journey southward in pursuit of racial justice, Woodward's essay was rife with contemporary relevance. It was no coincidence that this condemnation appeared as the contest for civil rights reached a series of crossroads. As part of the broader pursuit of equality, black leaders began questioning the pacifist model of Martin Luther King Jr. Not surprisingly, nearly all these figures evoked John Brown in their public discourse. However, King, arguably the most important thinker on social justice and racial equality in the second half of the twentieth century, avoided Brown completely.[14] King had countless opportunities to discuss Brown, and his silence is especially noteworthy because he was the keynote speaker at a centennial celebration of John Brown at the University of Minnesota in 1959. The event was described as an opportunity to discuss "the relevance of John Brown's raid to the Negro problem today." King delivered his address without once mentioning the abolitionist.[15]

Although both Brown and King believed that America was a project worth salvaging, King proposed a contrary set of intertwining steps toward that end. Brown's experience in antebellum America showed him the inevitability, necessity, and legitimacy of violence as a catalyst for transformative change. King's experience in the twentieth century led him to the opposite conclusion. Both men believed that race was an illegitimate basis for social organization, but King's life and mission were largely a repudiation of Brown's. With his silence on the radical abolitionist, King refused to honor Brown's actions and beliefs by awkwardly endorsing or condemning him. Instead, King led by example, not through Brown.

In contrast, Malcolm X chose to use Brown, directly confronting C. Vann Woodward, Robert Penn Warren, and popular interpretations of Brown as a villainous madman. "White people call John Brown a nut," Malcolm said in a speech to the Organization of Afro-American Unity in 1964. "Go read the history, go read what all of them say about John Brown. They're trying to make it look like he was a nut, a fanatic. . . . Why I would be afraid to get near John Brown if I go by what other white folks say about him." The radical black leader readily identified the cause of this treatment. "They depict him in this image because he was willing to shed blood to free the slaves. And any white man who is ready and willing to shed blood for your freedom — in sight of other whites, he's nuts. . . . So when you want to know good white folks in history where black people are concerned, go read the history of John Brown."[16]

Brown's ability to raise radical conceptions of violence, equality, and change laid bare the chasm between King and Malcolm. "I totally disagree with many of [Malcolm X's] political and philosophical views," King told Alex Haley in 1965. "Violence is not going to solve our problem." "I feel that Malcolm has done himself and our people a great disservice," King continued. "Urging Negroes to arm themselves and prepare to engage in violence, as he has done, can reap nothing but grief."[17] Malcolm X's response was simple. John Brown was "the only good white the country's ever had," he explained in 1965. "If you are for me, when I say *me* I mean us, our people — then you have to be willing to do as old John Brown did."[18]

Other black Americans found compelling historical evidence for Brown's use of violence. Robert F. Williams was another leader seeking alternatives to the peaceful protest model personified by King. The FBI monitored Williams because he publicized his willingness to use weapons. One agent told J. Edgar Hoover that Williams had become "something of a 'John Brown' to Negroes . . . and they will do anything for him."[19] Williams had more than just an affinity with Brown; he claimed to always carry a copy of Thoreau's "Plea for Captain John Brown" in his pocket.[20] Williams cherished Thoreau's admonishment to "never have anything to do with any war, unless it were a war for liberty."[21]

Throughout the 1950s and 1960s, that war led many to carefully consider Brown's righteous violence. H. Rap Brown personified this transition to more radical solutions. Although he had once served as director of the Student Nonviolent Coordinating Committee, H. Rap Brown eventually became the justice minister of the Black Panther Party. Infamous for his statements that "violence is as American as cherry pie" and "if America don't come around, we going to burn it down," it is unsurprising that he referred to John Brown with some frequency.[22] In addition to calling the abolitionist "the blackest white man anyone had ever known," he also commented that "John Brown was the only white man I could respect and he is dead."[23]

John Brown's adoption by groups like the Panthers represented the abolitionist's increasing distance from mainstream American discourse. His extreme dedication to a cause and willingness to use violence to achieve his goals intensified his association with fringe groups on the political left and right. The Weather Underground, the violent far left group of the late 1960s and early 1970s, named its newsletter *Osawatomie* after the site of Brown's baptism of violence. The paper identified itself as "the revolutionary voice" that would reveal socialism as the solution to America's problems. Inspired by Brown's violence, the Weather Underground expressed its "certainty that we will see revolution in our lifetime."[24]

At this time, Brown largely ceased to be the subject of mainstream works of visual and literary art. Instead, new groups began to ignore his beliefs and utilize him solely as a representative of revolutionary violence or simple extremism. Brown's pursuit of liberty and equality for black Americans was overshadowed by his use of violence. During the 1980s, a series of abortion clinics in Florida were bombed, burgled, and ransacked. John Burt, an ex-Marine convicted for his role in the violence, had been inspired by many historical figures, but he singled out Brown. Perhaps, he speculated, the events would become "like Harpers Ferry, [which brought] the evils of slavery into focus." "These bombings," Burt reasoned, "may do the same thing on the abortion issue."[25]

The anti-abortion movement's embrace of Brown's moral guidance and violence was a signal of the abolitionist's precarious future. Stripped of his racial purpose, Brown might become a mere symbol of violent extremism. Just as radicals appeared to have hijacked Brown as a symbol, the abolitionist began to reemerge in American art, perhaps most strikingly in the work of black artist Kara Walker.

Born in Stockton, California, in 1969, Walker spent her teenage years in the Atlanta suburb of Stone Mountain after her father was offered a position at Georgia State University. Stone Mountain was not merely the birthplace of the modern-day Ku Klux Klan but the site of annual Klan rallies into the 1980s. Like the poet Stephen Vincent Benét after his move to Georgia in 1911, Walker experienced severe culture shock in Stone Mountain. However, as a black woman, Walker constantly had to confront more than the moonlight-and-magnolia image of the antebellum South that Atlanta openly celebrated.[26] For Walker, the social and cultural legacies of the Jim Crow era were a living reality.

When Walker became an artist, particularly after she began graduate school at the Rhode Island School of Design, she avoided depicting blacks to pursue more "universal" subject matter. "When I took a step back," she recalled, "I realized [my art] was Eurocentric, white-male identified." She responded by shifting to a medium that twisted that perspective against itself. Working with silhouettes, a form popular among eighteenth-century middle-class whites, Walker began creating visually arresting tableaus about race, sex, and other contemporary taboos.

"I often compare my method of working to that of a well-meaning freed woman in a Northern state who is attempting to delineate the horrors of Southern slavery," Walker said, with "some paper and a pen knife and some people she'd like to kill."[27] In Walker's hands, these cut paper silhouettes, black profiles on white gallery and museum walls, offer a devastating panorama of race in American history.[28] The majority of Walker's art depicts interracial antebellum scenes with all manner of sexual, historical, and bodily horrors: kinky-headed slave women perform fellatio on plantation owners, a man roasts the heads of slaves over an open fire, a white boy seems to hang from the breast of a topless slave woman. Rape, incest, torture, and murder all figure prominently in Walker's work. The artist draws these shadows of history and memory from racist boilerplate like D. W. Griffith's *Birth of a Nation*, abolitionist fantasy like Harriet Beecher Stowe's *Uncle Tom's Cabin*, and the many stereotypes of contemporary American culture. These characters populate Walker's surreal landscapes.[29] Visually straightforward, her work is simultaneously horrifying, titillating, and captivating.[30]

Although Walker's art has enjoyed enormous popularity, her use of racial stereotypes and sexuality has been the source of constant controversy.[31] "You know when it comes to our sordid racist past and our sordid racist relationship with *Race*," Walker told an interviewer, "there is going to be some shouting."[32] Regardless of criticism, Walker has maintained an unwavering focus on the legacy of America's great trauma of slavery.[33] Her "work is all about the now," Walker has written, because "a black subject in the present tense is a container for specific pathologies from the past and is growing and feeding off those maladies. Racist pathology is the muck."[34]

Walker is powerfully engaged with the nation's historical memory and uses the past to forcefully critique contemporary society. Walker told an audience in 1999 that "it was not until I escaped the South (where I still found it impossible to speak) that I began to seek out any references to Interracial Romance, American Chattel Slavery, Black Womanhood and the Fictions of the South."[35] African American history "has been absorbed and worked in strange ways," Walker told one interviewer. "That's what I wind up drawing from in the popular consciousness. Not just contemporary black intellectual thought, but popular black thought."[36]

Walker documents national understandings through the visual tropes of American art and the contested narrative of American history. Walker's attraction to a "particularly racialized history" is achieved, according to the art historian Gwendolyn DuBois Shaw, by "radically transfiguring and subverting specific sources culled from nineteenth-century American visual, political, and literary culture: from slave narratives and sentimental novels, from abolitionist propaganda and scientific literature."[37]

The immense power of Walker's art is that the past and the present meld together, circulating constantly, in a dynamic flow. Walker wrestles with "memory, whether or not there is such a thing as a past and a present, or if the present is just like the past with new clothes on."[38] Walker wrote in an early exhibition catalogue that "history is carried like a pathology, a cyclical melodrama immersed in artifice and unable to function without it."[39] Again and again, the artist has described her goal as getting people to think about "how it is that we produce and reproduce memory."[40]

Given her interests, it is unsurprising that Walker has been drawn to John Brown more than once. Her investment in America's visual history is plainly evident in her use of Civil War *Harper's Weekly* illustrations, frontispieces from abolitionist literature, and her trademark silhouettes. But one of Walker's keenest historical refutations is a large watercolor and gouache painting from 1996 simply titled *John Brown* (figure E.1).

In this painting, Walker not only rejects the most infamous of Brown's legends, his embrace of a slave child as he heads to the gallows, but she twists the teleology of Brown's artistic representations in an effort to completely reorient (as well as disorient) our understandings of the abolitionist. Walker confronts the stories and visual threads of Whittier, Ransom, Noble, Hovenden, Sanborn, and others by altering the power dynamic of the embrace. Walker "almost obsessively" examines "social conflicts that have a racial or racist overtone, thinking about the ways that the romanticized version of black history comes into play as a dynamic."[41] In Walker's revisioning of this classic image, the slave child suckles at Brown's dried-out teat. This initial portrait of Brown is tame next to Walker's other Brown image, part of a series of etchings inspired by Goya. *Untitled (John Brown)* was included in Walker's first gallery show, the exhibition that launched her career (figure E.2). In this image, Brown performs fellatio on the slave child as the mother kicks a white child under her skirt.

In both images, Walker emphasizes the abolitionist's last moments as a spectacle. She tweaks the visual and historical myths in order to challenge Brown's relevance to another generation. As in nearly all her work, Walker forces viewers to acknowledge their complicity in these voyeuristic moments.[42] "Part of my project has really been about simplifying," Walker has

Figure E.1. Kara Walker, John Brown, 1996. Watercolor and gouache on paper, 65 × 51 inches. Sikkema Jenkins & Co., New York.

Figure E.2. Kara Walker, Untitled (John Brown), *1997. Etching with Chine Collé, 18 × 14 inches. Sikkema Jenkins & Co., New York; © Landfall Press Inc. and Kara Walker.*

noted, "reducing to very easily graspable pairs of opposites, object/ground, figure/ground, black/white, sex/death, love/hate, good/bad."[43] Walker returns again and again to the antebellum American South for those opposites, and in Brown, as Albion Tourgée explained in the 1880s, there was good, bad, black, white, and more.

For Walker, there was also a rich visual history. "I have always used historic picture files as references," Walker remarked in one interview. "Going into picture files and going to research an image. . . . They are works I could draw from as freely as I might a Delacroix or something."[44] Walker is quick to point out that she complicates the history from the start: "I am too aware of the role of my overzealous imagination interfering in the basic facts of history. A collusion of fact and fiction . . . has informed me probably since day one."[45]

In both Brown pieces, Walker, to borrow the words of art historian Phillip Vergne, "mutilates the constructed national memory and fabricated myth of self-sacrificing white liberators perpetuated by such characters, and harshly criticizes submissive faith in and dependence on such martyr myths."[46] In the hands of previous artists, particularly those that painted the embrace of the slave child as a moment worthy of reverence, Brown was the martyr. This dynamic guided encounters between the races long before the abolitionist, but the John Browns of Sanborn and Villard underscored the importance of the white liberator-martyr. This trope has been, in the words of Linda Williams, the "fundamental mode by which American mass culture has 'talked to itself' about the enduring moral dilemma of race."[47] Whether it be Abraham Lincoln as the Great Emancipator or Brown the violent liberator, this white hero has been immensely important in discussions of race and American history.

In the first image, Walker rejects this hero. In so doing, she also attacks the spurious premise of the *New York Tribune* article from 1859 and the subsequent paintings by Ransom, Noble, and Hovenden. The positioning of the central characters changes the power dynamic immediately. The slave child no longer requires Brown's blessing. Walker's rejection of both the nineteenth-century white saint and the black revolutionist of Lawrence and Du Bois is clear. For Walker, Brown's martyrdom is a problem for all Americans; neither heroic vision of the abolitionist clarifies or solves the nation's racial problems.

Both images show Walker's typical tweaking of artistic and historical sources. In this case, Walker deftly reimagines Caritas Romana (Roman Charity) for Brown and the postracial moment.[48] Rubens, Carvaggio, and

Vermeer all painted versions of the ancient story of Pero secretly breastfeeding her father Cimron after his sentence of death by starvation.[49] Walker alters Caritas Romana in two different ways, both equally unflattering to Brown's legacy in American memory. Walker's image suggests that Brown is unable to provide sustenance to African Americans. Unlike the generations of plantation children raised on slave milk, Brown is unable to reciprocate.[50] Walker's conclusion is clear: Brown has limited importance to African Americans. The painting is an emphatic answer to the questions of Jacob Lawrence's series of Brown paintings, which inquired whether the abolitionist was a martyr for black freedom. Walker also confronts the long history of African American adulation of Brown. As Gwendolyn DuBois Shaw explains, "Walker highlights the moral vacuity of Brown's status as a martyr for African American culture." Brown's pained expression and stretched-out teat underscore that this man is no martyr; he has not even been helpful in survival.[51]

It is fascinating to consider Walker's painting as a draft version for her untitled etching. For that work, Walker makes the visual cues of her artistic predecessors impossible to miss. An armed soldier, reminiscent of Ransom, Noble, and Hovenden, stands guard over the scene. Like the limp noose of the Hovenden painting and taut one in Lawrence's final Brown panel, the bearded abolitionist, in leather codpiece and boots, has a thick rope around his neck. As a nappy-headed slave woman kicks a white child out from under her skirt, she offers her naked boy to Brown, who sucks the black child's penis.[52] Inverting the original image and Caritas Romana, Brown engages in an act of sexual deviance, submission, and sustenance.[53] Where the first painting establishes the folly of African Americans' enshrining Brown, Walker's etching condemns the white liberal power structure for honoring Brown as a martyr-hero. In this sense, Walker is equally appalled by white liberal celebration of Brown the saintly patriarch as she is by the alternative black radical narrative of Brown the crusading revolutionist.

Like *John Brown*, the etching invokes the sexual perversions and inversions of Caritas Romana. But in making the slave child's penis the vessel of survival, Walker challenges Brown even more dramatically. Walker's etching raises questions about the quality of Brown's racial egalitarianism that have long loomed over the abolitionist. The later image also complicates the sexual exploitations of slavery and abolitionism.[54] Brown is not simply useless to black Americans, but he leeches off of them, deviantly, for his survival, gratification, and approval.

To be sure, there is a quality in Walker's work that delights in shocking audiences. There is always humor in the horrors she depicts; Walker clearly enjoys the role of iconoclastic provocateur.[55] However, in the depth of her readings of the visual and documentary history of gender, race, slavery, and violence, Walker proves the seriousness of her messages. Walker says she would be happy if people, when they looked at her work, felt ashamed, "ashamed because they have . . . simply believed in the project of modernism."[56] The shameless belief in progress, and in the absence of right and wrong in history, is anathema to her imagery and purpose. Where Ransom, Noble, Hovenden, and Lawrence sought in Brown a lesson of redemption for past traumas, Walker sees none.

"I don't know how much I believe in redemptive stories, even though people want them and strive for them," Walker has explained. "They're satisfied with stories of triumph over evil, but then triumph is a dead end. Triumph never sits still. Life goes on. People forget and make mistakes. Heroes are not completely pure, and villains aren't purely evil. I'm interested in the continuity of conflict, the creation of racist narratives, or nationalist narratives, or whatever narratives people use to construct a group identity and to keep themselves whole—such activity has a darker side to it, since it allows people to lash out at whoever's not in the group. That's a constant thread that flummoxes me."[57]

In *John Brown* and *Untitled (John Brown)*, Walker takes the dominant narratives of Brown's place in American memory and rejects them almost violently. She does so to challenge our sense of racial identity, just as her challenge threatens our understanding of the past. The art historian Robert F. Reid-Pharr argues that Walker questions whether "there is a clear and constant connection between current generations of Black Americans and enslaved Africans, or between white Americans and the enslavers of Africans."[58]

The writer Ralph Ellison clarified the meaning of these tensions in our racial identities. "Obviously the experiences of Negroes—slavery, the grueling and continuing fight for full citizenship since Emancipation, the stigma of color, the enforced alienation which continually knifes into natural identification with our country—have not been [those] of white Americans," he explained. "And though as passionate believers in democracy Negroes identify themselves with the broader American ideals, their sense of reality springs, in part, from an American experience which most white men not only have not had, but one with which they are reluctant to identify themselves even when presented in forms of the imagination."[59]

Walker's art visualizes, questions, and elaborates on Ellison's divisions.

Her images ask us to parse America's traumatic racial identities, sorting the various pieces of cultural and historical detritus. John Brown, for one, is simply a mess of superimposed identities. Walker argues with these images that the abolitionist has not helped Americans navigate their past and will not help them solve these deep conflicts in identity for the future. Brown's confused amalgamation of racial taboos, revolutionary violence, and sex are rickety staves. To the open question of Lawrence's *Legend of John Brown*, Kara Walker has answered emphatically that we should stop employing Brown's baggage.

And yet, as one has to expect from Brown, the pendulum simply continues to swing.[60] The most powerful symbol of postracial America, the forty-fourth president, Barack Obama, returns to John Brown in his own meditation on the legacy of slavery, the potent use of righteous violence, and the possibility of change. Obama lays out this elaborate framework in his second book, *The Audacity of Hope*. "The Constitution envisions a road map by which we marry passion to reason, the ideal of individual freedom to the demands of community," he writes. "But only once has the conversation broken down completely, . . . over the one subject the Founders refused to talk about," slavery. Clarifying slavery's divisive role, Obama uses the Declaration of Independence to explain that the "spirit of liberty didn't extend, in the minds of the Founders, to the slaves who worked their fields, made their beds, and nursed their children."[61]

"Deliberation alone could not provide the slave his freedom or cleanse America of its original sin," Obama continues. "In the end, it was the sword that would sever his chains." The first person to wield that sword was John Brown. "The best I can do in the face of our history is remind myself that it has not always been the pragmatist, the voice of reason, or the force of compromise, that has created the conditions for liberty." After mentioning the efforts of other abolitionists, Obama comes to his conclusion: "It was the wild-eyed prophecies of John Brown, his willingness to spill blood and not just words on behalf of his visions, that helped force the issue of a nation half slave and half free."[62]

Campaigning to become the first black president of the United States, Obama came under intense criticism for his association with the radical Reverend Jeremiah Wright. That association generated what is considered the most important speech of his campaign. In "A More Perfect Union," delivered in Philadelphia, Obama elucidated the reasons Brown remains such a potent medium.[63] "Working together we can move beyond some of our old racial wounds," Obama argued. "In fact, we have no choice if we are to continue on the path of a more perfect union." That means, he explained, "continuing to insist on a full measure of justice in every aspect of American life."[64]

Because John Brown gave his life in pursuit of that more perfect union, for some small piece of that justice, he remains a part of America's cultural consciousness. In *Audacity of Hope,* Obama explains that it is impossible to "brush aside the magnitude of the injustice done, or erase the ghosts of generations past, or ignore the open wound, the aching spirit, that ails this country still." "The blood of slaves reminds us that our pragmatism can sometimes be moral cowardice. Lincoln, and those buried at Gettysburg, remind us that we should pursue our own absolute truths only if we acknowledge that there may be a terrible price to pay."[65]

Brown wanted to alert his nation to "the accumulated wrongs and sufferings of more than three million [slaves]."[66] His life, death, and symbolism, twisted and labyrinthine, speak to our desire to make sense of the present and future through the past. Brown's principled purpose in invading Virginia, however clouded by personal glory, racial paternalism, and religious delusion, has always been confounded by his willingness to shed blood for his cause. As the characters and episodes in these pages have shown, Brown has been a conduit for conversations about violence, equality, and change for so long that it is hard to imagine his absence.

Obama highlights these contradictions in "A More Perfect Union." The journey to that destination, he explains, "means embracing the burdens of our past without becoming victims of our past."[67] Brown captures the obligations and hazards of historical memory. Misusing him through partisan means has led many astray, but embracing the burdens of the nation's past, to which Brown has been such an easy conduit, should finally lay him to rest. Until then, John Brown will live, forcing new generations to confront the incessant violence, racial traumas, and stubborn conservatism of the nation's past. He should be a beacon, not a martyr-hero or criminal madman but the wonderful and frightening combination of nobility and folly that has guided the United States since its inception.

Notes

Abbreviations

BDL	Bartow Darrach Letters, 1852–56, Beinecke Rare Book Library, Yale University, New Haven, CT
BSC	Boyd B. Stutler Collection, West Virginia State Archives, Charleston
DD Papers	Donald Davidson Papers, Special Collections, Jean and Alexander Heard Library, Vanderbilt University, Nashville, TN
JBL	John Brown Family Letters: Kansas, 1855–56, Beinecke Rare Book Library, Yale University, New Haven, CT
JSC Papers	John Steuart Curry Papers, Archives of American Art, Smithsonian Institution, Washington, DC
KSHS	Kansas State Historical Society, Topeka
OGV	Oswald Garrison Villard
OGV-JB Papers	Oswald Garrison Villard–John Brown Papers, Columbia Rare Book Library, Columbia University, New York, NY
OGV Papers	Oswald Garrison Villard Papers, Houghton Library, Harvard University, Cambridge, MA
RPW	Robert Penn Warren
RPW Papers	Robert Penn Warren Papers, Beinecke Rare Book Library, Yale University, New Haven, CT
SVB	Stephen Vincent Benét
SVB Papers	Stephen Vincent Benét Papers, Beinecke Rare Book Library, Yale University, New Haven, CT
WEBDB Papers	W. E. B. Du Bois Papers, University of Massachusetts, Amherst
WRB	William Rose Benét

Introduction

1. John Brown, "Statement," December 2, 1859. Brown's statement was widely reported following his execution, notably in the *Charleston (SC) Courier*, December 15, 1859, and the *Lowell (MA) Daily Citizen*, December 20, 1859, among others. See also John Brown Folder, OGV-JB Papers.

2. The paternalism of American abolitionists, including John Brown, has been much debated by historians. Recent work by John Stauffer (*Black Hearts of Men*) and Stanley Harrold (*Subversives*) has upended the negative assessments that long dominated the field. For those, see James Stewart, *Holy Warriors*; Pease and Pease, *They Who Would Be Free*; and Rossbach, *Ambivalent Conspirators*.

3. Quoted in Higginson, *Henry Wordsworth Longfellow*, 271.

4. Tourgée, *Hot Plowshares*, 608–9.

5. The abolitionists James Redpath and Franklin Sanborn, the philosophers Henry David Thoreau and Ralph Waldo Emerson, the activists W. E. B. Du Bois and Oswald Garrison Villard, the writers Stephen Vincent Benét and Robert Penn Warren, and the artists Thomas Hovenden, John Steuart Curry, and Jacob Lawrence were all drawn to Brown because he spoke to their historical moments in the thundering voice of a masculine hero or antihero. Not only did each man find in Brown something to apply to their historical moments, but all seemed to personally identify with parts of Brown's persona or become mesmerized by his heroic (or antiheroic) actions. Kara Walker's art attempts to dismantle this mythology through these very constructions.

6. Davis, "Remarks in the U.S. Senate," 260–61.

7. Even a decade into the twenty-first century, it is difficult to find middle ground with John Brown. Contemporary terrorism has recently prompted yet another round of reconsiderations. Descriptions of Brown asa "freedom fighter" or "terrorist" compare him to Osama Bin Laden and Timothy McVeigh. For more on Brown as a modern terrorist, see the debate between the historians Paul Finkelman and Clayton Cramer, "Analogies: Was Timothy McVeigh Our John Brown?" See also Blight, "John Brown."

8. This book explores visual art—mainly paintings, prints, and lithographs—as one manifestation of ongoing interpretations of Brown's symbolism. By literature, I refer to the fiction, poetry, and biography focusing on Brown. Nearly all of the art and literature discussed in these pages has an activist dimension because it was used to support a cause. However, there are also more strictly defined moments of activism in these pages. In such instances, *activism* refers to historical episodes where Brown was invoked in a physical demonstration or memorial.

9. Redpath, *Public Life*. Redpath has rightly been designated the chief "propagandist of the Brown legend." See Oates, *Our Fiery Trial*, 22–23. Following Redpath's method of glossing over the more problematic aspects of Brown's career were similar works by Brown's associates Franklin Sanborn and Richard Hinton. Sanborn, *Life and Letters*; Hinton, *John Brown and His Men*.

10. Du Bois, *John Brown* (1909); OGV, *John Brown*.

11. See Malin, *John Brown*, for Brown as a horse thief with no antislavery motives and Nevins, *Emergence of Lincoln*, for "Brown the madman." These works established the practice of labeling Brown as a psychopath and a monomaniac. See also Genovese, *Roll, Jordan Roll*; Donald and Randall, *Civil War and Reconstruction*; and Potter, *Impending Crisis*, for treatments of Brown with the derision and bluntness of the psychiatric straitjacket.

12. Oates, *To Purge This Land*; Reynolds, *John Brown*; Carton, *Patriotic Treason*. Of these, Oates and Reynolds follow Villard's painstaking (and often long-winded) research while Carton synthesizes and consolidates. Carton's is by far the most grounded and readable of the biographies. Merrill D. Peterson's short guide to Browniana, *John Brown*, supplements

the basic biographical material and offers a glimpse of the many rewards of Brown's memory. Bruce Ronda's recent *Reading the Old Man* elaborates on Peterson but focuses mainly on literary interpretations of Brown. Robert E. McGlone's new study, *John Brown's War*, is a meticulous account of Brown's life that unfortunately repeats many of the distortions of Malin, Donald, and Potter.

13. For this, Alfred Young, *Shoemaker and the Tea Party*, is a particular inspiration. Charting the public memory of the revolution and the Boston Tea Party through a shoemaker named George Hewes, Young expounds on the troubling mobilization of the past for partisan purposes and the moments when public memory is created and altered.

14. Memory studies enjoyed a certain vogue in the academy during the late 1990s and early 2000s. Merrill Peterson's two studies of major American presidents, *Lincoln in American Memory* and *The Jefferson Image*, are particularly notable. See also Kammen, *Mystic Chords of Memory* and *Meadows of Memory*. For more recent efforts, see Brundage, *Southern Past*; and Cobb, *Away down South*. The Spanish filmmaker Luis Buñuel argued that "memory is what makes our lives. Life without memory is no life at all. . . . Our memory is our coherence, our reason, our feeling, even our acting." Buñuel, *My Last Sigh*, 25. In the *Man Who Mistook His Wife for a Hat*, a fascinating book of clinical tales that features Buñuel, the popular neurologist Oliver Sacks offers several extended meditations surrounding amnesiac patients that show just how devastating the present can be without the "mooring" that an understanding of the past provides.

15. David W. Blight argues that "the study of historical memory might therefore be defined as the study of cultural struggle, of contested truths, of moments, or even texts in history that thresh out rival versions of the past which are in turn put to the service of the present." Blight, "W. E. B. Du Bois," 46.

Chapter 1

1. John Brown to Henry L. Stearns, July 15, 1857, John Brown Folder, OGV-JB Papers. An elderly Stearns recalled in 1902 that Brown wrote this letter at young Henry's request, in exchange for donating his allowance to the cause. But George Stearns, writing to give Brown access to one thousand dollars in Massachusetts Kansas Committee funds, asked Brown to write his son. George Stearns to John Brown, April 18, 1857, John Brown Folder, OGV-JB Papers.

2. Robert McGlone calls this Brown's "aphoristic memory" in *John Brown's War*, 53.

3. William Stevens, *London Spectator*, quoted in Winkley, *John Brown the Hero*.

4. "Mr. Bell's Story," *St. Louis Globe Democrat*, April 29, 1888.

5. See Alfred Young, *Shoemaker and the Tea Party*; Purcell, *Sealed with Blood*; and Raphael, *People's History*.

6. For more on the emergence of Calvinism in revolutionary America, see Hoogstra, *American Calvinism*; Howard, *Conscience and Slavery*; Joseph Washington, *Race and Religion*; Hirrel, *Children of Wrath*; and Gura, *American Transcendentalism*.

7. Disregarding the colorful tales in Brown's letter to Henry L. Stearns of July 15, 1857, there is compelling evidence that Brown was sympathetic to abolitionism long before he took up an active role in the movement. See McGlone, *John Brown's War*, 80–85.

8. Brown's eventual engagement with abolitionism, particularly his embrace of violent

means, threw into question what being an abolitionist really meant. Was financial or moral support of the cause enough?

9. It was the years in Hudson that produced the slightly less apocryphal story of Brown disciplining John Brown Jr. Lashing the boy with "blue-beech switch," he stopped halfway through and ordered the boy to deliver the remaining blows to his own (Brown Sr.'s) back. Brown Jr. and biographers alike have used the moment to show Brown practicing as he preached that the innocent should suffer equally for the collective guilt of mankind. See Sanborn, *Life and Letters*, 91–93.

10. When a mob came to destroy Lovejoy's printing press in Alton, Illinois, he was killed by a shotgun blast to the back. See Dillon, *Elijah P. Lovejoy*.

11. "Lovejoy Aftermath," John Brown Folder, OGV-JB Papers.

12. Oates, *To Purge This Land*, 69.

13. Sandage, *Born Losers*, 5.

14. Foner, *Life and Writings*, 49–50.

15. This portrait was just recently discovered and is thought to be the first one that Brown commissioned from Washington. However, Brown's jacket appears to be the same in both portraits, leading many to believe they were taken in the same session. Some scholars believe the portraits were taken closer to Brown's first meeting with Frederick Douglass in 1848. See Frederick Douglass to William C. Nell in *The North Star*, February 11, 1848. The daguerreotype, discovered in 2007, had stayed in John Brown's family through five generations. The other Augustus Washington portrait of Brown was auctioned in 1997 (for $115,000) and donated to the Smithsonian Institution's National Portrait Gallery.

16. "This extremely rare and riveting portrait . . . was made by the remarkable African-American photographer Augustus Washington," said Theresa Leininger-Miller, an art history professor at the University of Cincinnati. See Terry Kinney, "Rare John Brown Daguerreotype Sells for $97,750 in Cincinnati Auction," *Columbus (OH) Dispatch*, December 7, 2007.

17. Sandage, *Born Losers*, 188.

18. Carton, *Patriotic Treason*, 109–12.

19. "A Durable Memento: Augustus Washington, African American Daguerreotypist." http://www.npg.si.edu/exh/awash/brown2.htm. Brown's friend and chronicler Richard Hinton mentions a third Washington daguerreotype, depicting Brown alongside John Thomas, a free black man from Springfield, Massachusetts. Thomas holds Brown's "banneret marked 'S.P.W.'—Subterranean Pass Way," the name of Brown's imagined armed underground railroad. The whereabouts of this image are unknown, and Hinton is the only source for its existence. Hinton, *John Brown and His Men*, 716.

20. John Stauffer, in *Black Hearts of Men*, was the first scholar to carefully parse the meaning of Brown's self-conscious imagery. Louis DeCaro, in *"Fire from the Midst of You,"* 153–54, argues that Brown's imagery at this time was aspirational. See also DeCaro, "John Brown the Abolitionist."

21. Sandage, *Born Losers*, 188.

22. Richard Henry Dana, "How We Met John Brown," *Atlantic Monthly*, July 1871, 6–7; rpt. in Hinton, *John Brown and His Men*, 684. See also William S. McFeeley, introduction to Quarles, *Allies for Freedom*, vii.

23. Charles Torrey, a Yale graduate, had formulated similar plans to Brown's nascent 1840s

invasion plans. He wanted to establish a base in Baltimore to aid escaping slaves. He was imprisoned more than once for aiding fugitive slaves and eventually was condemned to six years of hard labor. He died in prison in 1846. See http://www.yaleslavery.org/Abolitionists/torrey.html. For more on the influence of the Fugitive Slave Act, see Collison, *Shadrach Minkins.*

24. Brown, "Words of Advice."

25. Stauffer, *Black Hearts of Men*, 170–74.

26. John Brown to John Brown Jr., August 21, 1854, John Brown Folder, OGV-JB Papers.

27. John Brown Jr. to John Brown, May 20, 24, 1855, John Brown Folder, OGV-JB Papers.

28. Brown also received letters from his daughter-in-law Wealthy. Beginning a new life in a makeshift tent in central Kansas, she wrote the Brown family of the many advantages of Kansas life. "Such a thing as a swamp I have yet to see, there is almost a constant breeze which makes it pleasant even in cool days," she wrote. "There is great plenty of timber and water also of stone with any quantity of nice prairie where there is not a stone or a stump to prevent ploughing as much as you want." After imploring her sister's relations to move to the territory to "enjoy the pioneer life," Wealthy Brown added that anyone "would be delighted with the country. I *certainly* never saw any region to compare in beauty and in richness." Wealthy blended high politics and daily life in the same way as her fellow settlers, invoking the opportunism and rabble-rousing that defined the territorial contest in Kansas. Wealthy had anticipated "fears and hardships" on the journey, but the boat ride through Missouri with "slaveholders and their wives with their slaves" was a real test of faith. When the ship got stuck in the shallow waters of the summer Missouri river, "there were 9 deaths," including John's son Austin. Stopping at Waverly, Missouri, to fix the rudder, "the captain told us he should not start until afternoon [but] . . . *the scamp* would not wait for us. . . . We think he cut up that trick on us because we were *Abolitionists*." Wealthy Brown to Ruth Brown, June 12, 1855, JBL.

Chapter 2

1. Sanborn, *Life and Letters*, 122, 117.

2. Ibid., 501–2.

3. For a general history, see Miner, *Kansas.*

4. In this sense, the symbolism of Kansas, embodied by John Brown, is the key to understanding how Brown simultaneously transcended the chaos of Kansas while acting in accord with the texture of the times. Ultimately, in addition to showcasing the wrongheadedness of so much Kansas history, these efforts should also underscore the set of contingencies emerging from Bleeding Kansas. No one could know what would materialize once the brutal violence calmed down. Harpers Ferry and the Civil War were certainly not foregone conclusions. Kansas was not the last word.

5. Determining if John Brown personally killed anyone during the Pottawatomie massacre, for instance, is nigh impossible. He was certainly present for all of the murders and instructed his men to carry out the killings. The meaning and impact of the massacre take on new significance, however, as the contours of this chaotic free-for-all are elucidated. Only then can we comprehend the futility of ascertaining which side stole more horses, burned more houses, or confiscated more property. James Malin's account is an exhaustive and ex-

hausting example of trying to establish these numbers, including a dogged focus on Brown's culpability. See Malin, *John Brown*, 87. Also RPW, *John Brown*. Both Malin and Warren tend to exaggerate the manipulations by historical actors, especially of Free Soilers lying about events to serve their own ends. Malin is particularly culpable in this regard, trusting the sources he deems trustworthy and ignoring the others. Malin questions a source's accuracy unless the account serves his purposes. For instance, Brown's letters are always treated as worthless, except when Malin needs them to prove a point. See Malin, *John Brown*, 649. For a concise and effective refutation of Malin's evidentiary choices, see Oates, *To Purge This Land*, 379. In the end, such accounting misses the point. Understanding Brown and sectional strife does not require determining the veracity of Brown's claims or the countless rights and wrongs committed by each side during the conflict. Histories of Kansas continue chasing that red herring, pursuing factual validation in service to a broader timeline that tries to apportion blame along some inevitable timeline of the Civil War.

6. Situating Brown in this manner contrasts with the interpretations of James Malin, Nicole Etcheson, and David Potter, among others. Malin's *John Brown* argues that Brown was essentially an opportunistic horse thief and criminal, but that he also had almost no tangible effect on Kansas affairs. Still, Malin maintains that the legend that developed around Brown's actions led inevitably to the Civil War. Etcheson, in *Bleeding Kansas*, argues that the only reason there was conflict in Kansas was the flawed interpretation of popular sovereignty. Furthermore, the issue that united Free State settlers was simply a belief in the political liberties of free whites, not a multiracial vision. Potter, in *Impending Crisis*, emphasizes the manipulation of apathetic settlers by outside interests, interests that bolstered the momentum toward war.

7. Jason Brown to mothers, brothers, sisters, July 22, 1855, Osawatomie, Kansas, John Brown Family Papers—Correspondence, Photos, Ephemera, 1838–1970, Huntington Library, mssHM 53560–75.

8. Like those settlers, I use the terms *Free Soil* and *Free State* interchangeably. All Free Staters and Free Soilers simply shared the belief that Kansas should not become a slave state.

9. "Bartow Darrach to Parents, May 30, 1856," BDL. For a similar and extensive published account by a Free State settler, see Brewerton, *War in Kansas*.

10. Bartow Darrach to Brother, [undated fragment after August 7 letter], BDL. Unfortunately, Kansas politicians could do little to ameliorate the situation. In August 1855, Governor Reeder, the first reasonably impartial governor of the territory, was dismissed. Every day there seemed to be a new election or a dispute over a previous election. Free Soilers were not unified and were consistently outnumbered when Missourian slavery supporters were brought across the border for booze-fueled voting parties. Some settlers, like the future candidate for governor, James Lane, refused to vote at all, avoiding tainted elections under arms. For more on the political wrangling of the Kansas territorial period, see Etcheson, *Bleeding Kansas*; Goodrich, *War to the Knife*; and Neely, *Border between Them*.

11. The image was later reproduced in many different formats, but the best surviving example comes from a *carte de visite* produced by the Boston photographer J. J. Hawes, owned by the Boston Aethenaeum. This particular card is signed by Amos A. Lawrence, Boston, 1881: "a likeness of old John Brown wh. he had taken at my request in 1856: when he went to Kansas." Amos Adams Lawrence was the son of the famous philanthropist Amos Lawrence. The younger Amos helped to finance the University of Kansas at Lawrence, made signifi-

cant contributions to the Massachusetts Emigrant Aid Company (which supported Free Soil settlers with money, arms, food, and more), and provided financial support to John Brown. See William Lawrence, *Life of Amos A. Lawrence.*

12. Wealthy Brown to Ruth Brown, June 12, 1855, JBL.

13. Oates, *To Purge This Land*, 97, 98, 119.

14. Bartow Darrach to Brother, November 6, 1855, BDL.

15. Ibid.

16. Bartow Darrach to Brother, December 6, 1855, BDL.

17. Ibid. See also Malin, *John Brown*, 16.

18. Ibid.

19. Winkley, *John Brown the Hero*, 36. Winkley moved to Kansas at the height of territorial conflict and lived near Blackjack, fought in the Battle of Osawatomie (the response to the Pottawatomie massacre), and was personally acquainted with John Brown.

20. Oates, *To Purge This Land*, 108.

21. "Editorial: Kansas," *St. Louis Interpreter*, September 6, 1856.

22. Ruchames, *John Brown*, 99–100.

23. The arrangement was reached by the dubiously elected Governor Wilson Shannon and the military opportunist cum journalist James H. Lane. Shannon served as governor from September 7, 1855, until June 24, 1856, and July 7, 1856, through August 18, 1856. Lane, previously a congressman who had voted for the Kansas-Nebraska Act, was later elected a Senator when Kansas was admitted to statehood.

24. Oates, *To Purge This Land*, 110.

25. "John Brown to Wife and Children," December 16, 1855, John Brown Collection, KSHS.

26. Etcheson, *Bleeding Kansas*, 91.

27. Wealthy Brown to Ruth Brown, February 12, 1856, JBL.

28. Ibid.

29. For more on this dynamic, see Gilpin, "National Precipice."

30. On the afternoon of May 21, Preston Brooks, a congressman from South Carolina, had attacked Charles Sumner, an abolitionist senator from Massachusetts, inside the Senate chamber, beating him bloodied to the floor. Historians have long speculated that the news of Charles Sumner's beating prompted Brown's retribution. Stephen Oates in particular tells a compelling story about that sequence of events. See Oates, *To Purge This Land*, 129. See Etcheson, *Bleeding Kansas*, 99–100, for an excellent account of how symbolic the Sumner attack was for both Free State and slavery supporters. There is no direct evidence linking the Sumner news to the massacre, however, only conjecture. Robert McGlone makes a convincing case that it would have been impossible for Brown or anyone in Kansas to learn of the beating until May 26 at the earliest. See McGlone, *John Brown's War*, 74, 350.

31. Ibid., 129.

32. Etcheson, *Bleeding Kansas*, 108–10.

33. Bartow Darrach to Parents, May 30, 1856, BDL. Darrach also points out that in their last raid, Missourians had "stolen all the horses they could find and a great many cattle." Darrach's account of the most infamous incident of Bleeding Kansas is notable for its subtlety. Not only did he refrain from blessing Brown's massacre, he also directly contradicted many historians' relentless focus on John Brown as the only horse thief in territorial Kansas. By

the middle of 1856, horse thievery was the standard byproduct of military raids. In "terror-stricken southeastern Kansas," the Brown biographer Stephen Oates wrote, "Missourians and their Southern allies ransacked the area, plundering homesteads, taking horse and cattle and everything else . . . as they searched for the Pottawatomie killers." See Oates, *To Purge This Land*, 144–45. James Malin interprets Brown's and Free Soilers' thefts in a vacuum, chalking proslavery raids and horse thievery up to revenge or payback for previous Free Soil actions, while describing Free Soil thievery as archvillany. See Malin, *John Brown*, 624–25.

34. Darrach's attribution is especially notable in the long anti-Brown historiography. Malin, Warren, and many others argued that Free Soilers never attributed the massacre to Brown. In addition to his connection to Brown, Samuel Adair was the pastor of the First Congregational Church of Osawatomie. He was paid by the American Missionary Association in New York City—a prominent supporter of the Free State cause.

35. Ibid.

36. Jason Brown to Brown family, June 28, 1856, JBL. Jason's brother John Jr., who witnessed the massacre firsthand, did not recover. After the night of May 23, John Jr. "appeared very much excited," Jason wrote, and "he became more and more confused in mind till . . . he was quite insane."

37. Ibid.

38. Ibid. Jason further noted that his captors were mostly "kind hearted men. Especially among Kentuckians." Stephen Oates described the situation as "chaos. . . . Dozens of settlers—proslavery as well as free-state—had fled the region out of fear for their lives." Oates, *To Purge This Land*, 146. Nicole Etcheson remains unconvinced by this reasoning, which she argues was only created after the massacre as a rationale by the Browns. See Etcheson, *Bleeding Kansas*, 111. Darrach also cited the threat to the young female school-teacher, which most historians believe was completely fictitious.

39. Winkley, *John Brown*, 31, 33.

40. Etcheson, *Bleeding Kansas*, 105.

41. While Redpath would eventually become a close friend of men like Horace Greeley, Mark Twain, and Thomas Nast, his beginnings were humble. Emigrating from Scotland, Redpath joined two of his elder brothers in America in 1850, moving to Allegan County, Michigan. Redpath soon traveled to Kalamazoo, where he camped out on the local newspaper editor's stoop and convinced the man to take him on. Redpath's writings in papers across the Midwest gained notice, and one day he received a barely legible letter, whose only clear sentiment was "come to New York." The note's scrawled signature read, Redpath believed, "Horace Greeley." Thus his career began. See Horner, *Life of James Redpath*, 10–15.

42. Redpath, *Public Life*, 106–7.

43. Redpath's interviews were collected in his first book, originally published in 1859. Redpath, *Roving Editor*, 300. See also McKivigan, *Roving Editor*.

44. "A GENERAL STAMPEDE OF THE SLAVES [would occur] if the Abolitionist would send down a trustworthy Band of 'Liberators' provided with compasses, pistols, and a little money for the fugitives." See *The Liberator*, September 1, 1854; and *National Anti-slavery Standard*, December 2, 1854.

45. Redpath later recalled, with a bit of embroidery: "I believed that a civil war between the North and South would ultimate in insurrection, and that the Kansas troubles would probably create a military conflict of the sections. Hence I left the South, and went to Kansas;

and endeavored, personally and by my pen, to precipitate a revolution." See Redpath, *Roving Editor*, 300.

46. McKivigan, *Forgotten Firebrand*, 11, 15–17.

47. Redpath, *Public Life*, 113.

48. Ibid., 113–14. As Redpath's biographer John McKivigan describes, Redpath left the meeting having "certainly become an active partisan." See McKivigan, *Forgotten Firebrand*, 29. If Redpath's background as a cunning risk-taker brought him to Brown, his fervent and lifelong belief in the abolition of slavery bound the men together. Redpath's knack for self-promotion and his astuteness in developing and marketing Brown made their partnership that much closer. See Horner, *Life of James Redpath*, 15.

49. Bangs and Co., *Library of James Redpath*, February 19, 1894, Mudd Library, Yale University.

50. McKivigan, *Roving Editor*, 8.

51. Sara Robinson, *Kansas*, 276–77.

52. Redpath, *Public Life*, 134.

53. Bartow Darrach to Parents, June 13, 1856, BDL.

54. Jason Brown to Brown family, August 13, 1856, JBL.

55. Ibid. See also Etcheson, *Bleeding Kansas*, which argues exactly this point, that Free Soilers were just as racist as proslavery settlers, and wanted a free white state without slavery. Malin also advances this interpretation; Malin, *John Brown*, 513.

56. Winkley, *John Brown*, 50.

57. Ibid., 60–61.

58. Bartow Darrach to Parents, September 2, 1856, BDL.

59. Winkley, *John Brown*, 82, 79.

60. Both Hinton and Redpath published well-known accounts of territorial Kansas and Brown's exploits there. William Phillips also put out a volume on the subject: *The Conquest of Kansas*.

61. *New York Daily Tribune*, January 12, 1857.

62. John Brown, "An Idea of Things in Kansas," 1857, John Brown Collection, KSHS.

63. John Brown, "Speech to Massachusetts Legislative Committee," February 18, 1857, BSC.

64. Reflecting the underlying chaos of territorial Kansas, Redpath chose Doniphan because it had a large enough Free Soil population to support his radical paper. On the day the first issue appeared, a Free Soil settler was shot in broad daylight on Main Street in Doniphan by proslavery settlers.

65. McKivigan, *Forgotten Firebrand*, x, 48.

66. Redpath, *Roving Editor*, iv.

67. Winkley, *John Brown*, 46. Despite Brown's best efforts to force freedom on Kansas, no decision for statehood was made during his lifetime. So while Brown had done nothing particularly heroic, he had matched proslavery supporters' violence. In this way, he distinguished himself in Kansas, and the notoriety of his few acts allowed Brown to fashion himself into a symbol of all that had transpired. See also Etcheson, *Bleeding Kansas*, 101. Typically, historians have viewed Brown's Kansas escapade as either crazy and cruel or heroic and principled. Most of these accounts make his eventual hanging in December 1859 the endpoint of a narrative that began in Kansas's territorial contest. Nonetheless, James Malin and others

portray the raid on Harpers Ferry as an inevitable consequence of the military and psychological strategies of Bleeding Kansas. Malin derides the historians who "became accessories after the fact in the massacre, and such complicity may have been a factor in the later evolution of the Brown legend." But somehow, after seven hundred pages of condemning Brown as "a master criminal and horse-thief," Malin admits that the Pottawatomie massacre "was not unique in brutality." See Malin, *John Brown*, 624, 673, 750, 753.

68. One popular *carte de visite*, from 1857, was owned by James H. Holmes, a Kansan associate of Brown's during the 1850s. A Free Stater who arrived in the territory in late 1855, Holmes emigrated with a typical cocktail of goals: to make Kansas free but also to support vegetarianism and education. After fighting alongside the Old Hero near Osawatomie in the summer of 1856, Brown left Holmes in charge of his men, asking him to "carry the war" to the South. Holmes took up the charge, conducting raids in Missouri, eventually being labeled "John Brown's little hornet" by Kansas authorities. See http://abolitionist-john-brown.blogspot.com/2007/06/carte-de-visite-of-john-brown-to-be.html.

69. This has been a real problem in recent studies of Brown, where the exposure seems to show an even more weathered and severe-looking man. The symbolic implications of overexposure often dovetail with broader interpretations of Brown's character.

70. John Stauffer dedicates much discussion to abolitionist imagery (particularly the Bowles daguerreotype) in *Black Hearts of Men*, 56–59. For a critique of Stauffer's analysis, see Bay, "Abolition and the Color Line."

71. James Stewart, *Holy Warriors*, 151.

72. Stauffer, *Black Hearts of Men*, 36.

73. Whitehill, "John Brown of Osawatomie," 263–64.

74. Sumner, like many politicians, was forced to take a complicated position on John Brown after the Harpers Ferry raid. Conceding that Brown's actions "must be deplored," Sumner admitted his admiration for "the singular courage and character of Brown." Sumner "refrained from entering the debates on Brown's raid, giving as his reason his doctor's advice against overexertion," but he found the space to complement Brown for his spirit of "the Covenanter, the Puritan, and even the early Christian martyr." Donald, *Charles Sumner*, 293.

75. James Redpath to Elias Nason, April 10, 1874, BSC, MS09-0014 A-V. The Reverend Elias Nason was then writing *Life and Times of Charles Sumner*. David Donald confirms the account in *Charles Sumner*. See also Scott, *Secret Six*, 230.

Chapter 3

1. He also wrote that the raid was "the first overt act that led to the Civil War." Zittle, *Correct History of the John Brown Invasion*, 1.

2. Benjamin Quarles makes a convincing argument that black attitudes about the Pottawatomie massacre were much different than even the most ardent white abolitionists. Any sobering effect the five murders might have had on the black community was immediately put in the context of the "nearly five million of their kind subject by their color to a killing of their dreams, a snuffing out of their manhood and womanhood, day-in and day-out." Quarles, *Allies for Freedom*, 35.

3. Redpath, *Public Life*, 134, 220.

4. John Brown, "John Brown's Parallels: Letter to the Editor of the *New York Tribune*," January 1859, John Brown Folder, OGV-JB Papers.

5. Ibid.

6. James Newton Gloucester to John Brown, February 19, 1858, in OGV-JB Papers.

7. Ibid.

8. Du Bois, *John Brown* (1909), 76.

9. A. Bronson Alcott, Concord, January 1, 1864, in Various John Brown (box 18), OGV-JB Papers.

10. Hinton, *John Brown and His Men*, 153.

11. Trodd and Stauffer, *Meteor of War*, 199.

12. Sanborn, *Life and Letters*, 418–68.

13. Historian Edward Renehan called this "Brown's deadpan nonchalance . . . [about] the prolonged punitive slave uprising—with all its attendant violence, destruction, and terror." Renehan, *Secret Six*, 135–37.

14. Martin, "Speech on December 2, 1859," 216.

15. OGV, *John Brown*, 327.

16. John Brown to John Brown Jr., April 8, 1858, BSC, MS02-0019. This letter raises the important issue of Yankee masculinity, a quality Brown's Northeastern supporters were especially enthusiastic about. Because antebellum Southerners had declared male conduct their arena of expertise, the beating of Sumner as a case in point, Brown offered a Yankee response to Southern claims of male/martial superiority. For more on this, see John Brown to E. B., November 11, 1860, in Sanborn, *Life and Letters*, 582–83.

17. John Brown, "Provisional Constitution and Ordinances for the People of the United States," May 8, 1858, John Brown Folder, OGV-JB Papers.

18. Ibid.

19. Ibid.

20. Virginia had been the location for two of the most dramatic slave rebellions of nineteenth-century America: those led by Gabriel Prosser and Nat Turner. The repressions that followed both were notoriously brutal. See Egerton, *Gabriel's Rebellion*; and Greenberg, *Nat Turner*.

21. Redpath, *Roving Editor*, iv, 300.

22. Douglass, quoted in Clay MacCauley, "Warning John Brown," *Boston Transcript*, February 3, 1909. See also Douglass, *Life and Times*, 319–20.

23. MacCauley, "Warning John Brown." See also Douglass, *Life and Times*, 320.

24. Anderson, *Voice from Harper's Ferry*, 31.

25. Leech, *Raid of John Brown*.

26. The best book on the raiders and their background is still Richard Hinton's *John Brown and His Men*. A forthcoming book by Horwitz, *Midnight Rising*, promises to greatly expand our knowledge and understanding of the raiders.

27. Brown sent three whites and three blacks: Leary, Green, Stevens, Cook, Tidd, and Anderson.

28. "Statement of Mr. John Thomas Allstadt, Kearneysville, WV, April 15, 1909, on the Harper's Ferry Raid," given to Katherine Mayo, in OGV-JB Papers.

29. "In Honor of John Brown," *Weekly Republican* (Springfield, MA), May 16, 1907.

Tucker's husband had been sold just before the raid, and she had fought back "the best way [she] could." After taking to the woods in protest, where she managed to survive for several weeks, she was captured and put in jail until she calmed down.

30. "Statement of Mr. John Thomas Allstadt."

31. Ibid.

32. "In Honor of John Brown."

33. Lee, *Recollections*, 21.

34. "Statement of Mr. John Thomas Allstadt."

35. Lee, *Recollections*, 21.

36. "Statement of Mr. John Thomas Allstadt."

37. For an excellent account of Brown's trial, see Weiner, *Black Trials*. Brian McGinty's *John Brown's Trial* focuses mainly on its legal strategies and implications.

38. As the final American slave revolt (notwithstanding Steve Hahn's assertions about wartime emancipation), this fear was Southerners' most constant and powerful response (aside from repression) to slave uprisings. See Dubois, *Avengers of the New World*; Egerton, *Gabriel's Rebellion*; Franklin and Schweninger, *Runaway Slaves*; and Frey, *Water from the Rock*.

39. *Baltimore American and Commercial Advertiser*, December 2, 1859.

40. "Untitled," *New York Herald*, November 16, 1859, 1.

41. John Brown, "Last Address to the Virginia Court," John Brown Folder, OGV-JB Papers.

42. Edwin Coppoc to Uncle, December 13, 1859, Coppoc Folder, OGV-JB Papers.

43. John Brown to E. B., November 1, 1859, John Brown Folder, OGV-JB Papers.

44. John Brown to Rev. H. L. Vaill, November 15, 1859, John Brown Folder, OGV-JB Papers.

45. John Brown to Wife, November 16, 1859, John Brown Folder, OGV-JB Papers.

46. Redpath, *Public Life*, 324; Reynolds, *John Brown*, 387.

47. Reynolds, *John Brown*, 387–88.

48. Redpath, *Public Life*, 388.

49. John Brown to J. B. Musgrave, Esqr., November 17, 1859, John Brown Folder, OGV-JB Papers.

50. John Brown to Wife, Sons, & Daughters, every one, November 30, 1859, John Brown Folder, OGV-JB Papers.

51. John Brown, "Statement," December 2, 1859, John Brown Folder, OGV-JB Papers, original in Chicago Historical Society.

52. Given the tension in Virginia, only one black man witnessed Brown's execution. William Brent, a body servant of Governor Wise, described the event for newspapers. "The body was allowed to hang about ten minutes," he said. "While it was hanging a man walked up to it, raised the cap and made a pencil picture of the face." See "Was Witness to the Hanging of Old John Brown," *Leavenworth (KS) Times*, November 2, 1911. The pencil picture was for Lydia Maria Child, the noted author and abolitionist. The artist who did this brutal deed was David H. Strother, the "Porte Crayon" of *Harper's Weekly*. As for the stories of Brown kissing a slave baby on the way to the scaffold, Brent said there was "no truth in the story. . . . No one was allowed to approach the prisoner except the guards from the time he left the jail until he was dead."

53. Despite his distaste for Brown's goals, Booth was also intrigued by the "rugged old hero." Booth learned from Brown that a symbolic death could reach thousands of Americans. As Booth wrote, "John Brown was a man inspired, the grandest character of this century!" See Goodrich, *Darkest Dawn*, 60–61.

54. John Wilkes Booth to brother-in-law, x-x-64, reprinted in *New York Tribune*, April 20, 1865.

55. Stedman, *Raid of John Brown*. For more on the poetry Brown inspired, see Ronda, "Whittier and Melville," 25–45.

56. "Tablet for John Brown," *Springfield (MA) Daily Republican*, August 24, 1916.

57. William Lloyd Garrison to Dr. A. M. Ross, August 25, 1876, Garrison Folder, OGV-JB Papers.

58. "Editorial," *Daily Cleveland Herald*, October 26, 1859. The proliferation of similar editorials contradicts Bruce Ronda's arguments in his recent cultural exploration of Brown. Ronda makes Thoreau "the founder" of the school that explored "the problem of John Brown"; the "Old Man's complex and contradictory behavior, motivations, and impact to those who wished to interpret or explain him." Ronda asserts that "a large segment of Northern public opinion . . . did shift its view of the abolitionist warrior" after Thoreau began writing. Ronda, *Reading the Old Man*, 21–22.

59. "The Independent and John Brown," *Oberlin (OH) Evangelist*, December 21, 1859.

60. "The Union and Old John Brown," *Freedom's Champion* (Atchison, KS), November 5, 1859.

61. *Cleveland Weekly Leader*, December 7, 1859.

62. *Ashtabula (OH) Sentinel*, December 15, 1859, vol. 28, 401.

63. Ibid.

64. Letter from E. C. Lamson, January 3, 1908, Various John Brown (box 3) Folder, OGV-JB Papers. Five raiders were captured during the raid and later executed. Five others escaped: Osborne Anderson, Owen Brown, Barclay Coppoc, Francis Meriam, and Charles Tidd.

65. Reverend J. H. McNeilly, "John Brown's Soul Goes Marching On," *Nashville Banner*, September 17, 1910.

66. Ibid.

67. Some of Brown's supporters (many of the same characters who proposed to break Brown out of prison) imagined that Brown's coffin would be paraded throughout the North, rallying support for the antislavery cause. Mary Brown refused to cooperate in such a lengthy and potentially explosive ordeal. See John Brown Folder, OGV-JB Papers.

68. Reverend J. S. Martin, "Speech," *The Liberator*, December 9, 1859.

69. Quarles, *Allies for Freedom*, 135.

70. *Weekly Anglo-African* (Detroit), December 17, 1859.

71. Ibid.

72. Redpath, *Public Life*, 4.

73. De Witt, *Life, Trial and Execution*.

74. McKivigan, *Forgotten Fireband*, x.

75. Ibid., 53.

76. McKivigan describes Brown as man who pioneered "cultural entrepreneurialism and helped to forge modern concepts of celebrity." Ibid., xiv.

77. Ibid., 59.

78. Redpath, *Public Life*, 5.

79. Ibid., 3–4.

80. Ibid., 266, 404, 188.

81. Ibid., 7.

82. Ibid., 36, 48.

83. Ibid., 205.

84. Redpath's 1860 collection of Brown-related speeches, letters, and ephemera was another brick in this edifice. Redpath, *Echoes of Harper's Ferry*.

85. General L. V. Bierce, "Address Delivered at Akron, Ohio on the evening of the Execution of John Brown, December 2, 1859" (Columbus: Ohio State Journal Steam Press, 1865).

86. Ibid.

87. Patton, *Execution of John Brown*.

88. Thoreau, "Plea for Captain John Brown," 42.

89. Emerson, in Sanborn, *Life and Letters*, 119.

Chapter 4

1. McFeely, *Frederick Douglass*, 211–15.

2. The black newspaper editor Thomas Hamilton had made similar comparisons immediately following Brown's execution. In an editorial, Hamilton made the strange case that Brown's peaceful invasion and Turner's violent uprising were the "fearful choices" facing the South. If the South could not deal with Brown, then Hamilton argued that the region would soon be "drenched in blood." Thomas Hamilton, "The Nat Turner Insurrection," *Weekly Anglo-African* (New York), December 31, 1859.

3. Anderson, *Voice from Harper's Ferry*, 3, 7, 8, 62.

4. George Kimball, "Origin of the John Brown Song," *New England Magazine*, n.s. 1 (1890): 376.

5. The tune, "Say Brothers Will You Meet Us," fashioned into "The John Brown Song," was also rewritten, in Julia Ward Howe's "Battle Hymn of the Republic." Howe penned the new lyrics when a friend suggested, "Why do you not write some good words for that stirring tune?" See Kimball, "Origin," 377.

6. See Stutler, "John Brown's Body"; Annie Randall, "Censorship of Forgetting."

7. Charlotte Forten, Diary, November 10, 1862, Francis James Grimké Papers, 1833–1937, Manuscript Division, Moorland-Spingarn Research Center, Howard University. Forten eventually married Francis J. Grimké, the famous writer and pastor of the Fifteenth Street Presbyterian Church in Washington, DC.

8. Eventually the song was employed in other causes as well. John Brown's daughter Annie, who had assisted with the raid at Harpers Ferry, moved to California after the war. She began teaching at a local black school and boarding with a black family, while Brown's widow, Mary, tried to purchase a home in Red Bluff, a small town on the Sacramento River. When locals discovered Mary's family identity and her predicament, they collected money to build her a house. The editor of Red Bluff's newspaper argued that, "if every man, woman, and child in California who has hummed 'John Brown's Body Lies Mouldering in the Grave' will throw in a dime, his family will have a home." See Weber, "John Brown's Family," 4. The

governor of California led the fundraising charge and in January 1866 a cottage was presented triumphantly to Mary Brown. Brown's sacrifices and his enduring relevance continually prompted both whites and blacks to support the family. The "colored ladies" of New York were "a band of sisters" who would "collect our weekly pence, and pour it lovingly in [Mary's] lap." But these women, among many others, explicitly described John Brown as "our honored and dearly-loved brother." Black Women to Mary A. Brown, November 23, 1859, in Quarles, *Blacks on John Brown*, 17–19.

9. The Shiloh Presbyterian Church boasted a long tradition of radical black leadership. It was founded as the First Colored Presbyterian Church by Samuel Cornish in 1822. Cornish helped found *Freedom's Journal*, the nation's first black newspaper. The church's second pastor, Theodore Wright, was a founding member of the American Anti-slavery Society, and its third pastor was the fiery Henry Highland Garnet. All three were great thinkers, speakers, and leading abolitionists. See http://maap.columbia.edu/place/37.html.

10. "Lincoln and John Brown: Coupled by Colored Men as Martyrs in Freedom's Battle," December 3, 1879, in John Brown: Some Later Estimates Folder, OGV-JB Papers.

11. Ibid.

12. Ibid.

13. Garnet's remarks did celebrate Brown's moral leadership: "None can express a more profound admiration than I feel and have ever felt for that hero and martyr, whose friendship I enjoyed and whose campaign against slavery I endeavored to aid, it was at first defeated, but how gloriously it has now succeeded—far above our expectation, though not beyond the confident hope of John Brown." Until that point, Garnet could have been reading one of Sanborn's soliloquies. Curiously enough, a parishioner rose and read a letter from Franklin Sanborn eulogizing Brown in his typical manner; Brown was a Christian leader, dedicated to a peaceful and heroic emancipation.

14. Ibid.

15. McKivigan, *Forgotten Firebrand*, 122.

16. Douglass, "John Brown," 205.

17. Ibid., 210.

18. Henry Samuels Olcott was a journalist and lawyer who eventually earned the rank of colonel in the United States Army during the Civil War. He was also a cofounder and the first president of the American Theosophical Society. Olcott was one of the earliest Westerners to convert to Buddhism. He is still widely admired in Sri Lanka for his efforts to spread Buddhism.

19. John Greenleaf Whittier, "Brown of Osawatomie," *New York Independent*, December 22, 1859.

20. Unfortunately, Ransom's painting was donated to Oberlin College, where it was badly looked after. It was eventually lent to a high school in Washington, DC. Its whereabouts are currently unknown. It only survives as a deteriorating photograph. Robert S. Fletcher does an excellent job of tracing the painting's history in "Ransom's John Brown Painting." See also Fletcher, "John Brown and Oberlin," 141.

21. Ibid.

22. George William Curtis, "The Lounger," *Harper's Weekly*, June 13, 1863, 371.

23. *A Rare Picture*, pamphlet (Oberlin College, 1886), cited in Fletcher, "John Brown and Oberlin."

24. Ibid.

25. Ibid.

26. Certainly, Ransom began circulating the ideas of miscegenation with the image. Ransom had done this intentionally, but Currier and Ives transformed the image to be less polemical. On the wider specter of miscegenation in American art, see Wilson, "Optical Illusions."

27. Ransom gave the lithograph a title that fully explained his debt to the *Herald Tribune* and to Whittier: *John Brown Meeting the Slave-Mother and Her Child on the Steps of Charlestown Jail on His Way to Execution*: "The artist has represented Capt. Brown regarding with a look of compassion a Slave-mother and Child who obstructed his passage on the way to the Scaffold. . . . Capt. Brown stooped and kissed the Child . . . then met his fate." This posed image, where Brown does not actually bend to kiss the baby, was painted by Thomas Satterwhite Noble in 1867, *John Brown's Blessing*, owned by the New York Historical Society. Noble's giant canvas (84 ¼ inches × 60 ⅜ inches) shows a serious European influence; the scene seems to take place in a European jail.

28. Gwendolyn DuBois Shaw traces the lineage of Ransom, Currier and Ives, Noble, Hovenden, and others in her fascinating study of the contemporary African American artist Kara Walker. See Shaw, *Seeing the Unspeakable*.

29. Terhune, *Thomas Hovenden*, 101, 136.

30. Hovenden wrote a friend that "artistically to me, at least, [*Last Moments*] afforded less opportunity to show what I could do than almost any other incident in his thrilling and varied career. . . . While I was at work on the picture I made an illustration . . . of John Brown wounded in the guard house of Harper's Ferry. This was what I would have painted had I been thinking of myself. . . . [But] I think there is as good work in [*Last Moments*] as any I have ever done." This alternate image was initially painted as a "monochromatic oil sketch of Brown lying on the guardroom floor addressing his captors." The original painting is lost, but on the back of the canvas, Hovenden inscribed a quote from Brown that he found in Sanborn: "You may dispose of me very easily, I am nearly disposed of now, but this question is still to be settled—this negro question, I mean." Hovenden eventually sold the image to *Century Illustrated Monthly Magazine*, where it appeared in July 1883 inside Sanborn's article "Comment by a Radical Abolitionist."

31. Ransom, Noble, and Hovenden all relied on the Heywood Brown (see figure 3.4) but Hovenden's takes a new angle and thus gains some freedom from the visual source. Noble in particular exaggerates the split and size of Brown's beard. Hovenden may have even seen Ransom's original canvas at P. T. Barnum's museum before the Draft Riots forced its removal. See Terhune, *Thomas Hovenden*, 133.

32. In addition to the correspondence with Battell, Hovenden also revealed his admiration for Whittier's poem. When lithographs were made of *Last Moments*, Hovenden etched the first three stanzas of Whittier's poem on his copperplate of the painting.

33. The confusion in representing Brown as New Testament versus Old Testament spoke not just to Brown's controversial embrace of tactics from both books. The artist John Steuart Curry would literally confuse them when he gave his vengeful Brown a rifle in one hand and the Alpha and Omega (from Revelation 1:8, 21:6, and 22:13 in the New Testament) in the other hand.

34. Shaw argues convincingly that the image reassured viewers "that the racial hierarchies they had grown up with would endure." Shaw, *Seeing the Unspeakable*, 82–83.

35. See Cameron, *Transcendental Youth and Age.*

36. Sanborn, "Comment by a Radical Abolitionist."

37. Sanborn, *Recollections*, 1:20.

38. Ibid.

39. Sanborn, *Recollections*, 2:315.

40. Ibid., 320.

41. Menand, *Metaphysical Club*, 73.

42. Sanborn, *Recollections*, 2:443.

43. Oates, *To Purge This Land*, 181; Wells, *Dear Preceptor*, 104.

44. Oates, *To Purge This Land*, 181, 183; Sanborn, *Recollections*, 1:73.

45. Ibid., 181.

46. Sanborn, *Recollections*, 1:82.

47. Ibid., 103–6.

48. Sanborn, "John Brown," 371; Sanborn, *Recollections*, 1:147.

49. Sanborn, *Recollections*, 1:147.

50. Ibid., 146.

51. The other five were Gerrit Smith, George Luther Stearns, Thomas Wentworth Higginson, Samuel Gridley Howe, and Theodore Parker.

52. Sanborn, *Recollections*, 1:185.

53. Franklin Sanborn to Mother, December 1, 1859, Channing-Sanborn Papers, bMS Am 1898, Houghton Library, Harvard University.

54. George W. Cooke, "The Two Thoreaus," *The Independent*, December 10, 1896; Dean and Hoag, "Thoreau's Lectures after *Walden*," 311.

55. Sanborn, *Recollections*, 1:183.

56. In this sense, Sanborn revealed one of the strange commonalities among biographers, chroniclers, artists, and politicians captivated or repulsed by Brown. This masculine extremist did things that they only imagined doing.

57. A. Bronson Alcott, January 1, 1864, OGV-JB Papers.

58. Franklin Sanborn, "John Brown in Massachusetts," *Atlantic Monthly*, April 1872, 427.

59. John Brown, "Provisional Constitution and Ordinances," 110.

60. In their introduction to Brown's constitution, Trodd and Stauffer (*Meteor of War*) note that despite the embarrassment this document causes most Brown biographers, these "revolutionary constitutions" were being drawn with great frequency in different parts of the world. Still, modern accounts (most sympathetic to Brown's ultimate goal of emancipation and racial equality) tend to excuse the treasonous act of drafting this document, which Brown certainly intended to implement if he succeeded.

61. Sanborn, "John Brown," in Orcutt, *History of Torrington*, 315, 357, 324, 350, 358, 331.

62. *Weekly Times* (Leavenworth, KS), September 6, 1877.

63. Sanborn edited the primary documents in the book for clarity, confusing and frustrating historians for years to come.

64. "The John Brown Anniversary," *Springfield (MA) Republican*, May 10, 1900.

65. Ibid.

66. In the summer of 1887, Nicolay and Hay cemented Brown's place in the American imagination when they serialized the latest section of their exhaustive forty-seven-hundred-page biography of Abraham Lincoln. Appearing in the August issue of *The Century* magazine was a mostly innocuous account of John Brown's ill-fated attack on Harpers Ferry, Virginia, as it related to Lincoln's presidency. Nicolay and Hay wrote plainly, if a little skeptically, of Brown's religious faith, his probable presence at the Pottawatomie massacre, and his fundraising and military actions leading up to the Harpers Ferry raid. Nicolay and Hay concluded that, "on the whole, the principal results of [Harpers Ferry] were, to sectionalize parties more completely, ripen Southern sentiment towards secession, and combine wavering voters in the free States." For what was essentially a "Republican campaign tract" by two former Lincoln secretaries, Nicolay and Hay succeeded in reducing Harpers Ferry to its key political dimensions. In short, nothing terribly contentious could be found in the conclusions they drew from the infamous episode. Just days after the article appeared, Sanborn penned a rebuttal for his regular column in the *Springfield (MA) Republican*. He lashed out at the incompetence and prejudice that plagued Nicolay and Hay's treatment of Brown. At the most fundamental level, Sanborn wrote, "the broad ocean of history is too much for them." The biographers had made the mistake of treading on what Sanborn had come to consider his exclusive historical beat. Nicolay and Hay betrayed their total ignorance of John Brown, their "piddling conceit of knowledge," and Sanborn declared their ten-volume biography of Lincoln destined "for oblivion." See J. J. Nicolay and John Hay, "Abraham Lincoln: A History," *The Century: A Popular Quarterly*, August 1887, 509–34; Burlingame, "Nicolay and Hay," 1; and Franklin Sanborn, "John Brown Revised," *Springfield (MA) Republican*, August 18, 1887, 4, cols. 3–4.

67. Howells, *Literary Friends*, 59.

68. William Roscoe Thayer to Villard, August 31, 1910, OGV Papers.

69. This exchange with Villard was Sanborn's fiercest battle in his John Brown turf war. Since the early 1890s, Villard—William Lloyd Garrison's grandson, heir to the family railroad fortune, and owner, editor, and publisher of *The Nation* and the *New York Evening Post*—had slowly been gathering momentum to attempt his own biography of Brown. He and Sanborn corresponded frequently on various Brown matters, trading documents and contacts. Their friendly correspondence turned sour when Villard commissioned this devastating editorial review. Not only did these articles condemn Sanborn's scholarship, they also highlighted the treasonous efforts of the Secret Six and questioned Sanborn's loyalty to the antislavery cause.

70. Sanborn to Villard, August 24, 1909, OGV-JB Papers.

71. Ronda, *Reading the Old Man*, 20, 23.

72. Sanborn, *Recollections*, 1:81–82.

73. Ibid., 81.

74. Franklin Sanborn, "John Brown: Apostle and Martyr," *Springfield (MA) Republican*, September 2, 1916, 7, cols. 2–3.

75. Ibid.

76. Sanborn, *Recollections*, 1:252.

77. Pleasant's recollections were quite typical of the memorial fever that swept the country. Local newspapers, particularly in Kansas and the Northeast, were filled with residents claiming powerful connections with the martyr of Harpers Ferry. For more on Mary Pleasant and her relationship with Brown, see Hudson, *Making of "Mammy Pleasant,"* 24–44.

78. Sam P. Davis, "How a Colored Woman Aided John Brown," *Augusta (ME) Comfort,* November 1903.

79. Quarles, *Allies for Freedom,* 170.

80. "In Honor of John Brown," *Weekly Republican* (Springfield, MA), May 16, 1907.

81. Ibid.

82. Thomas Featherstonhaugh to Oswald Villard, October 20, 1907, various John Brown (box 8) files, OGV-JB Papers.

83. The racial invective and paternalistic tone of the Featherstonhaugh letters notwithstanding, both men called attention to a long-standing issue. It was not until the 1930s that memorials, particularly those funded by black Americans, began to be erected. This paucity of concrete tributes to Brown can be attributed to a number of factors. First, Brown was always a controversial figure. An entire book could be dedicated to the controversies surrounding public memorializations of him. Second, Lincoln often took Brown's place as a figure more interracially palatable and easier to comprehend.

84. Thomas Featherstonhaugh to Oswald Villard, December 4, 1907, various John Brown (box 8) files, OGV-JB Papers.

85. Forter, "Dedicatory Address."

86. Aptheker, *Pamphlets and Leaflets,* 53–54.

Chapter 5

1. Du Bois, *Autobiography,* 249.

2. Ibid., 251.

3. Smith, "Introduction," xxi.

4. Julie Husband explores Du Bois's vision of Brown and his teleology of African American heroes and socialist politics in "W. E. B. Du Bois's *John Brown*" but spends little time discussing Villard. Louis DeCaro, in "Black People's Ally, White People's Bogeyman," takes a historiographical approach, contrasting several racially inspired approaches to Brown, including those of Du Bois and Villard.

5. Wolters, *Du Bois and His Rivals,* 13.

6. Ellis Paxon Oberholtzer to W. E. B. Du Bois, November 21, 1903, WEBDB Papers.

7. This competition soon grew into fevered critiques, backbiting, and outspoken rivalry, with Du Bois and the more established Washington fighting to determine who would lead American racial reform. In some ways, this conflict can be seen as performing the fault line between adjacent generations. It was during this episode, however, that Du Bois's particular kind of ambition emerged. Throughout his career, Du Bois seemed to believe that to get ahead, one must trample one's rivals. For more detail on the dynamic between Du Bois and Washington, see Wolters, *Du Bois and His Rivals,* 40–77.

8. Ellis Paxon Oberholtzer to W. E. B. Du Bois, February 3, 1904, and February 16, 1904, WEBDB Papers.

9. Du Bois, *Dusk of Dawn,* 15.

10. Broderick, *W. E. B. Du Bois,* 82.

11. Du Bois, preface to *John Brown* (1909).

12. Ibid.

13. Quarles, *Allies for Freedom*; Stauffer, *Black Hearts of Men*; and DeCaro, *"Fire in the*

Midst of You," are notable exceptions. In addition to Quarles's secondary work on blacks and John Brown, he also published a collection of primary documents in 1972 as a companion to *Allies for Freedom*: Quarles, *Blacks on John Brown.*

14. Du Bois's biographer David Roediger argues that Du Bois put Brown at the head of "a river of African American adulation." See Roediger, introduction to Du Bois, *John Brown* (2001), xv. The "river" that Roediger mentions was tentatively charted in Quarles's landmark *Allies for Freedom*, a major inspiration for my own analysis of Du Bois and Villard. Quarles was not new to the analysis of memory and memorialization. His *Lincoln and the Negro* explored black approaches to Lincoln as it told the story of Lincoln's attitudes toward blacks. Quarles's illumination of the documentary record of blacks' relationship to Brown is fascinating, especially his argument that this narrative was developed by a black America only tenuously connected to the mainstream.

15. As the historian John David Smith explains, the book "provides a relatively unobscured window to Du Bois's heart and mind—his obsession with the breaking of racial and class lines." See Smith, "Introduction," xxi.

16. Francis Broderick has taken particular issue with Du Bois's opinion of *John Brown.* Broderick writes that Du Bois's praise of "his flimsiest work" is merely a pathetic attempt by him to claim infallibility. While it is impossible to deny Du Bois's capacity for self-involvement and self-justification, the truth is slightly more complicated. See Broderick, *Du Bois*, 227.

17. David W. Blight examines this very dynamic in his captivating essay on Du Bois's books *Souls of Black Folk* and *Black Reconstruction.* Blight, "W. E. B. Du Bois," 46–48. In particular, Blight argues that from his 1890 Harvard commencement address until his 1968 *Autobiography*, Du Bois attempted "to dislodge American history from its racist moorings," even if he often exaggerated his interpretations to reset the balance.

18. Du Bois, *Autobiography*, 343.

19. As Blight has argued, Du Bois "understood how deeply embedded the problem of racism was in American historical narratives, as well as how much those narratives continued to shape the future." See Blight, "W. E. B. Du Bois," 52. For examples of Du Bois fighting against the prevailing grand narratives, see Du Bois, *World and Africa* and *Negro.*

20. Most modern critics have dealt with the book rather harshly, but their comments underscore its ultimate value. As Francis Broderick complained, there was nothing new in *John Brown* except its call for further scholarship. The book was "largely a pastiche from earlier writings," Broderick sniped, even if "Du Bois's commentary on the legacy of John Brown to the twentieth century . . . served as a bridge to a critique of race relations in 1909." Broderick, *Du Bois*, 49.

21. Du Bois, preface to *John Brown* (1909).

22. Ibid., 3.

23. In this sense, Du Bois's selection of episodes from Brown's life clearly mirrors each partisan effort, from Redpath to Sanborn to James Malin. For example, Brown's business failures played no role in Du Bois's grand narrative of American slavery and John Brown. This was in sharp contrast to later Brown biographers Hill Peebles Wilson, Robert Penn Warren, and James Malin, all of whom used Brown's business acumen, or lack thereof, to indict him as a petty thief and con man. James Malin's text is particularly one-sided, because it focuses only on Brown's time in Kansas. See Malin, *John Brown*; Wilson, *John Brown*; and RPW, *John Brown.*

24. Du Bois, *John Brown* (1909), 38.

25. Ibid., 41.

26. The historian Herbert Aptheker has argued that Du Bois saw himself as part of the very same timeline, one Du Bois had also utilized in *Souls of Black Folk*. Du Bois's attachment to Turner, L'Ouverture, and John Brown was "perfectly logical," Aptheker wrote. "There is no doubt that [Du Bois] was conscious of himself as a continuation of their purposes" (as Brown believed himself to be following Turner and L'Ouverture). Aptheker, *Literary Legacy*, 91. Keith Byerman seconds this interpretation in his account of Du Bois's biographical influences, "Du Bois, as historian of John Brown, takes on the same role as his subject, battling for justice. . . . Although the times and modes are different, the principles remain the same. The struggle for the black world that was Brown's story becomes the struggle for a black world in Du Bois's experience." Byerman, *Seizing the Word*, 178.

27. Du Bois, *John Brown* (1909), 41.

28. Ibid., 69, 71.

29. Du Bois attempted to explain how this chaos was central to understanding the shape of Bleeding Kansas. "To comprehend [Kansas]," Du Bois argued, "one must pick from the confused tangle of Kansas territorial history the main thread of its unraveling and then show how Brown's life twined with it." Ibid., 76.

30. Du Bois, *John Brown* (1909), 76, 75, 79. While Du Bois gave ample space to Brown's heroic exploits, he was careful to point out that his subject was most definitely not "the central figure of Kansas territorial history. . . . Rather he seemed and was but a humble co-worker."

31. Ibid., 81, 165. Du Bois also offered a reconsideration of Brown's raid. "The failure at Harpers Ferry," he wrote, "does not prove it a blunder from the start." Du Bois did not spare Brown critiques, he merely approached Brown's plan on its merits: a financially backed, utterly unexpected attack by a band of men willing to sacrifice their lives—revolutions have succeeded with less.

32. Ibid., 202.

33. Du Bois, *Autobiography*, 148. See Blight's discussion of history as one of Du Bois's "strategies" in Blight, "W. E. B. Du Bois," 47. As Blight keenly observes, for Du Bois, history became less a discipline than a "weapon" in his struggle against prevailing American historical narratives that had systematically excluded blacks.

34. Du Bois, *John Brown* (1909), 203, 202.

35. Ibid., 146.

36. Ibid., 225, 230. For more on this ancient Christian idea, particularly its origins, misapplications, and the debates over its merits, see Vollman, *Rising Up and Rising Down*.

37. OGV, *Fighting Years*, 24.

38. Ibid., 30.

39. Henry had also been a reporter during the Lincoln-Douglas debates and eventually befriended the future president, whom he greatly admired, in a small way. As Southern secession gained momentum, Henry was sent by the strongly anti-Lincoln *New York Herald* to follow the president-elect until his inauguration.

40. Villard de Borchgrave and Cullen, *Villard*, 189–90.

41. OGV, *Fighting Years*, 5, 7; Chapman, *William Lloyd Garrison*, 165.

42. OGV, *Fighting Years*, 4–5. Villard's only biographer, D. Joy Humes, highlighted Vil-

lard's belief in his ability to see the "moral implications in all things." See Humes, *Oswald Garrison Villard*, 3.

43. F. J. Garrison to OGV, January 4, 1905; OGV to F. J. Garrison, March 18, 1902, OGV Papers.

44. Villard de Borchgrave and Cullen, *Villard*, 385.

45. OGV, *Fighting Years*, 17.

46. OGV, "To Henry Villard," 145, 157, 158.

47. OGV, *Fighting Years*, 80–81. Villard had particular praise for the president of Harvard, Charles W. Eliot, "the outstanding figure in American education." This was the same Eliot who "openly deplored miscegenation, denounced any admixture of racial stocks, and endorsed the absolute separation of races." Kellogg, *NAACP*, 5.

48. Villard's publishing and activism did eventually earn him an honorary Phi Beta Kappa key from Howard, which he displayed prominently for the rest of his life. He also received honorary doctorates from Howard, Washington and Lee, Lafayette, and the University of Oregon. He was also president of numerous businesses, from the Fort Montgomery Iron Company to several realty companies and a half-dozen banks in the New York metropolitan area. He served as vice president of the elite New York City Club, president of the Philharmonic Society, and was a member of countless other clubs in New York and beyond.

49. Humes, *Oswald Garrison Villard*, 3.

50. OGV, *Fighting Years*, 62.

51. Humes, *Oswald Garrison Villard*, 4. Villard, however, traced his involvement with black equality not to his grandfather but to his own "interest in Negro education." This interest, like his occasional John Brown document-gathering, brought Villard to the merchant-philanthropist Robert C. Ogden, who led safaris throughout the South. With journalists in tow, Villard and other reform-minded high-society passengers got a glimpse of the former Confederate states. Villard met his wife, Julia Sandford, a native Georgian (who would figure prominently in many of the NAACP schisms with Du Bois), on the trip. He also claimed to have discovered his personal passion for African American reform during the journey. See OGV, *Fighting Years*, 172; and "What Is Doing in Society," *New York Times*, Nov. 14, 1902, 7.

52. William English Walling, "Race War in the North," *The Independent*, September 3, 1908.

53. Ovington, *Walls*, 196. According to Villard's retelling, he was one of the principal organizers of the NAACP. However, as Ovington described in her autobiography (and Kellogg confirms in his definitive account of the NAACP), only she, Walling, and Moskowitz "met in Walling's apartment" for the true founding moment of the NAACP.

54. Ovington, *Walls*, iii. See also Kellogg, *NAACP*, 12.

55. *The Call*, OGV Papers; also reprinted in Kellogg, *NAACP*, Appendix A. *The Call* also posed the following intimidating question: "How far has [the nation] lived up to the obligations imposed upon it by the Emancipation Proclamation?" The tone was aggressive and critical; the document's bold subtitle was "To Discuss Means for Securing Political and Civil Equality for the Negro." Turning to bleak assessments, *The Call* said Lincoln "would see the black men and women for whose freedom a hundred thousand of soldiers gave their lives" denied "the best exercise of citizenship."

56. Ibid.

57. Ibid. In keeping with his self-centered conception of the organization's origins, Vil-

lard's account embroidered his own role. "The NAACP was founded by four people on February 12, 1909," Villard recalled in 1938. "On that day there met a national conference to discuss the grave situation of the Negro and the shameful injustices to which he was and is subjected and that conference was called by Mary White Ovington, William English Walling, Henry Moskowitz and myself."

58. OGV, "Rise of the NAACP."

59. A curious aspect of this desire was Villard's almost total lack of firsthand experience with anyone from these underprivileged groups. His autobiography makes clear that his friends and associates were all upstanding members of the patrician class, having attended Harvard, and sometimes Yale. See OGV, *Fighting Years*, 120–30.

60. "He felt duty-bound by his heritage," Villard's biographer described. See Humes, *Oswald Garrison Villard*, 78. In one of his many moments of hyperbolic egotism, Villard called the NAACP "one of the movements which I helped to originate . . . in which I can take unqualified satisfaction." See OGV, *Fighting Years*, 194.

61. Villard "spoke disparagingly that other descendants of the abolitionists had abdicated the cause." See Humes, *Oswald Garrison Villard*, 78.

62. Ovington, *Walls*, 100.

63. Walling wrote, "Yet who realizes the seriousness of the situation, and what large and powerful body of citizens is ready to come to their aid!" Walling, "Race War in the North," *The Independent*, September 3, 1908. After reading Walling's Springfield article in 1908, Ovington reached out to the author, not Du Bois, because the latter was busy "working with his own race." In Walling, Ovington had identified something that would define the new organization, "a white man who called upon both races, in the spirit of the abolitionist, to come forward and right the nation's wrongs." After the 1909 meeting in Moskowitz's New York apartment, they wrote up a draft of a mission statement and sent it to Villard, their "best chance for publicity." Ovington, *Walls*, 100–102.

64. Villard had finally realized that Booker T. Washington was a threat to any competing racial reform organization, even if the editor had ignored Du Bois's warnings on that subject in 1905. At a Hampton Institute fundraiser in 1909 headlined by President Howard Taft and Washington, Villard definitively abandoned the Tuskegee camp. Needless to say, he did not simply join Du Bois, but his recollection of the evening reveals just how close he and Du Bois could be in their thinking. "I grow weary of hearing it said that Hampton and Tuskegee provide the absolute solution," Villard wrote to his uncle. "It is always the same thing, platitudes, stories [and] high praise for the Southern white man who is helping the negro up." OGV to W. L. Garrison, February 24, 1909, OGV Papers.

65. Ovington, *Walls*, 109.

66. Kellogg, *NAACP*, 17.

67. Ibid., 24, 33.

68. Even stranger, Villard had written to Du Bois for help with his own biography in 1907, a gesture that made his *Nation* review even more inconsiderate. At the time of the early correspondence, Du Bois cordially responded that he was focusing mainly on "interpretation" and was "afraid I can't be of very much assistance to you, but of course, if there is any way in which I can, I shall be very glad to." Du Bois to OGV, November 15, 1907, OGV-JB Papers. Villard also received Du Bois's assurance that the book would not conflict with Villard's own, a claim Villard repeated in a letter to the John Brown bibliographer Thomas Featherston-

haugh: "It will [not] in any way conflict with mine." Villard also noted that Du Bois was "a Harvard graduate" and "intellectually the ablest of his race." OGV to Thomas Featherston-haugh, November 20, 1907, OGV-JB Papers.

69. Villard had long been aware of Du Bois's biography, and the review itself was not a last-minute assignment but the culmination of at least two years of assumptions about a competitor's work. As Villard had written to the elderly Brown biographer Franklin Sanborn in 1907: "While Du Bois's forthcoming book is to be an appreciation, mine is to be more of an historical study, giving such new light as I may be able to discover." OGV to Franklin Sanborn, November 30, 1907, OGV-JB Papers.

70. OGV, "Harper's Ferry and Gettysburg," *The Nation*, October 28, 1909, 405.

71. Ibid.

72. W. E. B. Du Bois to Paul E. More, November 6, 1909, November 15, 1909, November 20, 1909, WEBDB Papers.

73. Du Bois to Paul E. More, November 15, 1909.

74. In a letter to his assistant, Katherine Mayo, Villard mentioned the uproar. "We have another nasty note from Du Bois," Villard wrote. "He says that I deliberately ran down his book unjustly to put it out of the way for the arrival of my own volume. Isn't it incredible? I am not sure whether I shall reply or not." OGV to Katherine Mayo, November 22, 1909, OGV-JB Papers.

75. Du Bois to Paul E. More, November 15, 1909, WEBDB Papers.

76. Ibid. Du Bois's feelings seem even more justified by Villard's private correspondence. Writing Franklin Sanborn, Villard asked if he had "seen Du Bois's John Brown now out? It has many errors of fact on almost every page and shows an amazing lack of research. . . . I am very sorry indeed, because I have the highest opinion of Du Bois and his ability, and nothing would have gratified me more than to have had him produce from the point of view of the negro a great biography. It would have helped create interest in mine." OGV to Franklin Sanborn, October 26, 1909, OGV-JB Papers.

77. OGV to Francis J. Garrison, November 17, 1909, OGV Papers.

78. Francis J. Garrison to OGV, November 23, 1909, OGV Papers.

79. Francis J. Garrison to OGV, May 18, 1910, OGV Papers.

80. W. E. B. Du Bois, "NAACP," *The Crisis*, December 1910.

81. *Washington (DC) Bee*, November 5, 1910, November 12, 1910. As Charles Kellogg wrote in his history of the organization, "The problem of white leadership and white control was to haunt the work of the association for many years." Kellogg, *NAACP*, 54.

82. OGV to Francis J. Garrison, March 9, 1910, OGV Papers.

83. For his published resignation from *The Nation* in 1940 (Villard's pacifism was no longer compatible with the magazine), Villard invoked his grandfather's *Liberator* masthead. "It is not, of course, easy to thrust away at the injustice on every hand," he declared, "but it is far worse to be a compromiser; to be a toady to things as they are; to bow the knee to Baal; to seek only to advance one's own interest and let the devil take the hindmost. . . . Nobody can, I hope, truthfully aver that I ever compromised on a principal, or failed to tell the truth as I saw it." OGV, "Radio Address."

84. Whereas Du Bois has been celebrated as the oracle of race in America, Villard has most often been lauded as the prototypical elite benefactor and philanthropist. "He crusaded zealously and faithfully," his biographer wrote in 1960, "to extend individual rights and equal

opportunity and protection to minority and underprivileged groups." But the truth was much more complicated. Villard's supposed selflessness and principle regarding Du Bois and the NAACP have never been critiqued in any serious way. This seems even odder considering that Villard's pacifism, a stance inherited and relentlessly adhered to, forced him to sell first the *New York Evening Post* (during World War I) and his beloved *The Nation* (during World War II). Villard's pacifist writings, letters, and speeches are collected in Gronowicz, *Oswald Garrison Villard*.

85. Kellogg, *NAACP*, 89.

86. OGV, *Fighting Years*, 198.

87. Ibid., 18.

88. Ibid., 97, 81.

89. Ibid., 99, 242.

90. Mayo, *Mother India*.

91. Ibid., 242.

92. OGV to Katherine Mayo, August 31, 1908, OGV-JB Papers.

93. Mayo's extensive interviews are in the various John Brown folders, OGV-JB Papers.

94. OGV to Katherine Mayo, December 5, 1908, OGV-JB Papers.

95. OGV, *John Brown*, viii.

96. OGV to Katherine Mayo, November 3, 1910, OGV-JB Papers.

97. OGV, *John Brown*, preface.

98. Ibid.

99. Ibid.

100. Ibid., viii.

101. Ibid., 7.

102. Ibid., 42, 44–45. "In November, 1834," Villard wrote, "[Brown] first expressed on paper a wish to aid his fellow-Americans in chains." At this early stage, violence was still far from Brown's mind and he then was arguing that merely educating blacks "would shatter the whole system of slavery." Villard showed a similar eagerness to play up the parallels to Garrisonian abolition in his novel analysis of Brown's provisional constitution of 1851, that vaguely treasonous document made infamous after the Harpers Ferry invasion. The constitution defined "slavery as war . . . the keynote to Brown's philosophy," Villard wrote, so it "explains better than anything else why it was consistent with his devout religious character for him to kill, and to plunder for supplies in Kansas, and to take up arms against slavery itself. There was no such thing as peace so long as there were chains upon a single slave." See ibid., 334–36. Understanding Villard's personal distaste for religiously inspired violence makes his measured analysis all the more notable. "The constitution," Villard concluded, "simply emphasize[d] anew Brown's belief that he really could engage in warfare against slavery."

103. Ibid., 28. "In these and other schemes," as Villard described another botched enterprise, "John Brown became so deeply involved that he failed during the bad times of 1837, lost nearly all his property by assignment to his creditors, and was then not able to pay all his debts."

104. OGV-JB Papers. See also OGV, *John Brown*, 28. Villard narrated Brown's move to Kansas in identical terms. Villard wrote that Brown was now "free to move where he pleased, to devote every thought to his battle with the slave-power. . . . The metamorphosis was now complete." See ibid., 77–78.

105. OGV, *John Brown*, 77–78.

106. Ibid., 185.

107. Ibid., 185–88.

108. "Fanatical, Brown's mind was," Villard explained. "If to be devoted to one idea, or to a single cause, is to be a monomaniac, then the world owes much of its progress toward individual and racial freedom to lunacy of this variety." Ibid., 509–10. Stephen Oates fiercely defended Brown's sanity in his 1970 study, critiquing those historians who accepted the "insanity defense" affidavits from Brown's trial "at face value." Echoing Villard, Oates argues that "sanity" is a singularly unhelpful concept when dealing with "a revolutionary who believed himself called by God to a special destiny." To label Brown as "insane" would be to ignore two fundamental concepts: (1) Brown's "tremendous sympathy . . . for the suffering of the black man in the United States"; and (2) the "piercing insight" he showed that the raid, "whether it succeeded or whether it failed," would inflame "sectional tensions that already existed between North and South." See Oates, *To Purge This Land*, 331, 333.

109. Ibid., 538.

110. Ibid., 586.

111. Ibid., 588. "Not often in history," Villard wrote, "is there recorded such a rise to spiritual greatness of one whose hands were so stained with blood, whose judgment was ever so fault, whose public career was so brief."

112. Ibid., 586–87.

113. *Emporia (KS) Gazette*, October 2, 1910. Villard's book also earned him respect from professional historians after being lauded in the *American Historical Review*. A "most painstaking, judicial, finely humane book," reviewer James Hosmer wrote. "Inferences are drawn with nice discrimination; the detail is as nearly exhaustive as the most exacting reader can require." Hosmer cautioned his colleagues that Brown was only a hero in spite of his lawlessness and massacres, for the Old Hero "had the gravest limitations and could never have been a great leader." In the broader historical context, Brown was important because he "impressed friends and foes, the unlettered and the very flower of American culture. The border jayhawker and Emerson at Concord alike felt his spell, the one struck with terror, the other with admiration." Finally, Hosmer concluded, "excepting Lincoln, our time of trial offers to the biographer no worthier subjects." Hosmer, review of OGV, *John Brown*, 648.

114. William MacDonald, *The Nation*, October 20, 1910, also in *New York Evening Post*, October 22, 1910.

115. OGV, *Fighting Years*, 242.

116. January 6, 1911, for instance, marked an important centennial: that of the birth of Charles Sumner, the famous Massachusetts abolitionist. In planning for a celebration, Du Bois demonstrated his own difficulties in working with others, steamrolling a plan for a celebration at Boston's Faneuil Hall without consulting any local NAACP leaders. Villard clashed with Du Bois over the issue but also tried to torpedo the efforts of one of those local leaders, Charles Trotter, whom in 1905 Villard had called "dangerous" and "irresponsible." True to his principles, Villard had not changed his mind on Trotter, and the three men "were either unwilling or unable to submerge themselves for the good of the cause." Indeed, collegiality, enforced, unwilling, or otherwise, was essential to any success the NAACP would enjoy. Moorfield Storey, the first president of the organization, along with Villard, found the internal factionalism of the NAACP deeply counterproductive.

117. Storey to Villard, October 17, 1911, October 20, 1911, Storey Collection, Library of Congress.

118. OGV to Francis J. Garrison, October 23, 1906, OGV Papers.

119. OGV to Francis J. Garrison, February 7, 1913, February 11, 1913, OGV Papers.

120. Du Bois to OGV, March 18, 1913, April 3, 1913, OGV Papers; OGV to Du Bois, April 3, 1913, WEBDB Papers.

121. Du Bois to OGV, March 18, 1913, OGV-JB Papers. Charles Kellogg, in his history of the NAACP, which goes to great lengths to excuse Villard, still admits that "in spite of his good intentions [his letters] often show a patronizing attitude toward the Negro." Kellogg goes on to say that therein lay another difference between Du Bois and Booker T. Washington. While Washington "could tolerate [the patronizing approach] it must have been extremely trying to Du Bois, who was sensitive enough to observe every 'shadow.'" Kellogg, *NAACP*, 103.

122. OGV to Ovington, October 6, 1917, OGV Papers.

123. In Villard's view, his involvement with the NAACP had earned him a certain status. As he humorously recalled in his autobiography, there were moments when his activism and outspoken agitation for black rights helped him transcend race. During World War I, a Cincinnati newspaper described him, along with Moorfield Storey and Du Bois, as "the three most prominent Negroes in the United States." Even if it was the sole occasion he had "earned the adjective 'black,'" Villard was proud that his efforts had convinced ignorant people that he was on the right side. See OGV, *Fighting Years*, 241.

124. Mary White Ovington to OGV, November 25, 1913, OGV-JB Papers.

125. Ibid.

126. Mary White Ovington to OGV, November 10, 1915, OGV-JB Papers.

127. OGV to Mary White Ovington, November 11, 1915, OGV-JB Papers.

128. Ibid. Villard added that Du Bois "does not hesitate, however, to call upon me when he wants favors for his friends." In a letter to Ovington in 1917, he wrote, "I cannot work with Dr. Du Bois and I feel so strongly about it that I am going to again insist that I be allowed to leave. . . . I will not lend my name as the treasurer to the Association unless it becomes, as I think it should, efficient, and the first step toward that efficiency and public confidence should be the removal of Dr. Du Bois as editor. . . . I enclose the latest sample of the written things that he is doing." OGV to Mary White Ovington, October 6, 1917, OGV-JB Papers.

129. OGV to Jessie Fauset, February 24, 1920, OGV Papers. About the review, Villard replied that he could not possibly do so, "because it should be unfavorable [and] it would simply subject me to abuse and attack by Dr. Du Bois." See OGV to Mary White Ovington, August 11, 1915, OGV-JB Papers.

130. Caroline Janney has a terrific section on McDonald and his complicated position on racial equality in her fascinating essay about the competing memorials erected at Harpers Ferry, one for the free black railroad porter Heyward Shepherd, the other for John Brown. See Janney, "Written in Stone," 133–34. See also Shackel, *Memory in Black and White*, for excellent essays on the incredible transmutations of both the Heyward Shepherd Memorial and the John Brown Fort: "Southern Heritage and the Faithful-Slave Monuments: The Heyward Shepherd Memorial" and "The John Brown Fort: Unwanted Symbol, Coveted Icon."

131. Shackel, *Memory in Black and White*, 51–76.

132. *The Crisis*, July 1932, 219. The fort was purchased in 1910 for two thousand dollars.

133. Ibid., 219. The tablet's fate after 1950 is unknown. The NAACP does not know of its whereabouts. A replica of the stone now stands where the John Brown fort was located in 1932.

134. Janney, "Written in Stone," 134.

135. *Baltimore Afro-American*, June 4, 1932. Fortunately, the event was documented carefully; several newspaper reporters were in attendance to cover an elaborate meal prepared to follow the tablet's unveiling.

136. Janney, "Written in Stone," 133.

137. Du Bois published a nearly identical speech by Villard in *The Crisis*, July 1925. Speaking at the third annual pilgrimage of the John Brown Memorial Association (a black fundraising organization) Lake Placid, New York, Villard trumpeted his dedication to race reform: "I have now reached the age when I can look back on three decades of service to the colored people," Villard declared, "to work for them and with them. I think their progress has been amazing." Villard regretted that sometimes "their shortcomings, their lack of leadership," made him go "faint and weary." Beyond the deficiencies of the race he claimed to be so dedicated to, Villard focused on Brown. "Again I do not uphold his methods of force," he argued, "but I do urge whole-heartedly that the colored people of America make of John Brown the moral crusader their inspiration and their model, and they devote themselves without stint and without question to the cause of freedom which was but half won when Lee surrendered, and emancipation became a reality." Villard admitted that his "impatient nature" made him long "to see some of the causes to which I have given my life triumph in my lifetime, precisely as it was given to my grandfather to initiate the militant fight for emancipation and live to see its fulfillment." "I cannot help praying day by day for a greater solidarity among the colored people," he lectured, "a more militant sprit of determination to achieve justice and equality, an abjuring of the easy and the pleasant thing of life for the hardnesses, the bitternesses, the defeats and the victories of the struggle for complete emancipation." Villard reminded his audience that "with solidarity the colored people could achieve those rights in short time indeed . . . precisely as John Brown made the nation face the issue, made it realize that certain wrongs were beyond being borne any longer." OGV, "John Brown the Crusader," *The Crisis*, July 1925, 117–18.

138. OGV, "Address at Harper's Ferry," May 21, 1932, OGV Papers.

139. Ibid.

140. "Not Particular How John Brown Hit Slavery," *Baltimore Afro-American*, May 28, 1932. "STORER PREXY RUNS AWAY," headlined the entire issue. As Caroline Janney notes, "Therefore Brown, even though a white man, proved a more useful symbol of violence, authority, agency, and courage. As Henry McDonald's conflicted reverence for Brown but opposition to the NAACP tablet revealed, Brown's legacy of violence continued to divide white and black proponents of African American rights." Janney, "Written in Stone," 135.

141. "Pres. McDonald Leaves the John Brown Meeting: Du Bois Raps Storer College Head and Its Trustees: Had Barred Brown Tablet—Objected to 'Guilty Nation' Inscription," *Afro-American*, May 28, 1932, 1–2.

142. Ibid.

143. *The Crisis*, July 1932, 219.

144. Du Bois, *John Brown* (1909), 234.

Chapter 6

1. Bruce Ronda speculates that Benét might have read Robert Penn Warren's John Brown biography (examined in depth in the next chapter), but only Warren's inner circle read drafts of the work. Furthermore, Benét's epic poem was published several months before Warren's biography. Ronda, *Reading the Old Man*, 97.

2. SVB quoted in John Dickson to Rosemary Benét, October 6, 1947, SVB Papers.

3. Fenton, *Stephen Vincent Benét*, 10, 23–27.

4. See Izzo and Konkle, *Stephen Vincent Benét*, 4–5. For more on Lindsay, see Masters, *Vachel Lindsay*; and Mark Harris, *City of Discontent*.

5. In particular, see Morris, "Haystack in the Floods," and one of Morris's many historical epics, *A Dream of John Ball*. SVB, *Young Adventure* and *Heavens and Earth*.

6. Fitzgerald, *This Side of Paradise*, 315; Fenton, *Stephen Vincent Benét*, 57.

7. Benét's papers are full of references to his shoddy finances and his profligacy.

8. Douglas Moore, CBC talk, June 17, 1953, SVB Papers.

9. SVB to Wilbur Cross, September, 1925, SVB Papers.

10. SVB to Phelps Putnam, March 7, 1928, SVB Papers.

11. Fenton, *Stephen Vincent Benét*, 189.

12. WRB to SVB, February 27, 1926, SVB Papers.

13. SVB, *John Brown's Body*, vii. Nicolay and Hay, *Abraham Lincoln*; Goldthwaite, *Four Brothers in Blue*; Jones, *Rebel War Clerk's Diary*.

14. SVB to WRB, March 7, 1928, SVB Papers.

15. SVB to WRB, March 2, 1927, SVB Papers. For his epic poem, Benét would find an epic historical model in the four-volume compendium by Johnson and Buel, *Battles and Leaders of the Civil War*. Originally commissioned by *The Century* magazine, the series was a collective hagiography of Confederate and Union veterans.

16. Fenton, *Selected Letters*, 129.

17. SVB to WRB, March 20, 1927, SVB Papers.

18. SVB to WRB, April 25, 1927, SVB Papers.

19. SVB to Robert Nathan, May 21, 1927, SVB Papers.

20. WRB to SVB, November 8, 1927, SVB Papers.

21. WRB to Rosemary Benét, August, 1928, SVB Papers.

22. As Benét's biographer described it, "the entire nature of his life [was] changed and the future pattern of his career established"; Fenton, *Stephen Vincent Benét*, 224.

23. Pulitzer Prize Committee to SVB, May 6, 1929, SVB Papers.

24. Benét was not the only poet attracted to John Brown. Brown had first been celebrated by John Greenleaf Whittier and E. C. Stedman in 1859, but the 1920s and 1930s represented another high point in poems about the abolitionist. Bruce Ronda discusses contemporary efforts in his book on Brown. See Ronda, *Reading the Old Man*, 90–97.

25. Melville, "Portent."

26. SVB, *John Brown's Body*, xxxiii, foreword.

27. Ibid., xxxiii.

28. SVB to John Farrar, July 1, 1927, SVB Papers. In this letter to his publisher, Benét spoke of the urgent need for demythologizing biographies of Robert E. Lee, William Bedford Forrest, Ulysses S. Grant, and Jefferson Davis.

29. SVB, *John Brown's Body*, xxxiii.

30. Ibid., xxxvii.

31. Ibid., 18.

32. Ibid., 18.

33. Ibid., 29.

34. Ibid., 53, 59.

35. Ibid., 200.

36. SVB to Mrs. James Walker Benét, November 5, 1927, SVB Papers.

37. SVB, *John Brown's Body*, 200.

38. Ibid., 200, 363.

39. Blight, *Race and Reunion*, 397.

40. Ibid., 397. Blight writes that it was a struggle "even to know one another across [these] separate societies [and] anguished history."

41. William Minor Lile to SVB, January 29, 1929, SVB Papers.

42. Ibid.

43. Meredith Nicholson to SVB, January 22, 1929, SVB Papers.

44. Lile to SVB, January 29, 1929, SVB Papers.

45. Stokes, *D. W. Griffith's "The Birth of a Nation."*

46. Wade, *Fiery Cross*, 138.

47. Griffith, *Abraham Lincoln*.

48. Margaret Mitchell to SVB, July 9, 1936, in *Margaret Mitchell's "Gone with the Wind" Letters*, 34–36.

49. Ibid.

50. SVB, *John Brown's Body*, 363.

Chapter 7

1. Mencken, *Religious Orgy in Tennessee*. See also http://www.law.umkc.edu/faculty/ projects/ftrials/scopes/scopes.htm.

2. Mims, *Advancing South*, x, 301–3.

3. Hobson, *Serpent in Eden*, 148.

4. RPW, "Episode at the Dime Store," unpublished essay, box 232, folder 4391, RPW Papers. This essay eventually appeared in print in *Southern Review* 30 (1994).

5. Ibid.

6. For more on that process, see Davidson, *Southern Writers*, 10–19; and Underwood, *Allen Tate*, 31.

7. Davidson, "New South," 20–21, in DD Papers.

8. Winchell, *Where No Flag Flies*, 7–8.

9. Rubin, *Wary Fugitives*, 330.

10. Winchell, *Where No Flag Flies*, 18–19.

11. Ibid., 19.

12. Rubin, *Wary Fugitives*, 162; Thomas Daniel Young, *Waking Their Neighbors Up*, 9.

13. Underwood, *Allen Tate*, 171.

14. Tate had also imagined the South not as a region but as what his biographer Thomas Underwood called "an organized religion." See Underwood, *Allen Tate*, 157. On the very con-

cept of *Southern* being more than just a word, even more than a legend, "a body of notions that hold their hands up and answer present when one says southern," see Davidson, "*I'll Take My Stand*: A History," *American Review* 5 (Summer 1935): 309. The Fugitives' imagined South was not beholden to facts. The entire notion of their lost antebellum world was a matter of faith. This faith was so powerful that Warren still articulated pieces of the Fugitives' historical project in the 1980s: "Before the Civil War, [there was] a strong emancipation sentiment in the South," and important segments of southern society were "pro-emancipationist, as were many influential men." The logical question that followed was why the North had to wreck that inevitable, self-imposed end to slavery. Warren's sequence of events summed up the Fugitives' logic: "Then came the slave rebellion of Nat Turner and the brand of abolitionism fostered by William Lloyd Garrison, who would fanatically burn the Constitution. These developments stopped the movement in the South to free the slaves." Here, Warren offered the Fugitives' explanation of the history of the abuse of the South. The region was prepared to give up slavery, but the North was taken over by fanatics. Thus, the North was ultimately at fault for a pointless and horrific war. "Can Democracy Survive in a World of Technology? A Conversation with Robert Penn Warren," *U.S. News and World Report*, August 18, 1980, 64.

15. Allen Tate to Donald Davidson, March 17, 1927, DD Papers.

16. Davidson, *Southern Writers*, 62.

17. Ibid., 62.

18. Allen Tate to Donald Davidson, May 5, 1927, DD Papers.

19. Ibid.

20. Allen Tate to Donald Davidson, April 28, 1927, DD Papers.

21. Allen Tate to Donald Davidson, May 5, 1927, DD Papers.

22. Blight, *Race and Reunion*, 273.

23. Allen Tate to Donald Davidson, August 10, 1929, DD Papers. See also Bradbury, *Fugitives*, 3.

24. In the planning for the "Southern Symposium" that eventually became *I'll Take My Stand*, Donald Davidson voiced this exact concern. On the essay dealing with "the Negro Question," Davidson lamented "that the second Ku Klux Klan came along when it did" because the Fugitives/Agrarians would have to be particularly "careful not to fall into that slough." Donald Davidson to Allen Tate, October 26, 1929, in Fain and Young, *Literary Correspondence*, 236.

25. See Oates, *To Purge This Land*, x: "Slavery was entrenched . . . safeguarded by the Constitution and a web of court decisions and national and state laws, it was booming and expanding in the 1850s, not dying out." This argument has been explored and reinforced by several excellent pieces of scholarship. See Fehrenbacher and McAfee, *Slaveholding Republic*; and Wills, *Negro President*.

26. This interpretation plainly anticipated the work of the historian Avery Craven and the Revisionist school, which argued that Northern impatience, not slavery, was to blame for the Civil War. Craven would soon publish his landmark biography, *Edmund Ruffin, Southerner*. The Revisionist interpretation was first articulated in 1929 by Charles Ramsdell at the University of Texas and was rapidly taken up by others in the field. Revisionists rejected the reigning interpretations of Civil War causality, which blamed slavery (and by implication) the South for the war. See Ramsdell, "Natural Limits." Ramsdell argued that slavery had finished expanding by 1860; therefore war was unnecessary to prevent further growth. For

Ramsdell, James G. Randall (an influential professor at the University of Illinois), Craven, and Frank Owsley (a Vanderbilt faculty member, contributor to *I'll Take My Stand*, and long-time president of the Southern Historical Association), the Civil War had virtually nothing to do with slavery; Northern high-mindedness and aggression were to blame for the great conflict. As the Revisionists quickly set out to attack slavery-based interpretations of the war, its causes and villains, John Brown became a key target. For more on this historiographical conflict, see Tulloch, *Debate on the American Civil War Era*. An equally comprehensive account can be found in Pressly, *Americans Interpret Their Civil War*.

27. Winchell, *Where No Flag Flies*, 129. In contrast, Louis Rubin's chapter on Tate treats the two biographies Tate wrote as intimately connected to his family history and personal psychological issues. See Rubin, *Wary Fugitives*, 64–135.

28. Tate, *Stonewall Jackson*, 39. In his next biography, Tate argued that "the modern system is probably inferior to that of slavery"; Tate, *Jefferson Davis*, 301.

29. Tate, *Stonewall Jackson*, 39.

30. Allen Tate to Donald Davidson, August 10, 1929, DD Papers.

31. Emerson was considered the most villainous of these higher-law fanatics. The Fugitives had long decried New England intellectuals, who they believed had crippled voluntary Southern emancipation, caused the Civil War, and continued to beat the South down at every opportunity. While William Lloyd Garrison and John Brown were primary targets, Ralph Waldo Emerson quickly became the personification of the compounded evils of New England. Tate labeled him the "Lucifer of Concord," and the "light bearer who could see nothing but light and was fearfully blind." Davidson argued that "Emerson helped cause the Civil War" because "his voice was not the voice of America but of New England, and his plan of salvation was to result not in peaceful unification but in bloody disunion." Warren described Emerson as "a man who lived in words, big words, and not in facts." This virulent anti-Emerson feeling was not an isolated passion. For the group, Emerson simply represented the zenith of the Northern mindset, the same worldview that had interpreted the Constitution via "abstract right" in order to "destroy the social and political structure of the United States by force of arms." Vilifying Emerson formed one corner of an argument that disparaged abolitionists, excused the South from any serious blame, and generally sought to establish a new narrative for the defeat and resurrection of their beloved region. For more on Emerson's prominent role in anti-abolitionist thought, see Lewis Simpson's excellent book *Mind and the American Civil War*; Tate, "Emily Dickinson," 285; Davidson, "Regionalism and Nationalism," 59; RPW, *John Brown*, 245; and Tate, *Stonewall Jackson*, 60–61.

32. Tate, *Stonewall Jackson*, 56, 57.

33. Allen Tate to Malcolm Cowley, June 14, 1929, Malcolm Cowley Papers, Special Collections, Newberry Library, Chicago.

34. Allen Tate to Andrew Lytle, July 31, 1929, in Young and Sarcone, *Lytle-Tate Letters*, 34. Action Française was an anti-Semitic, proto-fascist political organization founded in 1898 by Charles Maurras. Many members embraced fascism and supported the Vichy regime following the Nazi invasion of France. For more, see Kalman, *The Extreme Right in Interwar France*.

35. RPW to Allen Tate, fall 1929; quoted in Blotner, *Robert Penn Warren*, 98.

36. Allen Tate to Donald Davidson, August 10, 1929, DD Papers.

37. Cullick, *Making History*, 30.

38. Rubin, *Wary Fugitives*, 98.

39. Allen Tate to Andrew Lytle, May 15, 1927, in Young and Sarcone, *Lytle-Tate Letters*, 5.

40. Lytle, "Journey South," 8–10.

41. Allen Tate to Andrew Lytle, July 1928, in Young and Sarcone, *Lytle-Tate Letters*, 12.

42. Lytle, "Journey South," 10.

43. Ibid., 10.

44. Allen Tate to Andrew Lytle, May 4, 1929, in Young and Sarcone, *Lytle-Tate Letters*, 26.

45. For a thorough analysis of the Fugitive ideology and their simultaneous interest in Civil War projects, see Rock, "Making and Meaning of *I'll Take My Stand*."

46. Allen Tate to Virginia Lyne Tunstall, August 19, 1928, in Underwood, *Allen Tate*, 135.

47. Warren recognized that America, in the words of William Bedford Clark, was "not short on myths, many of which [were] self deluding and pernicious," but Warren and his compatriots hoped to replace them with what they saw as their "painfully honest appraisal of society and self in which the whole truth, however difficult it may be to face, is allowed to merge on its own terms." Clark, *American Vision*, 14.

48. RPW, *Legacy of the Civil War*, 102.

49. As Warren wrote in his most famous work, "History is blind but man is not." RPW, *All the King's Men*, 462.

50. Andrew Lytle to Allen Tate, January 31, 1929, in Young and Sarcone, *Lytle-Tate Letters*, 16.

51. RPW to W. F. Payson, Esq., September 8, 1928, RPW Papers.

52. Redpath, *Echoes of Harpers Ferry*; Villard, *John Brown*; Sanborn, *Life and Letters*.

53. Hinton, *John Brown and His Men*; Wilson, *John Brown*.

54. RPW to Payson, September 8, 1928, RPW Papers.

55. Ibid.

56. RPW to Allen Tate, September 17, 1929, RPW Papers.

57. Allen Tate to Donald Davidson, October 24, 1928, DD Papers.

58. Allen Tate to Andrew Lytle, May 4, 1929, in Young and Sarcone, *Lytle-Tate Letters*, 26.

59. RPW, *John Brown*, 21.

60. Ibid., 30–32. This was also one of Warren's favorite tropes later in life. When asked about racism in the South, he would note that New England whites sent thousands of dollars to help blacks in Mississippi but were unwilling to give any money to help blacks in nearby slums. See "Can Democracy Survive in a World of Technology? A Conversation with Robert Penn Warren," *U.S. News and World Report*, August 18, 1980, 64.

61. Ibid., 38, 32, 339, 277. In contrast to Warren's portrait of blacks and the raid, we should recall Shields Green's impulsive decision to join Brown just before the attack on Harpers Ferry. The moment demonstrates free blacks' complex agency as well as Brown's very real charisma.

62. Ibid., 331–32.

63. Ibid., 283. Warren explained that slaves had everything provided for them, so freedom was going to be nearly impossible to navigate.

64. These hackneyed arguments for slavery were part of a broad defense of the Old South, one that harkened back to the father of the proslavery school of Southern history, Ulrich

Bonnell Phillips. Phillips, a historian at Columbia, professionalized the study of the South in the 1920s by defending slavery, calling it a system of "gentleness, kind-hearted friendship and mutual loyalty," concepts which guided several generations of historians. Ulrich Bonnell Phillips, *American Negro Slavery*, 18.

65. Ibid., 332.

66. Ibid., 441.

67. Casting abolitionists' invocations of "higher law" as treasonous was a crucial component to the Lost Cause. An excellent essay on Southern concerns is Holden, "John Brown as 'Lawless Fanatic.'" For more on this topic, see William Seward's landmark speech in the Senate on March 11, 1850, in which he railed against slavery as a temporary institution. "But there is a higher law than the Constitution," Seward declared, "which regulates our authority over the domain, and devotes it to the same noble purposes." In Baker, *Works of William H. Seward* 70–93; Carter, "Use of the Doctrine of Higher Law."

68. RPW, *John Brown*, 25, 134. Warren also believed that the war irrevocably weakened the Constitution.

69. Ibid., 45.

70. This interpretation is wholly unfair, given how common financial failure was in nineteenth-century America; see Sandage, *Born Losers*, 9. Sandage examines Brown's case specifically as part of his argument that failure was unbelievably commonplace; stories like Brown's were "everywhere, if we can bear to hear them."

71. RPW, *John Brown*, 166.

72. Ibid., 211. For Frederick Brown, Brown's son, shot in cold blood in Kansas, Warren demonstrated none of the compassion he professed to feel for the innocent proslavery victims at Pottawatomie. He wrote callously that "the first blood of the Brown family had been shed in the fight for freedom, for cattle and horses, for plunder," even though Frederick was not involved, even tangentially, in the Free State marauding of his father.

73. Ibid., 444, 304.

74. Etcheson, *Bleeding Kansas*, 202.

75. RPW, *John Brown*, 262, 348.

76. Ibid., 211, 128, 349, 314.

77. Ibid., 314.

78. Ibid., 314.

79. Ibid., 350.

80. Payson and Clarke, Ltd., Correspondence, RPW Papers.

81. Of more than 150 reviews from publications across the country, the majority lauded Warren's approach and analysis, often citing from the same passages. See folders 2790–92, RPW Papers.

82. As noted earlier, Craven would become one of the principle Revisionists, the group that came to dominate the historical profession by the mid-1930s. In a series of lectures later in that decade, Craven defined slavery as a "humane" system of "close friendships" among blacks and whites. But Craven's real fury, like Warren's and the Fugitives', was for crusading Northern zealots and their "distorted picture" of slavery, misguidedly convincing themselves "that the Negro was rebellious and much abused." "Less interested in realities than in effective weapons with which to wage his battle," the abolitionist, Craven wrote, set "a

people of common blood and common heritage . . . on the road to civil war." See Craven, *Repressible Conflict*, 27, 56, 52, 61, 62; Ramsdell, *Behind the Lines*; Craven, *Coming of the Civil War*; James Randall, *Civil War and Reconstruction*; and Owsley, *Plain Folk*. For an excellent analysis of the Revisionists, see Bonner, "Civil War Historians"; and the more recent Fladeland, "Revisionists vs. Abolitionists."

83. Avery Craven, "The John Brown the South Saw," *New York Herald Tribune*, January 12, 1930.

84. It is important to note that Craven did produce a good deal of methodically researched and evenhanded work. However, his broader perspective on the Civil War seems deeply suspect in its minimization of the horrors of slavery and his marginalization of slavery's importance to the war's causes, course, and impact.

85. Donald Davidson to RPW, January 20, 1930, RPW Papers.

86. Donald Davidson, "John Brown's Ghost Is Laid," *Commercial Appeal* (Memphis, TN), February 9, 1930 (printed in several other Tennessee newspapers, including the *Knoxville Journal*, February 9, 1930, and the *Nashville Tennessean*, February 9, 1930). Davidson also thought the review necessary to confront higher-law abolitionists and their obvious descendents, *New York Times* reviewers. Davidson argued that these misguided souls merely saw in John Brown something "congenial to their own prejudices and beliefs."

87. Ibid.

88. Ibid. Bruce Ronda also uses Davidson's review in his analysis of Warren's Brown moment, but Ronda does little to problematize Warren's intellectual roots or the reception of this fruit of his labor. See Ronda, *Reading the Old Man*, 75–87.

89. "John Brown's 'Martyrdom,'" *Beaumont (TX) Enterprise*, December 8, 1929.

90. "John Brown's Place in History," *Wichita Falls (TX) Times*, December 10, 1929.

91. H. L. Mencken, "The Library," *American Mercury*, January 1930.

92. For an excellent account of the *New York Amsterdam News*, see Ottley, *"New World a-Coming,"* 268–88.

93. "God's Madman," *New York Amsterdam News*, January 22, 1930. See also J. F. G., "Soul of John Brown Goes Marching on Despite the Sneers," *Brooklyn Times*, January 5, 1930.

94. "John Brown: Rationalist," *Clearfield (PA) Progress*, February 4, 1930.

95. William MacDonald, *The Nation*, July 2, 1930.

96. Emmett, "Dixie."

97. Allen Tate to Donald Davidson, August 10, 1929, DD Papers.

98. Andrew Lytle to Allen Tate, January 31, 1929, and Tate to Lytle, May 4, 1929, in Young and Sarcone, *Lytle-Tate Letters*, 16, 26.

99. Ibid.

100. John Crowe Ransom to RPW, January 20, 1930, RPW Papers.

101. Ibid.

102. Ibid.

103. Ibid.

104. Donald Davidson to RPW, March 10, 1930, RPW Papers.

105. Donald Davidson to RPW, (postmarked March 23, 1931), RPW Papers.

106. Underwood, *Allen Tate*, 156.

107. Donald Davidson to RPW, March 17, 1930, RPW Papers. Joseph Blotner cites the letter but does not mention the word "animals," nor does he attempt to analyze the notion that these men saw the need to march on their enemies. See Blotner, *Robert Penn Warren*, 106.

108. The best study of the volume is Rock, "Making and Meaning of *I'll Take My Stand.*"

109. RPW to Allen Tate, July 1928, box 44, Allen Tate Papers, Manuscripts Division, Rare Books and Special Collections, Princeton University Library.

110. Allen Tate to the Contributors to the Southern Symposium, July 24, 1930, DD Papers.

111. Allen Tate to Donald Davidson, September 2, 1930, DD Papers.

112. Allen Tate to Malcolm Cowley, December 19, 1930, Malcolm Cowley Papers.

113. Donald Davidson to Allen Tate, July 21, 1930, in Fain and Young, *Literary Correspondence*, 251. Not surprisingly, Warren's critics have spun his essay as that thoughtful departure from the Southern hardliners. In his study of Warren, Hugh Ruppersburg positions Warren's essay as an example of his many acts of rebellion, arguing that "Warren's nonfiction critiques of American culture and society present the ideas of a man who has passed much of his life reacting against the tenor of modern American life." Ruppersburg also argues that the importance of Warren's intellectual circle "has been obscured by their public image — partially justified — as reactionary, racist apologists for the Old South, a view which barely allows for objective understanding." See Ruppersburg, *Robert Penn Warren*, 170.

114. RPW, "Briar Patch," 247.

115. RPW, *John Brown*, 331–32.

116. RPW, "Briar Patch," 247.

117. Ibid., 247, 258, 259.

Chapter 8

1. More novels, plays, short stories, and poems about John Brown were produced from 1930 and 1940 than during any ten years since 1859–69. Talbert, "John Brown in American Literature," 590. See also Wardenaar, "John Brown."

2. Dennis, *Rethinking Regionalists*, 62. Dennis also, somewhat erroneously, calls Curry a "civil rights activist [for painting] an array of crucial African American experiences from the early thirties to the early forties." As this chapter will show, that vision often emphasized reunion over racial justice.

3. Bruce Ronda also discusses Curry, but he uses the artist to highlight the work of the novelist Truman Nelson. Ronda is primarily interested in Nelson's defiant act of spitting at the Kansas statehouse mural. Ronda, *Reading the Old Man*, 124–26.

4. Curry to Margit Varga, February 23, 1942, JSC Papers.

5. Edward Alden Jewell, *New York Times*, December 7, 1930.

6. "Curry believed American painting should be charged with a historically accurate, stop-action intensity: exciting, vital, and personally real in expression." Dennis, *Rethinking Regionalists*, 65.

7. Benton, *An American in Art*, 151.

8. Dray, *At the Hands of Persons Unknown*, 307–15.

9. Sitkoff, *New Deal for Blacks*, 1:268–97. See also Zagrando, *NAACP Crusade against Lynching*.

10. Curry was one of the only artists who had already shown paintings on the subject. His

painting, *The Manhunt*, a depiction of a posse hunting a fugitive, was sometimes thought to be a lynching, but the subject matter was drawn, like much of Curry's work, from a white incident of his youth in Kansas. One of the founding members of the NAACP, Arthur Spingarn, was the first owner of Curry's *Manhunt*.

11. A copy of the exhibition catalog is available in the Lynching Folder, Schomburg Collection, New York Public Library.

12. "Kansas Heals Breach with a Native Son," *New York Herald Tribune*, rpt. in *Topeka Capital*, February 10, 1935, KSHS.

13. In 1934, when the artist George Biddle started writing his high school classmate Franklin D. Roosevelt, the president was largely unaware that Biddle was trying to convince him to start a government funded art corps, but he soon became convinced of its utility. First organized under the Treasury Department, the federal government created a Section of Painting and Sculpture, eventually dubbed the Section of Fine Arts. For more on the establishment of this division, Curry's selection, and George Biddle's efforts, see Biddle, *An American Artist's Story*. On the overlapping institutions involved in New Deal art and the various artists affiliated with each, see Jonathan Harris, *Federal Art and National Culture*.

14. When Orozco came to Dartmouth College in 1932, his work in Mexico had come to be seen as a new civic art form. Orozco's *Epic of American Civilization*, a twenty-four-panel mural completed in 1934, convinced civic- and artistic-minded Americans that public art was essential for a thriving national art culture. See Schmeckebier, *John Steuart Curry's Pageant*, 89, 69.

15. Ibid., 273.

16. Other prominent examples of federally funded civic art projects include Ben Shahn's mural of the New Deal Resettlement project in Roosevelt, New Jersey, and Philip Evergood's *Story of Richmond Hill*, his depiction of the history of Queens for the Queens Borough Public Library. See also Linden, Weinberg, and Anreus, *Social and the Real*.

17. Schmeckebier, *John Steuart Curry's Pageant*, 262–63.

18. William Lloyd Garrison's great-grandson Lloyd K. Garrison, dean of the University of Wisconsin Law School, rescued Curry's Justice Building sketches in 1942. Garrison raised the funds personally for the mural commission, largely from a then anonymous donor, Robert Uihlein. Uihlein was enthusiastic about the emancipation scene "because of family associations with the Civil War and a family tradition of friendship for the Negroes." See Kendall, *Rethinking Regionalism*, 76. As Curry commented at the time, "I feel that in this painting I have made a work that is historically true, and I also feel it is prophetic of that which is to come." See Mimeograph from Wisconsin Law School, 284–307, University of Wisconsin Archives, Madison, WI. Also Reidinger, "Law School's Curry Mural."

19. As the art historian Matthew Baigell has observed, the black man in Curry's paintings functioned as "an Americanized noble savage who had been brutally ravaged by whites, a symbol of the destruction of the myths that had once sustained the country." But Curry also emphasized "the black man as the crucified American who at the same time offered the possibility of rebirth, the new American rising from the death of the old." See Baigell, "Relevancy of Curry's Paintings of Black Freedom," 21.

20. Ibid., 21, 24. Baigell pointed out that, rather than depicting salvation, it might have been more useful to paint "the despairing condition of the blacks in the 1930s . . . so that the effects of their continued bondage might better be understood. . . . [But] Curry fell into the

234 Notes to Pages 148–53

trap of most regionalists—he was retrospective when he should have pointed aggressively for change."

21. Schmeckebier, *John Steuart Curry's Pageant*, 285.

22. Dennis, *Rethinking Regionalists*, 63. For more on the conflicts over New Deal art projects, see Contreras, *Tradition and Innovation*.

23. John Steuart Curry, "Address," Madison Art Association, January 19, 1937, Madison, WI.

24. "Curry of Kansas," *Life Magazine*, January 23, 1936.

25. Ibid.

26. Allen to Curry, May 19, 1937, JSC Papers. John Brown was being painted by other American muralists at this same time. Etaro Ishigaki's 1937–38 FAP/WPA mural for the Harlem courthouse shows Brown in a large interracial crowd, wedged between Frederick Douglass and Abraham Lincoln. Brown is bearded and grasps a modern pump-action shotgun barrel in his enormous hand. Arthur Covey's *Episodes in the Life of John Brown*, painted in 1937 for the Torrington, Connecticut, post office, is an odd assortment of scenes from Brown's life. One scene shows his childhood home in Torrington, where he interacts with farm animals. Another shows him swearing enmity to slavery in his early adulthood. One scene shows a yoke for oxen. The central panel shows Brown, rifle over shoulder bathed in God's light, leading two oxen and a wagon laden with slaves. This scene seems to derive from Brown's liberation of Missouri slaves in 1858. For more on Covey, see Marling, *Wall to Wall America*, 75, 237.

27. Mrs. Allen quoted in Edna Reinbach, "Biographical Sketch," KSHS.

28. "Curry Controversy Is Stimulating Interest in Art," *Topeka State Journal*, August 27, 1937, John Steuart Curry File, KSHS.

29. *Topeka State Journal*, June 14, 1937.

30. John Steuart Curry, "Description of Murals for Kansas State Capitol," SP725.1, K13, pam. V, KSHS.

31. "Must Be Sane," *Art Digest*, August 1, 1937, 13. Curry also learned in August 1937 that he had been selected to produce a mural for the Department of Interior building in Washington, DC. See Contreras, "New Deal Treasury Art Programs."

32. Ibid.

33. *Topeka State Journal*, August 11, 1937.

34. "Iron in Kansas People Must Be Portrayed in Murals, Says Curry," *Topeka Capital*, August 5, 1937, John Steuart Curry Folder, KSHS.

35. Kendall, *Rethinking Regionalism*, 86.

36. *Scribner's Magazine*, January 1938, 37–98.

37. *Topeka State Journal*, August 4, 1937.

38. *Topeka State Journal*, August 11, 1937. Curry solicited support for including Brown in the mural by explaining that he did not "intend to leave out all the disagreeable things. . . . The people would hate me for that."

39. John Steuart Curry, "Description of Murals."

40. *Topeka State Journal*, November 12, 1937.

41. Bret Waller, "Interview with Mrs. John Steuart Curry," in Waller, *John Steuart Curry*, 7.

42. Santway, *Brief Sketch*, 1.

43. Schmeckebier, *John Steuart Curry's Pageant*, 312.

44. *Kansas City Star*, November 16, 1937.

45. John Steuart Curry to Reverend A. Christensen, January 12, 1940, JSC Papers.

46. *Topeka State Journal*, April 15, 1939.

47. *Topeka State Journal*, April 26, 1939.

48. *Kansas City Times*, June 1, 1939.

49. Schmeckebier, *John Steuart Curry's Pageant*, 312.

50. *Topeka State Journal*, January 28, 1941.

51. Ibid.

52. *Topeka State Journal*, March 31, 1941.

53. "Curry Will Not Sign Kansas Murals," *Topeka Capital*, August 30, 1946.

54. Ibid.

55. "Page Boys in Mock Session Vote $1.15 to Finish Murals," *Topeka Capital*, March 4, 1943.

56. Waller, "Interview with Mrs. John Steuart Curry," 10.

57. Bret Waller, "Interview with Mrs. Daniel Schuster," in Waller, *John Steuart Curry*, 16.

58. Curry quoted in Waller, *John Steuart Curry*, 321. It should be no surprise that Curry's paintings are today a great tourist attraction. In the statehouse gift shop, T-shirts and posters of the Brown mural are for sale. In addition, the picture is used frequently for book covers, conferences, and all things advertising John Brown.

Chapter 9

1. John Brown artwork was produced by many black artists during this period. The art historian Richard J. Powell, in his discussion of the artist William H. Johnson, who painted three different Brown images, credits the seventy-fifth anniversary of the Thirteenth Amendment with triggering an increase in Brown and the history of slavery. See Powell, *Homecoming*, 71. The black painter Horace Pippin also produced a series of three John Brown paintings in 1942 as well as a crucifixion scene (1943) and an Abe Lincoln series (1943), with content similar to that of Lawrence's Brown series. Pippin might have been exposed to Lawrence's Brown series before he began his own paintings.

2. Patricia Hills notes that Lawrence had a "special gift for communicating [the] great epic[s] of American history in dynamic modernist terms." See Hills, "Jacob Lawrence's Migration Series," 141.

3. Wheat, *Jacob Lawrence: The Frederick Douglass and Harriet Tubman Series*, 45, 43.

4. When the series was screen printed, a poem was commissioned by the prominent African American poet Robert Hayden. Hayden's poem, "John Brown," was a sensitive meditation on Lawrence's imagery. "Shall we not say," Hayden concluded in the poem, that Brown "died for us?" Hayden actually had many intersections with Brown in American memory prior to the Lawrence commission. After reading Stephen Vincent Benét's *John Brown's Body*, Hayden dreamed of becoming "the one who'd fulfill Benet's prophecy" in that poem, the singer of "the black spear." Hayden's unfinished *The Black Spear* was "a self-conscious effort in his quest to create a noble race memory." Like Lawrence, Hayden began his career by writing elegies for African American heroes. As a graduate student at the University of Michigan, he wrote a play, *Go Down, Moses*, about Harriet Tubman. Hayden also produced an accentual sonnet, "Frederick Douglass," published in the *Atlantic Monthly* in 1947. See

Harper, "Metaphysics of *American Journal*"; and Nesbett and DuBois, *Over the Line*, 11. For more on Lawrence's place in the broader context of African American art, see Powell, *Black Art*. Art historians called the series "an unparalleled artistic accomplishment, interpreting with great originality and poetic sensitivity a pivotal figure in American history." In Jacob Lawrence, *Legend of John Brown*, 12.

5. Saarinen, *Jacob Lawrence*, 5.

6. Hills, "Jacob Lawrence's Migration Series," 142.

7. In Jacob Lawrence, *Legend of John Brown*, 7. The young painter regularly attended the sermons of Reverend Adam Clayton Powell Sr. at Harlem's Abyssinian Baptist Church, furthering the powerful sense of black consciousness that pervaded the neighborhood. As Richard Wright described it in a WPA guide from 1935, "Negro Harlem, into which are crowded more than a quarter of a million Negroes from southern states, the West Indies and Africa," was a vital space for black Americans. "To Negro college graduates," Wright continued, "it is an opportunity to practice a profession among their own people; to those aspiring to racial leadership it is a domain where they may advocate their theories unmolested; to artists, writers and sociologists it is a mine of rich material; to the mass of Negro people it is the spiritual capital of Black America." Richard Wright, *WPA Guide*, 257.

8. Wheat, *Jacob Lawrence: American Painter*, 34–35.

9. The artist drew inspiration from the characters of the neighborhood. The art historian Jeffrey Stewart offers the following description: "from barefoot prophets to shell-shocked World War I veterans, from street-corner Garveyites . . . to soapbox Communists . . . all clamoring, all gesturing, all transforming a northern ghetto into a creative crucible called Harlem." Jeffrey Stewart, "(Un)Locke(ing) Jacob Lawrence's Migration Series," 41.

10. Jacob Lawrence, "Spingarn Medal Acceptance," *The Crisis*, August–September 1970, 266–67.

11. Milton Brown and Louise Parks called this Lawrence's "distinct Black resonance." Brown and Parks, *Jacob Lawrence*, 10. It was not just the bleak aspects of Harlem that captured Lawrence's eye but the fruit sellers, the soapbox preachers, even the sounds and smells of the city seemed to find a place in his art. Lawrence methodically traveled the streets of Harlem to ingrain "people and events in his memory in an attempt to learn about and understand the history of black people." Willis, "Schomburg Collection," 35.

12. Wheat, *Jacob Lawrence: American Painter*, 31.

13. Romare Bearden and Harry Henderson argue that the difference between black artists in the Harlem Renaissance and WPA was gainful employment. "What strongly differentiated this period from the Harlem Renaissance was that the employment of a large number of African American artists gave them self-respect, the feeling that they were worthy of their pay and not dependent on patrons who felt sorry for them. These African American artists believed that art was a means through which they could win new respect for their people." Bearden and Henderson, *History of African-American Artists*, 234.

14. King-Hammond, "Inside-Outside," 69.

15. "Opinion of W. E. B. Du Bois: In Black," *The Crisis* 20 (October 1920). This notion was nothing new. Many members of the Harlem community echoed the words of Frederick Douglass. In an essay from 1849, Douglass argued that blacks would never be fairly portrayed by white artists. "Artists, like all other white persons, have adopted a theory respecting the distinctive features of negro physiognomy," Douglass argued. "We have heard many white

persons say that 'negroes look all alike.' . . . This theory, impressed strongly on the mind of an artist, exercises a powerful influence over his pencil, and very naturally leads him to distort and exaggerate those peculiarities." See Frederick Douglass, "Negro Portraits," *The Liberator*, April 20, 1849, 62.

16. For a vivid account of this social, cultural, and artistic ferment, see Corbould, *Becoming African Americans.*

17. Bearden and Henderson, *Six Black Masters*, 104–5.

18. Charles Christopher Seifert, originally a carpenter, became a sort of amateur Schomburg. Seifert owned a building at 313 West 137th Street that he dubbed the Ethiopian School of Research History. Seifert plied his homegrown black studies program on the streets of Harlem. See Hills, *Painting Harlem Modern*, 23.

19. Bearden and Henderson, *Six Black Masters*, 105.

20. Bearden and Henderson, *History of African-American Artists*, 260.

21. Donaldson, "Generation '306,'" 106–7.

22. Other examples of mural form include Dürer's biblical print cycles, the engraved novels of Hogarth, Ben Shahn's Haggadah illustrations and Dreyfus Case watercolors as well as his Syracuse mural of Sacco and Vanzetti, and others of Tom Mooney and Prohibition.

23. Wheat, *Jacob Lawrence: The Frederick Douglass and Harriet Tubman Series*, 16. The idea of painting a series instead of an individual painting was not without historical precedent; from Egyptian wall painting to the mural cycles of the Middle Ages and the Renaissance. In the twentieth century, Mexican muralists like Orozco gave new life to this form, which was quickly taken up in the WPA mural initiatives as well.

24. Bannarn also decried the use of history for propagandistic purposes: "I don't like anything which is obvious because I believe that subtleties are more powerful." Marvel Cooke, "Carving for Posterity," *New York Amsterdam News*, November 12, 1937.

25. Unpublished document, Detroit Institute of Arts, quoted in Sharp, "Legend of John Brown," 21. As Lawrence himself recalled, "People would speak of these things on the street. I was encouraged by the community to do [narrative] works of this kind; they were interested in them." See Wheat, *Jacob Lawrence: American Painter*, 42. See also Wheat, *Jacob Lawrence: The Frederick Douglass and Harriet Tubman Series*, 17. "As the spirit of black consciousness grew during the Harlem Renaissance and the years immediately following," Lawrence's biographer wrote, "such inspiring figures . . . became sources of racial pride."

26. William was no relation to W. E. B. Du Bois. *Haiti* was produced by the Federal Theater Project and opened in Harlem in 1938.

27. Fax, *Seventeen Black Artists*, 153.

28. Gates, "New Negroes," 20.

29. King-Hammond, "Inside-Outside," 70.

30. Wheat, *Jacob Lawrence: American Painter*, 28.

31. The art historian Patricia Hills notes that the 1930s were rife with leftist artists celebrating "historical rebels who had advocated revolutionary struggle to advance the cause of the oppressed." Hills, *Painting Harlem Modern*, 57. L'Ouverture presented Lawrence with his first rebel; the series allowed him to translate Bannarn's "idea that his work could be a transforming educational force in the Black community" so he might serve "as a cultural interpreter of his people's history." Jeffrey Stewart, "(Un)Locke(ing) Jacob Lawrence's Migration Series," 49.

32. Saarinen, *Jacob Lawrence*, 8. The art historian Elizabeth Turner made grander claims for the transition: "Lawrence's story had become too big for a wall, his form too radical, too far from traditional constraints to be affixed in one time or space." Turner, *Jacob Lawrence*, 14.

33. In this first series, Lawrence made factual errors and sometimes failed to communicate the heroic message he meant to illustrate. In panel 28, which showed the framing of the Haitian constitution, the caption read, "The constitution was prepared and presented to Toussaint on the 19th day of May, 1800, by nine men he had chosen, right of whom were white proprietors and one mulatto. Toussaint's liberalism led him to choose such a group to draw up the constitution. He was much criticized for his choice, but the constitution proved workable." The only people the constitution benefited were the white planters and the mulatto managerial class. Hills explains that Lawrence "wanted to point out that Toussaint made a tragic mistake by not including blacks," but the caption and image give no indication of this desire. Hills also acknowledges that Lawrence "simplified the history." Hills, *Painting Harlem Modern*, 60–61, 70. Lawrence also made errors in the Brown series. With an image of blood on the snow and fleeing figures in panel 16, Lawrence wrote the somewhat historically dubious, "In spite of a price on his head, John Brown, in 1859, liberated 12 negroes from Missouri plantations."

34. For specific scenes of armed black revolution, see *The Life of Toussaint L'Ouverture*, Nos. *12, 17, 18, 19, 21, 23, 25, 29, 33, 34.*

35. "To Lawrence," Patricia Hills explains, "the narrative's moral declared that if oppressed people fight against their oppressors, they will eventually win." See Hills, *Painting Harlem Modern*, 60. This was the moment when Lawrence seemed to take on the mission that "African American art could be a redemptive force that could provide the black community with the spiritual empowerment to fulfill its possibilities as a group and as a submerged nation in America." Jeffrey Stewart, "(Un)Locke(ing) Jacob Lawrence's Migration Series," 43.

36. Ibid., 61.

37. Art historians Milton Brown and Louise Parks called the captions "laconically factual with a primer-like simplicity, as if written for Black school children," even if Lawrence's prose was "quite sophisticated, apt, and often poetically moving." Brown and Parks, *Jacob Lawrence*, 11. Another scholar compared the captions to stanzas of a poem, text that "guarantees that each scene will be, like poetry or music, experienced in a particular order and in time." Hills, "Jacob Lawrence's Expressive Cubism," 18. Hills tracked down a fascinating radio interview with Lawrence from 1943 in which Lawrence explained, "I found that captions gave the pictures a continuity and clarity that individual titles didn't." He also told the interviewer that Gwendolyn (Lawrence's wife) helped him with the captions. Ibid., 60, 297.

38. The captions use the imagery (and vice versa) to draw the viewer into Lawrence's narrative. Ellin Wheat makes that connection explicit. The series, and particularly their written component, all descend, she argued, "from the black oral tradition[;] . . . each painting is illustrative of and illuminated by its narrative caption." Wheat, *Jacob Lawrence: American Painter*, 48.

39. Alain Locke, Recommendation for Jacob Lawrence for Rosenwald Fund grant, 1940, Julius Rosenwald Fund Archives, Fisk University Library, Nashville, TN.

40. *New York Amsterdam News*, June 3, 1939.

41. Many elements of Toussaint's story "appealed to Lawrence for [their] description of

the hero as acting for a cause larger than himself or even his immediate community. He acts for all of humanity even when redressing wrongs inflicted on a specific group of oppressed people." See Hills, *Painting Harlem Modern*, 69.

42. Karlstrom, "Jacob Lawrence," 235. See in particular *The Life of Toussaint L'Ouverture, No. 10*, and Lawrence's "Interior Scene" (1937). One notable exception is *The Life of Toussaint L'Ouverture, No. 11*, which showed British abolitionists. The caption read, "The society of the Friends of the Blacks was formed in England, 1778, the leading members being Price, Priestly, Sharp, Clarkson and Wilberforce."

43. Lawrence continued to paint the series as before. As he commented, "I work on all 33 panels at a time, this keeps them as a complete unit and not as an individual easel painting." See Hills, *Painting Harlem Modern*, 43.

44. Wheat, *Jacob Lawrence: The Frederick Douglass and Harriet Tubman Series*, 71, 105, 43. In the Douglass series, eighteen of thirty-two images depict whites, including the Brown scenes. In six of the images, whites appear as allies, but often ignorant or unwitting ones. In the Tubman series, whites appeared in six other scenes of the thirty-one in the series. In two, they are the calculating and heartless masters selling slaves at auction and hunting down fugitives. In another, they are the anonymous, unsympathetic crowd of Northerners who "welcome [Tubman] to the land of freedom." Image 21 shows astonished antislavery whites as Tubman describes her experience. Image 22 shows Underground Railroad operator Thomas Garrett helping Tubman and her "cargo" after a trying escape. Finally, image 24 shows a disembodied white hand giving Tubman a coin.

45. Saarinen, *Jacob Lawrence*, 7.

46. Brown and Parks, *Jacob Lawrence*, 10.

47. Saarinen, *Jacob Lawrence* 7.

48. Harmon Foundation, Jacob Lawrence Biographical Sketch, November 12, 1940, Archives of American Art, Smithsonian Institution, Washington, DC, microfilm roll ND 5.

49. For more on the new bondage that Lawrence alluded to, see Blackmon, *Slavery by Another Name*.

50. Ibid.

51. Sanborn, *Life and Letters*, 626–29.

52. Ralph Waldo Emerson, "Courage," delivered in Boston, November 8, 1859.

53. In Lawrence, *Legend of John Brown*, 12.

54. The John Brown series went through two iterations: the original *The Life of John Brown* (1941) was retitled *The Legend of John Brown* (1977) for restoration and screen printing. By the 1970s, the original paintings were in such poor condition they could only be viewed at the Detroit Institute of Arts. Lawrence helped Ives-Stillman of New Haven, CT, produce a series of identically sized prints, which were displayed with the original captions and packaged with a new poem by Robert Hayden called "John Brown." The differences between Lawrence's originals and the 1977 prints are subtle. Most notable is the lack of brush strokes in the backgrounds. The panels' colors were made more consistent, strengthening the interpretative choices of hue and contrast.

55. Many commentators have been particularly enthusiastic about Lawrence's use of symbolism for these historical paintings. Aline Saarinen argues that Lawrence's use of symbolic forms in the Brown cycle was crucial to "convey a world of feelings that would have been lost had the artist interjected more realistic details into his painting." See Saarinen, *Jacob Law-*

rence, 5. Richard Powell makes a similar argument in his study of Lawrence. Brown's "inflammatory, zealous call for the slaves to rise up and slay their masters is skillfully articulated by the inclusion of a few eloquent [visual] components." See Powell, *Jacob Lawrence*, 2.

56. See *The Life of Frederick Douglass, Nos. 1, 3, 26, 29, 31; The Life of Harriet Tubman, Nos. 2, 6, 8, 9, 14, 17, 20, 26, 31.*

57. This is especially clear with Lawrence's choices in panels 11 and 12, which show the fighting in Kansas. Panel 11, of Brown fighting guerrilla war from his horse, draws on Lawrence's imagery in *The Life of Toussaint L'Ouverture*, particularly panels 21 and 34. Panel 12 in the Brown series also recalls the battle sequence in *The Life of Toussaint L'Ouverture, Nos. 18, 21, 34, 35.*

58. Lawrence's use of the map in *The Legend of John Brown, No. 13*, recalls *The Life of Frederick Douglass, No. 24*, as well as *The Life of Toussaint L'Ouverture, Nos. 4, 14, 24*. Most notably, the composition of the image recalls Toussaint in *The Life of Toussaint L'Ouverture, No. 22.*

59. "Frequently the figures exist in airless, unmeasurable areas made spaceless and unreal by planes of color or complex, over-all pattern. When they do exist in space, it is usually a constructed, box-like space, often narrow as a coffin and usually tipped upward. These are spaces which may relate back to the stage sets which Lawrence made in shoeboxes during his adolescence. When light illuminates his figures, it is apt to be intense side light, like that directed from the tormentors on the sides of a stage." Saarinen, *Jacob Lawrence*, 5.

60. The panel's caption makes no mention of these issues, furthering the contrast between image and text that Lawrence cultivated throughout the series. The abolitionist's hagiographers were particularly drawn to the sanctity of Brown's religiosity. See DeCaro, "*Fire from the Midst of You*." A typical assertion was Tubman's supposed recollection of Brown: "It was not John Brown that died at Charlestown. It was Christ—it was the Saviour of our people." See Earl Conrad, *Harriet Tubman*, 143.

61. Lawrence painted the image twice, rejecting his first attempt because it lacked the thematic and symbolic elements he hoped to communicate. The alternate image, "John Brown's Arsenal," is owned by the Maier Museum of Art at Randolph-Macon Woman's College in Lynchburg, Virginia.

62. This image powerfully echoes *The Life of Toussaint L'Ouverture, No. 23*, which shows L'Ouverture's black troops en route to capture San Miguel. Such parallels reinforce the interracial questions of the Brown series.

63. Patricia Hills writes that Lawrence's art revolved around this concept. That "reminders of historical gains would spur collective action toward securing better social and economic conditions for the whole community. He felt that artists could make a difference by visualizing inspiring themes, just as the griot can verbalize hopes in the most ordinary of us." Hills, "Jacob Lawrence's Migration Series," 145. See also Hills, "Jacob Lawrence as Pictorial Griot."

64. Despite the lack of resolution, the first exhibition of the John Brown series in 1945 met with instant success. Jacob Lawrence, *Art Digest* wrote, "has made of this saga a powerful and compelling series. Simplified in approach, and, in several instances, highly abstract, they are never obscure in their import and their message is amplified through the technique employed." Ben Wolf, "The Saga of John Brown," *Art Digest*, December 15, 1945. Lawrence's biographer saw the Brown series as "the apogee of Lawrence's dramatic narrative abilities,

[exploring] the universality of the theme in which a man lays down his life in a struggle for freedom and justice." Wheat, *Jacob Lawrence: American Painter*, 65, 43.

65. Jacob Lawrence, "May 10, 1978," in Lawrence, *Legend of John Brown*, 14.

66. More than any specific message of reform, Aline Saarinen argues that Lawrence saw "Negroes' struggle for liberty and freedom as part of the struggle of *all* men to achieve human dignity." For these reasons, writes Saarinen, Lawrence's historical series were "full of blood and violence and oppression as well as courage and hope," because he was painting "neither sermons nor pamphlets[, just] telling compelling stories the only way he knows—pictorially." Lawrence's universal vision resonates powerfully with Abraham Lincoln's speech to Congress in December 1862. "We—even we here," Lincoln said, "hold the power, and bear the responsibility. In giving freedom to the slave, we assure freedom to the free—honorable alike in what we give, and what we preserve. We shall nobly save, or meanly lose, the last best hope of earth." Saarinen, *Jacob Lawrence*, 9; Abraham Lincoln, "Annual Message to Congress," December 1, 1862.

67. Thomas Jefferson to William Smith, November 13, 1787, Library of Congress, Washington, DC.

Epilogue

1. The sole surviving typescript of Welles's drama resides in the Orson Welles Papers, Lilly Library, Indiana University.

2. For a particularly powerful meditation on this theme, see Welles's last major film, *F Is for Fake* (1974).

3. Leaming, *Orson Welles*, 55.

4. Callow, *Orson Welles*, 121. Welles was never able to stage his Brown production because the play was deemed "unsuitable for the market." See Leaming, *Orson Welles*, 57. The director stewed over his ideas, characters, and themes until he began filming *Citizen Kane*. In fact, Welles was so interested in John Brown he even recorded some of the abolitionist's statements, most notably his well-known "Speech to the Court at His Trial" from November 2, 1859. Welles performed the speech for "gramophone in 1945." See Peter Conrad, *Orson Welles*, 314.

5. SVB, *John Brown's Body*, 18.

6. Aaron, *America in Crisis*.

7. Woodward tellingly dedicated his book to his friend and fellow Southern expatriate Robert Penn Warren. However, while Warren had published his anti-Brown biography in 1929 and *Segregation*, his apology for the separation of the races, in 1956, Woodward had just written his transformative history *The Strange Career of Jim Crow* (1955). Woodward's publishers still use a Martin Luther King Jr. quotation praising *Strange Career* as "the historical Bible of the civil rights movement." Although the quote has been occasionally disputed by skeptics because the remark does not appear in any independent accounts, William Leuchtenburg, William Rand Kenan Jr. Professor Emeritus of History at the University of North Carolina–Chapel Hill, was with Woodward and King "on the Montgomery march and heard King say it." William Leuchtenburg, e-mail to the author, October 26, 2010. Martin Luther King Jr., quoted in Roper, *C. Vann Woodward, Southerner*, 11. See also Roper, *C. Vann Woodward: A Southern Historian*.

8. Woodward, *Burden of Southern History*, 41.

9. Ibid., 43.

10. Ibid., 55.

11. Ibid., 43.

12. Woodward also made the spurious argument that Brown partisans admitted that Harpers Ferry had not resulted in any "gain for the extremist cause." Ibid, 60.

13. Ibid., 68.

14. The only time King seems to have spoken or written the words "John Brown" was in reference to the song "John Brown's Body," in his interview for *Playboy*. Martin Luther King Jr., in Alex Haley, "The *Playboy* Interview: Martin Luther King," *Playboy*, January 1965. When King was asked about "We Shall Overcome," he replied that "In a sense, songs are the *soul* of a movement. Consider, in World War Two, *Praise the Lord and Pass the Ammunition*, and in World War One, *Over There* and *Tipperary*, and during the Civil War, *Battle Hymn of the Republic* and *John Brown's Body*."

15. King felt Lincoln was the antebellum era's lasting hero and strongly urged President Kennedy to issue a second Emancipation Proclamation on the one hundredth anniversary of that document. Peterson, *John Brown*, 155.

16. Malcolm X, "Speech for Organization of Afro-American Unity," 81–82.

17. King admitted that "some historical victories have been won by violence; the U.S. Revolution is certainly one of the foremost." But King clarified that "the struggle of the Negro in America, to be successful, must be waged with resolute efforts, but efforts that are kept strictly within the framework of our democratic society. This means reaching, educating and moving large enough groups of people of both races to stir the conscience of the nation." If King's rhetoric recalled an antebellum figure, it was William Lloyd Garrison, not John Brown. As King concluded, "Before we can make any progress, we must avoid retrogression—by doing everything in our power to avert further racial violence." Martin Luther King, Jr., quoted in Haley, "The *Playboy* Interview."

18. Reynolds, *John Brown*, 498.

19. Timothy Tyson, *Radio Free Dixie*, 84.

20. Robert Williams, *Negroes with Guns*, 122.

21. Thoreau, "Plea for Captain John Brown."

22. "CRIME: Cherry Pie," *Time Magazine*, October 25, 1971; and Norrell, *House I Live In*, 254.

23. H. Rap Brown, *Die, Nigger, Die*, 116.

24. *Osawatomie* 1, no. 1 (Spring 1975).

25. Blanchard and Prewitt, *Religious Violence and Abortion*, 257.

26. Shaw, *Seeing the Unspeakable*, 12.

27. Armstrong, "Kara Walker Interviewed," 106.

28. The art historian Annette Dixon writes that "the visual vocabulary of Walker's fantasy slave plantation world evokes stereotypical images from black memorabilia, folklore, historical novels, movies, cartoons, old advertisements, present-day steamy Harlequin Romances, and the nineteenth-century slave autobiography. Desire and miscegenation, sex and torture, violence and play intermingle thematically in her scenes." Dixon, "Negress Speaks Out," 12.

29. From the moment Walker burst onto the contemporary art scene, she showed a keen

awareness of the antebellum and postbellum cultural constructions of slavery. Her nom de plume—"the negress"—was lifted from Thomas Dixon's *The Clansman*. Ibid., 13.

30. The art historian Robert Storr offers particular insight into this aspect of Walker's art: "What defines us a social entity is the fact that the specific manifestations of our innate dividedness are universally rooted in the heritage of slavery. That terrible institution and its divisive legacy are as much what makes us Americans as the Declaration of Independence and the Constitution. In every way that they seem to pit us against each other, slavery and racism also bind us together. . . . They are what every American has in common with every other American. The bond they have created cannot be broken, the taint they have left can never be completely removed, and the demons they have engendered can never be definitively exorcised. Despite everything, though, there is humor in the situation. . . . Walker makes abundantly obvious in her work [that] the joke—irresistibly but piercingly funny—is on us all." Storr, "Spooked," 73.

31. Walker's creations have been purchased and exhibited by the Whitney Museum, the Guggenheim, and the Museum of Modern Art. In 1997 she became the youngest person ever awarded a MacArthur Fellowship. The MacArthur award was the spark for widespread criticism of Walker's work. As Kathy Halbreich has written, Walker was a victim of a generational divide. Black artists from the 1960s like Betye Saar felt that Walker's views on slavery were "twisted and not inspirational" and that she was a naive victim of the white art establishment. In this formulation, she succeeded only because her art "served their racist ends." See Halbreich, foreword to *Kara Walker*, 1–2. See also Culture Shock, "You Decide."

32. *Deutsche Bank Art Magazine*, "Interview/Conversation." Walker's humor comes out in her extended comments. "I was having a show [at Harvard] of a large suite of silhouette pieces. And [Henry Louis] Gates organized a weekend-long series of lectures and films around the slippery slope of race and representation. It included a panel with Betye Saar, who started a censorship/hatemail campaign against my work and against my positive reception by the art market/MacArthur Award folks, Howardina Pindell, and Michael Ray Charles (also much-hated for his *pickaninny art*). And from the reports of my disappointed friends, dissed because I wasn't there, Mr. Charles couldn't hold up his end of the argument—and he has an advertising background, for shame! Now, if I hadn't been on a much-anticipated trip to the German Oma and Opa, they anticipating their first and only grandchild, I would have simply sat on the stage and nursed my Quadroon baby and said nothing."

33. The art historian Mark Reinhardt replies to Walker's critics by admitting that her art's "terrible beauty is shocking, but the shock is a means and not the end. The end is the viewer's (and, not trivially, the artist's) engagement with both the violent, pain-saturated character of America's racial history and the ways that history lives on in everyday fantasy and social interaction." Reinhardt, "Art of Racial Profiling," 118.

34. Golden, "Kara Walker"; Kara Walker, *After the Deluge*, catalog (New York: Metropolitan Museum of Art, 2006).

35. Kara Walker, "Fireside Chat," sponsored by the Society for the Encouragement of Contemporary Art (San Francisco Museum of Modern Art), April 25, 1999.

36. Golden, "Kara Walker," 49.

37. Shaw, *Seeing the Unspeakable*, 42.

38. Harvey, "Kara Walker," 5.

39. Kara Walker in Jenkins, *Look Away!*, 26.

40. Reid-Pharr, "Black Girl Lost," 33.

41. Golden, "Kara Walker," 44.

42. Reinhardt describes this process as the viewer becoming "hopelessly entangled with that of the creator." Reinhardt, "Art of Racial Profiling," 125.

43. Obrist, "Interview with Kara Walker," 14.

44. Golden, "Kara Walker," 45–46.

45. Armstrong, "Kara Walker Interviewed," 107.

46. Vergne, "Black Saint," 17.

47. Linda Williams, *Playing the Race Card*, xiv.

48. See Rosenblum, "Caritas Romana"; and Steensberg, *Caritas Romana*.

49. "Such is the case, for example in the prison scene known as Caritas Romana where a young lady, Pero by name, saves the life of her aged father by offering him her breast, a demonstration of loving-kindness praised by Pliny, depicted in Roman wall paintings, much favored by the Baroque, gracefully metamorphosed by Guy de Maupassant, and last observed (or so he says) by Mr. Steinbeck near Route 66 in California." Panofsky, *Early Netherlandish Painting*, 53. See also Balass, "Female Breast as a Source of Charity."

50. Yasmil Raymond reminds us that in slave auctions women were sold and separated from their infants while breastfeeding. "Paternal lactation is further displaced" in Walker's *Brown*. "Walker's portrayal of him as a dry father figure, a 'failed patriarch' brings into question his authority and entitlement in the pantheon of African American idols. . . . Mouths depicted in these compositions are guided not only be penury and hunger but also, certainly, by libidinal desire. The appetites seem to be driven by a deep longing for something that extends beyond food and warmth to comfort and pleasure beyond sexual pleasure to a lust for life." Raymond, "Maladies of Power," 365–67.

51. Gwendolyn DuBois Shaw also mentions Caritas Romana, drawing attention to the feminization of Brown's body in Walker's painting. Shaw's discussion of the dress and positioning of Brown, comparing it to J. T. Zealy's 1850 daguerreotype *Delia*, is particularly interesting. For Walker, "Brown has become a hollow icon, empty of meaningful nourishment for the descents of the black folk who have kept the memory of his martyrdom alive." Walker's Brown also "revokes the sexual power of the white male body by transforming significant paternalistic devices" like Brown's benevolent gaze in the Ransom painting and the blessing kiss in Hovenden. By removing Brown's clothing, Shaw writes, "Walker consciously subverts the messianic patriarch" and becomes the mammy character. In so doing Walker frees the slave mother "from slavery while imprisoning him within his martyrdom." This choice raises a perplexing question about the contrasts between Walker and Ransom, Noble, and Hovenden. The earlier paintings privilege Brown's "impending pain" over the pain of the slave mother and child. Walker's image also challenges that premise. Whose pain is more important? Walker inverts and upsets that idea. See Shaw, *Seeing the Unspeakable*, 72, 83, 84, 92–93.

52. Walker's work draws extensively on taboo sexual fantasy and nightmare. This etching is a particularly sharp reshaping of long-standing tropes of slave women's sexual subservience to white men. Gwendolyn DuBois Shaw draws out the visual evolution of "hegemonic sexual codes." See ibid., 75–85. Walker herself draws a fascinating connection between American historical sources and the sexual subtext of her work: "I read somewhere about

how Frederick Douglass's narrative, or variations on his narrative, have this very American rags-to-riches or boy-to-man construction, whereas—and maybe I just intuited this—
women's narratives are confronted with silences: rape, child death, illegitimate childbirth. . . .
That's where women always end up being women: you can do x, y, and z to become a human
being, but you're suddenly confronted with being a woman again in a very limited sense:
being a sexual object, and a sexual object who might also become a mother, willingly or un-
willingly." Harvey, "Kara Walker," 5.

53. Walker has said her primary influences are "bad romance novels and porno, because
it's a given that the reader should experience titillation. My experience also includes a heavy
dose of shame. [There is] so much irritating fucking truth about us and our reliance on the
old master/slave dialectic to define and redefine our selves and our history." *Deutsche Bank
Art Magazine*, "Interview/Conversation."

54. Philip Vergne argues that Walker "uses representations of alleged sexual excesses and
what is perceived as sexual deviancy and equates them with the perception and nature of
history." Walker's work "is a radical demystification of religious, moral, political, and verbal
power. Playing with what we see as the danger of filth, she uses abjection—and the eroticiza-
tion of abjection—as well as defilement and pollution to expose the absurdity and frailty of
a social order based on discrimination." Vergne, "Black Saint," 23.

55. Asked if there are "people in other genres that you feel a certain kinship with," Walker
replies, "Mark Twain is high on the list. I sometimes conjure up imaginary conversations
with him about his characters, their frankness. I query him about Huck and Jim and their
urgency to survive. I ask if he ever felt disappointed that his political stories were misunderstood as children's tales, or if he was perfectly jaded by human foibles and certain that 'children's tales' are all we produce anyway." Quoted in Harvey, "Kara Walker," 11.

56. McEvilley, "Primitivism," 54.

57. Kara Walker, quoted in D'Arcy, "Eye of the Storm," 59.

58. Reid-Pharr, "Black Girl Lost," 32. Reinhardt elaborates on this idea, writing that "the
implicit premise of [Walker's] enterprise is that the primal scenes of the psychodrama of
American racism still play out in our imaginations, a persistence many of us deny, even to
ourselves: we hide our affective investments and commitments behind a façade of propriety,
and struggle mightily to keep it in place. By restaging these scenes in shocking detail, Walker
seeks to pry open the cracks in the façade and sketch what lies beneath." Reinhardt, "Art of
Racial Profiling," 111.

59. Ellison, "Twentieth-Century Fiction," 25.

60. One notable entry after Walker's images is Russell Banks's popular novel *Cloudsplitter*. The novel's protagonist is John Brown's son Owen, but the story is narrated largely
through the interviews of Oswald Garrison Villard's assistant Katherine Mayo. While the
book fudges some of the historical facts, Banks's work is widely read and underscores many
of the themes that Orson Welles used Brown to explore in his 1932 play. *Cloudsplitter* probes
the meaning of unreliable narration, moral extremism, violence, and religious fanaticism
through Brown's raid. Marilynne Robinson's novel *Gilead* takes up these threads through a
fictional creation named John Ames and his grandfather, who fought with John Brown in
Kansas. Both books sold well, were widely reviewed, and won important awards. Most important, Banks has been working on a film of his novel. The *Cloudsplitter* movie would likely
be the most widespread interpretation of Brown since the extensive newspaper coverage in

the fall and winter of 1859. When that film is released (or if it is ultimately quashed), Banks's work will be better appreciated in the long study of Brown in American memory.

61. Obama includes a terrific paragraph on the historiography of these constitutional questions, parsing whether the founders were hypocrites or whether the real wisdom of the founding documents was creating "the space for abolitionists to rally and the debate to proceed," that space where amendments "could be passed, and the Union finally perfected." See Obama, *Audacity of Hope*, 95–96.

62. Ibid., 96, 97. "The hard, cold facts remind me that it was unbending idealists like William Lloyd Garrison who first sounded the clarion call for justice; that it was slaves and former slaves, men like Denmark Vesey and Frederick Douglass and women like Harriet Tubman, who recognized power would concede nothing without a fight." Obama continues: "I'm reminded that deliberation and the constitutional order may sometimes be the luxury of the powerful, and that it has sometimes been the cranks, the zealots, the prophets, the agitators, and the unreasonable—in other words, the absolutists—that have fought for a new order. Knowing this, I can't summarily dismiss those possessed of similar certainty today— the anti-abortion activist who pickets my town hall meeting, or the animal rights activist who raids a laboratory—no matter how deeply I disagree with their views. I am robbed even of the certainty of uncertainty—for sometimes absolute truths may well be absolute." Ibid., 97.

63. On February 27, 1860, Abraham Lincoln was forced to give a similar speech. At the Cooper Institute in New York City, Lincoln had to answer for Brown's raid in Virginia. Fifteen hundred New Yorkers watched the Republican presidential candidate confront his country's past, present, and future. "Who were our fathers that framed the Constitution?" Lincoln inquired, reminding his audience that the founders were divided over slavery but came together in a spirit of compromise. As Lincoln moved to present concerns, he tried to downplay the recent misadventure of the insurrectionist John Brown. "John Brown was no Republican," Lincoln tried to explain. "Some of you admit that . . . but still insist that our doctrines and declarations necessarily lead to such results. . . . We know we hold to no doctrine, and make no declaration, which were not held to and made by 'our fathers who framed the Government under which we live.'" Explaining away how Brown had flung slavery into the center of the 1860 election, Lincoln shifted the focus to political frustrations and legal intricacies. "Wrong as we think slavery is," Lincoln maintained, invoking the spirit of compromise, "we can yet afford to let it alone." Lincoln, "Cooper Union Address."

64. Obama, "More Perfect Union."

65. Obama, *Audacity of Hope*, 97, 98.

66. John Brown, "Words of Advice."

67. Obama, "More Perfect Union."

BIBLIOGRAPHY

Manuscript Collections

Archives of American Art, Smithsonian Institution, Washington, DC
    John Steuart Curry Papers
Beinecke Rare Book Library, Yale University, New Haven, CT
    Charles G. Athearn Correspondence
    Steven Vincent Benét Papers
    John Brown Family Letters: Kansas, 1855–56
    Bartow Darrach Letters, 1852–56
    William Swift Journals
    Samuel Tappan Letters
    Robert Penn Warren Papers
Columbia Rare Book Library, Columbia University, New York, NY
    Oswald Garrison Villard–John Brown Papers
Fisk University Library, Nashville, TN
    Julius Rosenwald Fund Archives
Houghton Library, Harvard University, Cambridge, MA
    Channing-Sanborn Papers
    Oswald Garrison Villard Papers
Huntington Library, San Marino, CA
    John Brown Family Papers
    James Eldridge Collection
Jean and Alexander Heard Library, Vanderbilt University, Nashville, TN
    Donald Davidson Papers
Kansas State Historical Society, Topeka
    John Steuart Curry Files
    Territorial Kansas Collection
Library of Congress, Washington, DC
    Storey Collection
Lilly Library, Indiana University, Bloomington, IN
    Orson Welles Papers
Mudd Library, Yale University, New Haven, CT
    Library of James Redpath, February 19, 1894

Newberry Library, Chicago, IL
    Malcolm Cowley Papers
New York Public Library, New York, NY
    Schomburg Collection
Princeton University Rare Book and Special Collections, Princeton, NJ
    Allen Tate Papers
University of Wisconsin Archives, Madison, WI

Microfilm Collections

W. E. B. Du Bois Papers, University of Massachusetts, Amherst

Online Articles and Collections

"A Durable Memento: Augustus Washington, African American Daguerreotypist." http://
    www.npg.si.edu/exh/awash/brown2.htm.
Balass, Golda. "The Female Breast as a Source of Charity: Artistic Depictions of Caritas
    Romana." http://www.hit.ac.il/staff/boazT/files/The%20Female%20Breast%20as%20
    a%20Source%20of%20Charity.doc.
Boyd Stutler Collection, West Virginia State Archives. http://www.wvculture.org/HiStory/
    wvmemory/imlsintro.html.
Culture Shock. "You Decide: The Art of Kara Walker." http://www.pbs.org/wgbh/
    cultureshock/provocations/kara/warning.html.
DeCaro, Louis A. "John Brown the Abolitionist: A Biographer's Blog." http://abolitionist-
    john-brown.blogspot.com/2007/12/john-brown-daguerreotype-resurfaces.html.
Deutsche Bank Art Magazine. "An Interview/Conversation via Email between Darius James
    and Kara Walker." http://www.db-artmag.de/02/e/magazin-interview-walker.php.
Douglass, Frederick. "Address at Harpers Ferry," May 30, 1881. http://www.nps.gov/hafe/
    douglass.htm.
Finkelman, Paul, and Clayton Cramer. "Analogies: Was Timothy McVeigh Our John
    Brown?" July 6, 2001. http://hnn.us/articles/139.html.
"John Brown the Abolitionist: A Biographer's Blog." http://abolitionist-john-brown
    .blogspot.com/2007/12/john-brown-daguerreotype-resurfaces.html.
Libby, Jean. "Chronology of John Brown Portraits." http://www.alliesforfreedom.org.
Lincoln, Abraham. "Cooper Union Address." New York, February 27, 1860. http://showcase
    .netins.net/web/creative/lincoln/speeches/cooper.htm.
Obama, Barack. "A More Perfect Union." Philadelphia, March 18, 2008. http://my.barack
    obama.com/page/content/hisownwords.
Pierce, President Franklin. "State of the Union, December 31, 1855." http://www.infoplease
    .com/t/hist/state-of-the-union/67.html.
Scopes Trial Resource. http://www.law.umkc.edu/faculty/projects/ftrials/scopes/scopes
    .htm.
Yale Slavery Pages. http://www.yaleslavery.org/Abolitionists/torrey.html.

Newspapers and Periodicals

American Mercury
American Review
Art Digest
Ashtabula (OH) Sentinel
Atlanta Journal
Atlantic Monthly
Augusta (ME) Comfort
Baltimore Afro-American
Baltimore American and Commercial Advertiser
Baltimore Evening Sun
Beaumont (TX) Enterprise
Book World
Bookman
Boston Transcript
Brooklyn Times
The Call
The Century: A Popular Quarterly
Charleston (SC) Courier
Charleston (WV) Gazette
Cincinnati Enquirer
Clearfield (PA) Progress
Cleveland Plain Dealer
Cleveland Weekly Leader
Columbus (OH) Dispatch
Commercial Appeal (Memphis, TN)
The Crisis
Daily Cleveland Herald
Emporia (KS) Gazette
Federal Council Bulletin
Freedom's Champion (Atchison, KS)
Hammond (IN) Lake Co. Times
Harper's Weekly
The Independent
The Jewish Journal
Kansas City Star
Kansas City Times
Knoxville (TN) Journal
Leavenworth (KS) Times
The Liberator
Life Magazine
London Spectator
Lowell (MA) Daily Citizen

Macon (GA) Telegraph
Nashville Banner
Nashville Tennessean
The Nation
National Anti-slavery Standard
New England Magazine
The New Republic
New York Amsterdam News
New York Daily Tribune
New York Evening Post
New York Herald
New York Herald Tribune
New York Independent
New York Tribune
New York Times
Norfolk Virginian Pilot
North American Review
Oberlin (OH) Evangelist
Osawatomie
Outlook and Independent
Philadelphia Ledger
Plain Talk
Playboy
Portland Express
Portland (ME) News
Proceedings of the Massachusetts Historical Society
Scribner's Magazine
Springfield (MA) Republican
St. Louis Globe Democrat
St. Louis Interpreter
Time Magazine
Topeka (KS) Capital
Topeka (KS) Daily Commonwealth
Topeka (KS) State Journal
U.S. News and World Report
Washington (DC) Bee
Weekly Anglo-African (Detroit)
Weekly Anglo-African (New York)
Weekly Republican (Springfield, MA)
Weekly Times (Leavenworth, KS)
Wichita Falls (TX) Times

Published Sources

A Rare Picture. Pamphlet. Oberlin College, 1886.

Aaron, Daniel, ed. *America in Crisis: Fourteen Crucial Episodes in American History.* New York: Knopf, 1952.

Anderson, Osborne P. *A Voice from Harper's Ferry.* Boston: Printed for the author, 1861.

Aptheker, Herbert, ed. *The Literary Legacy of W. E. B. Du Bois.* White Plains, NY: Kraus International, 1989.

————. *Pamphlets and Leaflets by Du Bois.* White Plains, NY: Kraus International, 1985.

Armstrong, Elizabeth. "Kara Walker Interviewed by Liz Armstrong, 7/23/96." In *No Place Like Home*, ed. Elizabeth Armstrong. Minneapolis: Walker Art Center, 1997.

Baigell, Matthew. "The Relevancy of Curry's Paintings of Black Freedom." In *John Steuart Curry: A Retrospective Exhibition of His Work Held in the Kansas State Capitol, Topeka, October 3–November 3, 1970.* Lawrence: University of Kansas Press for the University of Kansas Museum of Art. Reprinted from *Kansas Quarterly* 2 (1970).

Baker, George E., ed. *The Works of William H. Seward.* Vol. 1. New York: Redfield, 1853.

Banks, Russell. *Cloudsplitter.* New York: Harper Flamingo, 1998.

Barker, John. *The Superhistorians: Makers of Our Past.* New York: Scribners, 1982.

Barnes, Gilbert. *Antislavery Impulse, 1830–1844.* New York: D. Appleton-Century, 1933.

Bay, Mia. "Abolition and the Color Line." *American Quarterly* 55, no. 1 (March 2003).

Bearden, Romare, and Harry Henderson. *A History of African-American Artists from 1792 to the Present.* New York: Pantheon, 1993.

————. *Six Black Masters of American Art.* New York: Zenith, 1972.

Benét, Stephen Vincent. *Heavens and Earth.* New York: Henry Holt, 1920.

————. *John Brown's Body.* New York: Farrar and Rinehart, 1928.

————. *Young Adventure.* New Haven, CT: Yale University Press, 1918.

Bennett, Lerone, Jr. *The Challenge of Blackness.* Chicago: Johnson, 1972.

Benton, Thomas Hart. *An American in Art: A Professional and Technical Autobiography.* Lawrence: University of Kansas Press, 1969.

Berry, Ian, Darby English, Vivian Patterson, and Mark Reinhardt, eds. *Kara Walker: Narratives of a Negress.* New York: Rizzoli, 2007.

Biddle, George. *An American Artist's Story.* Boston: Little, Brown, 1939.

Bierce, General L. V. "Address Delivered at Akron, Ohio, on the Evening of the Execution of John Brown, December 2, 1859." Columbus: Ohio State Journal Steam Press, 1865.

Blackmon, Douglas A. *Slavery by Another Name: The Re-enslavement of Black Americans from the Civil War to World War II.* New York: Anchor, 2008.

Blanchard, Dallas A., and Terry James Prewitt. Religious Violence and Abortion: The Gideon Project. Gainesville: University Press of Florida, 1993.

Blight, David W. "John Brown: Triumphant Failure." *American Prospect*, November 30, 2002.

————. *Race and Reunion: The Civil War in American Memory.* Cambridge: Harvard University Press, 2001.

————. "W. E. B. Du Bois and the Struggle for American Historical Memory." In *History and Memory in African-American Culture*, ed. Genevieve Fabre. New York: Oxford University Press, 1994.

Blotner, Joseph. *Robert Penn Warren: A Biography*. New York: Random House, 1997.

Bonner, Thomas N. "Civil War Historians and the 'Needless War' Doctrine." Journal of the History of Ideas 17, no. 2 (April 1956).

Bradbury, John. *The Fugitives: A Critical Account*. Chapel Hill: University of North Carolina Press, 1958.

Breitman, George, ed. *By Any Means Necessary: Speeches, Interviews and a Letter*. New York: Pathfinder, 1970.

Brewerton, G. Douglas. *The War in Kansas*. Freeport, NY: Books for Libraries, 1971.

Broderick, Francis. *W. E. B. Du Bois: Negro Leader in a Time of Crisis*. Stanford, CA: Stanford University Press, 1959.

Brown, H. Rap. *Die, Nigger, Die*. New York: Dial, 1969.

Brown, John. "Provisional Constitution and Ordinances for the People of the United States, May 8, 1858." In *Meteor of War: The John Brown Story*, ed. Zoe Trodd and John Stauffer. Maplecrest, NY: Brandywine, 2004.

———. "Words of Advice" (1851). In *Meteor of War: The John Brown Story*, ed. Zoe Trodd and John Stauffer. Maplecrest, NY: Brandywine, 2004.

Brown, Milton W., and Louise A. Parks. *Jacob Lawrence*. New York: Whitney Museum of American Art, 1974.

Brundage, W. Fitzhugh. *The Southern Past: A Clash of Race and Memory*. Cambridge, MA: Belknap, 2005.

Buñuel, Luis. *My Last Sigh: The Autobiography of Luis Buñuel*. New York: Knopf, 1983.

Burlingame, Michael. "Nicolay and Hay: Court Historians." *Journal of the Abraham Lincoln Association* 19, no. 1 (Winter 1998).

Byerman, Keith. *Seizing the Word: History, Art and Self in the Work of W. E. B. Du Bois*. Athens: University of Georgia Press, 1994.

Cady, Edwin H. *Young Howells and John Brown: Episodes in a Radical Education*. Columbus: Ohio State University Press, 1985.

Callow, Simon. *Orson Welles*. Vol. 1, *The Road to Xanadu*. New York: Penguin, 1995.

Cameron, Kenneth Walker. *Transcendental Youth and Age: Chapters in Biography and Autobiography*. Hartford, CT: Transcendental, 1981.

Carter, George Edward. "The Use of the Doctrine of Higher Law in the American Anti-slavery Crusade." PhD diss., University of Oregon, 1970.

Carton, Evan. *Patriotic Treason: John Brown and the Soul of America*. New York: Free Press, 2006.

Chapman, John Jay. *William Lloyd Garrison*. Boston: Atlantic Monthly, 1921.

Clark, William Bedford. *The American Vision of Robert Penn Warren*. Lexington: University of Kentucky Press, 1991.

Cobb, James C. *Away down South: A History of Southern Identity*. New York: Oxford University Press, 2005.

Collison, Gary L. *Shadrach Minkins: From Fugitive Slave to Citizen*. Cambridge: Harvard University Press, 1997.

Conrad, Earl. *Harriet Tubman*. New York: Paul S. Eriksson, 1943.

Conrad, Peter. *Orson Welles: The Stories of His Life*. New York: Faber and Faber, 2004.

Contreras, Belisario R. "The New Deal Treasury Art Programs and the American Artist: 1933–1943." PhD diss., American University, 1967.

———. *Tradition and Innovation in New Deal Art*. Lewisburg, PA: Bucknell University Press, 1983.

Corbould, Clare. *Becoming African Americans: Black Public Life in Harlem, 1919–1939*. Cambridge: Harvard University Press, 2009.

Craven, Avery. *Coming of the Civil War*. New York: Scribner and Sons, 1942.

———. *Edmund Ruffin, Southerner: A Study in Secession*. New York: D. Appleton, 1932.

———. *The Repressible Conflict, 1830–1861*. Baton Rouge: Louisiana State University Press, 1939.

Cullick, Jonathan. *Making History: The Biographical Narratives of Robert Penn Warren*. Baton Rouge: Louisiana State University Press, 2000.

Curry, John Steuart. "Address." Madison Art Association, Madison, WI, January 19, 1937.

D'Arcy, David. "The Eye of the Storm." *Modern Painters*, April 2006.

Davidson, Donald. "The New South and the Conservative Tradition." Lecture at Biennial Institute of Bowdoin College. April 26, 1958.

———. *Southern Writers in the Modern World*. Athens: University of Georgia Press, 1958.

———. "Regionalism and Nationalism in American Literature." In Davidson, *Still Rebels, Still Yankees and Other Essays*. Baton Rouge: Louisiana State University Press, 1953.

Davis, David Brion. *Ante-bellum Reform*. New York: Harper and Row, 1967.

———. "The Emergence of Immediatism in British and American Antislavery Thought." *Mississippi Valley Historical Review* 49 (September 1962): 209–230.

———. *In the Image of God: Religion, Moral Values, and Our Heritage of Slavery*. New Haven, CT: Yale University Press, 2001.

———. *The Problem of Slavery in the Age of Revolution, 1770–1823*. Ithaca, NY: Cornell University Press, 1975.

———. *The Problem of Slavery in Western Culture*. Ithaca, NY: Cornell University Press, 1966.

———. *Slavery and Human Progress*. New York: Oxford University Press, 1984.

Davis, Jefferson. "Remarks in the U.S. Senate," December 8, 1859. In *Meteor of War: The John Brown Story*, ed. Zoe Trodd and John Stauffer. Maplecrest, NY: Brandywine, 2004.

Dean, Bradley P., and Ronald Wesley Hoag. "Thoreau's Lectures after *Walden*: An Annotated Calendar." In *Studies in the American Renaissance*, ed. Joel Myerson. Charlottesville: University Press of Virginia, 1997.

de Borchgrave, Alexandra Villard, and John Cullen. *Villard: The Life and Times of an American Titan*. New York: Doubleday, 2001.

DeCaro, Louis A. "Black People's Ally, White People's Bogeyman: A John Brown Story." In *The Afterlife of John Brown*, ed. Andrew Taylor and Eldrid Herrington. New York: Palgrave, 2005.

———. *"Fire from the Midst of You": A Religious Life of John Brown*. New York: New York University Press, 2002.

Dennis, James M. *Rethinking Regionalists: The Modern Independence of Grant Wood, Thomas Hart Benton and John Steuart Curry*. Madison: University of Wisconsin Press, 1998.

De Witt, Robert, pub. *The Life, Trial and Execution of Captain John Brown*. New York: De Witt, 1859.

Dillon, Merton. "The Abolitionists: A Decade of Historiography, 1959–1969." *Journal of Southern History* 35 (1969): 500.

———. *Elijah P. Lovejoy, Abolitionist Editor*. Urbana: University of Illinois Press, 1961.

Dixon, Annette. "A Negress Speaks Out: The Art of Kara Walker." In *Kara Walker: Pictures from Another Time*, ed. Annette Dixon. Ann Arbor: University of Michigan Press, 2002.

Donald, David. *Charles Sumner and the Coming of the Civil War*. New York: Knopf, 1960.

Donald, David, and J. G. Randall. *Civil War and Reconstruction*. Boston: Heath, 1961.

Donaldson, Jeff Richardson. "Generation '306': Harlem, New York." PhD diss., Northwestern University, 1974.

Douglass, Frederick. "John Brown: An Address at the Fourteenth Anniversary of Storer College," May 30, 1881. In *Meteor of War: The John Brown Story*, ed. Zoe Trodd and John Stauffer. Maplecrest, NY: Brandywine, 2004.

———. *The Life and Times of Frederick Douglass*. Hartford, CT: Park, 1881.

Dray, Philip. *At the Hands of Persons Unknown: The Lynching of Black America*. New York: Modern Library, 2003.

Dubois, Laurent. *Avengers of the New World: The Story of the Haitian Revolution*. Cambridge: Belknap, 2004.

Du Bois, W. E. B. *The Autobiography of W. E. B. Du Bois: A Soliloquy on Viewing My Life from the Last Decade of Its First Century*. New York: International, 1968.

———. *Dusk of Dawn: An Essay toward an Autobiography of a Race Concept*. New York: Harcourt, 1940.

———. *John Brown*. Philadelphia: G. W. Jacobs, 1909.

———. *John Brown*. Armonk, NY: M. E. Sharpe, 1997.

———. *John Brown*. New York: Modern Library, 2001.

———. *The Negro*. New York: Henry Holt, 1915.

———. *The World and Africa: An Inquiry into the Part Which Africa Has Played in World History*. New York: Viking, 1947.

Dumond, Dwight, ed. *Letters of James Gillespie Birney, 1831–1857*. New York: D. Appleton-Century, 1938.

Dumond, Dwight, and Gilbert H Barnes, eds. *Letters of Theodore Dwight Weld, Angelina Grimké Weld and Sarah Grimké, 1822–1844*. New York: D. Appleton-Century, 1934.

Egerton, Douglas. *Gabriel's Rebellion: The Virginia Slave Conspiracies of 1800–1802*. Chapel Hill: University of North Carolina Press, 1993.

Elkins, Stanley. *Slavery: A Problem in American Institutional and Intellectual Life*. New York: Universal Library, 1963.

Ellison, Ralph. "Twentieth-Century Fiction and the Black Mask of Humanity." In Ellison, *Shadow and Act*. New York: Vintage, 1995.

Emmett, Daniel Decatur. "Dixie." New York: Firth, Pond, 1860.

Etcheson, Nicole. *Bleeding Kansas: Contested Liberty in the Civil War Era*. Lawrence: University of Kansas Press, 2004.

Fabre, Genevieve, ed. *History and Memory in African-American Culture*. New York: Oxford University Press, 1994.

Fain, John Tyree, and Thomas Daniel Young, eds. *The Literary Correspondence of Donald Davidson and Allen Tate*. Athens: University of Georgia Press, 1974.

Fax, Elton C. *Seventeen Black Artists*. New York: Dodd, Mead, 1971.

Fehrenbacher, Don, and Ward M. McAfee. *Slaveholding Republic: An Account of the United States Government's Relations to Slavery*. New York: Oxford University Press, 2001.

Fenton, Charles A. *Stephen Vincent Benét: The Life and Times of an American Man of Letters*, 1898–1943. New Haven, CT: Yale University Press, 1958.

———, ed. *Selected Letters of Stephen Vincent Benét*. New Haven, CT: Yale University Press, 1960.

Finkelman, Paul, ed. *His Soul Goes Marching On: Responses to John Brown and the Harpers Ferry Raid*. Charlottesville: University Press of Virginia, 1993.

Finkelman, Paul, and Peggy A. Russo, eds. *Terrible Swift Sword: The Legacy of John Brown*. Athens: Ohio University Press, 2005.

Fitzgerald, F. Scott. *This Side of Paradise*. New York: Scribner, 1920.

Fladeland, Betty L. "Revisionists vs. Abolitionists: The Historiographical Cold War of the 1930s and 1940s." Journal of the Early Republic 6, no. 1 (Spring 1986).

Fletcher, Robert S. "John Brown and Oberlin." *Oberlin Alumni Magazine*, February 1932.

———. "Ransom's John Brown Painting." *Kansas Historical Quarterly* 9, no. 4 (November 1940).

Foner, Philip S. *Life and Writings of Frederick Douglass*. New York: International, 1955.

Forter, Emma E. "The Dedicatory Address." Topeka, KS: Women's Relief Corps, 1909.

Franklin, John Hope, and Loren Schweninger. *Runaway Slaves: Rebels on the Plantation*. New York: Oxford University Press, 1999.

Frey, Sylvia. *Water from the Rock: Resistance in a Revolutionary Age*. Princeton, NJ: Princeton University Press, 1991.

Gates, Henry Louis, Jr. "New Negroes, Migration, and Cultural Exchange." In *Jacob Lawrence: The Migration Series*, ed. Elizabeth Hutton Turner. Washington, DC: Rappahannock, 1993.

Genovese, Eugene. *Roll, Jordan Roll*. New York: Pantheon, 1974.

Gilpin, R. Blakeslee. "The National Precipice: Rumor and Violence in John Brown's Kansas." Paper delivered at Western Historical Association meeting, Scottsdale, AZ, October 15, 2005.

Golden, Thelma. "Kara Walker: A Dialogue." In *Kara Walker: Pictures from Another Time*, ed. Annette Dixon. Ann Arbor: University of Michigan Press, 2002.

Goldthwaite, Robert. *Four Brothers in Blue*. New York: Washington, 1913.

Goodman, Susan, and Carl Dawson. *William Dean Howells: A Writer's Life*. Berkeley: University of California Press, 2005.

Goodrich, Thomas. *The Darkest Dawn: Lincoln, Booth, and the Great American Tragedy*. Bloomington: Indiana University Press, 2005.

———. *War to the Knife: Bleeding Kansas, 1854–1861*. New York: Bison, 2004.

Greenberg, Kenneth, ed. *Nat Turner: A Slave Rebellion in History and Memory*. New York: Oxford University Press, 2003.

Griffith, D. W. *Abraham Lincoln*. United Artists, 1930.

Gronowicz, Anthony, ed. *Oswald Garrison Villard: The Dilemmas of the Absolute Pacifist in Two World Wars*. New York: Garland, 1983.

Gura, Philip. *American Transcendentalism: A History*. New York: Hill and Wang, 2007.

Halbreich, Kathy. Foreword to *Kara Walker: My Complement, My Enemy, My Oppressor, My Love*, ed. Philip Vergne. Minneapolis, MN: Walker Art Center, 2007.

Harlan Louis R., and Raymond W. Smock, eds. *The Booker T. Washington Papers*. Urbana: University of Illinois Press, 1976.

Harmon Foundation. *Jacob Lawrence Biographical Sketch*, November 12, 1940.

Harper, Michael S. "The Metaphysics of American Journal." *American Poet*, Spring 2001.

Harris, Jonathan. *Federal Art and National Culture: The Politics of Identity in New Deal America*. Cambridge: Cambridge University Press, 1995.

Harris, Mark. *City of Discontent: An Interpretative Biography of Vachel Lindsay*. New York: Permanent, 1990.

Harrold, Stanley. *Subversives: Antislavery Community in Washington, D.C., 1828–1865*. Baton Rouge: Louisiana State University Press, 2003.

Harvey, Matthea. "Kara Walker." *BOMB* 100 (Summer 2007).

Hess, Thomas B., and Linda Nochlin, eds. *Woman as Sex Object: Studies in Erotic Art, 1730–1970*. New York: Allen Lane, 1972.

Higginson, Thomas Wentworth. *Henry Wordsworth Longfellow*. Boston: Houghton Mifflin, 1902.

Hills, Patricia. "Jacob Lawrence as Pictorial Griot." *American Art* 7, no. 1 (Winter 1993).

———. "Jacob Lawrence's Expressive Cubism." In *Jacob Lawrence: American Painter*, ed. Ellin Harkins Wheat. Seattle: University of Washington Press, 1986.

———. "Jacob Lawrence's Migration Series: Weavings of Pictures and Texts." In *Jacob Lawrence: The Migration Series*, ed. Elizabeth Hutton Turner. Washington, DC: Rappahannock, 1993.

———. *Painting Harlem Modern: The Art of Jacob Lawrence*. Berkeley: University of California Press, 2009.

Hinton, Richard. *John Brown and His Men: With Some Account of the Roads They Traveled to Reach Harpers Ferry*. New York: Funk and Wagnalls, 1894.

Hirrel, Leo. *Children of Wrath: New School Calvinism and Antebellum Reform*. Lexington: University of Kentucky Press, 1998.

Hobson, Fred C. *Serpent in Eden: H. L. Mencken and the South*. Baton Rouge: Louisiana State University Press, 1974.

Holden, Charles J. "John Brown as 'Lawless Fanatic': A Usable Past for the Postwar South." In *Terrible Swift Sword: The Legacy of John Brown*, ed. Paul Finkelman and Peggy A. Russo. Athens: Ohio University Press, 2005.

Hoogstra, Jacob T. *American Calvinism: A Survey*. Grand Rapids, MI: Baker Book House, 1957.

Horner, Charles. *The Life of James Redpath and the Development of the Modern Lyceum*. New York: Base and Hopkins, 1926.

Horwitz, Tony. *Midnight Rising: John Brown's Raid and the Start of the Civil War*. New York: Henry Holt, forthcoming.

Hosmer, James K. Review of Oswald Garrison Villard, *John Brown, 1800–1859: A Biography Fifty Years After. American Historical Review*, April 1911.

Howard, Victor. *Conscience and Slavery: The Evangelistic Calvinist Domestic Missions, 1837–1861*. Kent, OH: Kent State University Press, 1990.

Howells, William Dean. *Literary Friends and Acquaintances*. New York: Harper and Bros., 1900.

Hudson, Lynn. *The Making of "Mammy Pleasant": A Black Entrepreneur in Nineteenth-Century America*. Urbana: University of Illinois Press, 2003.

Humes, D. Joy. *Oswald Garrison Villard: Liberal of the 1920s*. Syracuse, NY: Syracuse University Press, 1960.

Husband, Julie. "W. E. B. Du Bois's *John Brown*: Placing Racial Justice at the Center of a Socialist Politics." In *The Afterlife of John Brown*, ed. Andrew Taylor and Eldrid Herrington. New York: Palgrave, 2005.

Izzo, David Garrett, and Lincoln Konkle, eds. *Stephen Vincent Benét: Essays on His Life and Work*. Jefferson, NC: McFarland, 2003.

Janney, Caroline. "Written in Stone: Gender, Race, and the Heyward Shepherd Memorial." *Civil War History* 52, no. 2 (2006).

Jenkins, Sidney. *Look Away! Look Away! Look Away!* Annandale-on-Hudson, NY: Center for Curatorial Studies, Bard College, 1996.

Johnson, R. U., and C. C. Clough Buel. *Battles and Leaders of the Civil War*. New York: Century, 1887–88.

Johnson, Walter. *Soul by Soul: Life inside the Antebellum Slave Market*. Cambridge: Harvard University Press, 1999.

John Steuart Curry: A Retrospective Exhibition of His Work Held in the Kansas State Capitol, Topeka, October 3–November 3, 1970. Lawrence: University of Kansas Press for the University of Kansas Museum of Art. Reprinted from *Kansas Quarterly* 2 (1970).

Jonas, Gilbert. *Freedom's Sword: The NAACP and the Struggle against Racism in America, 1909–1959*. New York: Routledge, 2005.

Jones, John B. *A Rebel War Clerk's Diary*. Philadelphia: Lippincott, 1866.

Kaiser, Ernest. "John Brown: A Review." *Freedomways*, Summer 1963.

Kalman, Samuel. *The Extreme Right in Interwar France*. Aldershot, England: Ashgate, 2008.

Kammen, Michael. *Meadows of Memory: Images of Time and Tradition in American Art and Culture*. Austin: University of Texas Press, 1992.

———. *Mystic Chords of Memory: The Transformation of Tradition in American Culture*. New York: Knopf, 1991.

Karlstrom, Paul J. "Jacob Lawrence: Modernism, Race and Community." In *Over the Line: The Art and Life of Jacob Lawrence*, ed. Peter T. Nesbett and Michelle DuBois. Seattle: University of Washington Press, 2000.

Kellogg, Charles Flint. *NAACP: A History of the National Association for the Advancement of Colored People*. Vol. 1, *1909–1920*. Baltimore: Johns Hopkins, 1967.

Kendall, M. Sue. *Rethinking Regionalism: John Steuart Curry and the Kansas Mural Controversy*. Washington, DC: Smithsonian Institution Press, 1986.

King-Hammond, Leslie. "Inside-Outside, Uptown-Downtown: Jacob Lawrence and the Aesthetic Ethos of the Harlem Working-Class Community." In *Over the Line: The Art and Life of Jacob Lawrence*, ed. Peter T. Nesbett and Michelle DuBois. Seattle: University of Washington Press, 2000.

Lawrence, Jacob. *The Legend of John Brown*. Detroit: Detroit Institute of Arts, 1978.

Lawrence, William. *Life of Amos A. Lawrence, with Extracts from His Diary and Correspondence*. Boston: Houghton Mifflin, 1899.

Leaming, Barbara. *Orson Welles: A Biography*. New York: Limelight, 2004.

Lee, Robert E. *Recollections and Letters of General Robert E. Lee*. New York: Doubleday, 1904.

Leech, Samuel Vanderlip. *The Raid of John Brown at Harper's Ferry As I Saw It, by Rev. Samuel Venderlip Leech, D.D.* Washington, DC: Published by author, 1909.

"The Legend of John Brown and the Series by Jacob Lawrence." *Bulletin of the Detroit Institute of Arts* 67, no. 4 (1993).

Lewis, Daniel Levering. *W. E. B. Du Bois: Biography of a Race*. New York: Henry Holt, 1993.

Linden, Diana L., Jonathan Weinberg, and Alejandro Anreus, eds. *The Social and the Real: Political Art of the 1930s in the Western Hemisphere*. University Park: Pennsylvania State University Press, 2006.

Lynn, Kenneth. *William Dean Howells: An American Life*. New York: Harcourt, 1970.

Lytle, Andrew. "A Journey South." *Kentucky Review* 1 (Spring 1980).

Malin, James. *John Brown and the Legend of Fifty-Six*. Philadelphia: American Philosophical Society, 1942.

Marable, Manning. *W. E. B. Du Bois: Black Radical Democrat*. Boston: Twane, 1986.

Marling, Karal Ann. *Wall to Wall America: Post Office Murals in the Great Depression*. Minneapolis: University of Minnesota Press, 1982.

Martin, J. S. "Speech on December 2, 1859." In *Meteor of War: The John Brown Story*, ed. Zoe Trodd and John Stauffer. Maplecrest, NY: Brandywine, 2004.

Masters, Edgar Lee. *Vachel Lindsay: A Poet in America*. New York: Bibio-Moser, 1969.

Mayo, Katherine. Mother India. New York: Harcourt, Brace, 1927.

McEvilley, Thomas. "Primitivism in the Works of an Emancipated Negress." In *Kara Walker: My Complement, My Enemy, My Oppressor, My Love*, ed. Philip Vergne. Minneapolis, MN: Walker Art Center, 2007.

McFeely, William S. *Frederick Douglass*. New York: W. W. Norton, 1995.

McGinty, Brian. *John Brown's Trial*. Cambridge: Harvard University Press, 2009.

McGlone, Robert E. *John Brown's War against Slavery*. Cambridge: Cambridge University Press, 2009.

McKivigan, John. *Forgotten Fireband: James Redpath and the Making of Nineteenth-Century America*. Ithaca, NY: Cornell University Press, 2008.

McKivigan, John R., ed. *Antislavery Violence: Sectional, Racial, and Cultural Conflict in Antebellum America*. Knoxville: University of Tennessee Press, 1999.

———. *History of the American Abolitionist Movement: A Bibliography of Scholarly Articles*, vols. 1–5. New York: Garland, 1999.

———. *Religion and the Antebellum Debate over Slavery*. Athens: University of Georgia Press, 1998.

———. *The Roving Editor, or Talks with Slaves in the Southern States by James Redpath*. University Park: Pennsylvania State University Press, 1996.

Melville, Herman. "The Portent" (1859). In Melville, *Battle-Pieces and Aspects of the War*. New York: Harper and Brothers, 1866.

Menand, Louis. *The Metaphysical Club*. New York: Flamingo, 2001.

Mencken, H. L. *A Religious Orgy in Tennessee*. New York: Melville House, 2006.

Mims, Edwin. *The Advancing South*. New York: Doubleday, 1926.

Miner, Craig. *Kansas: The History of the Sunflower State, 1854–2000*. Lawrence: University Press of Kansas, 2002.

Mitchell, Margaret. *Margaret Mitchell's "Gone with the Wind" Letters, 1936–1949*. New York: Macmillan, 1976.

Morris, William. *The Defence of Guenevere, and Other Poems*. London: Bell and Daidy, 1858.

———. *A Dream of John Ball*. London: Reeves and Turner, 1888.

Myerson, Joel, ed. *Studies in the American Renaissance*. Charlottesville: University of Virginia Press, 1997.

Nason, Reverend Elias. *Life and Times of Charles Sumner*. Boston: B. B. Russell, 1874.

Neely, Jeremy. *Border between Them: Violence and Reconciliation on the Kansas-Missouri Line*. Columbia: University of Missouri Press, 2007.

Nesbett, Peter T., and Michelle DuBois, eds. *Over the Line: The Art and Life of Jacob Lawrence*. Seattle: University of Washington Press, 2000.

Nevins, Allan. *Emergence of Lincoln*. New York: Scribner, 1950.

Nicolay, John G., and John M. Hay. *Abraham Lincoln: A History*. New York: Century, 1890.

Nixon, H. C. "Paths to the Past: The Presidential Addresses of the Southern Historical Association." *Journal of Southern History* 16, no. 1 (February 1950).

Norrell, Robert. *The House I Live In: Race in the American Century*. New York: Oxford University Press, 2005.

———. *Up from History: The Life of Booker T. Washington*. Cambridge, MA: Belknap, 2009.

Nudelman, Franny. *John Brown's Body: Slavery, Violence, and the Culture of War*. Chapel Hill: University of North Carolina Press, 2004.

Oates, Stephen. *Our Fiery Trial: Abraham Lincoln, John Brown, and the Civil War Era*. Amherst: University of Massachusetts Press, 1979.

———. *To Purge This Land with Blood: A Biography of John Brown*. Amherst: University of Massachusetts Press, 1984.

Obama, Barack. *The Audacity of Hope: Thoughts on Reclaiming the American Dream*. New York: Random House, 2006.

Obrist, Hans-Ulrich. "Interview with Kara Walker." In *Safety Curtain: Kara Walker*, ed. Johannes Schlebrugge. Vienna: Museum in Progress in Cooperation with Vienna State Opera House and P & S Wien, 2000.

Orcutt, Samuel. *History of Torrington, Connecticut*. Albany, NY: J. Munsell, 1878.

Ottley, Roi. *'New World a-Coming': Inside Black America*. Boston: Houghton Mifflin, 1943.

Ovington, Mary White. *The Walls Came Tumbling Down*. New York: Arno, 1964.

Owsley, Frank. *Plain Folk of the Old South*. Baton Rouge: Louisiana State University Press, 1949.

Panofsky, Erwin. *Early Netherlandish Painting*, vol. 1. New York: Harper Collins, 1971.

Patton, Rev. W. W. *The Execution of John Brown: A Discourse, Delivered at Chicago, December 4, 1859, in the First Congregation Church*. Chicago: Church, Goodman, and Cushing.

Pease, Jane H., and William H. Pease. *They Who Would Be Free: Blacks' Search for Freedom, 1830–1861*. New York: Athenaeum, 1974.

Peterson, Merrill D. *The Jefferson Image in the American Mind*. Charlottesville: University of Virginia Press, 1998.

———. *John Brown: The Legend Revisited*. Charlottesville: University of Virginia Press, 2002.

———. *Lincoln in American Memory*. New York: Oxford University Press, 1994.

Phillips, Ulrich Bonnell. *American Negro Slavery*. New York: D. Appleton, 1918.

———. *Course of the South to Secession*. New York: Appleton-Century, 1939.

———. *Life and Labor in the Old South*. Boston: Little, Brown, 1929.

Phillips, William. *The Conquest of Kansas by Missouri and Her Allies*. Boston: Phillips, Sampson, 1856.

Potter, David. *The Impending Crisis*. New York: Harper and Row, 1976.

Powell, Richard J. *Black Art: A Cultural History*. London: Thames and Hudson, 2002.

———. *Homecoming: The Art and Life of William H. Johnson*. New York: Norton, 1993.

———. *Jacob Lawrence*. New York: Rizzoli International, 1992.

Pressly, Thomas J. *Americans Interpret Their Civil War*. Princeton, NJ: Princeton University Press, 1954.

Purcell, Sarah J. *Sealed with Blood: War, Sacrifice, and Memory in Revolutionary America*. Philadelphia: University of Pennsylvania Press, 2002.

Quarles, Benjamin. *Allies for Freedom and Blacks on John Brown*. New York: Da Capo, 2001.

———. *Lincoln and the Negro*. New York: Oxford University Press, 1962.

Quarles, Benjamin, ed. *Blacks on John Brown*. Urbana: University of Illinois Press, 1972.

Ramsdell, Charles. *Behind the Lines in the Southern Confederacy*. Baton Rouge: Louisiana State University Press, 1944.

———. "The Natural Limits of Slavery Expansion." *Mississippi Valley Historical Review* 16 (Sept. 1929).

Randall, Annie J. "A Censorship of Forgetting: Origins and Origin Myths of 'Battle Hymn of the Republic.'" In Annie J. Randall, *Music, Power, and Politics*. New York: Routledge, 2004.

———. *Music, Power, and Politics*. New York: Routledge, 2004.

Randall, James G. *Civil War and Reconstruction*. Boston: D. C. Heath, 1937.

Raphael, Ray. *A People's History of the American Revolution: How Common People Shaped the Fight for Independence*. New York: New Press, 2001.

Raymond, Yasmil. "Maladies of Power: A Kara Walker Lexicon." In *Kara Walker: My Complement, My Enemy, My Oppressor, My Love*, ed. Philip Vergne. Minneapolis, MN: Walker Art Center, 2007.

Redpath, James. *The Public Life of Captain John Brown*. Boston: Thayer and Eldridge, 1860.

———, ed. *Echoes of Harper's Ferry*. Boston: Thayer and Eldridge, 1860.

———. *The Roving Editor; or, Talks with Slaves in the Southern States*. Boston: A. B. Burdick, 1859.

Reidinger, Paul. "The Law School's Curry Mural: One of the Grandest and Most Distinguished Works of Art in Wisconsin." *Gargoyle* 10 (Summer 1985).

Reid-Pharr, Robert F. "Black Girl Lost." In *Kara Walker: Pictures from Another Time*, ed. Annette Dixon. Ann Arbor: University of Michigan Press, 2002.

Reinhardt, Mark. "The Art of Racial Profiling." In *Kara Walker: Narratives of a Negress*, ed. Ian Berry, Darby English, Vivian Patterson, and Mark Reinhardt. New York: Rizzoli, 2007.

Renehan, Edward J., Jr. *The Secret Six: The True Tale of the Men Who Conspired with John Brown*. New York: Crown, 1995.

Reynolds, David S. *John Brown, Abolitionist: The Man Who Killed Slavery, Sparked the Civil War, and Seeded Civil Rights*. New York: Knopf, 2005.

Robinson, Marilynne. *Gilead*. New York: Farrar, Straus, and Giroux, 2004.

Robinson, Sara T. *Kansas: Its Interior and Exterior Life*. Boston: Bosby, Nichols, 1856.

Rock, Virginia Jean. "The Making and Meaning of *I'll Take My Stand*: A Study of Utopian-Conservatism, 1925–1939." PhD diss., University of Minnesota, 1964.

Roediger, David. Introduction to W. E. B. Du Bois, *John Brown*. New York: Modern Library, 2001.

Ronda, Bruce A. *Reading the Old Man: John Brown in American Culture*. Knoxville: University of Tennessee Press, 2008.

———. "Whittier and Melville." In Bruce A. Ronda, *Reading the Old Man: John Brown in American Culture*. Knoxville: University of Tennessee Press, 2008.

Roper, John Herbert. *C. Vann Woodward: A Southern Historian and His Critics*. Athens: University of Georgia Press, 1997.

———. *C. Vann Woodward, Southerner*. Athens: University of Georgia Press, 1987.

Rosenblum, Robert. "Caritas Romana after 1760: Some Romantic Lactations." In *Woman as Sex Object: Studies in Erotic Art, 1730–1970*, ed. Thomas B. Hess and Linda Nochlin. New York: Allen Lane, 1972.

Rossbach, Jeffrey. *Ambivalent Conspirators: John Brown, the Secret Six, and a Theory of Slave Violence*. Philadelphia: University of Pennsylvania Press, 1982.

Rubin, Louis. *The Wary Fugitives: Four Poets and the South*. Baton Rouge: Louisiana State University Press, 1978.

Ruchames, Louis. *John Brown: The Making of a Revolutionary*. New York: Grosset and Dunlap, 1969.

———, ed. *A John Brown Reader*. London: Abelard-Schuman, 1959.

Ruppersburg, Hugh M. *Robert Penn Warren and the American Imagination*. Athens: University of Georgia Press, 1990.

Saarinen, Aline B. *Jacob Lawrence*. New York: American Federation of Arts, 1960.

Sacks, Oliver. *The Man Who Mistook His Wife for A Hat*. New York: Touchstone, 1998.

Sanborn, Franklin. "Comment by a Radical Abolitionist." *Century Magazine* 26 (July 1883).

———. "John Brown." In Samuel Orcutt, *History of Torrington, Connecticut*. Albany, NY: J. Munsell, 1878.

———. *Life and Letters of John Brown*. Concord, MA: Roberts Brothers, 1885.

———. *Recollections of Seventy Years*. Vols. 1 and 2. Boston: Richard G. Badger, 1909.

Sandage, Scott. *Born Losers: A History of Failure in America*. Cambridge: Harvard University Press, 2005.

Santway, Alfred A. *A Brief Sketch of the Life of John Brown, the Martyr-Emancipator.* Watertown, NY: Alfred A. Santway, 1934.

Schlebrugge, Johannes, ed. *Safety Curtain: Kara Walker.* Vienna: Museum in Progress in Cooperation with Vienna State Opera House and P & S Wien, 2000.

Schmeckebier, Laurence E. *John Steuart Curry's Pageant of America.* New York: American Artists Group, 1943.

Scott, Otto J. *The Secret Six: John Brown and the Abolitionist Movement.* New York: New York Times Book, 1979.

Shackel, Paul. *Memory in Black and White: Race, Commemoration, and the Post-bellum Landscape.* Lanham, MD: Altamira, 2003.

Sharp, Ellen. "The Legend of John Brown and the Series by Jacob Lawrence." *Bulletin of the Detroit Institute of Arts* 67, no. 4 (1993).

Shaw, Gwendolyn DuBois. *Seeing the Unspeakable: The Art of Kara Walker.* Durham, NC: Duke University Press, 2004.

Simpson, Lewis. *Mind and the American Civil War: A Meditation on Lost Causes.* Baton Rouge: Louisiana State University Press, 1989.

Sitkoff, Harvard. *A New Deal for Blacks: The Emergence of Civil Rights as a National Issue.* Vol. 1, *The Depression Decade.* New York: Oxford University Press, 1978.

Smith, John David. "Introduction: Historical Biography as Social Activism." In W. E. B. Du Bois, *John Brown.* Armonk, NY: M. E. Sharpe, 1997.

Stauffer, John. *Black Hearts of Men: Radical Abolitionists.* Cambridge: Harvard University Press, 2001.

Stedman, E. C. *Voice from Harper's Ferry.* Boston: Printed for author, 1861.

Steensberg, Axel. *Caritas Romana: The Concept of Culture.* Copenhagen: National Museum of Denmark, 1976.

Stewart, James B. *Holy Warriors: The Abolitionists and American Slavery.* New York: Hill and Wang, 1976.

———. "Politics and Belief in Abolitionism: Stanley Elkins' Concept of Anti-institutionalism and Recent Interpretations of American Antislavery." *South Atlantic Quarterly* 75 (1976).

Stewart, Jeffrey C. "(Un)Locke(ing) Jacob Lawrence's Migration Series." In *Jacob Lawrence: The Migration Series,* ed. Elizabeth Hutton Turner. Washington, DC: Rappahannock, 1993.

Stokes, Melvyn. *D. W. Griffith's "The Birth of a Nation": A History of the Most Controversial Motion Picture of All Time.* New York: Oxford University Press, 2007.

Storr, Robert. "Spooked." In *Kara Walker: My Complement, My Enemy, My Oppressor, My Love,* ed. Philip Vergne. Minneapolis, MN: Walker Art Center, 2007.

Strong, Sydney, ed. *What I Owe to My Father.* New York: Henry Holt, 1931.

Stutler, Boyd. "John Brown's Body." *Civil War History* 4 (1958).

Talbert, Joy K. "John Brown in American Literature." PhD diss., University of Kansas, 1941.

Tate, Allen. "Emily Dickinson." In Tate, *Essays of Four Decades.* Chicago: Swallow, 1968.

———. *Jefferson Davis: His Rise and Fall, a Biographical Narrative.* New York: Minton, Balch, 1929.

———. *Stonewall Jackson: The Good Soldier.* New York: Minton, Balch, 1928.

Taylor, Andrew, and Eldrid Herrington, eds. *The Afterlife of John Brown*. New York: Palgrave, 2005.

Terhune, Anne Gregory, with Patricia Smith Scanlan. *Thomas Hovenden: His Life and Art*. Philadelphia: University of Pennsylvania Press, 2006.

Thoreau, Henry David. "A Plea for Captain John Brown." In *Echoes of Harper's Ferry*, ed. James Redpath. Boston: Thayer and Eldridge, 1860.

Tourgée, Albion. *Hot Plowshares*. New York: Fords, Howard, and Hulbert, 1883.

Trodd, Zoe, and John Stauffer, eds. *Meteor of War: The John Brown Story*. Maplecrest, NY: Brandywine, 2004.

Tulloch, Hugh. *The Debate on the American Civil War Era*. New York: Manchester University Press, 1999.

Turner, Elizabeth Hutton, ed. *Jacob Lawrence: The Migration Series*. Washington, DC: Rappahannock, 1993.

Twelve Southerners. *I'll Take My Stand: The South and the Agrarian Tradition*. New York: Harper, 1962.

Tyson, Timothy. *Radio Free Dixie: Robert F. Williams and the Roots of Black Power*. Chapel Hill: University of North Carolina Press, 1999.

Underwood, Thomas. *Allen Tate: Orphan of the South*. Princeton, NJ: Princeton University Press, 2000.

Vergne, Philip. "The Black Saint Is the Sinner Lady." In *Kara Walker: My Complement, My Enemy, My Oppressor, My Love*, ed. Philip Vergne. Minneapolis, MN: Walker Art Center, 2007.

———, ed. *Kara Walker: My Complement, My Enemy, My Oppressor, My Love*. Minneapolis, MN: Walker Art Center, 2007.

Villard, Oswald Garrison. *Fighting Years: Memoirs of a Liberal Editor*. New York: Harcourt, Brace, 1939.

———. *John Brown, 1800–1859: A Biography Fifty Years After*. Boston: Houghton Mifflin, 1910.

———. "Radio Address" (1940). In D. Joy Humes, *Oswald Garrison Villard: Liberal of the 1920s*. Syracuse, NY: Syracuse University Press, 1960.

———. "The Rise of the NAACP." Radio Speech, WEVD, December 2, 1938.

———. "To Henry Villard." In *What I Owe to My Father*, ed. Sydney Strong. New York: Henry Holt, 1931.

Vollman, William T. *Rising Up and Rising Down: Some Thoughts on Violence, Freedom and Urgent Means*. New York: Ecco, 2004.

Von Holst, Hermann, and Frank Preston Stearns, eds. *John Brown*. Boston: Cupples and Hurd, 1889.

Wade, Wyn Craig. *The Fiery Cross: The Ku Klux Klan in America*. New York: Oxford University Press, 1998.

Waller, Bret. *John Steuart Curry: A Retrospective Exhibition of His Work Held in the Kansas State Capitol, Topeka, October 3–November 3, 1970*. Lawrence: University of Kansas Press for the University of Kansas Museum of Art. Reprinted from *Kansas Quarterly* 2 (1970).

Wardenaar, Leslie. "John Brown: The Literary Image." PhD diss., University of California, 1974.

Warren, Robert Penn. *All the King's Men*. New York: Harcourt, Brace, 1946.

———. "The Briar Patch." In Twelve Southerners, *I'll Take My Stand: The South and the Agrarian Tradition*. New York: Harper, 1962.

———. *John Brown: The Making of a Martyr*. Nashville: J. S. Sanders, 1993.

———. *The Legacy of the Civil War*. New York: Random House, 1961.

———. *Segregation: The Inner Conflict of the South*. New York: Random House, 1956.

Washington, Booker T. *The Future of the American Negro*. Boston: Small, Maynard, 1899.

Washington, Joseph. *Race and Religion in Early Nineteenth-Century America, 1800–1850*. Lewiston, NY: E. Mellen, 1988.

Watkins, Floyd, John T. Hiers, and Mary Louise Weaks, eds. *Talking with Robert Penn Warren*. Athens: University of Georgia Press, 1990.

Webb, Richard D. *Life and Letters of John Brown*. London: Smith, Elder, 1860.

Weber, Sandra. "John Brown's Family: A Living Legacy." *Civil War Times*, February 2004.

Weiner, Mark S. *Black Trials: Citizenship from the Beginnings of Slavery to the End of Caste*. New York: Vintage, 2006.

Wells, Anna Mary. *Dear Preceptor: The Life and Times of Thomas Wentworth Higginson*. Boston: Houghton Mifflin, 1963.

Wheat, Ellin Harkins. *Jacob Lawrence: American Painter*. Seattle: University of Washington Press, 1986.

———. *Jacob Lawrence: The Frederick Douglass and Harriet Tubman Series of 1938–1940*. Hampton, VA: Hampton University Museum, 1991.

Whitehill, Walter Muir. "John Brown of Osawatomie in Boston, 1857." *Proceedings of the Massachusetts Historical Society* 69 (1950).

Williams, Linda. *Playing the Race Card: Melodramas of Black and White from Uncle Tom to O. J. Simpson*. Princeton, NJ: Princeton University Press, 2001.

Williams, Robert F. *Negroes with Guns*. New York: Marzani and Munsell, 1962.

Willis, Deborah. "The Schomburg Collection: A Rich Resource for Jacob Lawrence." In *Jacob Lawrence: The Migration Series*, ed. Elizabeth Hutton Turner. Washington, DC: Rappahannock, 1993.

Wills, Gary. *Negro President: Jefferson and the Slave Power*. Boston: Houghton Mifflin, 2003.

Wilson, Hill Peebles. *John Brown, Soldier of Fortune: A Critique*. Lawrence, KS: H. P. Wilson, 1913.

Wilson, Judith. "Optical Illusions: Images of Miscegenation in Nineteenth and Twentieth Century Art." *American Art* 5, no. 3 (Summer 1991).

Winchell, Mark. *Where No Flag Flies: Donald Davidson and the Southern Resistance*. Columbia: University of Missouri Press, 2000.

Winkley, W. W., MD. *John Brown the Hero: Personal Reminiscences*. Boston: James H. West, 1905.

Wolters, Raymond. *Du Bois and His Rivals*. Columbia: University of Missouri Press, 2002.

Woodward, C. Vann. *The Burden of Southern History*. 3rd ed. Baton Rouge: Louisiana State University Press, 1993.

———. *The Strange Career of Jim Crow*. New York: Oxford University Press, 1955.

Wright, Richard. *The WPA Guide to New York City*. New York: Random House, 1982.

Wyatt-Brown, Bertram. "Stanley Elkins' *Slavery*: The Antislavery Interpretation Reexamined." *American Quarterly* 25 (1973).

X, Malcolm. "Speech for Organization of Afro-American Unity" (July 5, 1964). In *By Any Means Necessary: Speeches, Interviews and a Letter*, ed. George Breitman. New York: Pathfinder, 1970.

Young, Alfred. *The Shoemaker and the Tea Party: Memory and the American Revolution.* Boston: Beacon, 1999.

Young, Thomas Daniel. *Waking Their Neighbors Up: The Nashville Agrarians Rediscovered.* Athens: University of Georgia Press, 1982.

Young, Thomas Daniel, and Elizabeth Sarcone, eds. *The Lytle-Tate Letters: The Correspondence of Andrew Lytle and Allen Tate.* Jackson: University of Mississippi Press, 1987.

Zagrando, Robert Lewis. *NAACP Crusade against Lynching, 1909–1950.* Philadelphia: Temple University Press, 1980.

Zittle, John. *A Correct History of the John Brown Invasion at Harper's Ferry, West Va., Oct. 17, 1859–Compiled by the Late Capt. John H. Zittle of Shepherdstown, W. Va., Who Was an Eye-Witness to Many of the Occurrences, and Edited and Published by His Widow.* Hagerstown, MD: Mill, 1905.

Index

Note: JB = John Brown.